Human Rights Futures

In one collected volume, mainstream and critical human rights scholars together examine the empirical and normative debates around the future of human rights. They ask what makes human rights effective, what strategies will enhance the chances of compliance, what blocks progress, and whether the hope for human rights is entirely misplaced in a rapidly transforming world. *Human Rights Futures* sees the world as at a crucial juncture. The project for globalizing rights will either continue to be embedded or will fall backward into a maelstrom of nationalist backlash, religious resurgence and faltering Western power. Each chapter talks directly to the others in an interactive dialogue, providing a theoretical and methodological framework for a clear research agenda for the next decade. Scholars, graduate students and practitioners of political science, history, sociology, law and development will find much, both to challenge and provoke them, in this innovative book.

Stephen Hopgood is Professor of International Relations at SOAS, University of London, and author of *Keepers of the Flame: Understanding Amnesty International* (2006), which won the APSA Best Book in Human Rights Award in 2007, and *The Endtimes of Human Rights* (2013).

Jack Snyder is the Robert and Renée Belfer Professor of International Relations in the Political Science Department and the Saltzman Institute of War and Peace Studies at Columbia University in the City of New York. His books include *Ranking the World: Grading States as a Tool of Global Governance* (with Alexander Cooley, Cambridge University Press, 2015).

Leslie Vinjamuri is Associate Professor of International Relations, and Director of the Centre on Conflict, Rights and Justice at SOAS, University of London. Recent works include *The Distant Promise of a Negotiated Justice* (2017).

D0770512

Human Rights Futures

Edited by

Stephen Hopgood
SOAS, University of London

Jack Snyder
Columbia University, New York

Leslie Vinjamuri
SOAS, University of London

CAMBRIDGE
UNIVERSITY PRESS

CAMBRIDGE
UNIVERSITY PRESS

University Printing House, Cambridge CB2 8BS, United Kingdom

One Liberty Plaza, 20th Floor, New York, NY 10006, USA

477 Williamstown Road, Port Melbourne, VIC 3207, Australia

314-321, 3rd Floor, Plot 3, Splendor Forum, Jasola District Centre, New Delhi-110025, India

79 Anson Road, #06-04/06, Singapore 079906

Cambridge University Press is part of the University of Cambridge.

It furthers the University's mission by disseminating knowledge in the pursuit of education, learning and research at the highest international levels of excellence.

www.cambridge.org
Information on this title: www.cambridge.org/9781316644164
DOI: 10.1017/9781108147767

First published 2017
First paperback edition 2018

A catalogue record for this publication is available from the British Library

Library of Congress Cataloging in Publication data
Names: Hopgood, Stephen, author. | Snyder, Jack L.,
author. | Vinjamuri, Leslie, author.
Title: Human Rights Futures / Stephen Hopgood (School of Oriental
and African Studies, University of London), Jack Snyder (Columbia University,
New York), Leslie Vinjamuri (School of Oriental and African Studies,
University of London).
Description: Cambridge [UK] ; New York : Cambridge University Press,
2017. | Includes index.
Identifiers: LCCN 2016056473 | ISBN 9781107193352
Subjects: LCSH: Human rights.
Classification: LCC K3240 .H645 2017 | DDC 323–dc23
LC record available at https://lccn.loc.gov/2016056473

ISBN 978-1-107-19335-2 Hardback
ISBN 978-1-316-64416-4 Paperback

Contents

Figures

Contributors

ALEXANDER COOLEY is the Claire Tow Professor of Political Science at Barnard College and Director of Columbia University's Harriman Institute for the Study of Russia, Eurasia, and Eastern Europe. His books include *Great Games, Local Rules* and *Dictators Beyond Borders*.

GEOFF DANCY is an Assistant Professor in the Department of Political Science at Tulane University. His current book project is called *Beyond Backlash: A Pragmatist Approach to Human Rights Law and Activism*.

SHAREEN HERTEL is Associate Professor of Political Science at the University of Connecticut, jointly appointed with the university's Human Rights Institute. She is the author of *Unexpected Power: Conflict and Change Among Transnational Activists*, and editor of *The Journal of Human Rights*.

STEPHEN HOPGOOD is Professor of International Relations at SOAS, University of London, and author of *Keepers of the Flame: Understanding Amnesty International*, which won the APSA Best Book in Human Rights Award in 2007, and *The Endtimes of Human Rights* (2013).

ELIZABETH SHAKMAN HURD is Professor of Political Science and Religious Studies at Northwestern University. Her books include *The Politics of Secularism in International Relations* and *Beyond Religious Freedom: The New Global Politics of Religion*.

PEGGY LEVITT is Chair of the Sociology Department and the Luella LaMer Slaner Professor in Latin American Studies at Wellesley College and Co-Director of Harvard University's Transnational Studies Initiative. Her most recent book is *Artifacts and Allegiances: How Museums Put the Nation and the World on Display*.

SALLY ENGLE MERRY is Silver Professor of Anthropology at New York University and a Faculty Director of the Center for Human Rights and Global Justice at the New York University School of Law. Her most recent book is *The Seductions of Quantification: Measuring Human Rights, Gender Violence, and Sex Trafficking*.

SAMUEL MOYN is Professor of Law and Professor of History at Yale University. His books include *The Last Utopia: Human Rights in History* and *Christian Human Rights*.

THOMAS RISSE is Professor of International Relations at the Otto Suhr Institute of Political Science, Freie Universität Berlin, Germany. He is co-editor of *The Persistent Power of Human Rights. From Commitment to Compliance* (with Stephen Ropp and Kathryn Sikkink).

MATTHEW SCHAAF is a human rights advocate and serves as the director of Freedom House's office in Ukraine. He is an expert on human rights and democratic development in Ukraine, Russia, and Kyrgyzstan, and an expert on LGBTI rights across Eurasia.

KATHRYN SIKKINK is the Ryan Family Professor of Human Rights Policy at Harvard Kennedy School and the Carol K. Pforzheimer Professor at the Radcliffe Institute for Advanced Study. She is author of *The Justice Cascade: How Human Rights Prosecutions Are Changing World Politics*.

BETH A. SIMMONS is Andrea Mitchell University Professor of Law, Business Ethics and Political Science, University of Pennsylvania. She is the author of *Mobilizing for Human Rights: International Law in Domestic Politics*.

JACK SNYDER is the Robert and Renée Belfer Professor of International Relations in the Political Science Department and the Saltzman Institute of War and Peace Studies at Columbia University in the City of New York. His books include *Ranking the World: Grading States as a Tool of Global Governance* (with Alexander Cooley, Cambridge University Press, 2015).

ANTON STREZHNEV is a PhD Candidate in the Harvard University Department of Government. His research focuses on the politics of international investment arbitration and the role of private actors in global economic governance.

LESLIE VINJAMURI is Associate Professor of International Relations, and Director of the Centre on Conflict, Rights and Justice at SOAS, University of London. Recent works include *The Distant Promise of a Negotiated Justice* (2017).

Acknowledgments

Human Rights Futures grew out of a number of workshops held in London and New York. We would like to thank our colleagues at SOAS, University of London, and Columbia University in the City of New York for their valuable contributions. For their financial support, we thank SOAS, the Luce Foundation and the Institute for Religion, Culture, and Public Life at Columbia. For their participation at the workshops, or in reading and commenting on draft papers, we are extremely grateful to Amitav Acharya, Fiona Adamson, Elazar Barkan, Jonathan Blake, Carlo Bonura, Agnes Callamard, Thomas Carothers, Kate Cronin-Furman, Anthony Dworkin, Yasmine Ergas, Peter Katzenstein, Jennifer Lind, Andrew Nathan, Matthew Nelson, Rahul Rao, Christian Reus-Smit, James Ron, Elizabeth Sperber, Alfred Stepan, Ruti Teitel, Rachel Wahl, and Jennifer Welsh. In addition to writing chapters, Alexander Cooley and Shareen Hertel provided valuable comments on the Introduction and Conclusion. Tonya Putnam also gave us important extensive comments at an early stage. Finally, we would like to thank all our chapter writers for their time and patience in bringing this project to fruition.

STEPHEN HOPGOOD
JACK SNYDER
LESLIE VINJAMURI

1 Introduction: Human Rights Past, Present, and Future

Stephen Hopgood, Jack Snyder, and Leslie Vinjamuri

International human rights NGOs and institutions have been at the vanguard of multiple advocacy campaigns designed to galvanize global support for human rights. The impact of these initiatives has been dramatic. States have adopted human rights conventions, ratified treaties, supported new human rights committees and courts, and extended the mandate of existing international and regional organizations to include human rights. The sheer growth of human rights NGOs and the increased reference to human rights by states, international organizations, and other actors shows that human rights are now a major focal point for transnational mobilization. The global middle class, widely seen as a mainstay of human rights observance, is projected to increase from 1.8 billion in 2012 to 3.2 billion by 2020.[1]

Human rights research has also found cause for optimism. Some scholars argue we are living through a 'justice cascade' where transnational movements for human rights allied to international law have made accelerating gains in the elimination of human rights violations such as torture.[2] Some have even claimed that cruelty and killing are in decline,

---

[1] Homi Kharas and Geoffrey Gertz, "The New Global Middle Class: A Cross-Over from West to East," in Cheng Li (ed.), *China's Emerging Middle Class, Beyond Economic Transformation* (Washington DC: Brookings Institution Press, 2010). Although much of the projected growth is expected to take place in China and India where human rights advocates have so far struggled to make headway, the emergence of a global middle class is likely to narrow the material and cultural divides that slow the emergence of a global set of values. The mass of global polling data collected in the World Values Survey (WVS) provides empirical evidence of how economic development leads to value changes conducive to democracy. European Strategy and Policy Analysis System (ESPAS), *Global Trends 2030 – Citizens in an Interconnected and Polycentric World*, European Union Institute for Security Studies, 2012, p. 29: www.iss.europa.eu/publications/detail/article/espas-report-global-trends-2030-citizens-in-an-interconnected-and-polycentric-world/.

[2] Kathryn Sikkink, *The Justice Cascade: How Human Rights Prosecutions Are Changing World Politics* (New York: W. W. Norton & co, 2011); Margaret Keck and Kathryn Sikkink, *Activists Beyond Borders: Advocacy Networks in International Politics* (Ithaca: Cornell University Press, 1998); Beth A. Simmons, *Mobilizing for Human Rights: International Law*

1

due in no small part to the rights revolution.[3] Others suggest that even in a world where Western powers no longer dominate, international liberal norms embedded in global institutions will endure.[4] These advocacy and scholarly claims all sustain a hopeful story in which the future for human rights mobilization is a positive and enduring one.

But, as many of the chapters that follow will argue, this is not the only possible future for human rights. Alternative accounts to the mobilization narrative see a future that is much more one of ambivalence, ineffectiveness, failure, and even irrelevance. We group these critiques under four headings: scope conditions, backlash, localization, and utopias and endtimes.

Scope conditions for successful human rights activism include embedding mobilization within a broader social movement for political change that harnesses actors with varying motivations to the cause, an alliance with power to realize human rights ends when persuasion is not enough, and the material capacity of states to make real the legal commitments they have made. These favorable conditions hold when countries are at peace and when they already enjoy some institutional, economic, and social facilitating conditions for democracy. But the countries where rights abuses are worst are what we will call "hard cases," which lack these favorable conditions. Outside the scope conditions for the success of conventional mainstream approaches to rights advocacy, pragmatic innovations may be necessary.

Human rights mobilization not only fails because of its lack of anchorage in social coalitions, its inadequate alliance with state power, or a lack of state capacity, it also faces resistance. *Backlash* is driven by those threatened by human rights and powerful enough to resist. They sometimes exploit the opportunity to reframe or even demonize global rights to mobilize the many against the rights message, while at other times more subtle methods of non-engagement and resistance are employed. Backlash encompasses a wide variety of strategies, in other words, ranging

---

in Domestic Politics (Cambridge: Cambridge University Press, 2009); Christopher J. Fariss, "Respect for Human Rights Has Improved over Time: Modeling the Changing Standard of Accountability," *American Political Science Review* 108, no. 2 (2014): 297–318; Ann Marie Clark and Kathryn Sikkink, "Information Effects and Human Rights Data: Is the Good News about Increased Human Rights Information Bad News for Human Rights Measures?" *Human Rights Quarterly* 35, no. 3 (August 2013): 539–68; Jo Becker, *Campaigning for Justice: Human Rights Advocacy in Practice* (Stanford: Stanford University Press, 2012); Alison Brysk, *Speaking Rights to Power: Constructing Political Will* (New York: Oxford University Press, 2013).

[3] Steven Pinker, *The Better Angels of Our Nature: A History of Violence and Humanity* (London: Penguin, 2012); Joshua S. Goldstein, *Winning the War on War: The Decline of Armed Conflict Worldwide* (New York: Plume Books, 2012).

[4] G. John Ikenberry, *Liberal Leviathan: The Origins, Crisis and Transformation of American World Order* (Princeton: Princeton University Press, 2011).

from confrontation (openly resisting the obligations rights impose), to evasion (ignoring rights demands) or instrumentalization (e.g., using rights language to justify repressing individual speech or due process to protect the "rights of the community"). Democracies as well as autocracies can engage in behavior along this spectrum.

In an era that is marked by increasing political upheaval not only in many parts of the Global South, but also in the United States and Europe, we ask the question of whether backlash is increasing and what this means for human rights going forward. The recent assault on human rights in the United States provides a laboratory for evaluating the role of domestic institutions, civil society, and norms in securing human rights. Protests in support of rights in the weeks following the election of Donald Trump also remind us that backlash can be deployed in favor of, and not only against, human rights. Like previous critiques, backlash theorists underscore the need to trim unbending principles in the face of political reality. Pursuing some rights, such as religious freedom, may at times be counterproductive. Similarly, backlash in support of rights faces the challenge of tailoring principle to politics.

Human rights as they are understood in Western capitals have often been poorly integrated in struggles for freedom and equality in the South. To be effective, a greater awareness of local needs, actors, and strategies – manifest in different forms of advocacy, and in alternative campaign priorities – may be essential to achieve positive results. We label this *localization*. The most influential account of this process, where global principles are translated into local struggles, has been termed 'vernacularization' and we examine it in depth. We also acknowledge the agency that local human rights actors often display by examining how they use human rights in their own customized ways to achieve their priorities. This is all 'human rights activism,' but it may not look much like the human rights with which we are familiar.

Finally, in *utopias and endtimes*, some scholars ask whether there is really any future at all for human rights. They suggest that human rights may represent a mistaken path taken on the road to delivering more genuine freedom and equality, an illusion of a post-ideological world of liberal freedoms that actually serves to deflect us from real progress toward social and economic justice. Others claim that human rights may be an artifact of a postcolonial world dominated by Western states that are declining in the face of newly emerging non-liberal global powers, revitalized nationalism, resurgent religion, and the refusal of the middle classes to part with any of their privilege.

Although normative discussions are in evidence throughout the volume, we do not deal explicitly with the moral and philosophical basis of human rights. Questions about the foundations and justification of rights, about what a right is, what kinds of rights there are, about universality, about the conception of the person underlying rights, whether that person must necessarily be conceived in 'liberal' terms, the justifiability of natural rights claims, whether political rights have priority, deontology vs. utilitarianism, and the role of dignity as a moral foundation for rights are not explicitly addressed for three reasons.

First, other recent works have considered these normative issues in forensic detail.[5] Second, normative arguments can be made for or against both human rights as such, and against certain rights in particular. Such moral claims as these admit of no empirical resolution. However, for some participants in these normative debates, it makes a difference whether and how rights can be instantiated in specific real world conditions: *ought* implies *can*. In this spirit, we focus on what makes the difference in everyday success for human rights – the alignment of social and political forces, globally, nationally, and locally, and the interests they pursue, including but not limited to those in greater equality or freedom.

Third, following on from this, we see many of the sharpest debates about human rights at the present juncture as about the feasibility of making rights a reality and what tactics to use in pursuing that goal. So, while we do have chapters that stake out opposing normative positions in the debate, and while almost all the chapters discuss norms and normative beliefs as empirical facts, we focus in the main on the politics of making rights real rather than the strength of the moral argument behind them.

In Section 1, we give due attention to what are, on the face of it, the remarkable achievements of generations of human rights advocates. Following this, in Section 2, we take an audit of scholarship into human rights. In Section 3 we outline the four critiques introduced above in more depth. Section 4 is a brief conclusion.

1   Globalizing Human Rights

The emergence of human rights as a global discourse was the culmination of a long historical process. There is no consensus on the social and

---

[5] See, for example, Rowan Cruft, S. Matthew Liao, and Massimo Renzo (eds.), *Philosophical Foundations of Human Rights* (Oxford: Oxford University Press, 2015); Cindy Holder and David Reidy (eds.) *Human Rights: The Hard Questions* (Cambridge: Cambridge University Press, 2013); Costas Douzinas and Conor Gearty (eds.), *The Meanings of Rights: The Philosophy and Social Theory of Human Rights* (Cambridge: Cambridge University Press, 2014).

political origins of human rights.[6] Rights-like ideas and practices have been dated to antiquity, Roman law, late medieval European politics, Calvinism, the middle ages, and the evolution of humanist sensibilities in the eighteenth and nineteenth centuries.[7] The most influential narrative sees post-Enlightenment European revulsion with torture and slavery at the heart of a linear account of liberal progress, this "revolution in moral sentiment" then globalized in the name of civilization through the vector of empire.[8] Its culmination came in the period immediately following World War II and the Holocaust, when human rights were embedded through a series of bold institutional developments such as the Nuremberg trials, the Charter of the United Nations, the Universal Declaration of Human Rights, the Genocide Convention, and the revised Geneva Conventions.

Searching recent reassessments of this account have stressed the disjuncture between the 1940s and the 1970s. Rather than seeing human rights progress as a linear development, more attention is given to the lesser role that responses to the Holocaust actually played in stimulating human rights institutions in the immediate postwar period, and the ways rights displaced alternative organizing principles for justice and freedom (e.g., socialism, national self-determination). The role of non-Western actors in stimulating rights developments in the 1960s, particularly at the UN, also fits within this critical revisionism.[9]

---

[6] For recent historical scholarship see: Stefan-Ludwig Hoffmann, ed., *Human Rights in the Twentieth Century* (New York: Cambridge University Press, 2011); Akira Iriye, Petra Goedde, and William I Hitchcock (eds.) *The Human Rights Revolution: An International History* (New York: Oxford University Press, 2012); Samuel Moyn. *The Last Utopia: Human Rights in History* (Cambridge, MA: Belknap/Harvard University Press, 2010); Elizabeth Borgwardt, *A New Deal for the World: America's Vision for Human Rights* (Cambridge, MA: Belknap/Harvard University Press, 2005).

[7] Micheline R. Ishay, *The History of Human Rights: From Ancient Times to the Globalization Era* (Oakland: University of California Press, 2008); Christian Reus-Smit, *Individual Rights and the Making of the International System* (Cambridge: Cambridge University Press, 2013); Lynn Hunt, *Inventing Human Rights: A History* (New York: W. W. Norton & Co, 2007); Paul Gordon Lauren, *The Evolution of International Human Rights: Visions Seen*, 2nd edn. (Philadelphia: Penn Press, 2003); Mary Ann Glendon, *A World Made New: Eleanor Roosevelt and the Universal Declaration of Human Rights* (New York: Random House, 2001); Aryeh Neier, *The International Human Rights Movement: A History* (Princeton: Princeton University Press, 2012); Roger Normand and Sarah Zaidi. *Human Rights at the UN: The Political History of Universal Justice* (Bloomington: Indiana University Press, 2008); Moyn, *The Last Utopia*.

[8] Hunt, *Inventing Human Rights*, but also Stephen Hopgood, *The Endtimes of Human Rights* (Ithaca: Cornell University Press, 2013).

[9] The most influential account is Moyn, *The Last Utopia*. See also Steven L. B. Jensen, *The Making of International Human Rights; The 1960s, Decolonization, and the Reconstruction of Global Values* (New York: Cambridge University Press, 2016).

What is less contested in most of these histories is the importance of the 1970s as the moment of take-off for the modern human rights revolution, and of the 1990s as the decade in which human rights achieved truly global stature.[10] President Jimmy Carter made human rights a centerpiece of US foreign policy in 1977, the same year Amnesty International won the Nobel Peace Prize and a year before Helsinki Watch, the forerunner of Human Rights Watch, was formed. Building on international covenants on civil and political, and economic, social, and cultural rights ratified in the mid-1970s, conventions were established on discrimination against women (1981), against torture (1987), and on children's rights (1989). The UN secretary-general Boutros Ghali's *Agenda for Peace* of 1992 even announced a new era where human rights would increasingly impose conditions on legitimate sovereignty.[11]

As the Cold War ended, the era of *institutionalized* human rights familiar to us today gathered pace with 1993's UN Conference on Human Rights in Vienna, which established the UN Office of the High Commissioner of Human Rights. This was followed by ad hoc tribunals for Yugoslavia (1993) and Rwanda (1994), the Rome Statute (1998) and the International Criminal Court (2002), the Responsibility to Protect (2001/2005), the new Human Rights Council (2006), and the Universal Periodic Review (2008). These were all significant developments in the law and compliance regime of human rights. Many other agreements and institutions were set up or revitalized, at the regional and national levels, and soon almost all advocates who sought progress on norms and their implementation – from migrants to indigenous people to the disabled to those fighting against female genital mutilation – expressed their demands in the language of human rights. Even humanitarian organizations such as the ICRC and Oxfam followed suit.

Human rights are also now central to international condemnations of atrocity crimes by states. The UN's detailed report on the appalling conditions in which people live in North Korea, released in February 2014, uses human rights and their most far-reaching legalized expression – crimes against humanity – as the framework for demanding both referral to the ICC (now backed by the UN General Assembly) and even the use of coercive pressure under the label of R2P.[12] High-profile human rights

[10] Barbara J. Keys, *Reclaiming American Virtue: The Human Rights Revolution of the 1970s* (Cambridge, MA: Harvard University Press, 2014).
[11] UN Security Council, *An Agenda for Peace: Report of the Secretary-General Pursuant to the Statement Adopted by the Summit Meeting of the Security Council on 31 Jan 1992.* June 17, 1992.
[12] Report of the detailed findings of the commission of inquiry on human rights in the Democratic People's Republic of Korea, A/HRC/25/CRP.1, February 2014, available at:

campaigns – over Israeli shelling of Gaza, ISIS in Iraq, or civil war in Syria – now get publicity on a global scale. Within the UN system, there has been a major institutional shift with the implementation of a 'Rights Up Front' policy following what was seen as the UN's failure to protect human rights during the end of the Sri Lankan civil war in 2009. It is intended to embed human rights in every aspect of the UN's operational work.[13]

As for the future, various initiatives are currently being proposed whose aim is to fully globalize the reach of human rights law. For example, a convention on crimes against humanity is being discussed within the International Law Commission (as the Rome Statute was initially).[14] This convention will, advocates hope, be a powerful tool for condemning the worst state excesses, applying in peacetime as well as in war and filling in several gaps that the current network of treaties leaves open. Advocates for the convention even hope it might give impetus to prosecuting the crime of aggression, the fourth major international crime under the Rome Statute. As crimes against humanity are considered to be customary international law, this would open up almost all state behavior to binding legal accountability.

Second, the most ambitious proposal of all is perhaps a Swiss-led initiative for a World Human Rights Court. This court, while treaty-based, would apply to non-state actors as well as states, and would allow complaints to be heard against non-parties to the statute provided they were supported by the UN High Commissioner for Human Rights (in which case, they would constitute opinions, not legally binding judgments). The court would also be able to rule on the permissibility of reservations entered by states to human rights treaties.[15] The ICC's focus on individual criminal responsibility would be augmented by the WCHR's focus on state and non-state actor responsibility. The court might even, its advocates suggest, exercise judicial review of Security Council decisions.[16]

---

www.ohchr.org/EN/HRBodies/HRC/CoIDPRK/Pages/ReportoftheCommissionofInquiryDPRK.aspx.

[13] www.un.org/sg/en/content/ban-ki-moon/human-rights-front-initiative.

[14] See the Crimes Against Humanity Initiative, *Fulfilling the Dictates of Public Conscience: Moving Forward with a Convention on Crimes Against Humanity*, Washington St Louis School of Law (2014): http://law.wustl.edu/harris/documents/Final-CAHGenevaReport -071714.pdf, and Leila Nadya Sadat (ed.), *Forging a Convention for Crimes Against Humanity* (Cambridge: Cambridge University Press, 2014).

[15] Martin Scheinin, "Towards a World Court for Human Rights," advanced copy, European University Institute, June 2009, p. 8 (available at: www.eui.eu/Documents/ DepartmentsCentres/AcademyofEuropeanLaw/CourseMaterialsHR/HR2009/Scheini n/ScheininClassReading1.pdf).

[16] Ibid., 26. In a withering critique, Philip Alston finds the idea of the court thoroughly misconceived, a distraction from the difficult business of improving human rights by

This overview of significant institutional achievements gives us a sense of the aspirational character of the global human rights regime.[17] All of these developments in theory move us closer to the advocacy ideal of a *global constitution*, a set of binding laws about appropriate behavior by states, non-state actors, and individuals alike. In fact, though, each of these institutions has embedded protections for states, and exceptions or even exemptions for especially powerful ones. The ultimate prize – a law without boundaries, with universal jurisdiction, beyond explicit state consent that would move us "from consent to constitution," from "a state-centred world order to a new global order with [a] focus on the individual endowed with rights" – has been heavily compromised.[18] Institutional design rarely reflects the aspiration of advocates who seek a world where due process and the rule of law hold superior authority to state practice.

2   An Audit of Human Rights Scholarship

Empirical research on human rights has flourished over the past two decades, moving from a productive early phase of empirical theory development into a more recent phase of sophisticated, multi-method research and debate among different theoretical approaches and inference strategies. This research has been explanatory as well as descriptive, quantitative as well as qualitative, experimental as well as observational, and aimed at the development as well as the testing of theory.[19] Over time, claims for a difference in results based on method have been inconclusive.[20] Rather, different methods have complementary strengths that can compensate for corresponding weaknesses, with quantitative methods best at assessing general patterns and qualitative methods stronger at verifying

non-judicial as well as judicial means, which requires giving more attention to certain political realities; see "Against a World Court for Human Rights," *Ethics and International Affairs*, no. 2 (2014): 197–212.

[17] See Ruti Teitel, *Humanity's Law* (Oxford and New York: Oxford University Press, 2011).

[18] Scheinin, *Towards a World Court*, 9. Also Stephen Gardbaum, "Human Rights and International Constitutionalism," in *Ruling the World: Constitutionalism, International Law, and Global Governance*, edited by Jeffrey L. Dunoff and Joel P. Trachtman (Cambridge: Cambridge University Press, 2009), 233–57.

[19] Emilie Hafner-Burton and James Ron, "Seeing Double: Human Rights Impact through Qualitative and Quantitative Eyes," *World Politics* 61, no. 2 (April 2009): 360–401. For a randomized experiment on women's empowerment in Afghan villages, see Andrew Beath, Fotini Christia, and Ruben Enikolopov, "Empowering Women through Development Aid: Evidence from a Field Experiment in Afghanistan," *American Political Science Review* 107, no. 3 (August 2013): 540–57.

[20] Although compare, for e.g., Simmons' and Clark's largely confirmatory studies with Moyn's and Hopgood's largely skeptical historical and ethnographic studies.

causal mechanisms. As a result, researchers have converged on a substantial core of consensual findings on the conditions that facilitate good human rights outcomes.

Consensus About Facilitating Conditions for Rights

Broad consensus exists across all kinds of empirical researchers, including quantitative and qualitative, as well as critics and defenders of mainstream practices, about the conditions that promote and hinder positive rights outcomes. Quantitative studies report that two factors are the most important predictors of the quality of rights outcomes in a country: whether the country is at peace or at war, and how democratic the country is. Some might see the democracy finding as bordering on the circular, since most measures of democracy assume the existence of the civil liberties and legal apparatus that makes democracy possible. And so it is. But many of the other strong findings about the correlates of good rights outcomes are either causes, attributes, or consequences of democracy, which suggests that the link between democracy and rights is not just a tautology, but is based on a complex of mutually supporting causal factors that sustain rights outcomes. These include a reasonably high per capita income, which is the single strongest predictor of democracy; a fairly strong institutional capacity of the state, including an effective, impartial bureaucracy as well as strong representative and legal institutions, sometimes measured by the rough proxy of being a former British colony; and a progressive, socially inclusive ruling coalition that is "on the left."[21]

Findings about the risk factors for rights also echo findings for democracy. Economic inequality undermines both rights and democracy.[22] A large population is likewise a risk factor for rights abuse, possibly because of the difficulty of democratically governing culturally diverse peoples in a single state.[23] Some findings also suggest that there is "more murder in the middle": democratizing states endure similar levels of rights abuse to authoritarian states as a result of contentious mass mobilization in a context of weakly developed institutions for regulating mass political participation. These studies find that any benefit from

---

[21] Steven C. Poe, Neal Tate, and Linda Camp Keith, "Repression of the Human Right to Personal Integrity Revisited: A Global Cross-National Study Covering the Years 1976–1993." *International Studies Quarterly* 43, no. 2 (1999): 291–313.

[22] Todd Landman and Marco Larizza, "Inequality and Human Rights: Who Controls What, When, and How," *International Studies Quarterly* 53, no. 3 (2009), 715–36.

[23] In some studies, though, this apparent finding may stem from a failure to weight results by population.

democratization accrues only after passing a rather high threshold to nearly complete democracy.[24] Another well-established literature, in contrast, finds that treaty-signing and mainstream methods of legal and activist follow-up have their greatest benefit for rights improvement in democratizing states.[25]

These seemingly contradictory findings could be simultaneously true if violations rise mainly at the early phases of transition, when democracy is very poorly institutionalized, and they decline in the more advanced phases of transition. Alternatively, it could be that democratizers "in the middle" are deadly unless they enjoy favorable facilitating conditions, which mainstream rights methods try to encourage by treaty signing, NGO activism, and lobbying for judicial independence.

These statistical results track fairly closely with the list of limiting conditions set out by qualitative scholars for evaluating the spiral model of rights promotion, which is based on the establishment of legal and moral standards and the shaming and coercion of violators. *The Persistent Power of Human Rights* argues that such methods are less effective in authoritarian regimes, in very weak and very strong states, in issue areas where violations are socially decentralized, and where the rights-abusing state enjoys popular support.[26] *Persistent Power*'s summary list of facilitating scope conditions omits peace and per capita income, though these are implied in some of the empirical chapters. One, for example, notes that protecting rights becomes an "almost insurmountable" task in wartime, though some rebels may be restrained by a concern not to gain a reputation for being lawbreakers.[27]

[24] Bruce Bueno de Mesquita, Feyral Marie Cherif, George Downs, and Alastair Smith, "Thinking Inside the Box: A Closer Look at Democracy and Human Rights," *International Studies Quarterly* 49, no. 3 (2005), 439–58; Helen Fein, "More Murder in the Middle: Life Integrity Violations and Democracy in the World, 1987," *Human Rights Quarterly* 17, no. 1 (1995), 170–91. Simmons, *Mobilizing for Human Rights*, refers to this literature on p. 136, note 84. See also Christian Davenport and David Armstrong, "Democracy and the Violation of Human Rights: A Statistical Analysis from 1976 to 1996," *American Journal of Political Science* 48, no. 3 (2004), 538–54. See also Samuel Huntington, *Political Order in Changing Societies* (New Haven: Yale University Press, 1968), for relevant theory.

[25] Simmons, *Mobilizing for Human Rights*, 153; Davenport and Armstrong, "Democracy and the Violation of Human Rights," 547; Fein, "More Murder in the Middle," 177, 179, 181, 183. Simmons' graph of the theoretically *expected* value of political mobilization begins to arc upward as soon as autocracy ends, whereas Davenport's and Fein's charts of actual outcomes show rights abuse remaining high and even trending slightly up at that point and declining only in complete democracy.

[26] Risse, Ropp, and Sikkink (eds.), *Persistent Power*; see also Kenneth Roth, "Africa: The Attacks on the International Criminal Court," *New York Review of Books*, February 6, 2014, 32–5.

[27] Hyeran Jo and Katherine Bryant, "Taming of the Warlords," in Risse, Ropp and Sikkink (eds.), *Persistent Power*, 239.

Overall Trends in Human Rights Outcomes

Notwithstanding the consensus on facilitating conditions for rights in general, there is much less consensus in the research on outcomes and on the effects of tactical interventions designed to improve rights in a specific setting. Here, the research findings are often contradictory, limited by problems of data and research design, hedged by conditional hypotheses that are not yet corroborated by replicating or extending studies, or simply absent.

However, even when the full battery of methods is used in mutually supportive ways, the field still faces methodological challenges. Some originate in data problems. For example, comparing trends in human rights compliance over time is difficult because awareness of abuses and data collection has changed. Likewise, scales for measuring abuses that were designed to highlight the existence of even small numbers of rights violations may be insensitive to larger differences in the number of violations at the higher end of the scale.[28] More intractable are inference problems that hinge on unobservable or unmeasureable factors. For example, James Meernik et al. note that the power of rights-abusing spoilers is central to theories about the effects of trials on human rights, but, like the rest of the quantitative literature, their study lacks any way to measure this variable or include its conditional effects in the analysis.[29] Even qualitative studies have only had limited success so far in conceptualizing the power of spoilers in a way that permits reliable comparison across cases and causal process tracing.[30]

Critics of prevailing human rights strategies also argue that statistical measures of most rights outcomes, defined in terms of treaty compliance, have not improved in recent decades, despite the intense rhetoric and mobilization of the global rights movement.[31] Defenders of the achievements of the human rights movement argue that the apparent lack of progress is an optical illusion: improved data has turned up violations that previously would have gone unreported.[32] They also argue that real

---

[28] Clark and Sikkink, "Information Effects and Human Rights Data."

[29] James Meernik, Kimi King, and Angela Nichols, "The Impact of International Tribunals and Domestic Trials on Peace and Human Rights after Civil War," *International Studies Perspectives* 11, no. 4 (2010): 309–34.

[30] Kelly Greenhill and Solomon Major, "The Perils of Profiling: Civil War Spoilers and the Collapse of Intrastate Peace Accords," *International Security* 31, no. 3 (Winter 2006/07): 7–40.

[31] Emile M. Hafner-Burton, *Making Human Rights a Reality* (Princeton: Princeton University Press, 2013), 3. Improved data cuts both ways, civil war researchers frequently adjusting their numbers downward as time passes and information improves.

[32] Fariss, "Respect for Human Rights Has Improved Over Time," proposes a very complex, indirect method for calibrating biases in measuring rights violations due to increased data availability, and historically changing standards, by making use of comparisons to continually updated historical data on the worst atrocities. He claims this technique shows

improvements have occurred in some countries, especially democratizing countries that have signed human rights treaties, but not in countries that lie outside the scope conditions of current approaches.[33] Finally, they argue that it is too soon to judge the success of mainstream rights strategies, because strengthening global norms through persuasion and institutionalization is necessarily a gradual process. For example, despite the ICC's minimal conviction rate and Africa-dominated docket, they emphasize that the institutional base for future success has been established.[34] Thus, the lack of consensus is based on disputes about the validity of data and on theoretically informed differences about how to interpret evidence.

Tactical Interventions to Improve Rights

There is only partial consensus about the effects of different tactics, with limited convergence reflecting underlying agreement about scope conditions. Research suggests that mainstream rights approaches work well mainly in what might be called easy cases: countries that are already fairly democratic, have respectable administrative capacity, have somewhat independent courts, and tolerate robust activism by principled civil society groups.[35] There is little agreement, however, on the effects of different tactics in harder cases.

Results of statistical studies of shaming tactics, for example, are inconsistent and difficult to interpret. Many studies have attempted to identify the conditions in which shaming works, but with little convergence so far. Some studies find that shaming is often ineffective or even counterproductive, leading, for example, to backlash (see chapters by Vinjamuri, and Cooley and Schaaf, this volume). Hafner-Burton, based on statistical findings and numerous brief illustrations, finds that shaming is generally correlated with improvements in political rights but not physical integrity rights. She concludes that denunciations can have a "whack-a-mole" effect, leading the abuser to shift from more visible repression to other forms.[36] Jennifer Lind's detailed monograph, *Sorry States*, finds that

---

that rights outcomes are improving. Though an intriguing step forward, this methodology requires making several heroic assumptions, including confidence in updated atrocities data, which remains highly politicized. See Peter Andreas and Kelly M. Greenhill (eds.) *Sex, Drugs, and Body Counts: The Politics of Numbers in Global Crime and Conflict* (Ithaca: Cornell University Press, 2010), chapters 1, 6, 7, 8, and 11.

[33] Clark and Sikkink, "Informational Effects"; Simmons, *Mobilizing for Human Rights.*

[34] Thomas Risse and Kathryn Sikkink, "Conclusions," *Persistent Power*, 281–2, 294.

[35] Simmons, *Mobilizing for Human Rights.*

[36] Emilie Hafner-Burton, "Sticks and Stones: Naming and Shaming the Human Rights Enforcement Problem." *International Organization* 62, no. 4 (Fall 2008): 689–716;

repeated international demands that Japan apologize for its World War II atrocities have played into the hands of Japanese nationalists who were lobbying for official visits to the Shinto shrine where war criminals are interred.[37] Other studies stress more positive findings, many of them trying to identify the conditions under which shaming is effective. Ann Marie Clark, illustrating her statistical study with the example of Indonesia, finds that shaming reduces rights abuse in countries that have ratified rights treaties, even if they are non-democracies.[38] An entirely statistical study by Matthew Krain found that shaming reduced the severity of 29 genocides and mass killings from 1976 to 2008.[39] Another entirely statistical study by Amanda Murdie and David Davis, offered as a test of the spiral model, finds that shaming by human rights organizations improves human rights if local human rights activists are numerous and if third parties such as states echo the denunciations of the activists.[40]

Why do these studies find such varied results? One reason may be that they ask somewhat different questions, advancing hypotheses that are qualified in different ways, using different databases and research designs, and covering different time periods.[41] The influential study by Murdie and Davis also raises the issue of how to interpret causality in a multifaceted interaction among (1) shaming by rights organizations in a setting in which (2) the flourishing of local rights organizations is not

---

Darius Rejali makes a similar argument, claiming that pressure from human rights advocates has driven states to adopt torture techniques that are less visible; see Darius Rejali, *Torture and Democracy* (Princeton: Princeton University Press, 2008). A factor that is not sufficiently taken into account by some of these studies is that disproportionate publicity may be aimed at recalcitrant actors that are hardest to change. If this were so, results would be biased against shaming tactics.

[37] Jennifer Lind, *Sorry States: Apologies in International Relations* (Ithaca: Cornell University Press, 2008). See also Jelena Subotic, *Hijacked Justice: Dealing with the Past in the Balkans* (Ithaca: Cornell University Press, 2009).

[38] Ann Marie Clark, "The Normative Context of Human Rights Criticism: Treaty Ratification and UN Mechanisms," in Risse, Ropp, and Sikkink, *Persistent Power*, chapter 7, p. 143.

[39] Matthew Krain, "J'accuse! Does Naming and Shaming Perpetrators Reduce the Severity of Genocides or Politicides?" *International Studies Quarterly* 56, no. 3 (2012): 574–89.

[40] Amanda M. Murdie and David R. Davis, "Shaming and Blaming: Using Events Data to Assess the Impact of Human Rights INGOs," *International Studies Quarterly* 56, no. 1 (2012): 1–16.

[41] For example, the outcome variable in the Murdie and Davis study is improvement in physical integrity rights, coded yes or no. Since they find no effect when they use what they call the "raw scores" for physical integrity rights, it may be that their reworked measure is picking up very small improvements, which they magnify by their practice of binary coding. The lack of even the briefest case illustrations further hinders the effort to understand why studies report diverse findings. See also Oskar N. T. Thoms, James Ron, and Roland Paris, "State-level Effects of Transitional Justice: What Do We Know?" *International Journal of Transitional Justice* 4, no. 3 (2010): 329–54.

suppressed by the state and (3) powerful outside parties, including states, are also exerting pressure. Because all of these elements are included in the spiral model, it is hard to tell whether shaming per se is doing much causal work. A number of these studies imply that the scope conditions for effective shaming may be quite narrow, putting its usefulness as a widespread advocacy tactic in doubt.

Implications of Social Science Findings for Advocacy

From this preliminary audit, on which the chapters below reflect both explicitly and implicitly, we draw an important conclusion. Despite the sophistication of much contemporary scholarship, the only broad consensus is on the background conditions that facilitate human rights success (essentially, peace and democracy). Disagreement continues among scholars over what the available data says about human rights outcomes in general, and specific interventions in particular. Building on the groundbreaking earlier work of Sikkink and Simmons, the chapter in *Human Rights Futures* by Dancy and Sikkink makes a strong case for the effectiveness of human rights mobilization. Much of the most influential human rights scholarship draws on their arguments and data to substantiate the claim that human rights are improving, indicating that the efforts of transnational human rights movements using international and national law can succeed.

For many advocates, this conclusion is both welcome and useful. They often hold to a vision of human rights that is both *normative* and *universal*. Human rights norms emerge and prevail at least in part, advocates claim, because they are inherently persuasive to people's innate sense of justice and fairness, given exposure to information and arguments on their behalf. In addition, human rights are accepted when they result from an appropriate, largely voluntary, and substantially consensual process of normative deliberation, such as processes of negotiating and ratifying multilateral treaties. As a result, scholarly theories based on these assumptions study the effects of ratifying treaties, persuading audiences to adopt norms, institutionalizing them, and shaming and punishing violators.[42] These theories are sometimes based on an analogy to the workings of domestic law and moral social rules.[43]

---

[42] Keck and Sikkink, *Activists Beyond Borders: Advocacy Networks in International Politics*; Martha Finnemore and Kathryn Sikkink, "International Norm Dynamics and Political Change," *International Organization* 52, no. 4 (Autumn 1998): 887–918; Thomas Risse, Stephen C. Ropp, and Kathryn Sikkink (eds.) *The Power of Human Rights* (Cambridge: Cambridge University Press, 1999).

[43] Sikkink, *The Justice Cascade*, 170.

Thus, the assumptions behind this kind of social science theory of human rights processes and outcomes overlap to a considerable extent with the explicit or implicit assumptions of many human rights organizations themselves.[44] Indeed, influential scholarship drew lessons from the practices of principled transnational activist networks in the first place to develop causal theories of rights promotion, such as the foundational boomerang, norms cascade, and spiral models, as well as recent work on international law as a lever for empowering rights activism in transitional countries.[45] Nevertheless, these scholarly, practice-derived accounts of successful mobilization, embedding, and impact increasingly face a range of reservations, questions, and critiques, as we now outline in Section 3.

3   Human Rights Mobilization and Its Critics

In this volume, we have grouped the chapters under four broad headings. That the arguments made, and evidence presented, often spills over these artificial boundaries we readily accept. But at the heart of each of the four critiques is a distinct claim: that there are structural impediments to human rights progress (*scope conditions*), that the scale and intensity of the pushback against human rights is substantial (*backlash*), that global rights rhetoric too often works at cross-purposes with local social justice priorities (*localization*), and that the human rights project as a whole is living on borrowed time (*utopias* and *endtimes*).

Scope Conditions

Mainstream approaches traditionally assume considerable leeway for activism to make a difference even in the face of structural impediments. *The Power of Human Rights* (1999) suggested that the spiral model could work in a broad range of settings, including very poor countries with few facilitating conditions for rights or democracy. The follow-up book organized by the same team, *The Persistent Power of Human Rights* (2013), has much more to say about the limitations that structural parameters such as the strength of the state place on the action of individuals in promoting or abusing rights, but its message remains that meaningful progress is possible.

Another approach assumes, however, that rights emerge, if at all, from specific configurations of social power. It asks: who has control over

---

[44] Of course, there are many more skeptical practitioners as well who would embrace some aspects of the critiques outlined in *Human Rights Futures*.

[45] See the references by Sikkink and by Simmons.

resources and rule-setting, what rules are in their interest, and how do they struggle and bargain over the creation of rules and institutions to realize those interests?[46] If this background social power is too weak to sustain a popular reform coalition then the drive for human rights is like a general without an army.

For example, a standard textbook on the history of rights traces their incremental expansion as a result of social modernization from privileges of armed nobility in such decrees as the *Magna Carta*, through civil and political rights for urban commercial classes, and finally to social and economic protections for the politically empowered working class.[47] The research agenda that emerges from these assumptions tends to ask questions about the power, interests, and coalition potential of rights-promoting groups and of rights-abusing "spoilers." Tactically, the research focus is on conditional incentives, political bargaining, and investment in enforcement institutions as precursors to the emergence of rights.[48] In this view, politics tends to lead; norms tend to follow. Under *scope conditions*, we ask some searching questions of the norms-led narrative of progress by looking at three sets of structural barriers in more detail.

Snyder, for example, argues that successful movements for change have been backed by well-placed, diversely motivated coalitions of political actors whose existing power and influence can be used to align around rights claims. But these are not necessarily rights-driven actors.[49] Risse, meanwhile, examines the prospect of human rights observance in areas of limited statehood where the state is unable or unwilling to make its power count.

These accounts remain committed to the successful realization of human rights, but they take a pragmatic view of how that might be achieved. In contrast to the use of shaming, moral condemnation and persuasion, and the pursuit of 'human rights first' (that is, human rights as a process as well as an outcome), pragmatically minded scholars have argued for compromises that include bargaining with powerful spoilers

---

[46] Michael Mann, *The Sources of Social Power*, volume II, *The Rise of Classes and Nation-States, 1760–1914* (Cambridge: Cambridge University Press, 1993), ch. 6, discusses the relationship between structural and normative power in the French Revolution.

[47] Ishay, *The History of Human Rights*.

[48] Hafner-Burton, *Making Human Rights a Reality* and Emilie Hafner-Burton, *Forced to Be Good: Why Trade Agreements Boost Human Rights* (Ithaca: Cornell University Press, 2009); Jack Snyder and Leslie Vinjamuri, "Trials and Errors: Principle and Pragmatism in Strategies of International Justice," *International Security* 28, No. 3 (Winter 2003/04): 5–44.

[49] Hafner-Burton focuses on the necessity of allying rights claims to political power as well, making it clear that without the backing of major states the prospects for improvements in human rights globally are diminished: Hafner-Burton, *Making Human Rights a Reality*.

and striking amnesty deals that might reduce rights abuse by helping to consolidate peace.[50] They argue for the merits of sequencing the pursuit of specific rights or accountability measures, working first to create political or institutional conditions that make rights feasible.[51] On the geopolitical level, pragmatists stress the value of enlisting support for global advocacy campaigns from rising democratic powers such as India, South Africa, and Brazil, even if this means tailoring themes to their interests and sensibilities. They also accept that human rights progress requires making peace with the use of political and economic power to raise the costs of non-compliance.[52]

Having said this, the normative and the social power approaches are not mutually exclusive, and they do have some overlap. Both envision a role for material coercion, and both are concerned with institutional development. Nonetheless, they tend to prioritize different causal mechanisms in terms of importance and in temporal sequence, and thus make distinguishable empirical predictions that can be tested. Both also realize that there is a particular problem with "hard cases."

If debates about rights tactics sometimes sound like a dialogue of the deaf, one reason may be a failure to be clear about the distinction between easy and hard cases. Much empirical research portrays a division into three distinct worlds of rights compliance: stable democracies, where rights guarantees are routine notwithstanding peculiar "exceptionalisms" and lapses; transitional states with some democratic features and some liberal institutions, where violations may be common but mainstream legal and activist methods can be effective (the "easy cases" for rights promotion); and authoritarian states, where mainstream methods rarely work and alternative methods are not well conceptualized or studied (the "hard cases").

Better locating the dividing line between "easy cases," where mainstream rights methods are promising, and "hard cases," which are beyond

---

[50] Carolyn M. Moehling, "State Child Labor Laws and the Decline of Child Labor," *Explorations in Economic History* 36, no. 1 (January 1999): 72–106. For an argument that getting the right result by the wrong means is a violation of rights, not a success for rights, see Kathryn Sikkink, "The Role of Consequences, Comparison and Counterfactuals in Constructivist Ethical Thought," in Richard Price, ed., *Moral Limit and Possibility in World Politics* (Cambridge, UK: Cambridge University Press 2008), 83–111; Jack Snyder and Leslie Vinjamuri, "Principled Pragmatism and the Logic of Consequences," *International Theory.* 4, no. 3 (November 2012): 434–48.

[51] Remarks by Kenneth Roth, "Roth: In Syria Peace Talks, Keep Justice – Not Impunity – on the Table," *International Peace Institute,* January 17, 2014, www.ipinst.org/events/pa nel-discussions/details/509-roth-in-syria-peace-talks-keep-justicenot-impunityon-the-ta ble.html; Also, remarks by Aryeh Neier on the Arab Revolutions, *European Council on Foreign Relations,* London, March 9, 2011.

[52] Hafner-Burton, *Making Human Rights a Reality.*

the scope conditions of mainstream theories and methods, would be of great value for scholarship and human rights practice.

Backlash

Early theories of human rights promotion placed most of their emphasis on the persuasive or coercive initiatives of rights promoters. The targets of influence were typically portrayed as out-argued, out-gunned, or lured down the slippery slope of compliance. Updated versions of the spiral model, however, join the scope conditions, backlash, and localization approaches in acknowledging that rights promotion is often relentlessly contested by actors drawing on a deep well of social, cultural, ideological, material, and geographic resources.

In many of these cases, entrenched and powerful spoilers have pushed back against the encroachment of human rights on their autonomy, sometimes strengthening their domestic base of support by mobilizing alternative value systems, at other times creating alternative venues that bypass rights or reinterpreting the demands of those rights so they no longer conflict with sovereign prerogatives. As human rights advocacy has grown stronger and more intrusive, many state leaders have become increasingly strategic in their response – for example, turning to regional institutions to deflect and restrict international human rights or even to create counternorms (Vinjamuri, and Cooley and Schaaf, this volume).

Backlash is "a behavioral response to the application or clear anticipation of a specific policy or institutional practice that is perceived to be in opposition to the interests or values of a particular actor or set of actors. It is characterized by an attempt to alter, restrict, subvert, or otherwise resist this application of policy or practice" (Vinjamuri, this volume). Backlash does not need to be a direct response to the promotion of human rights norms, in other words, but may be pre-emptive. It may also range from great powers explicitly rejecting the reach of human rights (e.g., Russia, China, and the United States refusing to join the ICC), to medium-sized and smaller powers frustrating the due process of international human rights and international justice processes (e.g., Turkey and Egypt, or Kenya and South Africa over the ICC). Restricting the activities of human rights NGOs (by barring foreign funding, for instance, or changing tax and registration rules) or challenging human rights norms through a countervailing sovereignty and stability discourse are further examples.

In her chapter for this collection, Hurd points to a further irony: the very activities of human rights promoters may bring about a deterioration in the long-term prospects for human rights observance. By advocating the right to religious freedom, and thus accentuating the advantages – recognition, mobilization, influence – that come with identifying as a religious group, the possibility for conflict over fundamental norms may be enhanced. As an unintended consequence, human rights promotion helps create the very circumstances that it is most keen to avoid.

Advocates for the success of human rights might ask why be so concerned with backlash now – after all, there has always been resistance to human rights from both the left and the right, as well as from religious groups? One explanation is that the very ubiquity of rights, and their use as conditional aspects of global governance and foreign policy prescriptions (e.g., the United States and Venezuela), gives them a power and influence they have only had since the 1990s. They now threaten established authorities in a way they never have before. Moreover, in a world in which China is rising, the international system now has at least one great power (two, if we count Russia) that openly rejects the rights discourse, providing inspiration and diplomatic cover for other resistors.

Localization

A third approach assumes that, while rights concepts may have analogues in most of the world's cultures, they emerge in *local* forms using *vernacular* terminologies in different cultural settings. The research agenda that emerges from this perspective (associated most prominently with Sally Engle Merry, this volume, and Amitav Acharya) asks questions about how local discourses interact with the universalistic language of the contemporary global human rights movement.

These "vernacularizers" or "localizers" of rights have stressed the role of local brokers capable of adapting norms to local cultures.[53] This is not necessarily a unidirectional process. The current research agenda, while retaining the basic propositions of largely one-way influence models, now routinely accepts that all interactions on rights are two-way (or more likely multi-directional), involving "blocking," "backdooring," "multi-vocality," and phony compliance with norms of legal accountability (Hertel, this volume).[54]

[53] Peggy Levitt and Sally Engle Merry, "Making Women's Human Rights in the Vernacular: Navigating the Culture/Rights Divide," in *Gender and Culture at the Limit of Rights*, Dorothy Hodgson (ed.) (Philadelphia: University of Pennsylvania Press, pp. 81–100); Aaron Boesenecker and Leslie Vinjamuri, "Lost in Translation? Civil Society and the Negotiation of International Norms," *International Journal of Transitional Justice* (Special Issue on Civil Society) 5, no. 3 (2011): 345–65.

[54] In addition to *Persistent Power of Human Rights* and Shareen Hertel, *Unexpected Power: Conflict and Change among Transnational Activists* (Ithaca: Cornell University Press, 2006), see Kate Cronin-Furman, "Managing Expectations: International Criminal

Successful rights promotion outside the West, say advocates of vernacularization, requires more scope for domestic agents to draw on local culture to create normative alternatives that secure autonomy for locals. They need to do this, however, without potential converts to rights becoming alienated from the rights-compatible discourses and practices to which they are already committed. Vernacularization, they note, has been most successful when local brokers are anchored domestically and have good networks abroad that enable them to adapt international norms to local contexts. Grounding international norms in local culture reduces the risk that spoilers will be able to brand rights activists as handmaidens of imperialism. It is even possible to see "American exceptionalism" on this basis as a kind of vernacularization.

In some cases, cultural differences have driven a wedge through transnational human rights networks, separating international advocates from local activists. Human rights norms have failed to gain traction where they seem tangential to solving the most pressing problems, like endemic poverty, underdevelopment, climate change, or disease. In countries where elites can appeal to Islam, evangelical Christianity, and even the Catholic Church, pressures to embrace women's rights have been easily deflected. As a consequence, translating rights ideas into the vernacular may also at times grease a slippery slope toward transgression.

Scholarly research has addressed the effectiveness of different persuasion techniques to enrich and diversify global rights cultures across cultural boundaries, including analyzing both the modalities of decentralization and two-way dialogue.[55] Merry makes the point that the power of the human rights message for downtrodden constituencies in developing countries stems in large part from the idea that universal ideals propounded by the most powerful, successful societies in the world are being applied to their own situation, no matter what local norms say. Thus, she raises the question of the trade-off in effectiveness between the

Trials and the Prospects for Deterrence of Mass Atrocity," *International Journal of Transitional Justice* 7, no. 3 (2013): 434–54, first published online August 7, 2013 doi:10.1093/ijtj/ijt016; Subotic, *Hijacked Justice*; Boesenecker and Vinjamuri, "Lost in Translation?"; Amitav Acharya, "Norm Subsidiarity and Regional Orders: Sovereignty, Regionalism, and Rule-Making in the Third World,'" *International Studies Quarterly* 55, No. 1 (March 2011): 95–123, and Keck and Sikkink, *Activists Beyond Borders*, 67–77.

[55] Peggy Levitt and Sally Merry, "Vernacularization on the Ground: Local Uses of Global Women's Rights in Peru, China, India, and the United States," *Global Networks* 9, No. 4 (2009); Amitav Acharya, *Rethinking Power, Institutions, and Ideas in World Politics: Whose IR?* (London: Routledge, 2013); Lila Abu Lughod, "Do Muslim Women Really Need Saving? Anthropological Reflections on Cultural Relativism and Its Others," *American Anthropologist* 104, No. 3 (September 2002): 783–90; Andrew Moravcsik, "The Paradox of U.S. Human Rights Policy," in Michael Ignatieff (ed.) *American Exceptionalism and Human Rights* (Princeton: Princeton University Press, 2005), 147–97.

charisma of universality and the ease of adaptation into local language and practice. Like the question of the potential distortion – indeed, perversion – of rights concepts through vernacularization, this subject has been noticed but barely studied, let alone studied in a systematic way that asks when one horn of the dilemma predominates.

Empirical studies of vernacularization so far mainly serve the development and illustration of theory rather than the testing of it. Such illustrative studies include accounts of improvements in grass-roots women's rights practices in India without using rights language, and of the translation of universalistic rights arguments opposing female genital cutting into local Sufi religious doctrine in Senegal.[56] More mixed results, however, are reported in theory-building case studies of resistance to mainstream international rights frames by local activists in the global South who pursue different rights goals or prefer different kinds of rights justifications.[57] Similarly, scholars diverge in their estimation of whether local justice initiatives comply with or represent an unsettling departure from international human rights standards.[58] Finally, rights vernacularization studies also include unsettling accounts of human rights talk being used to justify the lynching of criminals by urban vigilantes as well as torture of suspects by police with special human rights training.[59] A next step for studies of vernacularization may be to specify conditions under which local translation facilitates or undermines adoption of rights thinking.

Utopias and Endtimes

A final approach to the future of human rights questions both the normative universalism of mainstream rights thinking and the global convergence assumptions of liberal modernization theory. Taking the vernacularization agenda a step further, this approach questions whether the cross-cultural impact of the human rights project is too superficial to thrive in the event of American hegemonic decline and the emergence of

---

[56] Levitt and Merry, "Vernacularization on the Ground"; Alfred Stepan, "Rituals of Respect: Sufis and Secularists in Senegal in Comparative Perspective," *Comparative Politics* 44, no. 4 (July 2012): 379–401.

[57] See Hertel, *Unexpected Power*, on blocking in Bangladesh and backdooring in Mexico.

[58] See Phil Clark, *The Gacaca Courts and Post-Genocide Justice and Reconciliation in Rwanda: Justice without Lawyers* (Cambridge: Cambridge University Press, 2010), and Lars Waldorf, "A Mere Pretense of Justice: Complementarity, Sham Trials, and Victor's Justice at the Rwanda Tribunal," *Fordham International Law Journal* 33, no. 4 (2010): 1221–77.

[59] Daniel Goldstein, *Outlawed: Between Security and Rights in a Bolivian City* (Durham: Duke University Press, 2012); Rachel Wahl, *Just Violence: Torture and Human Rights in the Eyes of the Police* (Stanford: Stanford University Press, 2017).

multiple modernities, including illiberal ones (Hopgood, this volume). It also suggests that Western liberalism has taken a wrong turn, over-investing in the rights approach to liberal progress and systematically sidelining both ideas (like freedom and equality) and alternative mobilizing principles (national self-determination, socialism) that promise more genuine normative progress (Moyn, this volume).

This research agenda asks whether human rights thinking is an unexportable product of liberal capitalism, whether it lacks the penetration power of earlier forms of cultural imperialism such as Christianity, whether the international human rights movement is recent and superficial, and whether it competes ideologically with and crowds out more promising mass-based movements for social justice?[60] These accounts are more critical of the whole enterprise of human rights. They suggest a future in which the aspiration to human rights is largely restricted to a zone of liberal-democratic states in the West. These accounts doubt the emancipatory potential of the transnational middle class and fear that the challenge to global liberal norms by Russia and China, as well as by populist nationalism in several Western states, including the United States, heralds a permanent reverse for human rights in an increasingly multipolar, even post-Western world. Increased backlash is evidence of existential contestation, in other words.

By monopolizing the liberal approach to freedom, rights have sidelined a much richer tradition of human progress and undermined their own emancipatory potential in the process. Furthermore, given the forces now arrayed against human rights, the narrow cultural roots of their underlying conception of the person and the distributional consequences they entail for equality in society are becoming clearer.

4   Conclusion

Contemporary rights practitioners have actively debated how to respond to these challenges, just as scholars have worked hard to figure out how to measure them. Many practitioners favor retaining a core focus on civil and political rights, a central role for legal tools in rights promotion, and adherence to universal standards. For many scholars and also advocates, the rights project is a long-term game; pushback and hypocrisy are inevitable, but temporary, setbacks. Growing participation in rights promotion by non-Western activists is an important objective, they agree, but not at the expense of watering down core principles. Others argue that

---

[60] Moyn, *Last Utopia*; Hopgood, *Endtimes*.

pragmatism is a realistic necessity in a world that's very different from that of the 1970s or even the 1990s.

To paraphrase Santayana, to get where you want to go you need to know where you have been, or at least your direction of travel. This is the spirit in which this volume was assembled. The chapters are written by scholars in political science, history, and anthropology whose work has shaped the development of debates about human rights over the past two decades. Our hope is to try to see the future through analyses of human rights that are rooted firmly in their past and present circumstances. We have seen that significant differences exist within the worlds of human rights advocacy and scholarship on a number of issues and these can be simplified into three questions: Have human rights improved? If so, why have they improved (and if not, why not)? And what are the alternatives to business as usual? Should we do more of the same in tackling hard cases, should we be more savvy (or cut our losses), or should we do something else entirely? There could hardly be more pressing questions to ask in the changing world we live in.

2   Human Rights Data, Processes, and Outcomes: How Recent Research Points to a Better Future

Geoff Dancy and Kathryn Sikkink

Introduction

Just as the end of the twentieth century brought with it brimming optimism around human rights ideals and interventions, the last decade has been flooded by pessimism aimed at the human rights movement. Historians are contending that the seeds of failure were planted deep within the foundations of human rights politics, which as a result of their minimalism cannot manage to produce an adequate vision of social justice.[1] Scholars now foretell the "endtimes of human rights" or the "twilight of human rights law."[2] The rise of this "paradoxical sensibility" among commentators might have begun with the onset of the Global War on Terror and the understandable fallout of cynicism it produced – or it might be the by-product of intellectuals' veiled nostalgia for wars over competing visions of the social good as opposed to fights over individual rights.[3] In any case, it would be hard to ignore the pervasive sense of pessimism in some current accounts. This pessimism seems warranted following 2016's "Brexit" and US presidential campaigns, which both evidenced an anti-globalist mood looming over the liberal West.[4]

---

[1] Samuel Moyn, *The Last Utopia: Human Rights in History* (Cambridge, MA: The Belknap Press of Harvard University Press, 2010). Compare to Robert Meister, *After Evil: A Politics of Human Rights* (New York: Columbia University Press, 2011).

[2] Stephen Hopgood, *The Endtimes of Human Rights* (Ithaca: Cornell University Press, 2013). Eric A. Posner, *The Twilight of Human Rights Law* (Oxford: Oxford University Press, 2014).

[3] For paradoxical sensibility, see Kenneth Cmiel, "The Recent History of Human Rights," *American Historical Review* 109, no. 1 (2004): 133. See also Steve J. Stern and Scott Straus, eds., *The Human Rights Paradox: Universality and Its Discontents* (Madison: University of Wisconsin Press, 2014). For the war on terror, see David Lubin, "The War on Terrorism and the End of Human Rights," *Philosophy and Public Policy Quarterly* 22, no. 3, Summer (2002). Michael Ignatieff, "Is the Human Rights Era Ending?," *The New York Times* February 5, 2002.

[4] See "Anti-globalists: Why They're Wrong." *The Economist* October 1, 2016.

Released into the current milieu, this volume concerns itself with the future of human rights, and, if successful, it will play a part in creating that future simply by imagining it. After all, science and philosophy are themselves productive. As political scientists by training, we take this productive potential seriously, and we make an attempt to guide our expectations of the future, immediate and distant, with careful research and theories that explain past events. We share many of the concerns raised by the measured and thoughtful Introduction to this volume, with its effort to categorize and synthesize a very diverse literature and provide compelling questions about human rights futures. We have some points of departure from the Introduction, however, including some disagreements about human rights outcomes. We share Hopgood, Snyder, and Vinjamuri's concerns with interrogating "contradictory" findings, and strengthening research into concrete policies meant to improve human rights practices – but we do not share the prevailing sense that tactical "interventions" have thus far been of limited use, nor do we think that law and activism will inevitably be crushed under the weight of resistant structures.

In order to construct our version of the future of human rights, our first task is to provide an account of human rights from past to present. In this chapter, we first plan on countering the viewpoint that human rights *outcomes* to date have been mostly unpromising or marginal. We do this by analyzing a series of new studies that focus on adjusting the biased datasets about human rights upon which many assessments are based. Our second aim is to show that positive outcomes have resulted in part from human rights *processes* including legal mobilization, transnational advocacy, and social movement resistance. Our third goal is to answer critical questions about *the mechanisms that link processes to outcomes*, and to suggest promising directions for future research.

This is not the place for a discussion of our intellectual commitments or traditions.[5] It is sufficient to stress that our major concern is with puzzle-driven or problem-oriented empirical research designed to address how to improve human rights practices in the world. Like others, we try to account for political realities, and we do not willfully ignore evidence of backlash. That said, our research typically does not *end* with an identification of paradoxes or intractable challenges. We also endeavor toward

---

[5] For a more autobiographical discussion of Sikkink's intellectual commitments, see Kathryn Sikkink. *Evidence for Hope: Making Human Rights Work in the 21st Century* (Princeton: Princeton University Press, 2017) and Kathryn Sikkink, "The Role of Consequences, Comparison and Counterfactuals in Constructivist Ethical Thought," in *Moral Limit and Possibility in World Politics*, ed. Richard M. Price (New York: Cambridge University Press, 2008) 83–111. For Dancy's intellectual assessments, see Geoff Dancy and Christopher Fariss, "Rescuing Human Rights Law from Legalism and Its Critics," *Human Rights Quarterly* 39, no. 1 (2017): 1–36.

practical solutions. In this sense, we do not think our project is out of tune with pragmatist concerns, and we have argued elsewhere that human rights legal activism is in fact quite pragmatic.[6] Moreover, our general approach is to theorize about politics and events, rather than to muse about intellectual currents. With this in mind, we choose to forego certain debates (for example with Samuel Moyn [Chapter 11 in this volume] about liberalism and ideology-driven research) because engaging with them would distract us from our main concern, which is to consider the future prospects of human rights on the ground.

In response to Moyn, however, we do not apologize at all for favoring the use of empirical evidence or sophisticated analytic methodologies. Exactly because of the disagreements highlighted in the Introduction to the volume, the field needs to continue to produce high-quality empirical and theoretical research, and collegial debates about the merits of this research. In this context, to critique political science research on human rights that "fetishizes" evidence-based empiricism would seem to be missing the point. While we recognize that not all readers will be satisfied with our approach, we at least make the plea that anyone engaging with this debate weighs the available evidence.

Human Rights Outcomes

The Introduction to this volume – with its breadth of topics, careful readings of previous research, and concise frameworking – is a valuable learning tool. One of the more helpful distinctions the chapter makes is between human rights conditions, "tactical interventions," and outcomes. However, we prefer to avoid the sense that all efforts to legalize or normalize human rights are "interventions," which connotes the outside disturbance of internal equilibrium. Not all human rights efforts are external shocks. In ways that are often hard to observe, human rights norms also change political "facilitating conditions" that Hopgood et al. outline. For this reason, we propose and use an alternative framework to discuss human rights research, involving two parts: processes and outcomes. Processes involve solidifying emerging legal norms, advocating transnationally for human rights, litigating in courts, and engaging in peaceful rights-based resistance. While these all may be valuable activities in themselves, most people assume such processes are useful actions only if they *causally* produce beneficial changes in rights outcomes. These outcomes include decreased use of torture and other

---

[6] Geoff Dancy, "Human Rights Pragmatism: Belief, Inquiry, and Action," *European Journal of International Relations* 22, no. 3 (2016): 512–35.

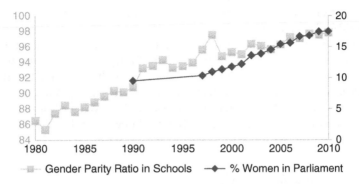

Figure 2.1: Global Trends in Women's Rights over Time.
Source: The Quality of Government Dataset.[1]

[1] Jan Teorell et al., *The Quality of Government Dataset, Version 20dec13* (University of Gothenberg: The Quality of Government Institute, www.qog.pol.gu.se, 2013).

violations to physical integrity, improved social and economic conditions in line with rights guarantees, and the protection of vulnerable groups.

We now have nearly decades of empirical research on human rights advocacy and law. At the same time, rights-based practices are rapidly evolving and shifting to "new human rights" issue areas such as women's human rights and LGBT rights.[7] In an effort to keep pace, empirical research has turned up a number of intriguing findings related to outcomes. For example, women's rights seem to provoke greater cultural and religious conflict than almost any other human rights issue.[8] Case in point, the CEDAW Convention has been the subject of more state reservations upon ratification than any other human rights treaty, and many of these reservations specifically mention culture and religion. And yet, we find that in the aggregate, women's political rights – including the right to run for and hold office, and to receive primary and secondary education – is gradually improving over time (see Figure 2.1).

[7] Clifford Bob, *The International Struggle for New Human Rights* (Philadelphia: University of Pennsylvania Press, 2009). Phillip M. Ayoub, "With Arms Wide Shut: Threat Perception, Norm Reception and Mobilized Resistance to LGBT Rights," *Journal of Human Rights* 13, no. 3 (2014).

[8] See the debate in Susan Moller Okin, *Is Multiculturalism Bad for Women?* (Princeton: Princeton University Press, 1999). Also see Catherine A. MacKinnon, *Are Women Human? And Other International Dialogues* (Cambridge, MA: Harvard University Press, 2006).

Furthermore, some of this is due to high progressive compliance with the CEDAW Convention.[9]

Research on women's rights and protections and sexual discrimination are crucial new directions for the future of human rights, along with the study of local and transnational efforts to mobilize around the right to a clean environment. However, most skeptics ask: What about the failed promise of the international bill of rights? What about stagnating global trends in the protection of physical integrity and social, economic, and cultural rights?

Physical Integrity Rights

In order to discuss whether or not human rights action has led to promising outcomes, we first need to specify what we mean by "outcomes." We assume that the editors of the volume, when they speak of the record of outcomes, do not mean to compare to utopic ideals. Needless to say, human rights outcomes often fall short of a perfect world. The work of the human rights movement is to continue to hold policy makers accountable to their commitments; the role of social scientists is to evaluate whether, how, and when progress has been made in relation to past practice. In order to conduct such evaluations, we need realistic yardsticks to measure human rights progress.

Ironically, progress toward the protection of physical integrity rights is at once hidden by and ascertainable through cross-national datasets. To explain, we first need to consider that large datasets of any kind are a blessing and a curse. They are both the culmination of a magnificent amount of synthesizing research and a repository of human bias and computational error. Datasets on civil and political rights are no exception. Early human rights researchers originally created events-based measures that focused on particular historical incidents of mass murder, genocide, or politicide that belonged to campaigns of state terror; however, by the late 1980s, events data were challenged for being uneven, biased, and difficult to compare.[10] Some country's events were simply

---

[9] Beth Simmons, *Mobilizing for Human Rights: International Law in Domestic Politics* (Cambridge: Cambridge University Press, 2009). Daniel W. Hill, "Estimating the Effects of Human Rights Treaties on State Behavior," *The Journal of Politics* 72, no. 4 (Oct 2010): 1161–1174. Yonatan Lupu, "The Informative Power of Treaty Commitment: Using the Spatial Model to Address Selection Effects," *American Journal of Political Science* 57, no. 4 (2013).

[10] See Steven C. Poe, "The Decision to Repress: An Integrative Theoretical Approach to the Research on Human Rights and Repression," in *Understanding Human Rights Violations: New Systematic Studies*, ed. Sabine C. Carey and Steven C. Poe (Burlington: Ashgate Publishing Company, 2004), 17–38. Christopher J. Fariss, "Respect for Human

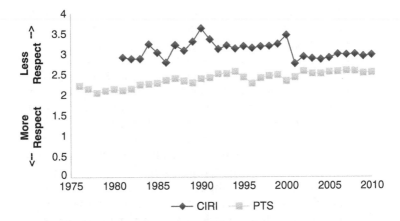

Figure 2.2: Global Average Standard-Based Human Rights Scores.
*The CIRI Physical Integrity Scale is 0–8, and the PTS scale is 0–5.
The PTS line here represents the average combination of PTS scores
derived from Amnesty and State Department Reports.

better recorded than others. For this reason, researchers moved toward
standard-based measures, which assign scores to every country in the
world in every year, based on subjective criteria applied to primary
sources documents.

Today, many statistical studies of international human rights change rely
on two prominent standard-based measures of states' human rights performance: the Political Terror Scale (PTS) and the Cingranelli-Richards
Human Rights Data Set (CIRI). These two measures in turn rely on two
annual reports that have been kept for decades, the *Amnesty International
Annual Report*, and the US State Department annual *Country Reports on
Human Rights Practices*. PTS and CIRI cover most countries of the world
and offer scholars data that can be used to test causal hypotheses about
human rights in a cross-national setting and over time.[11] When charted
over time, these popular datasets tend to show stagnant and unchanging
global levels of repression. Figure 2.2 shows that, despite minor fluctua-
tions, global average scores on PTS and CIRI have stayed mostly flat from

---

Rights Has Improved over Time: Modeling the Changing Standard of Accountability,"
American Political Science Review 108, no. 2 (2014): 304.

[11] Mark Gibney et al., "Political Terror Scale, 1976–2012," www.politicalterrorscale.org/
Retrieved February 14, 2014. David L. Cingranelli, David L. Richards, and K. Chad
Clay, "The Cingranelli-Richards (CIRI) Human Rights Dataset," (www
.humanrightsdata.com/p/data-documentation.html).

the late 1970s to 2010. This is the main evidence that has led many scholars to conclude that human rights progress has been less than promising.

But as Clark and Sikkink have argued at length elsewhere, it is likely that this apparently unchanging level of repression is due to greater human rights awareness and the increase in the quality and quantity of information about human rights around the world. Recent human rights source reports from Amnesty International and the US State Department typically contain much more and better information than earlier reports. More recent reports also tend to document a wider range of human rights violations. Keck and Sikkink have referred to this more generally as the "information paradox": as NGOs draw attention to new forms of human rights violations and make more information available about human rights, in some cases it may appear that the human rights situation is getting worse when in fact we simply have more information about human rights practices.[12] A clear example of this in the current period is the apparent increase in the use of rape as a tool of war. Few researchers think there is a *new* epidemic of rape in wartime. Rather, it would appear that the increasing awareness of rape as a war crime has contributed to an upsurge of reporting about rape both by victims and by NGOs, international organizations, and the press.[13]

Over time, diligent reporting on the world's horrors has led to a "changing standard of accountability": "Monitoring agencies look harder for torture, look in more places for torture, and classify more acts as torture."[14] An increase in the quality and quantity of information about human rights violations in the world and greater attention to the full range of human rights is good news for scholars and practitioners in this area, but it could have some unanticipated effects on the consistency of human rights measures such as CIRI and PTS and the explanatory power of research using solely those measures. Research based on this data, in turn, will be fighting against a bias in the data to show that *any* factors contribute to improvements in human rights.

Based on definitive new studies, however, we can now say with more confidence something that we have only speculated for a long while: repressive violence in the world is decreasing.[15] By repressive violence,

---

[12] Margaret Keck and Kathryn Sikkink, *Activists Beyond Borders: Advocacy Networks in International Politics* (Ithaca: Cornell University Press, 1998), 194.

[13] This upsurge is still uneven and at times obfuscating. See Amber Peterman et al., "Rape Reporting During War: Why the Numbers Don't Mean What You Think They Do," *Foreign Affairs*, August 1, 2011.

[14] Fariss, "Respect for Human Rights Has Improved over Time," 309.

[15] See, in particular, Fariss, "Respect for Human Rights Has Improved over Time," and Ann Marie Clark and Kathryn Sikkink, "Information Effects and Human Rights Data: Is the Good News About Increased Human Rights Information Bad News for Human Rights Measures," *Human Rights Quarterly* 35, no. 3 (2013).

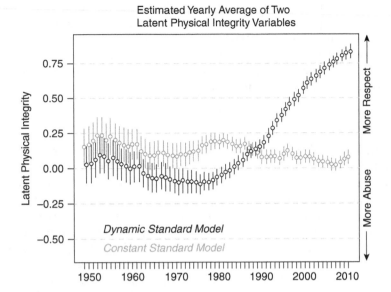

Figure 2.3: Fariss's Global Latent Respect for Physical Integrity.

(Reproduced with the permission of the author).

we mean violations of physical integrity, or the resort to campaigns of mass killing, torture, political imprisonment, and disappearances. Though far from eradicated from practice, these acts are much less likely to occur today than they were in 1800, 1900, 1970, or even 2000.[16]

Luckily, new computational methods allow researchers to estimate the latent, or true, levels of repression by both analyzing trends in multiple datasets and modeling the bias present in each one. In a new study that uses Bayesian statistical techniques, Chris Fariss analyzes a combination of 13 different events- and standard-based datasets used by analysts to study physical integrity violations. He finds that, when bias is accounted for, a clear global trend toward greater protection begins to climb upward in the mid-1980s (see Figure 2.3). These findings are most pronounced when it comes to torture. Over time, torture is at once less practiced and more thoroughly documented, making it *appear* interminable. Knowing that amassing information creates an illusion of decline allows us to say something about progress. But Fariss's research also goes some way to

---

[16] For the centuries-long account of declining violence, including human rights violations, see Steven Pinker, *The Better Angels of Our Nature: Why Violence Has Declined* (New York: Penguin Books, 2011).

demonstrating that this progress is neither linear nor inevitable. From the immediate postwar period to the late 1970s, governments in the world lurched toward greater abuse. Only then did the trend reverse. As we will argue further in the section entitled 'Human Rights Processes', it is no coincidence that this reversal corresponds directly to the meteoric rise of human rights processes in the world.

Social, Economic, and Cultural Rights

Though evidence indicates physical integrity outcomes are clearly improving, some may contend that this merely demonstrates the human rights movement's minimalism.[17] The movement might be an effective anti-authoritarian and pro-democracy force, but it cannot deliver a "lasting and tangible impact in people's daily lives" (Introduction, 12). Many argue that people's economic well-being, health, and overall human development are deteriorating, and human rights politics has done nothing to stop the decay. Meanwhile, the argument continues, human rights scholars continue to ignore economic and social outcomes in favor of civil and political outcomes, betraying their ideological preference toward Western neoliberalism.[18]

We isolate some problems with this criticism. First, it assumes that all human rights scholars are uniformly driven by some affinity to the same political tradition, which is not the case. Second, even more so than in the case of civil and political rights, it is not supported by general trends in the data. Much of the data that can be used to measure economic and social rights, such as literacy rates, life expectancy, or infant mortality, is not standard-based data and so does not suffer from some of the information paradox problems discussed earlier. For example, many of the measures in UNDP Human Development reports, with a notable exception of income and asset inequality data, show significant improvement over time (see Figure 2.4 for evidence of increasing levels of human development, as measured by the Human Development Index [HDI] and decreasing levels of the percentage of people living in poverty). Data on literacy, life expectancy, infant mortality, education levels, calorie intake, and some other measures of economic and social rights show similar upward trends. None of this is reason to be complacent or triumphalist;

[17] Wendy Brown, "'The Most We Can Hope for ...': Human Rights and the Politics of Fatalism,'" *South Atlantic Quarterly* 193, no. 2/3 (2004). Ran Hirschl, *Towards Juristocracy: The Origins and Consequences of the New Constitutionalism* (Cambridge, MA: Harvard University Press, 2004).

[18] Hopgood, *The Endtimes of Human Rights*, 104. Rosemary Nagy, "Transitional Justice as Global Project: Critical Reflections," *Third World Quarterly* 29, no. 2 (2008).

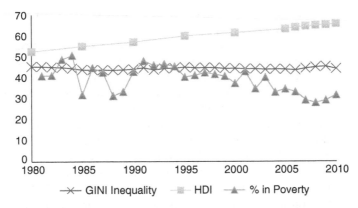

Figure 2.4: Global Average Economic and Social Conditions over Time
*GINI coefficient based on household gross income. HDI is the
UNDP's Human Development Index. Poverty figure is the World
Development Indicator's percent of the population below the national
poverty line.

(Teorell et al., *The Quality of Government Dataset, Version 20dec13*)

many people all over the world still live in situations of want and degradation. But in order to know how to work on such situations, we need to
know which economic and social rights outcomes are worsening, where,
and why. This is not aided by putting forward a general and misleading
impression that there is a broad trend in which people's economic well-
being, health, and overall human development are deteriorating.[19]

Economic and social conditions are imperfect and continue to be sub-
standard for many people around the world, but they are generally improving across time and space, with the important exception of income
inequality, which remains nearly constant over the last three decades.
Other forms of inequality, such as gender inequality, or health inequality
as measured by the differences in life expectancy and infant mortality rates
between low-income groups and high-income groups, have decreased
significantly in recent decades in comparison to earlier periods.[20] What
we cannot know, however, is if any of these improvements are linked to

[19] Charles Kenny, *Getting Better: Why Global Development Is Succeeding – and How We Can
Improve the World Even More* (New York: Basic Books, 2011).
[20] On gender inequality, see changes in the UNDP Gender Development Index (GDI) and
Gender Equality Measure (GEM) over time; on life expectancy and infant mortality,
see World Bank, World Development Indicators 2014: Mortality, http://wdi
.worldbank.org/table/2.21. The gap between average life expectancy in low-income

human rights processes involving law or activism (See "Human Rights Law and Institutions" section).

In repression studies, and in studies of international human rights law, academics have focused disproportionately on civil and political rights, but one primary reason is that when the human rights subfield was budding, scholars knew very little about the determinants of state-led political violence. Repression was largely conceived to be derivative of deeply ingrained "political-economic structures," rather than deliberate choices made by rational leaders attempting to maintain power.[21] It took decades of research to discover that political violence is also the result of choices by self-interested political leaders rather than the necessary result of systemic factors.[22] Shaking loose of structural determinism around social and economic rights concerns is even more difficult because human rights theorists have to contend with hundreds of years of economic theory. For economists, issues such as wages, employment, and labor laws are not rights issues at all, but the stuff of public policy aimed at improving the commonweal by providing the greatest good to the greatest number. A handful of studies have explored the link between human rights processes and economic and social indicators,[23] and they find that lagging respect for political freedoms and good governance corresponds to poor socioeconomic conditions. In other words, the two sets of human rights outcomes are in reality interdependent.[24]

Though civil and political rights and economic, social, and cultural rights were split at birth, and experienced different life cycles, human rights activists around the world, and especially in large countries of the Global South, are beginning to make headway on campaigning and

countries and high-income countries in 1990 was 22 years, and in 2012, it was 17 years; there was an 82 point difference in infant mortality rates between high- and low-income countries in 1990, which declined to a 51 point difference in 2012. The point is that mortality figures in both high- and low-income countries have been improving, but they have improved more rapidly in low-income countries.

[21] Christian Davenport, "State Repression and Political Order," *Annual Review of Political Science* 10, no. 1 (2007).

[22] See Poe, "The Decision to Repress"; Benjamin Valentino, *Final Solutions: Mass Killing and Genocide in the Twentieth Century* (Ithaca: Cornell University Press, 2004).

[23] Todd Landman and Marco Larizza, "Inequality and Human Rights: Who Controls What, When, and How," *International Studies Quarterly* 53, no. 3 (2009). V.N. Viswanathan, ed. *Corruption and Human Rights* (New Delhi: Allied Publishers Pvt Ltd, 2012); Reinhard Heinisch, "The Economic Nature of Basic Human Rights: Economic Explanations of Cross-National Variations in Governmental Basic Human Rights Performance," *Peace and Change* 23, no. 3 (1998): 333–72. Wesley T. Milner, "Economic Globalization and Rights: An Empirical Analysis," in *Globalization and Human Rights*, ed., Alison Brysk (Berkeley: University of California Press, 2002): 77–97.

[24] Amartya Sen, "An Argument for the Primacy of Political Rights: Freedoms and Needs," *The New Republic* 210, no. 2/3 (January 10, 1994).

litigating on behalf of economic and social rights, particularly in those few countries where living conditions are not markedly improving. Human rights organizations have brought cases to the courts that have led to important Supreme Court decisions in India on the right to food[25] and in South Africa on the right to health and housing.[26] The groups that protest the abuse of habeas corpus and lack of accountability in Sri Lanka are the same groups that work on helping women, Tamils, and minority Muslims avail themselves of their land rights.[27] Though major advocacy organizations such as Human Rights Watch and Amnesty International have chosen to prioritize civil and political rights, this is a choice not shared by many other organizations around the world that make no distinction between fulfillment of civil freedoms and fulfillment of personal needs.[28] For this reason, criticism aimed at the human rights movement for being unduly focused on one set of rights is deceptive because rights organizations are diverse and multidimensional. In many ways, they set their own local agendas.

Rights outcomes – of both political and economic varieties – have improved over the last thirty years. This bodes well for the future. Barring massive crises, catastrophic shocks, or other game-changing black swans, our notions of what level of violence is acceptable will continue to increasingly constrain political actors. Coupled with more information on abuses updated in real time, outrage will continue to limit the extent of repressive violence and suffering. This is our expectation because this is what has happened. In the next section, we will address claims that improvements in outcomes have had little to do with rights-based processes.

Human Rights Processes

Human Rights Law and Institutions

Just as in other areas of international law, treaty-drafting in the human rights area is intended to create international institutions to monitor

---

[25] See, for example, the case: *People's Union for Civil Liberties* v. *Union of India and Others*, In the Supreme Court of India, Civil Original Jurisdiction, Writ Petition (Civil) No. 196 of 2001.

[26] Sibonile Khoza, ed. *Socio-Economic Rights in South Africa, Second Edition* (University of the Western Cape: Community Law Centre, 2007).

[27] See, e.g., the Law & Society Trust, www.lawandsocietytrust.org, and in particular the extensive work of Kishali Pinto-Jayawardena.

[28] Elke Zuern, *The Politics of Necessity: Community Organizing and Democracy in South Africa*, ed. Steve J. Stern and Scott Straus, Critical Human Rights (Madison: University of Wisconsin Press, 2011).

compliance with treaties and to provide enforcement mechanisms to enhance treaty compliance. This process of drafting treaties with increasing levels of enforcement is not limited to human rights law, but is consistent with trends in international law more generally. We see similar developments in trade law, environmental law, humanitarian law, etc. Originally, because human rights violations do not involve collective goods issues, and do not impose externalities on other actors, international relations scholars expected that there would be lower levels of cooperation in the area of human rights than in other areas. So, what is surprising is not the uniqueness of developments in the area of human rights more generally, but, rather, that human rights legalization has flourished alongside legalization in other areas that may be more central to the material interests of states, such as trade law.

The first wave of studies on international law and process drew attention to a startling gap between states' treaty-based promises and trends in compliance.[29] One initial finding was that commitment to the Convention Against Torture is actually correlated with greater incidence of torture.[30] A second wave of studies has gone some way toward discrediting the findings in earlier work. The lesson is that the first-wave compliance studies failed to address the problem of causal inference: one simply cannot compare a country that has committed to human rights treaties to the same country in a counterfactual world where it had not committed. Using more complex methods, Beth Simmons and others have tackled this issue. Studies now clearly demonstrate that human rights law and institutions designed to implement that law have an impact on civil and political rights under certain conditions, specifically when countries are undergoing political transition toward greater democracy.[31] Because Simmons covers this material in Chapter 3, we will not elaborate further here. Suffice it to say that more evidence is emerging that international legal *processes* do indeed produce the observable improvement in *outcomes* depicted in Figure 2.3.

---

[29] Oona A. Hathaway, "Do Human Rights Treaties Make a Difference?," *The Yale Law Journal* 11, no. 8 (2002); Emilie M. Hafner-Burton and Kiyoteru Tsutsui, "Human Rights in a Globalizing World. The Paradox of Empty Promises," *American Journal of Sociology* 110, no. 5 (2005). For a more positive outlook from the first wave of studies, see Eric Neumayer, "Do International Human Rights Treaties Improve Respect for Human Rights?," *Journal of Conflict Resolution* 49, no. 6 (2005).

[30] Oona A. Hathaway, "The Promise and Limits of the International Law of Torture," in *Torture: Philosophical, Political and Legal Perspectives*, ed. Sanford Levinson (Oxford: Oxford University Press, 2004): 199–212. Emilie M. Hafner-Burton and Kiyoteru Tsutsui, "Justice Lost! The Failure of International Human Rights Law to Matter Where Needed Most," *Journal of Peace Research* 44, no. 4 (2007).

[31] Simmons, *Mobilizing for Human Rights*; Lupu, "The Informative Power of Treaty Commitment."

Compliance with treaties regulating social and economic rights is more difficult to observe empirically. One reason is that parts of these treaties were meant to be complied with progressively within available resources, meaning that less developed countries were given more time to make changes and they were only required to do so in relation to their level of development, not in relation to an absolute standard. Because of these greater complications, cross-national statistical indicators are less appropriate to studying compliance with economic and social rights agreements.[32] With that in mind, scholars have begun to develop metrics for evaluating compliance with these rights.

While we are coming to learn that international human rights law does influence state practices, what remains unclear is what mechanisms link treaties to positive improvements in human rights conditions. One idea is that the change comes from above; that is, through socialization into international institutions, leaders begin to slowly alter their practices.[33] Still, if elite socialization is the mechanism through which international human rights institutions exert their influence, it is not clear whether that socialization works best through "outcasting" or acculturation.[34] One common complaint from critics of institutions such as the Human Rights Council is that they allow abusive states such as Ethiopia, Russia, or Saudi Arabia to become members, which diminishes the influence of more "like-minded" states.[35] However, research into socialization has not done enough to suggest whether ostracizing rights-abusive states is in fact more effective than including them for the purpose of diplomatic intercourse and persuasion.

A second and more convincing idea is that the power of international law is defined by its ability to influence change from below – or from within states. Simmons, for example, develops a domestic politics theory of treaty compliance. In this theory, groups emboldened by state commitment to human rights agreements use them to change national policy agendas, to litigate to enforce protection of their newly guaranteed rights, and to engage in acts of social mobilization. The agenda-setting and social mobilization mechanisms have not yet been supported with systematic empirical evidence, but the litigation mechanism is receiving a good deal

---

[32] Sital Kalantry, Jocelyn E. Getgen, and Steven Arrigg Koh, "Enhancing Enforcement of Economic, Social, and Cultural Rights Using Indicators: A Focus on the Right to Education in the ICESCR," *Human Rights Quarterly* 32, no. 2 (2010): 284–5.

[33] Ryan Goodman and Derek Jinks, *Socializing States: Promoting Human Rights through International Law* (Oxford: Oxford University Press, 2013).

[34] Oona A. Hathaway and Scott J. Shapiro, "Outcasting: Enforcement in Domestic and International Law," *The Yale Law Journal* 121, no. 2 (2011).

[35] Emilie M. Hafner-Burton, *Making Human Rights a Reality* (Princeton: Princeton University Press, 2013).

of support. Studies have repeatedly discovered that the strength of domestic courts, which at times is boosted through regional and international legal networking, serves to enhance the effect of international commitments.[36] Some theorists have gone as far as to contend that the barriers between international and domestic sources of law are starting to erode.[37] Research is also suggesting that domestic courts are operating to enforce international law. Elsewhere, for example, we show that ratification of treaties with individual accountability provisions is empirically associated with a higher number of human rights prosecutions.[38] These human rights prosecutions – including both high-profile trials of leaders such as Peru's Alberto Fujimori and lower-level security forces who abuse their powers to use force – then lead to improvements in human rights practices through a combination of deterrence and normative communication.[39]

Transnational Advocacy

One area where we would distinguish our work from that of Simmons is that we place relatively more emphasis on transnational processes in contributing to human rights outcomes. We do not ignore or reject the importance of either human rights law or domestic mobilization, but argue that transnational advocacy networks and transnational legal processes also are often necessary to bring about positive human rights change, especially in societies where domestic social movements still face repression. Some countries, such as Argentina, rely primarily on domestic mobilization to ensure the greater use of human rights prosecutions, but prosecutions in many other countries are the result either of international imposition, such as in Serbia and Montenegro, or hybrid

---

[36] Anne-Marie Slaughter, *A New World Order* (Princeton: Princeton University Press, 2004). Yonatan Lupu, "Best Evidence: The Role of Information in Domestic Judicial Enforcement of International Human Rights Agreements," *International Organization* 67, no. 3 (2013). Courtenay R. Conrad, "Divergent Incentive for Dictators: Domestic Institutions and (International Promises Not to) Torture," *Journal of Conflict Resolution* 56, no. 5 (2012).

[37] Jeffrey K. Staton and Will H. Moore, "Judicial Power in Domestic Politics," *International Organization* 65, no. 3 (2011).

[38] Geoff Dancy and Kathryn Sikkink, "Treaty Ratification and Human Rights Prosecutions: Toward a Transnational Theory," *NYU Journal of Law and International Politics* 44, no. 3 (2012).

[39] Hunjoon Kim and Kathryn Sikkink, "Explaining the Deterrence Effect of Human Rights Prosecutions," *International Studies Quarterly* 54, no. 4 (2010). Geoff Dancy et al., "Stopping State Agents of Violence or Promoting Political Compromise? The Powerful Role of Transitional Justice Mechanisms," *American Political Science Association Meeting*, Chicago (2013).

forms of mobilization wherein international and regional institutions forge ties with domestic groups, as in the case of Uruguay.[40]

The role of non-governmental organizations and advocacy has been a subject of research since the late 1990s, and much of it has focused on the pejoratively termed act of "shaming." Some studies have argued that publicizing information about countries has a negative effect on human rights practices in those states, but those studies often fall prey to selection bias.[41] Human rights organizations target states that are *already* increasing repression, which makes shaming appear negative in cross-national comparison. Research that examines the same cases before and after shaming shows that, in fact, it produces moderately positive results.[42]

Other scholars have provided useful and sophisticated tests of some of the arguments put forward in earlier qualitative work on advocacy. So, for example, the extensive work of Amanda Murdie addresses, among other themes, the impact of global civil society actors, especially INGOs, and their tactics.[43] Murdie finds positive effects of targeted information campaigns, particularly when there are domestic groups within target states that also pressure for human rights change.[44] She also finds some "neighborhood effects" where very active INGOs in neighboring states can actually make an impact across borders. It appears that NGO information campaigns have both improved practices and changed the standard by which we judge rights-abusive countries (refer back to Figure 2.3).

There is a large literature on the causes of human rights violations, and we know that human rights activism is only one of the many factors that can contribute to human rights change. Most important among these factors are economic development, political democracy, and the absence of civil and international war. No human rights scholar thinks that human rights activism is the only, or even the most important factor contributing to human rights change. The main finding of Murdie's multiple quantitative studies, using a wealth of the best data on the topic, is that we can be

---

[40] Dancy and Sikkink, "Treaty Ratification and Human Rights Prosecutions." See also Ezequiel González Ocantos, "Persuade Them or Oust Them: Crafting Judicial Change and Transitional Justice in Argentina," *Comparative Politics* 46, no. 4 July (2014).

[41] Emilie M. Hafner-Burton, "Sticks and Stones: Naming and Shaming the Human Rights Enforcement Problem," *International Organization* 62, no 4 (2008).

[42] Matthew Krain, "*J'accuse!* Does Naming and Shaming Perpetrators Reduce the Severity of Genocides or Politicides?," *International Studies Quarterly* 56, no. 3 (2012).

[43] See, for example, Amanda M. Murdie, "The Impact of Human Rights INGO Activity on Human Rights Practices," *International NGO Journal* 4, no. 10 (2009): 421–440; Amanda Murdie and Tavishi Bhasin, "Aiding and Abetting: Human Rights Ingos and Domestic Protest," *Journal of Conflict Resolution* 55, no. 2 (2011); Amanda M. Murdie and David R. Davis, "Shaming and Blaming: Using Events Data to Assess the Impact of Human Rights INGOS," *International Studies Quarterly* 56, no. 1 (2012).

[44] Keck and Sikkink, *Activists Beyond Borders*.

cautiously optimistic about the impact of the work of human rights INGOs, including naming and shaming, but that in order to continue to be effective, it needs to be combined with efforts to build strong domestic advocacy sectors within states and not only bring pressure to bear from outside.

Some of the best evidence of human rights organizational influence is that many governments – Russia, Ethiopia, and Israel, to name a few – have recently sought to limit their activities by blocking their access to foreign funds or by forcing them to register as foreign agents.[45] This is dismaying, and it is evidence that authoritarian leaders are learning to engage in more diffuse forms of repression.[46] But the NGO crackdown is not evidence that transnationalism is not dead, nor should it be taken as proof that human rights advocacy is in full retreat. First, while some acknowledge that foreign funding of local organizations is at times corrupted, that it swells the ranks of a professional NGO class divorced from the grass-roots, or that it produces conservative reaction, no one is capable of arguing that funds should be discontinued.[47] Instead, what most commentators envision is a diversified response where some organizations make moves to localize funding, while others continue to accept external support. This would be a positive development indeed.

Second, the consequences of NGO crackdowns are likely going to be the opposite of what repressive states desire. By attacking the occupation of the rights advocate, state leaders may force NGO professionals more directly into social movement activism, which can be especially problematic for authoritarian rulers (See next section). Because we know that rights organizations are already inclined to indirectly support protest and resistance campaigns, staffers pushed out of work will likely find their way into solidarity groups that are pushing for more radical change.[48]

Third, we are likely to see more "multi-directionality" between elites and grass-roots actors in the near future.[49] The supposed difference between elite-led organizations and mass movements is starting to break

[45] Kendra Dupuy, James Ron, and Aseem Prakash, "Foreign Aid to Local NGOs: Good Intentions, Bad Policy," *opendemocracy.com*, November 15, 2012.

[46] William J. Dobson, *The Dictator's Learning Curve: Inside the Global Battle for Democracy* (New York: Double Day, 2012).

[47] For corruption and professionalization, see V. Suresh, "Funds and Civil Liberties," *open democracy.com*, January 6, 2014. For lack of an alternative, see James Ron's clarifying comments to Kendra Dupuy, James Ron, and Aseem Prakash, "Foreign Aid to Local NGOs: Good Intentions, Bad Policy."

[48] Murdie and Bhasin, "Aiding and Abetting: Human Rights INGOS and Domestic Protest." Linnea Beatty, "Interrelation of Violent and Non-Violent Resistance in Burma," in *American Political Science Association* (Seattle, WA 2011).

[49] Karina Ansolabehere, "Reforming and Transforming: A Multi-Directional Investigation of Human Rights," *opendemocracy.net*, December 4, 2013.

down with the proliferation of communication technologies and ready-made networking platforms. One example is the Facebook network "Stealthy Freedoms of Iranian Women," a group established by London journalist Masih Alinejad to represent women's resistance to enforcement of conservative religious laws in Iran. Though it has thousands of followers, many of whom are internationals, the group insists on local Iranian activism without financial support of Westerners or elites.[50] If social science is going to keep pace with these changes, researchers will need to produce a credible and up-to-date database on domestic human rights NGOs around the world, something that is regrettably still lacking. Second, it will need to engage more deeply with theories concerning the role of social movements in human rights developments.

Social Movements

One issue that is ripe for systematic exploration is the relationship between rights law and advocacy and social movement constituencies. We know from well-designed scholarship that widespread peaceful resistance is more effective at generating the downfall of dictatorships than armed resistance or constructive engagement.[51] Processes of peaceful resistance, then, have great potential to alter human rights outcomes. The question for human rights researchers is what role rights advocacy has played in the fomentation of effective pockets of social movement resistance. Skeptics argue that *the* human rights movement is removed from the masses, and that its legalism crowds out other forms of activism.[52] Others contend that social movements are crucially linked to rights advocacy, serving as the "hidden authors" of most human rights developments.[53] Some initial evidence suggests that social movements articulating rights-based claims have been relatively successful in pushing authoritarian governments toward democratic transition, a precondition for the improvement of human rights outcomes.[54] For Beth Simmons, the primary mechanism through which compliance with

---

[50] Saeed Kamali Dehghan, "Iranian Women Post Pictures of Themselves without Hijabs on Facebook," *The Guardian*, May 12, 2014.

[51] Erica Chenoweth and Maria Stephan, *Why Civil Resistance Works* (New York: Columbia University Press, 2011).

[52] Hopgood, *The Endtimes of Human Rights*; James Ron, David Crow, and Shannon Golden, "The Struggle for a Truly Grassroots Human Rights Movement," *opendemocracy.com*, June 18, 2013. Hirschl, *Towards Juristocracy: The Origins and Consequences of the New Constitutionalism*.

[53] Neil Stammers, *Human Rights and Social Movements* (London: Pluto Press, 2009).

[54] Geoff Dancy, *The Impact of Human Rights Law in Time* (PhD Dissertation: University of Minnesota, 2013).

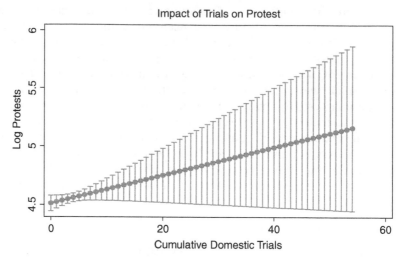

Figure 2.5: Correlation Between Human Rights Prosecutions and Protest Events over Time.
Sources: Trial data taken from the Transitional Justice Research Collaborative at www.transitionaljusticedata.com. Protest data from the GDELT Project at www.gdeltproject.org.

international law occurs is domestic mobilization, but while her data on the effect of international human rights law is persuasive, the link between domestic mobilization and human rights outcomes is still mainly hypothesized. In short, we do not yet have clear and concrete proof of a link between the human rights discourse and social movement processes.

Based on empirical evidence, we can make two modest contributions to this debate. First, against claims to the contrary, litigation does not seem to trade off with protest tactics. If anything, there appears to be a positive, though weak, correlation between number of human rights prosecutions and protests in states over time (See Figure 2.5).

Second, countering claims that human rights advocacy has abandoned notions of social welfare (See Moyn, Chapter 11), historically the resort to criminal litigation, does not necessarily crowd out the articulation of other socioeconomic concerns by civil society. Anthropologist Karen Ann Faulk has given extensive coverage to this issue with regard to Argentina. She finds, first, that "the focus on torture and disappearance within Argentina" has long been "contentious within the local human rights community."[55] Second, in reaction to neoliberal reforms in the 1990s, many Argentines began to demand redress for impunity not only for political crimes, but for economic crimes as well.[56] And third, when transitional justice re-emerged with the Kirchner administration, advocates began to protest not only for rights against violence, but also rights to "collective well being."[57] This is not to say that activism is curing the ills of years of neoliberal mismanagement, but based on Argentina, which has engaged extensively with transitional justice as well as experienced increased income inequality, one could argue that law and productive social movement activism have reinforced one another. In fact, the same groups that tirelessly fought for transitional justice have also struggled for social and economic rights *against* neoliberal inequality.[58]

Questions

The arguments we make above demonstrate the ways in which newer human rights research may give us leverage on questions of mechanisms, but, ultimately, theory remains open to debate. Our point is simply this: the debate about human rights futures should be centered on the ways in which various processes do or do not contribute to outcomes, rather than steadfast optimism or rejectionist pessimism. The nuanced views of the so-called pragmatists in this volume are welcome, and, in fact, we find that very few differences exist between our positions.[59] If anything, we propose a more agentic and possibilist model of change, as opposed to a mechanistic and structured model of change, where a powerful coalition has to be in place first before human rights change can proceed. For us, engagement in rights litigation, transnational advocacy, and social movement activisms can *create* conditions for change; where for others those conditions must *already exist.*

Neither of these models is intrinsically right or wrong. They are only more or less true to the paths we see on the ground. In other words, this is an empirical debate, and one worth having. Our claim is that more

---

[55] Karen Ann Faulk, *In the Wake of Neoliberalism: Citizenship and Human Rights in Argentina* (Stanford: Stanford University Press, 2013), 44.

[56] Ibid., 102.   [57] Ibid., 162.

[58] Geoff Dancy and Eric Wiebelhaus-Brahm, "Bridge to Human Development or Vehicle of Inequality? Transitional Justice and Economic Structures," *International Journal of Transitional Justice* 9, no. 1 (2015).

[59] We do not have space to elaborate here, but we resist the notion that our work is somehow not pragmatic. In fact, we consider ourselves to be devoted pragmatists on philosophical, methodological, and political grounds. For this reason, we place quotations around the term "pragmatist" through the rest of our chapter. See Geoff Dancy "Human Rights Pragmatism: Belief, Inquiry, and Action," *European Journal of International Relations* 22, no. 3 (2016).

agentic and possibilist model, as presented in Simmons, and in Risse, Ropp, and Sikkink, has more support if we look at the actual histories of countries that have made the transition from being less to more rights-conducive places. In our estimation, the slim theoretical differences between positions hinges on a few central questions: the reasons for differential "compliance gaps" in international law; whether human rights processes can have an effect in hard cases; the most effective way to bargain toward human rights outcomes; and the desirability of promoting the sequencing of reform. In this final section of the chapter, we will briefly attempt to address these tough issues.

Issue 1: Compliance Gaps

As opposed to first-wave studies of international law, which hold that compliance gaps are explained *mostly* by lack of enforcement, Risse, Ropp, and Sikkink argue that the centralization of the compliance decision is another of the factors that seems to explain variation in patterns of abuse and, ultimately, compliance with international law.[60] This makes sense from the principal–agent perspective. Those rights violations that are more difficult to control from the center – such as torture – will be subject to less compliance. Moreover, the weaker the institutional linkages between principals and agents, the more likely we are to see non-compliance with international law in general. For instance, if states use pro-government militias in the place of centralized militaries to engage in repression or to fight civil wars, we should expect greater gaps between promises to abide by rights restrictions and fulfillment of those promises.[61]

This insight could be expanded to suggest that in order to think about what mechanisms are responsible for compliance with human rights, we first have to specify the *location* of the compliance decision – who needs to comply in order to fulfill certain human rights. Traditionally, we have thought about the state as the source of all compliance decisions, but once we move beyond this legal fiction, it is clear that very diverse actors are responsible for abusing or fulfilling many rights. The appropriate mechanism to induce compliance depends upon the nature of the actors who need to comply. Even when the duty to respect rights rests in

---

[60] Thomas Risse, Stephen C. Ropp, and Kathryn Sikkink, eds., *The Persistent Power of Human Rights: From Commitment to Compliance* (Cambridge: Cambridge University Press, 2013).

[61] Sabine C. Carey, Neil J. Mitchell, and Will Lowe, "States, the Security Sector, and the Monopoly of Violence: A New Database on Pro-Government Militias," *Journal of Peace Research* 50, no. 2 (2013).

principle with the state, the actual compliance decision may be more or less centralized. So, for example, the decision to stop using the death penalty is quite centralized. Torture, on the other hand, can be practiced secretly in many police stations or military barracks, and even if the central state has made a commitment to end torture, it may continue in these far-flung locations. Simmons refers to this as a difference between what can be observed and monitored,[62] but it is also a difference in the centralization of the compliance decision. Similarly, the location of many compliance decisions about economic rights may rest in the private sector. This is the issue John Ruggie has grappled with in his Guiding Principles on Business and Human Rights. Ruggie's Guiding Principles clarify that the state has a *duty to protect* against human rights abuses, including those by business enterprises, while a corporation has a *responsibility to respect* human rights. While these may seem semantic, they point to realities the social scientist understands. Although states have a duty to protect women against employment discrimination, the *location* of the compliance decision is different for public sector employment than for private sector employment. This is the reason why, when Simmons tests the impact of CEDAW ratification on women's employment, she uses data on women's employment in the *public* sector. It is simply more realistic to expect a human rights treaty ratified by a state to have an impact on a compliance decision actually located within the state apparatus.

State repression (mass killing, torture, disappearance, and political imprisonment) is mainly committed by state security forces, military, and sometimes by armed insurgents. These are well-resourced individuals who use repression to secure state power. As both Ben Valentino and Steve Poe have argued separately, leaders use rational calculations to determine whether or not to use repression to secure their goals. Such individuals are unlikely to be subjects for normative socialization.[63] They may, however, be deterred from further human rights violations if the costs are clear and increasingly more probable to be incurred. We think that our research findings about the impact of human rights prosecutions on lowering repression mean that deterrence is one key mechanism for bringing about this kind of human rights change.

This does not mean that we think punishment or deterrence works for *all* human rights change. It depends on the location of the compliance decision and the kinds of individuals making choices about whether or not to violate rights. To the contrary, different kinds of actors may be

---

[62] Simmons, *Mobilizing for Human Rights*, 358.
[63] Poe, "The Decision to Repress." Valentino, *Final Solutions*.

influenced by different mechanisms. Since female genital cutting is practiced mainly in small villages with the permission of the families, it makes little sense to try to stop the practice by shaming or punishing governments that have already prohibited the practice. As Gerry Mackie has illustrated, tactics focused on community education and pledging ceremonies where families pledge not to cut their daughters and not to marry their sons to women whose genitals have been cut are far more effective in dealing with this kind of "human rights violation" committed by families who believe they are doing the best thing for their daughters by enabling them to be marriageable.[64]

More attention to the location of the compliance decision could help us better understand mechanisms and develop more effective tactics to bring about human rights change. Although "naming and shaming" has become the most common and most scrutinized tactic among many human rights actors, it is not and should not be the only or even the main tactic used. NGOs are aware of the need for innovation and are developing programs, such as "New Tactics in Human Rights," that research novel tactics used around the world in human rights work and then encourage activists to write up descriptions or workbooks on their methods and train other activists. Likewise, tactical mapping has been developed as a technique to help activists strategize about the location of the compliance decision and how to design more effective interventions that come closer to the individuals actually involved in the human rights violations.[65]

Issue 2: Easy and Hard Cases

Research showing that human rights law and/or human rights prosecutions have most impact in transitional countries is now taken as evidence that the human rights movement has been effective only in "easy" cases where it is less needed. Hafner-Burton and Ron argue, for example, "By some calculations, just over fifty states have begun a democratic transition since the 1960s. This suggests that only one-quarter of the world's countries could have been helped by international human rights laws and treaties."[66] Not only does this likely undercount the number of transitions since 1960,[67] this quantitative literalist interpretation also

---

[64] Gerry Mackie, "Ending Footbinding and Infibulation: A Convention Account," *American Sociological Review* 61, no. 6 (Dec 1996): 999–1017.

[65] www.newtactics.org/

[66] Emilie M. Hafner-Burton and James Ron, "Seeing Double: Human Rights Impact through Qualitative and Quantitative Eyes," *World Politics* 61, no. 2 (2009): 372.

[67] In our research, we count close to 110 transitions in over 80 countries. See www.transitionaljusticedata.com.

dismisses the fact that new political openings were created in dozens and dozens of cases once considered tough cases, such as Poland, South Korea, El Salvador, and Nigeria. Much of this was the direct *result* of human rights activism.

There is no doubt that, after the third wave of democracy, the remaining countries the human rights movement faces today are indeed "hard cases," of very entrenched authoritarian or semi-authoritarian regimes such as those in China, Sudan, Syria, and Russia. As the framework chapter notes, some of these countries, such as Russia and Azerbaijan, have also learned how to manipulate the system and give the appearance of democracy at the same time as they solidify a semi-authoritarian rule. The methods and even some of the institutions that the human rights movement has traditionally used (including such institutions as the Council of Europe) are now at times used by governments such as Azerbaijan to legitimate its regime.

This does *not* mean, however, that the work of the human rights movement to date has only worked in "easy cases" and thus is somehow insignificant because it is only relevant where it is needed less. First, what is an "easy case" or a "hard case" is often constructed ex post facto. In the 1980s, many countries that were once considered "hard cases" later became transitional countries. But at the time *no one* expected the USSR or the states of Eastern Europe to enter into transition to democracy. Ex post facto, for analysts to say that the human rights movement only succeeds in the "easy cases" and to include all of Eastern Europe in that camp is disingenuous and ahistorical. To be surprised that some of the countries of the former USSR are still "hard cases," and that somehow the human rights movement has been unable to easily contribute to change there, is equally disingenuous. As long as there are no definitions ahead of time as to what constitutes a hard case or an easy case, and the definition of an easy case seems to be that once it goes through a transition to democracy and improves human rights, it now counts as easy, we don't take this critique very seriously.

A more rigorous approach to this issue is to specify a priori what scope conditions make a country or a human rights issue more tractable or more difficult to change. As the editors note in the first chapter, the volume *The Persistent Power of Human Rights* represents an attempt to specify more carefully the scope conditions under which we would expect states to move from commitment to compliance.[68] In particular, the authors of that book recognize the difference in processes of human rights change in states that are *unwilling* to make change, compared to states that may be

---

[68] Risse, Ropp, and Sikkink, *The Persistent Power of Human Rights*.

unable to make such changes. The fact that there are scope conditions for human rights changes does not mean that change is impossible in countries that fail to meet these scope conditions. It simply means that it will be more difficult and time-consuming, and that different sets of tactics are required. So, for example, if a country is a "failed state" or what Risse and Börzel call "areas of limited statehood" that has the political will but not the state capacity to bring about change, it is likely that capacity-building tactics will be more useful than naming and shaming or other pressure tactics.

Issue 3: Backlash and Bargaining

One of the favorite claims of human rights skeptics, and social scientists in general, is that well-meaning actions will increase the probability of "negative unintended consequences."[69] This is no doubt true, much like deciding to drive will increase the risk of a car accident. Human rights gains are always made through struggle, and virtually always provoke backlash. Social scientists have done valuable work demonstrating that pro-violations constituencies exist, and that they will react negatively against efforts to protect the human rights of certain individuals.[70] As we write this, conservative groups in Mexico are rallying behind chants that "human rights are for criminals" and heavily armed anti-immigrant militias are patrolling the US border, ostensibly to target an influx of child refugees fleeing from Central American gang violence. Leaders such as Zimbabwe's Robert Mugabe and Sri Lanka's Mahinda Rajapaksa cling to power through onslaughts of repressive violence mixed with denouncements of human rights intervention from the outside. And militaries or armed groups that face accountability for their human rights violations agitatedly react with threats of violence and other types of "spoiler" behavior. All of these actions represent various kinds of backlash that we need to analyze and understand in greater depth.

However, we are not exactly sure what the implications are for human rights activists. Often, arguments about backlash turn into an appeal for the application of bargaining logics. These and other proposals of the "pragmatists," such as the merits of being patient or of building coalitions through engagement with local political actors, strike us as perfectly

---

[69] See Albert O. Hirschman, *The Rhetoric of Reaction: Perversity, Futility, Jeopardy* (Cambridge, MA: The Belknap Press of Harvard University Press, 1991).

[70] Sonia Cardenas, *Conflict and Compliance: State Responses to International Human Rights Pressure* (Philadelphia: University of Pennsylvania Press, 2007). Clifford Bob, *The Global Right Wing and the Clash of World Politics* (Cambridge: Cambridge University Press, 2012).

reasonable policy proposals. Mobilizing moderates in opposition groups and learning to negotiate with enemy groups are potentially beneficial steps, many of which are in fact being used in the world with greater frequency.[71] However, where we often depart from proponents of a bargaining model are over their policy recommendations (where they make them). For example, one recommendation is that human rights concerns should be abandoned, at least temporarily, in difficult situations while issues related to security or institution building are sufficiently addressed. This kind of claim was made in reference to the Dayton talks to end the Balkans Wars in November 1995. Rights advocates were chided for demanding that aggressive leaders be held accountable, which threatened peace negotiations.[72] Of course, had rights advocates been silenced, Milosevic might never have been discredited abroad and within Serbia, he may never have been ousted by the student-led Otpor campaign, and he may never have been tried by the ICTY.[73] We will never know what would have happened. But the desire to sweep rights issues off the table in the mid-1990s seems harsh and wrongheaded in retrospect.

More recently, backlash-based criticism has zeroed in on the ICC, which has been attacked both for bargaining too much and for not bargaining at all.[74] Political scientists have keenly advanced the position that in the context of conflict, what works better than the risk of prosecution is amnesty or exile.[75] The threat of trial will only cause violent groups to "dig in their heels."[76] In other words, if the international community would only allow rights-offending groups

---

[71] Arjun Chowdhury and Ronald R. Krebs, "Making and Mobilizing Moderates: Rhetorical Strategy, Political Networks, and Counterterrorism," *Security Studies* 18, no. 3 (2009). Stephan Sonnenberg and James L. Cavallaro, "Name, Shame, and Then Build Consensus? Bringing Conflict Resolution Skills to Human Rights," *Washington University Journal of Law & Policy* 39 (2012).

[72] Anonymous, "Human Rights in Peace Negotiations," *Human Rights Quarterly* 18 (1996).

[73] For more elaboration, see Peter Ackerman and Jack Duvall, *A Force More Powerful: A Century of Nonviolent Conflict* (New York: Palgrave, 2000). David Scheffer, *All the Missing Souls: A Personal History of the War Crimes Tribunals* (Princeton and Oxford: Princeton University Press, 2012).

[74] Phil Clark, "Law, Politics and Pragmatism: The ICC and Case Selection in Uganda and the Democratic Republic of Congo," in *Courting Conflict? Justice, Peace and the ICC in Africa*, ed. Nicholas Waddell and Phil Clark (Royal African Society, 2008). Adam Branch, "Uganda's Civil War and the Politics of ICC Intervention," *Ethics and International Affairs* 21, no. 2 (2007).

[75] Jack Snyder and Leslie Vinjamuri, "Trials and Errors: Principle and Pragmatism in Strategies of International Justice," *International Security* 28, no. 3 (2003/4).

[76] Julian Ku and Jide Nzelibe, "Do International Criminal Tribunals Deter or Exacerbate Humanitarian Atrocities?," *Washington University Law Quarterly* 84(2006). Philippe Sands, "The ICC Arrest Warrant Will Make Colonel Gaddafi Dig in His Heels," *The Guardian*, May 4, 2011.

and agents to exit the conflict, then they would happily oblige, and the situation would improve. The logical extrapolation is that the ICC should avoid involvement (though this argument is rarely made outright).

A few points should be made here. First, for hundreds of years, exile and amnesty were options for warring and rights-abusive leaders, and widespread peace was decidedly not the result. Leaders dug in their heels and fought because that is what risk-acceptant leaders do. Second, it has not been proven with any convincing evidence that amnesties, which are still being pursued at quite a high rate, actually decrease conflict recurrence.[77] Groups such as the M23 rebels in the Democratic Republic of Congo are amnestied and then only a few years later re-engage in battle. And countries such as Thailand chronically pass amnesties to no effect. Third, the argument that actors will initiate backlash can easily slip into an *apology* for individuals who do so. For example, in a closed-door meeting, African leaders recently voted sitting heads of state immunity from the new African Court of Justice and Human Rights, a move heavily criticized by regional rights advocates.[78] For the backlash theorist, is this a rational action to be prescribed based on political realities, or is it a deplorable act that should be disapproved? If backlash theorists care about making improvements, how would they stop leaders from trying to guarantee their own immunity? Oftentimes, the answer given is simply that human rights advocates should more smartly intervene in the future in order to struggle for accountability as well as peace. We would of course agree, but we also want to know more.

We would simply make the following observation: while backlash is certainly a constant risk, we see little evidence that actually forfeiting the cause of rights will lead to better rights outcomes than pursuing that cause. In fact, the evidence mostly suggests this is incorrect. As with any bargaining situation, human rights activists may wish to keep stressing their proposals in the hope of setting out a parameter within which a bargain or compromise can be struck, rather than surrendering at the outset. They may also seek to build support by translating their ideas into local idioms, customs, or political cultures (See Engle Merry and Levitt, Chapter 9, this volume). But they should not, for fear of backlash, cease making demands.

---

[77] Louise Mallinder, *Amnesty, Human Rights and Political Transition: Bridging the Peace and Justice Divide*, vol. 21, Studies in International Law (Oxford: Hart, 2008).
[78] Mike Pflanz, "African Leaders Vote to Give Themselves Immunity from War Crimes Prosecutions," *The Telegraph*, July 2, 2014.

Issue 4: Gradualism and Sequencing

No political scientist or human rights advocate should be naïve about the amount of time and struggle it will take to bring about change in a number of countries and regions. For example, to have expected Egypt in 2011 to move seamlessly from authoritarianism to democracy would have been unrealistic. But it is only one counterfactual speculation to believe that the attempt to demand democracy or human rights *too early* produced the backlash, where a more gradualist strategy would have succeeded. If anything, the problem for Egyptian liberals was not the timing or nature of their justice demands, but the mixed electoral system that was agreed upon prior to the 2012 elections.[79] Without the demands, there would have been no chance for political transformation in the first place.

Though the gradual development of rule of law institutions may be acceptable policy outcomes, there is no reason why human rights activists should necessarily *advocate* delay or exceptionality concerning rights issues. Recently, there has been increasing emphasis on "context, timing and sequencing" in the pursuit of justice for rights violations.[80] Some policies ought to precede others, the thinking goes, or, depending on the nature of the transition, policies should be arranged in an order conducive to the optimal generation of democratic consolidation and respect for rights. For example, maybe it makes the most sense to pass an amnesty to promote the demobilization of armed combatants, then develop a robust truth commission that gathers witness testimony and evidence, and only then move forward with trials for key rights violators beyond the realm of forgiveness. If these things are done out of order, the argument goes, or if they are timed improperly, they could result in a political backlash, in deleterious social relations, or in the resumption of civil war.

---

[79] Reem Abou-El-Fadl, "Beyond Conventional Transitional Justice: Egypt's 2011 Revolution and the Absence of Political Will," *International Journal of Transitional Justice* 6, no. 2 (2012). Samuel Tadros, "Egypt's Elections: Why the Islamists Won," *World Affairs*, March/April (2012).

[80] Snyder and Vinjamuri, "Trials and Errors: Principle and Pragmatism in Strategies of International Justice." Helena Cobban, "Think Again: International Courts," *Foreign Policy*, no. March/April (2006). Laurel Fletcher, Harvey M. Weinstein, and Jamie Rowen, "Context, Timing, and the Dynamics of Transitional Justice: A Historical Perspective," *Human Rights Quarterly* 31, no. 1 (2009); Alexander Dukalskis, "Interactions in Transition: How Truth Commissions and Trials Complement or Constrain Each Other," *International Studies Review* 13, no. 3 (2011). Cath Collins, *Post-Transitional Justice: Human Rights Trials in Chile and El Salvador* (University Park: Pennsylvania State University Press, 2010). Tricia D. Olsen, Leigh A. Payne, and Andrew G. Reiter, *Transitional Justice in Balance: Comparing Processes, Weighing Efficacy* (Washington, DC: United States Institute of Peace, 2010). Kieran McEvoy and Louise Mallinder, "Amnesties in Transition: Punishment, Restoration, and the Governance of Mercy," *Journal of Law and Society* 39, no. 3 (2012). Sonnenberg and Cavallaro, "Name, Shame, and Then Build Consensus?"

The central idea underlying these arguments is that efforts to acknowledge victims' suffering, hold leaders responsible for their depredations, and reinforce civil and political rights must wait for another day in the indeterminate future – a day when political equilibria will not be disturbed. According to Snyder and Vinjamuri, the amnesty-first plan described above must be preceded by even more, undescribed "political preconditions for the strengthening of law-abiding state institutions."[81] To the contrary, we advance the idea that human rights leaders should embrace the notion that change will only happen gradually, but they should not assume that they must move in a proper sequence. To date, no such successful sequence has been divined.[82] In each country, rights-based institutions develop unevenly, and in various sequences, but always on the backs of advocates who continue to push for their cause. In other words, we adopt the position of gradualism without sequencing.[83] Oftentimes, advances in human rights happen over long periods of time, with incremental improvements that become institutionalized and path-dependent. As scholars, we should be able to trace such changes, rather than noting only those perceived failures of rights activism in the short term.

Conclusion

The future we foresee is one that involves continued fights over rights and heightened outrage at bloody and brazen acts of violence. Rent-seeking state leaders, militaristic warlords, and exclusionary nativists will continue to use violence, and will seek to evade accountability. They will issue threats, and they will challenge people's resolve. Meanwhile, networks of individuals, which will penetrate more and more deeply into unreached populations, will continue to resist abuses of power, will adapt the law and discourse of human rights to their advantage using innovative tactics, and will translate rights-based ideals into local practices. Political and economic rights issues will merge more closely together, and conditions will improve – slowly, and in fits and starts.

Others do not share this vision. They stress that the human rights movement "risks rendering itself politically irrelevant outside Geneva, London, New York and a few other middle-class enclaves globally. Here the usefulness of human rights as ethical ideas and practical politics

---

[81] Snyder and Vinjamuri, "Trials and Errors: Principle and Pragmatism in Strategies of International Justice," 20.

[82] Geoff Dancy and Eric Wiebelhaus-Brahm, "Timing, Sequencing, and Transitional Justice Impact: A Qualitative Comparative Analysis of Latin America," *Human Rights Review* 16, no. 4 (2015).

[83] Thomas Carothers, "The 'Sequencing' Fallacy," *Journal of Democracy* 18, no. 1 (2007).

reaches its end." This creates an interesting dilemma. If the observer actually thinks the human rights movement is rendering itself irrelevant, then it is not clear why it is necessary to put up such a skeptical fuss. Why write books predicting the failure of the rights regime? Is the skeptics' effort intended to hurry along the demise of human rights? If so, what is their alternative vision for striving toward a better world?

Our survey of the human rights past and of recent human rights research strongly suggests that we are not at all in "an endtime" of human rights or the "twilight of human rights law." To the contrary, we are in a period of incredible dynamism in the human rights movement and in human rights law and institutions. Such dynamism does not mean that struggle or backlash disappears or that the end of history has emerged.

If we compare human rights ideals, and practices based on those ideals, to other actually existing belief systems, including the ambitious liberalism highlighted by Moyn in Chapter 11 of this volume or a Marxism that is often the unspoken lost utopia for many longing for deeper processes of emancipation, human rights aspirations and outcomes *may* appear to be minimalist. But if imperialism is held up as an accomplishment of the "aspirational confidence" of liberalism (See Moyn, Chapter 11), and we know that purges, gulags, and the killing fields were the results of Marxist ideals put into practice, the "minimalist" claims and accomplishments of the human rights movement are all the more impressive.

Human rights processes are one set of tools that have contributed to improvements in *some* human rights outcomes around the world. Compared to other actually existing tools, such as the build-up of military institutions and their equipment, or even other line items in the foreign aid budgets, the expenditures in time and money on human rights are not enormous, but, rather, quite moderate and acceptable in relation to the outcomes we document. Within our imperfect world, this looks to us like human rights processes have led to quite promising outcomes, and should be further developed, enhanced, and diversified to be able to continue to do so. One clear example of such change is the current work already going on among many human rights organizations in the global South, to pay more attention to economic, social, and cultural rights without ignoring the ongoing need to continue to protect civil and political rights. This change is not managed by gatekeepers in the global North, but is emerging from organizations based in the global South – just one more example of why the "endtime" or "twilight" metaphors are so misleading.[84]

---

[84] See, for example, blog posts by Cesar Rodriguez Garavito, "Against Human Rights Reductionism," July 30, 2013; and "Human Rights: Gated Community or Ecosystem," June 6, 2014. On Open Democracy, www.opendemocracy.net/author/c%C3%A9sar-rodr%C3%ADguez-garavito

References

Abou-El-Fadl, Reem. "Beyond Conventional Transitional Justice: Egypt's 2011 Revolution and the Absence of Political Will." *International Journal of Transitional Justice* 6, no. 2 (2012): 318–30.

Ackerman, Peter, and Jack Duvall. *A Force More Powerful: A Century of Nonviolent Conflict.* New York: Palgrave, 2000.

Anonymous. "Human Rights in Peace Negotiations." *Human Rights Quarterly* 18, no. 2 (1996): 249–58.

Ansolabehere, Karina. "Reforming and Transforming: A Multi-Directional Investigation of Human Rights." *opendemocracy.net*, December 4, 2013.

Ayoub, Phillip M. "With Arms Wide Shut: Threat Perception, Norm Reception and Mobilized Resistance to LGBT Rights." *Journal of Human Rights* 13, no. 3 (2014): 337–62.

Beatty, Linnea. "Interrelation of Violent and Non-Violent Resistance in Burma," in *American Political Science Association.* Seattle, WA 2011 [conference paper].

Bob, Clifford. *The Global Right Wing and the Clash of World Politics.* Cambridge: Cambridge University Press, 2012.

Bob, Clifford, ed. *The International Struggle for New Human Rights.* Philadelphia: University of Pennsylvania Press, 2009.

Branch, Adam. "Uganda's Civil War and the Politics of ICC Intervention." *Ethics and International Affairs* 21, no. 2 (2007): 179–98.

Brown, Wendy. "'The Most We Can Hope for ... ': Human Rights and the Politics of Fatalism." *South Atlantic Quarterly* 193, no. 2/3 (2004): 451–63.

Cardenas, Sonia. *Conflict and Compliance: State Responses to International Human Rights Pressure.* Philadelphia: University of Pennsylvania Press, 2007.

Carey, Sabine C., Neil J. Mitchell, and Will Lowe. "States, the Security Sector, and the Monopoly of Violence: A New Database on Pro-Government Militias." *Journal of Peace Research* 50, no. 2 (2013): 249–58.

Carothers, Thomas. "The 'Sequencing' Fallacy." *Journal of Democracy* 18, no. 1 (2007): 12–27.

Chenoweth, Erica, and Maria Stephan. *Why Civil Resistance Works.* New York: Columbia University Press, 2011.

Chowdhury, Arjun, and Ronald R. Krebs. "Making and Mobilizing Moderates: Rhetorical Strategy, Political Networks, and Counterterrorism." *Security Studies* 18, no. 3 (2009): 371–99.

Cingranelli, David L., David L. Richards, and K. Chad Clay. "The Cingranelli-Richards (CIRI) Human Rights Dataset." www.humanrightsdata.com/p/data-documentation.html, 2013.

Clark, Ann Marie, and Kathryn Sikkink. "Information Effects and Human Rights Data: Is the Good News About Increased Human Rights Information Bad News for Human Rights Measures?" *Human Rights Quarterly* 35, no. 3 (2013): 539–68.

Clark, Phil. "Law, Politics and Pragmatism: The ICC and Case Selection in Uganda and the Democratic Republic of Congo." In *Courting Conflict? Justice, Peace and the ICC in Africa*, edited by Nicholas Waddell and Phil Clark: Royal African Society, 2008: 37–46.

Cmiel, Kenneth. "The Recent History of Human Rights." *American Historical Review* 109, no. 1 (2004): 117–35.

Cobban, Helena. "Think Again: International Courts." *Foreign Policy* March/April (2006).

Collins, Cath. *Post-Transitional Justice: Human Rights Trials in Chile and El Salvador.* University Park: Pennsylvania State University Press, 2010.

Conrad, Courtenay R. "Divergent Incentive for Dictators: Domestic Institutions and (International Promises Not to) Torture." *Journal of Conflict Resolution* 56, no. 5 (2012): 1–34.

Dancy, Geoff. *"The Impact of Human Rights Law in Time."* PhD Dissertation: University of Minnesota, 2013.

"Human Rights Pragmatism: Belief, Inquiry, and Action," *European Journal of International Relations* 22, no. 3 (2016): 512–35.

Dancy, Geoff and Christopher Fariss, "Rescuing Human Rights Law from Legalism and Its Critics," *Human Rights Quarterly* 39, no. 1 (2017): 1–36.

Dancy, Geoff, Bridget Marchesi, Tricia Olsen, Leigh A. Payne, Andrew G. Reiter, and Kathryn Sikkink. "Stopping State Agents of Violence or Promoting Political Compromise? The Powerful Role of Transitional Justice Mechanisms." *American Political Science Association Meeting* Chicago, IL (2013).

Dancy, Geoff, and Kathryn Sikkink. "Treaty Ratification and Human Rights Prosecutions: Toward a Transnational Theory." *NYU Journal of Law and International Politics* 44, no. 3 (2012): 751–90.

Dancy, Geoff and Eric Wiebelhaus-Brahm. "Bridge to Human Development or Vehicle of Inequality?." *Transitional Justice and Economic Structures, International Journal of Transitional Justice* 9, no. 1 (2015): 51–69.

"Timing, Sequencing, and Transitional Justice Impact: A Qualitative Comparative Analysis of Latin America." *Human Rights Review* 16, no. 4 (2015): 321–42.

Davenport, Christian. "State Repression and Political Order." *Annual Review of Political Science* 10, no. 1 (2007): 1–23.

Dehghan, Saeed Kamali. "Iranian Women Post Pictures of Themselves without Hijabs on Facebook." *The Guardian*, May 12, 2014.

Dobson, William J. *The Dictator's Learning Curve: Inside the Global Battle for Democracy.* New York: Double Day, 2012.

Donnelly, Jack. *International Human Rights*, 4th edn. Boulder, CO: Westview Press, 2013.

Dukalskis, Alexander. "Interactions in Transition: How Truth Commissions and Trials Complement or Constrain Each Other." *International Studies Review* 13, no. 3 (2011): 432–51.

Dupuy, Kendra, James Ron, and Aseem Prakash. "Foreign Aid to Local NGOs: Good Intentions, Bad Policy." *opendemocracy.com*, November 15, 2012.

Fariss, Christopher J. "Respect for Human Rights Has Improved over Time: Modeling the Changing Standard of Accountability." *American Political Science Review* 108, no. 2 (2014): 297–318.

Faulk, Karen Ann. *In the Wake of Neoliberalism: Citizenship and Human Rights in Argentina.* Stanford: Stanford University Press, 2013.

Fletcher, Laurel, Harvey M. Weinstein, and Jamie Rowen. "Context, Timing, and the Dynamics of Transitional Justice: A Historical Perspective." *Human Rights Quarterly* 31, no 1 (2009): 163–220.

Gibney, Mark, Linda Cornett, Reed Wood, and Peter Haschke. "Political Terror Scale, 1976–2012." www.politicalterrorscale.org/. Retrieved February 14, 2014.

Goodman, Ryan, and Derek Jinks. *Socializing States: Promoting Human Rights through International Law.* Oxford: Oxford University Press, 2013.

Hafner-Burton, Emilie M. *Making Human Rights a Reality.* Princeton: Princeton University Press, 2013.

"Sticks and Stones: Naming and Shaming the Human Rights Enforcement Problem." *International Organization* 62, no. 4 (2008): 689–716.

Hafner-Burton, Emilie M., and James Ron. "Seeing Double: Human Rights Impact through Qualitative and Quantitative Eyes." *World Politics* 61, no. 2 (2009): 360–401.

Hafner-Burton, Emilie M., and Kiyoteru Tsutsui. "Human Rights in a Globalizing World. The Paradox of Empty Promises." *American Journal of Sociology* 110, no. 5 (2005): 1373–411.

"Justice Lost! The Failure of International Human Rights Law to Matter Where Needed Most." *Journal of Peace Research* 44, no. 4 (2007): 407–25.

Hathaway, Oona A. "Do Human Rights Treaties Make a Difference?" *The Yale Law Journal* 11, no. 8 (2002): 1935–2042.

"The Promise and Limits of the International Law of Torture." In *Torture: Philosophical, Political and Legal Perspectives*, edited by Sanford Levinson. Oxford: Oxford University Press, 2004: 199–212.

Hathaway, Oona A., and Scott J. Shapiro. "Outcasting: Enforcement in Domestic and International Law." *The Yale Law Journal* 121, no. 2 (2011): 252–348.

Hill, Daniel W. "Estimating the Effects of Human Rights Treaties on State Behavior." *Journal of Politics* 72, no. 4 (2010): 1161–1174.

Hirschl, Ran. *Towards Juristocracy: The Origins and Consequences of the New Constitutionalism.* Cambridge, MA: Harvard University Press, 2004.

Hirschman, Albert O. *The Rhetoric of Reaction: Perversity, Futility, Jeopardy.* Cambridge, MA: The Belknap Press of Harvard University Press, 1991.

Hopgood, Stephen. *The Endtimes of Human Rights.* Ithaca: Cornell University Press, 2013.

Ignatieff, Michael. "Is the Human Rights Era Ending?" *The New York Times*, February 5, 2002.

Johnston, Alistair Iain. "Treating International Institutions as Social Environments." *International Studies Quarterly* 45, no. 4 (2001): 487–516.

Kalantry, Sital, Jocelyn E. Getgen, and Steven Arrigg Koh. "Enhancing Enforcement of Economic, Social, and Cultural Rights Using Indicators: A Focus on the Right to Education in the ICESCR." *Human Rights Quarterly* 32, no. 2 (2010): 253–310.

Keck, Margaret, and Kathryn Sikkink. *Activists Beyond Borders: Advocacy Networks in International Politics.* Ithaca: Cornell University Press, 1998.

Kenny, Charles. *Getting Better: Why Global Development Is Succeeding and How We Can Improve the World Even More.* New York: Basic Books, 2011.

Khoza, Sibonile, ed. *Socio-Economic Rights in South Africa,* 2nd edn. University of the Western Cape: Community Law Centre, 2007.

Kim, Hunjoon, and Kathryn Sikkink. "Explaining the Deterrence Effect of Human Rights Prosecutions." *International Studies Quarterly* 54, no. 4 (2010): 939–63.

Krain, Matthew. "*J'accuse!* Does Naming and Shaming Perpetrators Reduce the Severity of Genocides or Politicides?." *International Studies Quarterly* 56, no. 3 (2012): 574–89.

Ku, Julian, and Jide Nzelibe. "Do International Criminal Tribunals Deter or Exacerbate Humanitarian Atrocities?." *Washington University Law Quarterly* 84, no. 4 (2006): 777–833.

Landman, Todd, and Marco Larizza. "Inequality and Human Rights: Who Controls What, When, and How." *International Studies Quarterly* 53, no. 3 (2009): 715–36.

Lewis, Hope. "'New' Human Rights? US Ambivalence Towards the International Economic and Social Rights Framework." In *Bringing Human Rights Home: A History of Human Rights in the United States,* edited by Cynthia Soohoo, Catherine Albisa, and Martha Davis. Philadelphia: University of Pennsylvania Press, 2009.

Lubin, David. "The War on Terrorism and the End of Human Rights." *Philosophy and Public Policy Quarterly* 22, no. 3 Summer (2002): 9–14.

Lupu, Yonatan. "Best Evidence: The Role of Information in Domestic Judicial Enforcement of International Human Rights Agreements." *International Organization* 67, no. 3 (2013): 469–503.

"The Informative Power of Treaty Commitment: Using the Spatial Model to Address Selection Effects." *American Journal of Political Science* 57, no. 4 (2013): 912–25.

MacKinnon, Catherine A. *Are Women Human? And Other International Dialogues.* Cambridge, MA: Harvard University Press, 2006.

Mallinder, Louise. *Amnesty, Human Rights and Political Transition: Bridging the Peace and Justice Divide.* Studies in International Law. Vol. 21, Oxford: Hart, 2008.

McEvoy, Kieran, and Louise Mallinder. "Amnesties in Transition: Punishment, Restoration, and the Governance of Mercy." *Journal of Law and Society* 39, no. 3 (2012): 410–40.

Meister, Robert. *After Evil: A Politics of Human Rights.* New York: Columbia University Press, 2011.

Moyn, Samuel. *The Last Utopia: Human Rights in History.* Cambridge, MA: The Belknap Press of Harvard University Press, 2010.

Murdie, Amanda, and Tavishi Bhasin. "Aiding and Abetting: Human Rights INGOS and Domestic Protest." *Journal of Conflict Resolution* 55, no. 2 (2011): 163–91.

Murdie, Amanda M., and David R. Davis. "Shaming and Blaming: Using Events Data to Assess the Impact of Human Rights INGOS." *International Studies Quarterly* 56, no. 1 (2012): 1–16.

Nagy, Rosemary. "Transitional Justice as Global Project: Critical Reflections." *Third World Quarterly* 29, no. 2 (2008): 275–89.

Neumayer, Eric. "Do International Human Rights Treaties Improve Respect for Human Rights?." *Journal of Conflict Resolution* 49, no. 6 (2005): 925–53.

Ocantos, Ezequiel González. "Persuade Them or Oust Them: Crafting Judicial Change and Transitional Justice in Argentina." *Comparative Politics* 46, no. 4 (July, 2014).

Okin, Susan Moller. *Is Multiculturalism Bad for Women?* Princeton: Princeton University Press, 1999.

Olsen, Tricia D., Leigh A. Payne, and Andrew G. Reiter. *Transitional Justice in Balance: Comparing Processes, Weighing Efficacy.* Washington, DC: United States Institute of Peace, 2010.

Peterman, Amber, Dara Kay Cohen, Tia Palermo, and Amelia Hoover Green. "Rape Reporting During War: Why the Numbers Don't Mean What You Think They Do." *Foreign Affairs*, August 1, 2011.

Pflanz, Mike. "African Leaders Vote to Give Themselves Immunity from War Crimes Prosecutions." *The Telegraph*, July 2, 2014.

Pinker, Steven. *The Better Angels of Our Nature: Why Violence Has Declined.* New York: Penguin Books, 2011.

Poe, Steven C. "The Decision to Repress: An Integrative Theoretical Approach to the Research on Human Rights and Repression." In *Understanding Human Rights Violations: New Systematic Studies,* edited by Sabine C. Carey and Steven C. Poe. Burlington: Ashgate Publishing Company, 2004: 17–38.

Posner, Eric A. *The Twilight of Human Rights Law.* Oxford: Oxford University Press, 2014.

Risse, Thomas, Stephen C. Ropp, and Kathryn Sikkink, eds. *The Persistent Power of Human Rights: From Commitment to Compliance.* Cambridge: Cambridge University Press, 2013.

Ron, James, David Crow, and Shannon Golden. "The Struggle for a Truly Grassroots Human Rights Movement." *opendemocracy.com* (June 18, 2013).

Sands, Philippe. "The ICC Arrest Warrant Will Make Colonel Gaddafi Dig in His Heels." *The Guardian*, May 4, 2011.

Scheffer, David. *All the Missing Souls: A Personal History of the War Crimes Tribunals.* Princeton and Oxford: Princeton University Press, 2012.

Sen, Amartya. "An Argument for the Primacy of Political Rights: Freedoms and Needs." *The New Republic* 210, no. 2/3 (January 10, 1994): 31–8.

Sikkink, Kathryn. "The Role of Consequences, Comparison and Counterfactuals in Constructivist Ethical Thought." In *Moral Limit and Possibility in World Politics,* edited by Richard M. Price. New York: Cambridge University Press, 2008: 83–111.

  Evidence for Hope: Making Human Rights Work in the 21st Century (Princeton: Princeton University Press, 2017).

Simmons, Beth. *Mobilizing for Human Rights: International Law in Domestic Politics.* Cambridge: Cambridge University Press, 2009.

Slaughter, Anne-Marie. *A New World Order.* Princeton: Princeton University Press, 2004.

Snyder, Jack, and Leslie Vinjamuri. "Trials and Errors: Principle and Pragmatism in Strategies of International Justice." *International Security* 28, no. 3 (2003/4): 5–44.

Sonnenberg, Stephan, and James L. Cavallaro. "Name, Shame, and Then Build Consensus? Bringing Conflict Resolution Skills to Human Rights." *Washington University Journal of Law & Policy* 39 (2012): 257–308.

Stammers, Neil. *Human Rights and Social Movements*. London: Pluto Press, 2009.

Staton, Jeffrey K., and Will H. Moore. "Judicial Power in Domestic Politics." *International Organization* 65, no. 3 (2011): 553–87.

Stern, Steve J., and Scott Straus, eds. *The Human Rights Paradox: Universality and Its Discontents*. Madison: University of Wisconsin Press, 2014.

Suresh, V. "Funds and Civil Liberties." *opendemocracy.com*, January 6, 2014.

Tadros, Samuel. "Egypt's Elections: Why the Islamists Won." *World Affairs*, March/April (2012).

Teorell, Jan, Nicholas Charron, Stefan Dahlberg, Sören Holmberg, Bo Rothstein, Petrus Sundin, and Richard Svensson. *The Quality of Government Dataset, Version 20dec13*. University of Gothenberg: The Quality of Government Institute, www.qog.pol.gu.se, 2013.

Viswanathan, V.N., ed. *Corruption and Human Rights*. New Delhi: Allied Publishers Pvt Ltd, 2012.

Zuern, Elke. *The Politics of Necessity: Community Organizing and Democracy in South Africa*. Madison: University of Wisconsin Press, 2011.

3   Human Rights *and* Human Welfare: Looking for a "Dark Side" to International Human Rights Law

Beth A. Simmons and Anton Strezhnev

International human rights law has attracted a barrage of criticism over the past decade or more. One critique views international human rights law as useless and argues that it has not managed to improve enjoyment of the rights it has set out to protect. Another critique goes further: it blames the legalization of international human rights norms for a series of negative outcomes, from the neglect of development to a crisis in the realization of social rights. Some even suggest that international legal obligations are to blame for the channeling of repressive tactics from areas that are clearly foreclosed by law to gray areas where rules are less clear.

These are important claims, because if true, they suggest that even if human rights treaties have improved some rights, the consequences might, on balance, be deleterious. If that is the case, we should rethink the strategy of legalizing human rights principles in formal agreements. But if these claims are wrong, they could undermine a global effort to improve the well-being of millions of people worldwide. Among liberal rights supporters, these claims, if correct, may reduce support for an international legal approach to human rights. Moreover, a vague belief that human rights norms have caused harm around the world adds fuel to an even more fundamental challenge: the "end times" of human rights that *all* governments should respect, and a concession to various religious entities, from the most humanitarian to the most brutal, to claim an unchecked moral authority to define and enforce, in any way they see fit, their own views of human rights and human wrongs.[1] We leave it to another paper to document the disastrous consequences for human well-being if either state or religious authority (or their combination) create alternatives to international human rights law that non-believers and non-nationals have no right to question.

---

[1] Stephen Hopgood, *The Endtimes of Human Rights* (Ithaca: Cornell University Press, 2013).

We argue that claims that international human rights law has had negative effects simply cannot be substantiated with evidence. We agree such law has not had positive effects everywhere, though the evidence of positive effects on average is quite strong. But claims of *harm* as a result of human rights law are utterly apocryphal. Even if, as the critics of international human rights law graciously admit, the glass is only "half-full,"[2] harms claims rest on weak logic and no evidence.

In this chapter, we provide an empirical review that might plausibly speak to these claims. This is no easy task, because to answer fully and properly would require a series of counterfactuals about the world without international human rights law. Nor are the claims of the critics always articulated in ways that are amenable to empirical investigation. We think that an attempt to confront harms claims should address the following: Has the attention to human rights – especially those defined in the major treaties that seem to be favored by the Western World – diverted attention from more important matters, such as economic development or social justice? Have rights obligations in certain areas simply driven repression further underground, where it is harder to observe? We find there is practically no evidence that would justify answering these questions affirmatively. These issues are important because international human rights law is undergoing a profound challenge. Stephen Hopgood, for example, claims that the international legal system is cracking under pressure by sovereign governments who claim it does not bind, and by resurgent religious organizations that claim it has lost – or never had – the moral authority to describe a set of universal rights in the first place.[3] The very legitimacy of the system seems to be under siege.

This chapter proceeds as follows. The first section outlines some of the claims in the literature about the deleterious consequences assumed to be associated with the postwar "obsession" with international human rights. We describe three claims about the net consequences of such attention. First, some commentators have suggested that when governments comply with one obligation (e.g., the rights contained in the ICCPR), they strategically and intentionally violate other rights (e.g., engage in disappearances of political opponents). Second, some commentators claim that attention to human rights has crowded out attention to economic well-being through economic development. Third, some claim that individual civil and political rights have crowded out attention to social rights, such as a right to be educated, a right to health, and a host of labor rights. All of these claims go beyond the observation that human rights are often

---

[2] Eric A Posner, *The Twilight of Human Rights Law* (Oxford University Press, 2014).
[3] Hopgood, *The Endtimes of Human Rights*.

involved in political and policy trade-offs and thus are rarely perfectly realized. Rather, these critiques suggest that the legal regime *has done net harm*. Such musings have never been seriously tested with data and sound methods.

The second section of this chapter searches high and low for empirical evidence of a dark side – i.e., of net harms of international human rights law. This is a real challenge, not least because many such claims are not articulated precisely enough to be tested with evidence. Nonetheless, we have attempted here to collect evidence relevant to the thrust of the above critiques. The third section presents some simple findings. We find no credible evidence that attention to and compliance with international human rights law is *causally* connected with any of the negative consequences advanced by its critics. This null finding has huge implications for policy going forward. It suggests that while human rights are obviously never easy to realize in full, international human rights law is not responsible for the series of bad outcomes critics have claimed. In conjunction with other research pointing to systematic improvements in the rights international law has sought to protect,[4] we argue that many detractors have been far off base. Governments may claim they cannot possibly achieve economic development or social rights and live up to their human rights obligations at the same time, and a few may strategically alter their repressive behavior to keep within the letter of the law, but, on average, there is no evidence that human rights law has forced, or even encouraged, such consequences.

1   Human Rights Research

Research on the state of the art with respect to compliance with international human rights agreements has been reviewed in detail elsewhere.[5] In this section, we provide only a very general discussion in order to set up the harms claimed by critics. For decades, there was little empirical research on the effects of treaty obligations. International lawyers seemed to assume human rights treaties were important and beneficial, while students of government (domestic and international) tended to be somewhat more skeptical. The most important empirical work on human rights in these fields was accomplished by scholars of non-governmental

---

[4] Beth A. Simmons, *Mobilizing for Human Rights: International Law in Domestic Politics* (New York: Cambridge University Press, 2009).
[5] Emilie Hafner-Burton, *Making Human Rights a Reality* (Princeton: Princeton University Press, 2013); Hans Peter Schmitz and Kathryn Sikkink, "International Human Rights," in *Handbook of International Relations*, ed. Walter Carlsnaes, Thomas Risse, and Beth A Simmons (London: Sage, 2012), 827–51.

organizations, but these did not center directly on the effects of legal agreements. Risse, Ropp, and Sikkink edited an important book of case studies showing that ratification of human rights treaties has, in fact, been one common step in a "spiral model" that ends up trapping governments in their own rights-rhetorical snares.[6] Treaties were largely seen as useful ways for governments to make tactical concessions, but whether governments actually complied with such agreements was not an explicit focus of study.

The "compliance debate" took an important evidentiary turn in 2002, when Oona Hathaway published ground-breaking – if controversial – evidence suggesting that treaties did not have much positive impact on the rights they were intended to protect.[7] Research to the contrary followed, often making fairly nuanced arguments about the conditions under which we might expect treaties to matter.[8] Many debates continue to surround the consequences of international human rights law. Some of these debates have been about the quality of data;[9] others are methodological.[10] Most of the research, however, has been focused on whether international human rights law has had its *intended* consequences; that is, they investigate whether treaty commitments are associated with improvements in rights practices that the treaties were designed to address.

While political scientists debated how to model causal inference, endogeneity, and selection effects surrounding treaties and their consequences, legal scholars began to question the entire project of "Human Rights" law, discourse, and advocacy. From the vantage of critical legal theory, David Kennedy criticized the "foregrounding"

---

[6] Thomas Risse, Steve C. Ropp, and Kathryn Sikkink, *The Power of Human Rights: International Norms and Domestic Change*, Cambridge Studies in International Relations; 66 (Cambridge, UK; New York: Cambridge University Press, 1999); Thomas Risse, Steve C Ropp, and Kathryn Sikkink, eds., *The Persistent Power of Human Rights: From Commitment to Compliance*, vol. 126, Cambridge Studies in International Relations; (Cambridge: Cambridge University Press, 2013).

[7] Oona Hathaway, "Do Human Rights Treaties Make a Difference?," *Yale Law Journal* 111, no. 8 (2002).

[8] Simmons, *Mobilizing for Human Rights: International Law in Domestic Politics*; Courtenay R. Conrad, "Divergent Incentives for Dictators: Domestic Institutions and (International Promises Not to) Torture," *Journal of Conflict Resolution* 58, no. 1 (2014); Emilia Justyna Powell and Jeffrey K.Staton, "Domestic Judicial Institutions and Human Rights Treaty Violation," *International Studies Quarterly* 53, no. 1 (2009).

[9] Christopher J Fariss, "Respect for Human Rights Has Improved over Time: Modeling the Changing Standard of Accountability," *American Political Science Review* 108, no. 02 (2014).

[10] Yonatan Lupu, "The Informative Power of Treaty Commitment: Using the Spatial Model to Address Selection Effects," *American Journal of Political Science* 57, no. 4 (2013).

of human rights as a way to address human well-being, adding a critique of the legal professionalization that had poured effort into the cause.[11] Intellectual and legal historian Samuel Moyn articulated a crisis of liberalism, which he argues has privileged individual civil and political rights, while hugely short-changing economic and social rights.[12] Using the logic of law and economics, Eric Posner took the opportunity to assert a strict budgetary trade-off between the whole project of human rights on the one hand and that of economic development on the other.[13] Even political scientists – once focused on the compliance debate – came to suggest that perhaps there was a risk in demanding adherence to treaties that governments would find a way to undermine by other, sometimes more atrocious, behavior.[14]

These critiques seem to contain important truths. We certainly acknowledge that governments make trade-offs involving human rights all of the time, at least in the short run. Michael Ignatieff, for example, has proposed a typology of trade-offs that governments often face, including derogations of human rights law for national security purposes; reservations to protect the primacy of domestic law; human rights compromises for foreign policy or diplomatic purposes; and trade-offs between competing human rights objectives themselves.[15] In this chapter, we do not dispute that trade-offs among human rights and sometimes between human rights and other values are never made; of course they are. Despite protests from some activists, most pragmatists would find it surprising were it otherwise. Instead, we are arguing against claims that international human rights norms may have had *net negative consequences* because they have *crowded out* other important objectives or have had *unintended negative consequences*. In other words, we do not claim what is practically impossible – that human rights are perfectly realized in the face of other objectives. Rather, we provide evidence that the worst fears of the cynics – that attention to human rights has been detrimental to human well-being – have no empirical basis.

[11] David Kennedy, "International Human Rights Movement: Part of the Problem?," *Harvard Human Rights Journal* 15 (2002); *The Dark Sides of Virtue: Reassessing International Humanitarianism* (Princeton: Princeton University Press, 2004).

[12] Samuel Moyn, *The Last Utopia: Human Rights in History* (Cambridge, MA: Belknap Press of Harvard University Press, 2010).

[13] Eric A. Posner, "Human Welfare, Not Human Rights," *Columbia Law Review* 108 (2008).

[14] Courtenay R. Conrad and Jacqueline H. R. DeMeritt, "Unintended Consequences: The Effect of Advocacy to End Torture on Empowerment Rights Violations," in *Examining Torture: Empirical Studies of State Repression*, ed. Tracy Lightcap and James P. Pfiffner (New York: Palgrave Macmillan US, 2014).

[15] Michael Ignatieff, "Human Rights and Politics: The Problem of Trade-Offs," *Harvard Human Rights Faculty Colloquium* March 3 (2016).

There are at least two possible responses to the claim that the international human rights regime has imposed net costs on human well-being. One is to deny that such a cost calculus is morally justified, and insist that we should not be having such discussions at all. The second is to subject the asserted trade-off to empirical investigation. We make the second of these responses, since the data and methods are available to consider at least some of the unintended negative consequences of the rights focus of the past four decades. But we insist that it is not enough to show that signing treaties is associated with various harms. Rather, those who claim that international human rights law has had negative consequences must show that these consequences result from efforts to implement legal obligations. In short, we must test for a trade-off or a diversion between international human rights obligations and other harms done. The unintended deleterious outcome must not just exist alongside the rights regime; critics instead are claiming various harms *result* from putting human rights law compliance first. They often conclude that too much effort has been put into the construction of the international legal regime, at the *expense* of social justice, human welfare, and economic growth. They claim that well-intended legalization has been *responsible* for crowding out other worthy projects to improve the human condition, and that treaties *create* incentives for strategic governments to avoid obvious violations while substituting violations that are harder to detect. In order to validate these causal claims, we examine them in detail.

In some ways, this is a return to an old debate. For decades, human rights have been resisted on the basis of expected costs of various kinds. As Jack Donnelly has noted, "Twenty-five years ago, most states justified routine violations of human rights not only by appealing to national security (as opposed to personal security) and cultural relativism (as opposed to universal human rights) but also by appealing to the 'higher' imperatives of development and democracy (as opposed to the interests of particular individuals and groups)."[16] Authoritarian governments have historically claimed that human rights essentially endanger a range of other values from development to political stability to local cultural practice. What is interesting is that mainstream Western academics are now making similar critiques, from very different perspectives.

2   Three "Trade-offs"

This section examines three kinds of causal claims about the negative consequences of the legal regime for international human rights. Each

---

[16] Jack Donnelly, "Human Rights, Democracy, and Development," *Human Rights Quarterly* 21, no. 3 (1999): 610.

involves a causal claim about the (largely unintended) consequences of insisting on legal protections for international human rights. First, some argue that the pressure to comply with easily observed human rights cause violation-shifting to less visible practices. Second, foregrounding human rights has been at the expense of development. Third, emphasizing civil and political rights has degraded social rights. We explore these claims in turn.

Rights Guarantees Shift Violations to Less Visible Practices

Commitment to international human rights treaties seems to have drawn attention to the problem of compliance, focusing intergovernmental, non-governmental, and domestic attention on specific and observable indicators of human rights performance. When torture is banned, governments are likely to move away from practices that leave obvious signs of abuse on the human body and toward practices that leave fewer traces of their perpetration. There is a constant demand for suppression. Treaty Obligations do not affect this underlying demand, they only displace it from one kind of violation to another. When torture is banned, governments will shift from "scarring torture" to "stealth torture."[17]

More generally, researchers have argued that when scrutiny focuses on one form of repression, governments find substitutes, with no or even negative impact on net repression. Conrad and DeMeritt argue that since not all forms of repression can be scrutinized and shamed, governments will decrease torture but ramp other forms of repression.[18] Similarly, Yonatan Lupu finds that ratification of the International Covenant on Civil and Political Rights (ICCPR) correlates with improved political rights *and* with increased victims of disappearances.[19] Based on this, Lupu suggests that the "results provide empirical evidence that such substitution may occur."[20] But because this claim is based on two separate models that do not actually connect these correlations to one another, it is not a direct test of the substitution hypothesis. In Section 3 we examine this substitution claim more closely, and show there is no reason to attribute negative *causal* effects to international human rights commitments.

---

[17] Darius M. Rejali, *Torture and Democracy* (Princeton: Princeton University Press, 2007). For discussion of torture data that makes the distinction see Ursula Daxecker, "Dirty Hands: Government Torture and Terrorism," *Journal of Conflict Resolution* (2015).

[18] Conrad and DeMeritt, "Unintended Consequences: The Effect of Advocacy to End Torture on Empowerment Rights Violations."

[19] Yonatan Lupu, "Best Evidence: The Role of Information in Domestic Judicial Enforcement of International Human Rights Agreements," *International Organization* 67, no. 03 (2013).

[20] Ibid., 492.

Human Rights at the Expense of Economic Development

There are many versions of the claim that developing countries must choose between human rights and development. Very few people make the crude claim anymore that there is a simple trade-off between civil and political liberties and development. While a few countries – China and Singapore are the most commonly cited examples – have achieved impressive growth and development under repressive regimes, no one has shown that repression has positively contributed to such development; at most, and only in these few cases, political repression and development seem compatible.[21]

One of the most vocal critics of the international legal regime for human rights has proposed that rights talk has crowded out developmental objectives. Eric Posner describes international human rights law as rigidly refusing "to allow states to trade off different values – for example, to allow states to violate political rights in order to enhance the overall well-being of the population."[22] He is right in this regard. But the argument defies logic. How do rights violations improve overall well-being? Posner believes international law gives far more attention to negative rights (the right to be free from repression, the right not to be tortured, the right to exercise freedom of conscience) rather than to positive rights (the right to a minimum income, for example).[23] He argues that governments regularly excuse their lack of attention to economic rights by pointing out their dedication to civil and political rights. By expending so much effort on such protections as fair trials, freedom of speech and association, and training security officers how not to torture, remaining resources are rendered scarce for the more important task of promoting general welfare through economic development. "In short," Posner claims, "human rights obligations interfere with welfare-promoting activities of the government, and these welfare-promoting activities should be given priority."[24] Posner is concerned that human rights and human welfare are literally in competition with each other for scarce resources: "It is possible," he ventures, "that a state might cite its positive rights obligation to supply health care under the ICESCR as a justification for its failure to fully respect the negative rights obligation not to torture under the ICCPR."[25] Budgets are limited, and states may "decide to reduce poverty rather than tackle negative rights violations committed by the police or military."[26] International law provides no guidance on such matters, but

---

[21] Donnelly, "Human Rights, Democracy, and Development," 627–28.
[22] Posner, "Human Welfare, Not Human Rights," 1763.   [23] Ibid., 1768.
[24] Ibid., 1771.   [25] Ibid., 1773.   [26] Ibid., 1775.

Posner suspects there is more external political pressure for human rights than there is for human welfare.

That state budgets are limited is an obvious point, but many of the negative rights Posner discusses are not especially costly – a right to privacy, a right to enjoy one's own culture, women's right to participate in community activities, to name just a few.[27] That said, some are health care, housing, and education, for example. But no one thinks the expensive items have to be achieved in the next budget cycle. And further, such rights contribute to productivity and to development; they can be expected in the medium-to-long run to *contribute* to the growth and development approach that Posner advocates.[28] The important question is: has attention to human rights really *crowded out* concerns about human welfare, or has it in fact legitimated them? A treaty calling for childhood immunization can be used in a debate about the relative value of providing basic health care versus renovating the presidential mansion. Human rights obligations are useful tools for a populace to demand more attention to basic human rights and needs than the state may be currently devoting. Posner insists rights are on a fixed budget and that advocates will have to fight it out among themselves for funding. But if there is any way to strengthen domestic demands for more humanely targeted development resources, international treaties could help – and certainly cannot hurt – in making the case. The logic for viewing human rights and human welfare as a trade-off is weaker than a logic which views these as mutually reinforcing.

Indeed, many human rights experts with some knowledge of development issues simply do not see a trade-off here. Philip Alston refers to the development agenda and the human rights agenda as disconnected, yes, but highly congruent: "two agendas resemble ships passing in the night, even though they are both headed for very similar destinations."[29]

[27] Posner, *The Twilight of Human Rights Law*.
[28] On the link between education and economic development see: Ingemar Fägerlind and Lawrence J. Saha, *Education and National Development: A Comparative Perspective* (Elsevier, 2014). On the positive developmental impact of closing the educational gap for disadvantaged ethnic groups see Matthew Calver, "Closing the Aboriginal Education Gap in Canada: The Impact on Employment, GDP, and Labour Productivity," *International Productivity Monitor*, no. 28 (2015). On the impact of both health and education on productivity and growth, see Shahzad Alvi and Ather Maqsood Ahmed, "Analyzing the Impact of Health and Education on Total Factor Productivity: A Panel Data Approach," *Indian Economic Review* 49, no. 1 (2014). On the impact of adequate housing on development see Richard Harris and Godwin Arku, "Housing and Economic Development: The Evolution of an Idea since 1945," *Habitat International* 30, no. 4 (2006).
[29] Philip Alston, "Ships Passing in the Night: The Current State of the Human Rights and Development Debate Seen through the Lens of the Millennium Development Goals," *Human Rights Quarterly* 27, no. 3 (2005).

Yet others view development and human rights as *positively* connected in the practical work of intergovernmental and non-governmental organizations.[30] Whether rights have indeed crowded out development is an empirical issue, which we test in Section 3.

Civil and Political Rights at the Expense of Social Justice

Finally, we turn from claims of budget constraints inspired by law and economics to claims of constraints on the political imagination of liberal thought itself. The final harm of the modern approach to human rights is an indictment of what liberalism itself has become. Samuel Moyn claims that contemporary liberalism's fascination with civil and political rights has crowded out greater ambitions for welfarism and even social justice: "The drastic curtailment of liberalism's ambition through the rise of its foreign policy of human rights promotion" has sent us back to the negative liberties of Hobbes and Locke.[31] Moyn speaks of civil liberties' "competing ideals – social peace, national emancipation, economic growth, and collective welfare prominent among them."[32] Setting aside for now his phobia of evidentiary demonstrations, Moyn registers his disappointment in liberalism's focus on civil and political rights to the detriment of social justice. Freedom has overtaken equality; the international human rights project reflects and even facilitates the death of justice beyond liberty. What use are human rights treaties in recovering liberalism's earlier glory? "And how plausible is it," he asks, "that ragtag activists 'mobilizing' to make use of the extra tool of international law to update their domestic citizenship in political terms will pave the way for a more generous transformation of citizenship that makes room for welfarist justice?"[33]

Perhaps not *utterly* unlikely, it turns out. Recent empirical work on social rights understood as some form of social equality does not support claims of a trade-off. In one important study, Wade Cole found that states that ratified the International Covenant of Economic Social and Cultural Rights (ICESCR) had better outcomes with respect to social justice than those that had not done so. Using a methodology that accounts for selection and reverse causality, he has shown that membership in the ICESCR is associated with more economic equality than among states

---

[30] Paul J. Nelson and Ellen Dorsey, "At the Nexus of Human Rights and Development: New Methods and Strategies of Global NGOS," *World Development* 31, no. 12 (2003).

[31] Samuel Moyn, "Human Rights and the Crisis of Liberalism," in *Human Rights Futures*, ed. Jack Snyder, Leslie Vinjamuri, and Stephen Hopgood (Cambridge University Press, 2017).

[32] Ibid.   [33] Ibid.

that are not parties. The finding was true for both developing and developed countries, although the effect was somewhat stronger for the developed states.[34]

Coming from a critical tradition, David Kennedy makes many of the same points as Samuel Moyn, though without any obvious nostalgia for the traditional liberal project. However, he agrees that social justice has fallen by the wayside, as international human rights law has drained attention of good people away from other important humanitarian concerns.[35] According to Kennedy: "Human rights foregrounds problems of participation and procedure, at the expense of distribution ... However useful saying 'that's my right' is in extracting things from the state, it is not good for extracting things from the economy, unless you are a property holder."[36] There is an "imbalance between civil/political and social/economic rights" and this reflects "power balances in the world."[37] Kennedy and Moyn both believe that human rights have swamped concerns for social welfare, basic fairness, and society-wide commitments to equality.

So what should we make of the world's (and many nations') growing inequality?[38] Clearly, the international human rights regime has not solved the problem of maldistribution of the world's wealth. But no one has produced convincing evidence that a devotion to rights – even an outsized attachment to negative rights – has caused or even contributed to the world's distribution of resources; indeed, Cole's evidence seems to suggest otherwise. Below we will explore whether states that ratify international human rights treaties to improve their civil and political rights have done so at the expense of improvements in social justice, or at the expense of throwing a higher proportion of their population into poverty.

3   Data and Testing

All of the arguments discussed above have a common structure: they suggest a specific mechanism for why international human rights law

[34] Wade M. Cole, "International Human Rights and Domestic Income Inequality: A Difficult Case of Compliance in World Society," *American Sociological Review* (2015).
[35] Kennedy, "International Human Rights Movement: Part of the Problem?," 119–20.
[36] Kennedy, *The Dark Sides of Virtue: Reassessing International Humanitarianism*, 11.
[37] Ibid.
[38] There are debates in the literature, which we set aside for purposes of argumentation, as to whether global income inequality is on the rise or on the decline. Much depends on the concept of inequality the analyst has in mind. See Branko Milanovic, "Global Income Inequality in Numbers: In History and Now," *Global Policy* 4, no. 2 (2013). Jan Luiten van Zanden et al., "The Changing Shape of Global Inequality 1820–2000; Exploring a New Dataset," *Review of Income and Wealth* 60, no. 2 (2014).

worsens human outcomes. One mechanism is that international human rights treaties lead states to *substitute between competing outcomes*. For example, a state wanting to engage in repressive behavior may, in response to a specific treaty commitment, choose to strategically substitute one form of repression (disappearances) for forms of repression banned by new civil or political rights guarantees (e.g., through the ICCPR). Alternatively, a government with a constrained political agenda may choose to allocate its limited political capital toward improving human rights in response to international pressure instead of policies aimed at growth or development (Posner's argument). Another mechanism is simply a general *crowding out* of international effort expended toward different objectives. The international community's obsession with human rights generally diverts energy from efforts at economic development, or the primacy of negative rights within public discourse crowds out arguments for a focus on social justice. In each of these cases, critics are making a causal argument about the mechanisms connecting specific legal obligations, families of human rights obligations (e.g., negative rights), or international human rights law generally to adverse outcomes. These are hypotheses in need of evidence. In the subsequent sections, we first illustrate how a researcher would go about uncovering evidence of such a mechanism from empirical data. We then demonstrate that the evidence for such trade-offs is very weak, if not non-existent.

Strategic Substitution: Formal Compliance With New Forms of Repression

When governments face a consistent need to repress in order to maintain security and control, they are thought highly likely to substitute less costly forms of repression for those that are banned. Despite its apparent simplicity, the strategic substitution hypothesis involved two distinct causal claims:

1) A commitment to protect human rights in one area (e.g., civil and political rights) causes some new forms of repression (e.g., disappearances) to crop up.
2) This effect is due to an improvement (e.g., in civil and political rights) in the first place.

The first part is a straightforward causal effect. Without it, there would be no evidence that negotiating or signing a treaty generates the negative outcome to begin with. The second component is a hypothesis about the mechanism through which the effect of treaty ratification is transferred. Without claim two, there would be no support for the idea that ratifying a treaty stimulates substitution between the two outcomes. Strategic substitution requires showing that any negative rights effect of ratification is causally attributable to an actual improvement in human rights in the first place. Otherwise, there would be no reason for the state to compensate by increasing repression in other ways. That is, there must in reality be a causal pathway such that **Ratification → Human Rights Improvement → Negative Outcome**. Rights improvements necessarily mediate the effect of law on new rights abuses in strategic substitution models.

To understand the intuition of why we need evidence of the full mechanism, suppose that international human rights law has no effect. If the trade-off hypothesis were true, without some rights improvements, governments would have no incentive to substitute alternative forms of repression. If blocking the causal pathway by intervening on both ratification *and* human rights practices does not mitigate the observed correlation between ratification and repression substitution, then there is either some other unrelated mechanism behind the effect of a treaty on the negative outcome, or else the correlation is simply spurious. Illustrating this difference in effects – with the causal pathway "on" (mediated by rights improve) and "off" (no mediating improvement) – is necessary to support a claim of trade-offs.

Evidence for this substitution effect cannot be demonstrated by a single regression model. Instead, we need two models – one for the effect of the mediator on the outcome, and a second model for the effect of the intervention on the outcome *after accounting for the effect of the mediator*. This approach allows us to estimate the "controlled direct effect" of an intervention, holding fixed some mediating variable.[39] If the difference between the overall effect with the mediator "on" and the "controlled" effect with the mediator "off" is negligible, then the causal story of substitution is simply not supported.[40] We therefore evaluate the strategic substitution hypothesis by testing the null of no substitution: that the total effect of ratification

---

[39] Blackwell, Acharya, and Sen argue that this quantity is appropriate for evaluating stories about causal mechanisms. They suggest researchers compare the total effect (TE) of an intervention to the controlled direct effect (CDE) in order to evaluate the general importance of a particular causal mechanism. They outline a simple approach to estimating the CDE using two regression models known as "sequential g-estimation." See Avidit Acharya, Matthew Blackwell, and Maya Sen. "Explaining causal findings without bias: Detecting and assessing direct effects." *American Political Science Review* 110.3 (2016): 512.

[40] In Blackwell et al.'s terms, if the Controlled Direct Effect is essentially equal to the total effect, then it is unlikely that the mediating mechanism explains much of the effect on the outcome.

on the negative outcome is equal to the controlled direct effect of ratification *holding constant* mediating conditions (a state's human rights practices).

To demonstrate how claims of strategic substitution are exaggerated relative to their empirical support, we test for evidence of substitution between forms of repression that is attributable to international human rights law. To illustrate, we re-examine the data in Lupu[41] on the relationship between ICCPR ratification and various measures of rights drawn from the Cingranelli et al. (CIRI) human rights dataset.[42] Lupu finds evidence of a marginal *positive* relationship between ICCPR ratification and CIRI indicators of freedom of association, freedom of speech, and religious freedom. However, there is also some evidence of an association between ICCPR ratification and *increased* incidence of disappearances. How likely is it that this indicates a trade-off? We start by plotting average levels for each of the four rights indicators over time, and split by states that have ratified the ICCPR and states that have not (Figure 3.1).

While it is difficult to draw causal claims from this figure as the population of states is changing over time (as more states ratify, fewer states make up the "non-ratifiers" population), we are able to check the face-validity of a trade-off claim. First, it is worth noting that disappearances tend to be both rarely used and fairly stable over time in this sample. Second, disappearance scores trend slightly toward *fewer* rights violations, while the remainder of the civil liberties indicators (speech/civil rights, personal integrity rights) exhibit mixed or downward movement overtime (more violations). This is the exact opposite of what we would expect if there were a trade-off developing over time. Nor is there a clear difference in general patterns over time between ratifiers and non-ratifiers, apart from year-to-year noise. The trade-off hypothesis would imply diverging trends for ratifiers but parallel trends for non-ratifiers. However, both ratifiers and non-ratifiers exhibit diverging trends in disappearances and religious freedom. Likewise, trends for freedom of association and disappearances are nearly parallel in both (barring the positive post-2000 shock for the non-ratifier sample). Obviously, we cannot draw inferences about individual state behavior from this time series. Nevertheless, Figure 3.1 does suggest that a sizable trade-off between rights and repression is implausible.

---

[41] Lupu, "Best Evidence," 2013.
[42] The CIRI data is described and can be accessed at www.humanrightsdata.com/

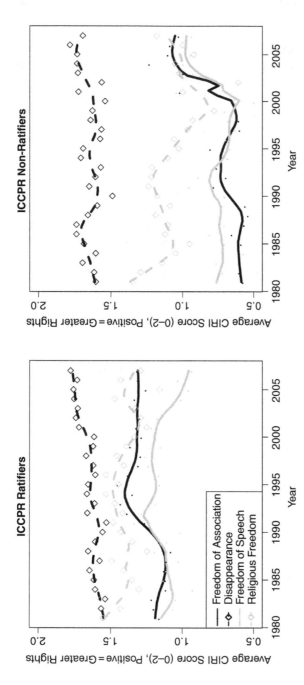

Figure 3.1: Mean CIRI Human Rights Scores over Time (1981–2007).
Lines denote smooth LOESS regressions fit to each time series.

To directly test the trade-off hypothesis, we replicate the analysis of Lupu (2013a) using the same set of control variables.[43] As described above, we estimate both the total effect of ICCPR ratification on disappearances *and* the effect controlling for each of the three other rights variables using sequential g-estimation. We fit a linear regression model on the estimate of the total direct effect of ICCPR ratification on the expected effect and compare it to the controlled direct effect.[44] To properly account for all of the uncertainty in our estimation, we compute standard errors and confidence intervals using a cluster bootstrap clustering on country.

Figure 3.2 plots the estimated average treatment effect of ICCPR ratification for a given country year on the expected CIRI disappearances scale. As negative values correspond to more disappearances (higher values denote greater respect for rights), this estimate implies that states that ratify the ICCPR do tend to be more likely to engage in disappearances, on average. Does this support strategic substitution? No. *When we estimated the controlled direct effects holding constant each of the other three rights mediators, the resulting point estimates are essentially identical to the average treatment effect.* Fixing the mediating rights variables has no appreciable change in the estimated effect of ratification on disappearances. Were the strategic substitution hypothesis true, the controlled direct effect would attenuate toward zero, since we would have blocked one of the crucial pathways through which the effect was supposed to be transmitted. In fact, there are no statistically significant differences between effects when the rights improvement mediating mechanism is "on" or "off."[45] While we do not have a clear explanation for the existence of the ICCPR correlation with disappearances in this case, we cannot

---

[43] Following Lupu (2013a), we include as pre-treatment controls measures of judicial independence, democracy, regime durability, incidence of civil and interstate war, log GDP per capita, log population, number of INGOs operating in the country, and outcomes lagged by one period, in addition to year fixed effects. Overall, our dataset contains 190 total countries and 2157–2160 total country-year observations. The total sample sizes differ slightly across each of the moderators as we have slightly different amounts of missingness in each CIRI variable.

[44] This is the only place where we diverge from the original model specification (which used an ordinal probit model). Sequential g-estimation requires us to assume linearity for the outcome in order to efficiently estimate the conditional expectation of the outcome. This is somewhat implausible given that the CIRI scale is bounded between 0–2 and is more properly ordinal. However, our results when using OLS to estimate the total effects are very similar to those from an ordered logistic model, suggesting that making the linearity assumption does not yield misleading implications.

[45] We directly test for whether there is a difference by computing the difference between the total and controlled effects for each bootstrapped sample. In all three cases, we fail to reject the null hypothesis that this difference is distinguishable from zero at $\alpha = .05$. While the largest difference does appear for religious freedom, the magnitude is still negligible and statistically indistinguishable from noise.

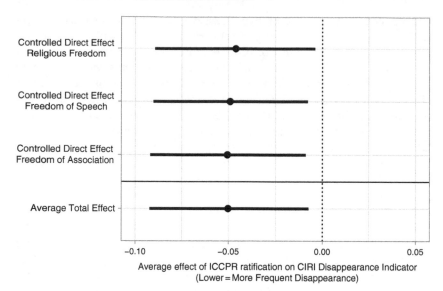

Figure 3.2: Total and Controlled Direct Effects of ICCPR Ratification on CIRI Disappearance Rating.

Lines denote 95 percent cluster bootstrapped confidence intervals.

attribute it to strategic substitution across other forms of repression. Perhaps there is some lurking variable driving the correlation or a different mediating mechanism. But we can conclude in this case that there is no evidence that states on average compensate for increases in civil and political rights by increasing repression via disappearances.

Crowding Out: Human Rights Versus Development

For the second test, we examine Posner's assertion that states' commitments to improve human rights directly crowd out efforts at promoting economic growth and development.[46] This argument takes a very similar form to the repression substitution. The effect of international human rights obligations on poor economic outcomes are mediated, in Posner's view, by the costly distraction of trying to comply with international human rights agreements. Lacking a good proxy for "effort" or "resources allocated," we understand this argument to suggest a head-to-head competition between rights realization and developmental outcomes.

[46] Posner, *The Twilight of Human Rights Law*; Posner, "Human Welfare, Not Human Rights."

Without improvements in rights, there is little reason to believe that Posner's rights-development trade-off would be very constraining.

Posner's argument grows out of a frustration with the proliferation of international human rights law. Treaty proliferation is a matter of historical record, and so is the fact that a growing number of states have ratified more and more human rights agreements over time.[47] The more human rights treaties a state ratifies, the more resources it is likely to devote to implementing its obligations (or so the argument goes). But to the extent that this is true, Posner claims there is a trade-off between rights and developmental outcomes, and the latter, he argues, are more clearly associated with human well-being generally.

Is this trade-off plausible? Interestingly, there has been no such trade-off for the international community as a whole. A quick look at official aid allocations suggests that if anything, the relationship is in the *opposite* direction to that Posner posits (Figure 3.3). According to the OECD database of official development aid, economic development assistance vastly outstrips human rights development assistance, and the growth over time in development assistance strongly counters Posner's claim that human rights efforts have crowded out development efforts.[48]

What about a budget constraint at the state level? The evidence above undercuts Posner's claim of a *hard* constraint, since state budgets for development have apparently been significantly augmented by the international community. But suppose the trade-off is real. We would then expect states that make more human rights commitments to underinvest in development. Posner suggests many measures of development that might conceivably reflect the human welfare concerns he has in mind. The first is GDP/capita: "Higher per capita GDP means that more goods and services are being consumed; because people want goods and services, an increase in consumption of goods and services would seem to indicate an increase in welfare."[49] The second is the United Nations Development Program's "Human Development Index" (HDI), which Posner mentions as a broader measure of factors that contribute to human well-being.[50]

---

[47] Simmons, *Mobilizing for Human Rights: International Law in Domestic Politics*, chapters 2 and 3.

[48] Richard A. Nielsen (2013). "Rewarding Human Rights? Selective Aid Sanctions Against Repressive States." *International Studies Quarterly* 57(4): 791–803.

[49] Posner, "Human Welfare, Not Human Rights," 1783.

[50] Ibid., 1789. The United Nations Development Program describes the HDI as "a summary measure of average achievement in key dimensions of human development: a long and healthy life, being knowledgeable and have a decent standard of living." See http://hdr.undp.org/en/content/human-development-index-hdi.

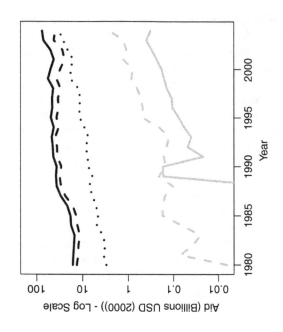

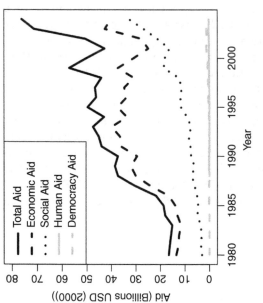

Figure 3.3: Aid Flows by Sector from 17 OECD Donors.
Source: OECD (2008), as presented in Nielsen (2013).

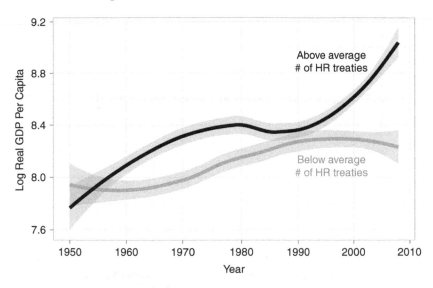

Figure 3.4: Patterns in per Capita GDP Among High-Commitment and Low-Commitment States (1950–2007).

Lines are LOESS smoothers for the conditional expectation of GDP per capita in a given year. Gray shading denotes the 95% confidence interval around the line.

Do more human rights obligations lead to underinvestment in economic development? A simple visualization does not support a trade-off. Using a count of ratification of the major human rights treaties[51] on the one hand and the log of GDP per capita[52] on the other, it is fairly clear that states that have ratified more treaties than average performed better economically than those who ratify fewer human rights treaties, contrary to the trade-off hypothesis (Figure 3.4). Posner's hypothesis sees little support here, as the average rate of change in per capita GDP tends to be generally parallel between the two groups. Since 2000, it even appears that the states with more human rights commitments grow at a more rapid rate. To test this hypothesis more explicitly, we regress countries' percent

[51] To measure levels of human rights commitment, we draw from Lupu's (2013b) dataset cataloguing the years in which states ratified universal UN human rights treaties. We generate a count for each state of how many of the 24 human rights treaties they have ratified in a given year.

[52] Time-series data on GDP is drawn from Version 6.0 of the Expanded Trade and GDP Data dataset. Kristian S. Gleditsch, "Expanded Trade and GDP Data," *Journal of Conflict Resolution* 46: 712–24 (2002).

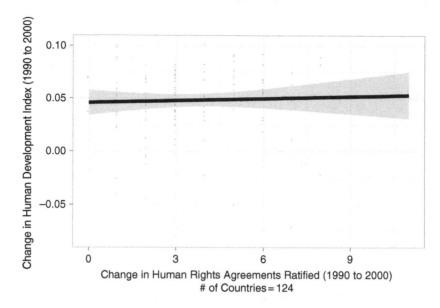

Figure 3.5: No Evidence of an Association Between Changes in HR Commitments and Changes in HDI.

change in GDP per capita on the number of human rights treaties that they sign, again using the same controls as we did above for Lupu (2013a). We find that for each additional treaty ratified, the expected change in growth rates is statistically indistinguishable from zero (95% confidence interval [0.11%–0.27%]).

We also find no evidence that the countries that expand their human rights commitments see weaker growth in terms of a more generalized index of development – the UN Human Development Index. While the HDI is not collected annually, nor does it cover every single state (particularly for earlier iterations of the survey), we do have two time points – 1990 and 2000 – that allow for some within-country comparisons. Figure 3.5 plots the change in HDI for each country for which data is available from the year 1990 to 2000 against the change in the number of human rights treaties that state signed between 1990 and 2000. We do not see the negative association that Posner's argument would imply. In fact, the slope of a simple regression fit to the bivariate relationship is statistically indistinguishable from zero. For conventional measures such as GDP per capita and more broad-based indices of development such as HDI, we find no evidence that states taking on greater human rights obligations are falling behind on development.

In short, there is practically no support for the claim that human rights obligations have interfered with the crucial project of economic development and attention to human welfare. Note what we are *not* arguing here. We agree that "[t]he notion that a government could legitimately put resources into economic growth, health care, or security rather than eliminating torture is highly controversial."[53] But it is fairly clear that the international legal system does not force, or even incentivize, such a controversial choice.

The Rights/Social Justice Trade-off: Individual Rights Versus Social Equity

Finally, we explore the contention that human rights have contributed to impoverished social justice. Unfortunately, the critics do not provide very clear guidance on exactly what constitutes social justice, or even whether this is a universal concept or culturally specific. David Miller defines social justice as "how the good and bad things in life should be distributed among the members of human society."[54] Europeans seem to have in mind some combination of attention to poverty prevention, equitable access to education, healthcare and labor market access, non-discrimination, and even intergenerational justice.[55] It is challenging to show that global social justice is improving or is at risk, because the concept only properly applies if we assume a society-wide consensus about the range of goods, services, and opportunities that members of a given society value (individual tastes notwithstanding).[56] Since that is not possible in the space of this short chapter, we have decided to test the concept of social justice as poverty prevention and equitable income distribution. We fully understand that this is too "flat" a conception,[57] and use it here only as prima facie empirical evidence of the claims advanced above.

We measure income inequality using the common Gini coefficient measure. With respect to within-country inequality, we find little evidence that countries that sign many human rights agreements have systematically greater inequality (higher Gini coefficients). The relationship is generally flat, if not somewhat negative, as countries that have signed

---

[53] Posner, "Human Welfare, Not Human Rights," 1794.

[54] David Miller, *Principles of Social Justice* (Harvard University Press, 1999), 1.

[55] See, for example, the content of the "Social Justice Index," which purports to measure the concept for states in the European Union; available at www.social-inclusion-monitor .eu/social-justice-index/.

[56] Miller, *Principles of Social Justice*, 8.

[57] A point made by many, including Cass R. Sunstein, *Free Markets and Social Justice* (Oxford University Press, 1999), 5.

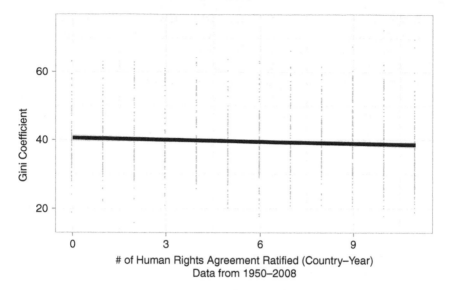

Figure 3.6: No Meaningful Relationship Between Measures of Income Inequality and Number of Human Rights Agreements Ratified.

many human rights treaties have (admittedly, negligibly) more *equal* income distributions. Figure 3.6 plots the bivariate relationship between Gini coefficients of countries from 1950 to 2008 against the number of human rights agreements that they have signed.[58] Indeed, the slope of the bivariate regression line is marginally negative, but the pattern is overall incredibly noisy. To adjust both for time-trends and other relevant covariates, we fit a regression of the Gini coefficient on the number of human rights agreements signed, along with controls and year fixed effects. We actually estimate a slight negative and statistically significant relationship between the two. All else being equal, a country that ratifies an additional human rights agreement can be expected to have a Gini coefficient that is *lower* – signifying greater income equality – by about 0.75 points (95% CI: [−1.47, −0.03]). This relationship is contrary to the claim that human rights have crowded out equality. However, the magnitude of the effect is so small that we should be cautious in inferring

[58] We use data on income inequality from the World Bank's "All the Ginis" Dataset (version: Autumn 2014), which aggregates multiple Gini coefficient measures from household surveys. Notably, there is sizable missingness in this time series as it relies only on available surveys. However, this dataset gives the widest coverage possible with respect to direct measures of income inequality without relying on estimates, imputation, or guesses.

anything from this result. Nevertheless, it does show, at a minimum, that there is no clear evidence that countries that allocate effort to ratifying human rights agreements have systematically disregarded social justice. If there is a trade-off in terms of countries' use of human rights instruments and actual distributional outcomes, it is essentially impossible to find evidence of it in the data.

4 Conclusion

Many claims have been made about how international human rights law works – and how it sometimes fails to do so. Most scholars have commented on the effectiveness of the regime as a whole, or have concentrated on the ability of human rights law to achieve its stated objectives. But in recent years, a few commentators have claimed, or at least implied, that Human Rights (with a capital H and a capital R, as Stephen Hopgood would have it) as a set of rules, a philosophy, or a strategy of claim-staking has had *negative* consequences. Sometimes, these consequences have not been fully anticipated, as the strategic substitution or the budget constraint arguments tend to suggest. In the case of liberalism's focus on negative rights over social justice, the consequences may be construed as a deliberate choice that suits specific coalitions in powerful countries, such as the United States.

We have specified three dynamics that some authors have alleged connect international human rights law with negative consequences. *Strategic substitution* is a common critique of law enforcement: enforcing the law in some situations incentivizes actors to violate other norms or standards in order to achieve their objective. Banning torture is said to lead to less visible forms of "enhanced interrogation": protecting civil rights that are observable is said to encourage repressive governments to simply cause their opponents to "disappear." In this view, the demand for repression is basically constant. Law, some have claimed, merely changes its format.

Others claim that Human Rights has caused harm by *distracting* humankind from other purposes and values. Stalled development and global economic disparities leave so many people around the world in misery that it is natural to try to find a cause for, or at least a contributing factor to, these realities. For some, Human Rights as a system of commitments is at least in part to blame. The crowding-out hypothesis blames rights law for diverting resources away from the crucial project of economic development. "Human Welfare, *not* Human Rights" is a posture that prioritizes the former rather than the latter. But why not both? Because, some have claimed, budgets are limited, and when push

comes to shove, people must eat, though they need not enjoy basic freedom from political and even physical repression. The consequence?
Allegedly, Human Rights has sapped efforts to tackle the bigger, broader
problem of global poverty.

Relatedly, it is claimed that Human Rights has pushed matters of
social justice into the background. In clinging to their negative liberties,
liberals have lost touch with richer notions of rights such as equity,
security, and justice. Over-legalization has become an end in itself;
Human Rights has metastasized to inhabit the whole of humanitarianism. Indeed, Human Rights has become part of *the problem* in the world
today.

This chapter is a humble empirical effort to ask, *really?* Empirical pushback against such sweeping claims is important because they imply clear
policy advice: drop the emphasis on Human Rights, and take up other
crucial issues such as democratic transition, poverty alleviation, and
"humanitarianism" writ large. Our findings suggest this drastic reorientation is unnecessarily destructive. It is also based on faulty empirics and
sometimes little more than emotive gestures that belie our own sense of
inadequacy in solving serious global problems.

We are aware that the basic empirics we offer in this chapter do not fully
respond to the sweeping indictments found in some of the literature. But
our discussion is designed simply to ask readers to stop and think for
a moment about the direction much of the critique of Human Rights has
taken. Unanticipated consequences have been described as *causal* outcomes on the basis of inappropriate empirical models. Crucial positions
have been staked on little more than supposition. Skepticism has been
fueled on the basis of thought experiments and possibilities. We want to at
least encourage readers to stop and ask, *what is the causal evidence that
international human rights law has contributed to any of these undesirable
outcomes?* For a decade or more, the presumption that law matters for
human rights has been the special evidentiary burden of those who
hypothesize positive effects. We insist that those who assign the international human rights regime negative consequences also have a burden to
demonstrate causality.

Ours is not just a position based on empirical social science versus
history, critical legal theory, philosophy, or any other academic discipline. All of these perspectives have a legitimate role in questioning the
rules of governance humankind have fashioned. But when it comes to
expounding on the consequences of choices we have made, it is essential
to realize the danger of damaging a fragile system without empirical
justification. As Stephen Hopgood has diagnosed, there *are* very powerful alternatives to Human Rights: for example, extreme forms of

religious authority and hard-shelled state sovereignty that we have recently rediscovered to be disastrous. Look at the evidence. Think again. Advocate wisely.

References

Acharya, Avidit, Matthew Blackwell, and Maya Sen. "Explaining Causal Findings without Bias: Detecting and Assessing Direct Effects." *American Political Science Review* Vol. 110, No. 3 (2016): 512.

Alston, Philip. "Ships Passing in the Night: The Current State of the Human Rights and Development Debate Seen through the Lens of the Millennium Development Goals." *Human Rights Quarterly* 27, no. 3 (2005): 755–829.

Alvi, Shahzad, and Ather Maqsood Ahmed. "Analyzing the Impact of Health and Education on Total Factor Productivity: A Panel Data Approach." *Indian Economic Review* 49, no. 1 (2014): 109–23.

Calver, Matthew. "Closing the Aboriginal Education Gap in Canada: The Impact on Employment, GDP, and Labour Productivity." *International Productivity Monitor*, no. 28 (Spring 2015): 27–46.

Cole, Wade M. "International Human Rights and Domestic Income Inequality: A Difficult Case of Compliance in World Society." *American Sociological Review* (March 2, 2015): 359–90.

Conrad, Courtenay R. "Divergent Incentives for Dictators: Domestic Institutions and (International Promises Not to) Torture." *Journal of Conflict Resolution* 58, no. 1 (February 1, 2014): 34–67.

Conrad, Courtenay R., and Jacqueline H. R. DeMeritt. "Unintended Consequences: The Effect of Advocacy to End Torture on Empowerment Rights Violations." In *Examining Torture: Empirical Studies of State Repression*, edited by Tracy Lightcap and James P. Pfiffner, 159–83. New York: Palgrave Macmillan US, 2014.

Daxecker, Ursula. "Dirty Hands: Government Torture and Terrorism." *Journal of Conflict Resolution* (September 18, 2015).

Donnelly, Jack. "Human Rights, Democracy, and Development." *Human Rights Quarterly* 21, no. 3 (1999): 608–32.

Fägerlind, Ingemar, and Lawrence J Saha. *Education and National Development: A Comparative Perspective*. Amsterdam: Elsevier, 2014.

Fariss, Christopher J. "Respect for Human Rights Has Improved over Time: Modeling the Changing Standard of Accountability." *American Political Science Review* 108, no. 02 (2014): 297–318.

Hafner-Burton, Emilie. "*Making Human Rights a Reality*." xvi. Princeton: Princeton University Press, 2013.

Harris, Richard, and Godwin Arku. "Housing and Economic Development: The Evolution of an Idea since 1945." *Habitat International* 30, no. 4 (2006): 1007–17.

Hathaway, Oona. "Do Human Rights Treaties Make a Difference?." *Yale Law Journal* 111, no. 8 (2002): 1935–2042.

Hopgood, Stephen. *The Endtimes of Human Rights*. Ithaca: Cornell University Press, 2013.

Ignatieff, Michael. "Human Rights and Politics: The Problem of Trade-Offs." *Harvard Human Rights Faculty Colloquium* (March 3, 2016): 1–19.

Kennedy, David. *The Dark Sides of Virtue: Reassessing International Humanitarianism*. Princeton: Princeton University Press, 2004.

"International Human Rights Movement: Part of the Problem?." *Harvard Human Rights Journal* 15 (2002): 101–26.

Lupu, Yonatan. "Best Evidence: The Role of Information in Domestic Judicial Enforcement of International Human Rights Agreements." *International Organization* 67, no. 03 (2013a): 469–503.

"The Informative Power of Treaty Commitment: Using the Spatial Model to Address Selection Effects." *American Journal of Political Science* 57, no. 4 (2013b): 912–25.

Milanovic, Branko. "Global Income Inequality in Numbers: In History and Now." *Global Policy* 4, no. 2 (2013): 198–208.

Miller, David. *Principles of Social Justice*. Harvard University Press, 1999.

Moyn, Samuel. "Human Rights and the Crisis of Liberalism." In *Human Rights Futures*, edited by Jack Snyder, Leslie Vinjamuri, and Stephen Hopgood. Cambridge University Press, 2017.

The Last Utopia: Human Rights in History. Cambridge, MA: Belknap Press of Harvard University Press, 2010.

Nelson, Paul J., and Ellen Dorsey. "At the Nexus of Human Rights and Development: New Methods and Strategies of Global NGOS." *World Development* 31, no. 12 (12/2003): 2013–26.

Nielsen, Richard A. "Rewarding Human Rights? Selective Aid Sanctions against Repressive States." *International Studies Quarterly* 57(4) (2013): 791–803.

Posner, Eric A. "Human Welfare, Not Human Rights." *Columbia Law Review* 108 (2008): 1758–801.

Posner, Eric A. *The Twilight of Human Rights Law*. New York: Oxford University Press, 2014.

Powell, Emilia Justyna, and Jeffrey K. Staton, "Domestic Judicial Institutions and Human Rights Treaty Violation." *International Studies Quarterly* 53, no. 1 (2009): 149–74.

Rejali, Darius M. *Torture and Democracy*. Princeton: Princeton University Press, 2007.

Risse, Thomas, Steve C Ropp, and Kathryn Sikkink, eds. *The Persistent Power of Human Rights: From Commitment to Compliance*. Vol. 126, Cambridge Studies in International Relations. Cambridge: Cambridge University Press, 2013.

The Power of Human Rights: International Norms and Domestic Change. Cambridge Studies in International Relations; 66. Cambridge, UK; New York: Cambridge University Press, 1999.

Schmitz, Hans Peter, and Kathryn Sikkink. "International Human Rights." In *Handbook of International Relations*, edited by Walter Carlsnaes, Thomas Risse, and Beth A. Simmons, 827–51. London: Sage, 2012.

Simmons, Beth A. *Mobilizing for Human Rights: International Law in Domestic Politics*. New York: Cambridge University Press, 2009.

Sunstein, Cass R. *Free Markets and Social Justice*. New York: Oxford University Press, 1999.

van Zanden, Jan Luiten, Joerg Baten, Peter Foldvari, and Bas van Leeuwen. "The Changing Shape of Global Inequality 1820–2000; Exploring a New Dataset." *Review of Income and Wealth* 60, no. 2 (2014): 279–97.

4   Empowering Rights Through Mass Movements, Religion, and Reform Parties

Jack Snyder

When asked to explain where the contemporary human rights movement gets its power, its advocates typically credit the rise of "global civil society."[1] Human Rights Watch has said that "its strength lies in its partnerships with local human rights groups, further extending its reach to the ground level and across the globe."[2]

The lore of the movement enshrines popular social mobilization as foundational to rights advocacy. Aryeh Neier, the founder of Human Rights Watch, portrays the British and American abolitionists as heroes whose relentless energy against the injustice of slavery should serve as the model for today's struggles for human rights.[3] Scholars sympathetic to the movement agree: the abolitionists prefigured contemporary rights activists in their uncompromisingly principled stance, their mobilization of civil society through moral rhetoric, and their tireless use of publicity to shame perpetrators and those who abetted them.[4] Likewise, Gandhi and Martin Luther King are iconic for their ability to make rights messages resonate with their mass constituencies.

But compared to these illustrious forbears, the contemporary human rights movement's vision of global civil society got small. After the collapse of the Berlin Wall, the US Agency for International Development allocated a significant percentage of its budget for "civil society" programs in transitional states, spurred in part by widely discussed social science research on the importance of grass-roots "social capital" to the

---

[1] Margaret Keck and Kathryn Sikkink, *Activists Beyond Borders* (Ithaca: Cornell University Press, 1998), 32–4, prefer the formulation "transnational civil society."

[2] Human Rights Watch "about us," n.d., quoted by the SUNY Levin Institute at www .globalization101.org/the-rise-of-non-governmental-organizations-ngos-and-global-civil -society/. As of October 8, 2016, Human Rights Watch said that "We work closely with a broad range of local and international civil society actors to maximize our impact . . . as part of a vibrant movement," www.hrw.org/about.

[3] Aryeh Neier, *The International Human Rights Movement: A History* (Princeton: Princeton University Press, 2012), 33–7.

[4] Keck and Sikkink, *Activists Beyond Borders*, 41–51.

thriving of democracy.[5] But much of this funding and its justifying terminology have been focused on "civil advocacy organizations," many of them elite, professionalized shamers and blamers documenting failures to comply with international law.[6] Although rights funders talk about "mobilizing" grass-roots constituencies such as labor and women, they often employ methods that bureaucratize activism, stilt the discourse of reform, skew local priorities, divert local talent, and distance reformers from their mass base.[7] As a corrective, some studies urge prioritizing popular social movements as an overlooked modality for promoting human rights.[8]

To be sure, masses of demonstrators continue to turn up in the central squares of the capital cities to protest corrupt, rights-abusing leaders' use of strong-arm tactics to win phony electoral victories. Scholars have documented the role of international networks in fostering "modular" color-revolutions-in-a-box in such places as Ukraine and Georgia.[9] But in many of these places the human rights movement has lacked the capacity to sustain the mobilization of a coalition to institutionalize liberal reform and rights practices. Even where leaders

[5] Robert Putnam, *Making Democracy Work: Civic Traditions in Modern Italy* (Princeton: Princeton University Press, 1993).

[6] "Constituencies for Reform: Strategic Approaches for Donor-Supported Civic Advocacy Programs," *USAID Evaluation Highlights*, No. 56 (Washington, DC: Center for Development Information and Evaluation, US Agency for International Development, March 1996); Sami Zabaida, "Civil Society, Community, and Democracy in the Middle East," in Sudipta Kaviraj, ed., *Civil Society: History and Possibilities* (New York: Cambridge University Press, 2001), 232–49, at 255.

[7] Rita Jalali, "Financing Empowerment? How Foreign Aid to Southern NGOS and Social Movements Undermines Grass-Roots Mobilization," *Sociology Compass* 7, no. 1 (2013): 55–73; Patrice McMahon, "Building Civil Societies in East Central Europe: The Effects of American NGOs on Women's Groups," in Peter Burnell and Peter Calvert, eds., *Civil Society in Democratization* (London: Frank Cass, 2004), 250–73, originally in *Democratization* 8, no. 2 (2001), 45–68; Steven Lawrence and Christen Dobson, *Advancing Human Rights: The State of Global Foundation Grantmaking* (New York: The Foundation Center, 2013).

[8] Maria Stephan, Sadaf Lakhani, and Nadia Naviwala, "Aid to Civil Society: A Movement Mindset," *Special Report* No. 361 (Washington, DC: US Institute of Peace, 2015); David Hulme and Michael Edward, eds., *NGOs, States, and Donors: Too Close for Comfort?* (New York: St. Martin's, 1997); Nicola Banks, David Hulme, and Michael Edwards, "NGOs, States, and Donors Revisited: Still Too Close for Comfort?" *World Development* 66 (2015): 707–18; Marina Ottaway and Thomas Carothers, eds., *Funding Virtue: Civil Society Aid and Democracy Promotion* (Washington, DC: Carnegie Endowment for International Peace, 2000), 11–13, 295–8.

[9] Mark R. Beissinger, "Structure and Example in Modular Political Phenomena: The Diffusion of Bulldozer/Rose/Orange/Tulip Revolutions," *Perspectives on Politics* 5, no. 2 (June 2007): 259–77; Valerie Bunce and Sharon Wolchik, "Transnational Networks, Diffusion Dynamics, and Electoral Change in the Postcommunist World," in Rebecca Kolins Givan, Kenneth Roberts, and Sarah Soule, eds., *The Diffusion of Social Movements* (New York: Cambridge University Press, 2010), 140–62.

were toppled, politics has usually slipped back into its accustomed abusive grooves.[10]

Often this happened not because there were no moderates who preferred a decent rights outcome, but because the mass of moderates was not organized around a cohesive strategy. In Egypt, for example, 49 percent of votes in the first round of the 2012 presidential election were split among three candidates with moderate views on rights, who the better organized campaigns of the Muslim Brotherhood and the military junta edged out for the two places on the run-off ballot. Agonizing over this unpalatable choice, some Cairo human rights advocates lamented that they lacked the Brotherhood's capacity for mass social movement and vowed to take steps to foster well-organized, sustainable ties with the villages and the street.[11]

Mass social movements in transitional developing countries often express social identities rooted in the networks of traditional society, normally ethnic and religious ones. Many of these movements, like many social movements throughout history, seek to advance the interests of their own group and are hostile to liberals' universalistic vision of human rights.[12]

Historically, however, religious motivations and organizations have been crucial to seminal progressive social movements in both developing and developed countries. The anti-slavery movement depended heavily on Quakers, English Dissenters, and American Evangelicals of the "Second Great Awakening," and on the ability of more secular politicians such as Abraham Lincoln to co-opt their gospel-tinged rhetoric.[13] Gandhi drew upon Hindu religious and cultural themes to mobilize a mass movement to oppose oppressive taxation, discrimination against lower castes, mistreatment of women, and colonial

[10] Henry Hale, "Regime Cycles: Democracy, Autocracy, and Revolution in Post-Soviet Eurasia," *World Politics* 58, no. 1 (October 2005): 133–65; Seva Gunitsky, "Complexity and Theories of Change in International Politics," *International Theory* 5, no. 1 (March 2015): 35–63, at 51–8.

[11] Leslie Vinjamuri's interview with Hossam Baghat, Cairo, June 2012; Jack Snyder's interview with Baghat, New York, February 26, 2014. For a similar argument applied to a wider range of cases, see Nancy Bermeo, *Ordinary People in Extraordinary Times: Citizenry and the Breakdown of Democracy* (Princeton: Princeton University Press, 2003), 221–4.

[12] Sheri Berman, "Civil Society and the Collapse of the Weimar Republic," *World Politics* 49, no. 3 (April 1997): 401–29; Amaney A. Jamal, *Barriers to Democracy: The Other Side of Social Capital in Palestine and the Arab World* (Princeton: Princeton University Press, 2008).

[13] Whitney R. Cross, *The Burned-Over District* (Ithaca: Cornell University Press, 1950); Roger Anstey, *The Atlantic Slave Trade and British Abolition, 1760–1810* (London: Macmillan, 1975); Eric Foner, *The Fiery Trial: Abraham Lincoln and American Slavery* (New York: Norton, 2010), xviii–xix.

rule.[14] Martin Luther King based his mobilization of the African-American community for effective civil disobedience on black churches, their social networks, their local authority figures, their distinctive rhetorical style, and their "turn the other cheek" philosophy.[15] Nowadays, however, the human rights movement is often characterized as the secular church of a professionalized liberal elite, whose rhetoric fails to mesh with the religious idiom of its clientele.[16]

Given the historical legacy of human rights as an inspiring mass movement, how has it come to pass that Human Rights Watch Executive Director Kenneth Roth now acknowledges "our relative weakness at mobilizing large numbers of people at this stage of our evolution"?[17]

Why the Turn Away from a Mass Rights Movement?

Four hypotheses might be offered to explain the global human rights movement's thin penetration of its supposed source of power, global civil society. Considered together, these conjectures imply a mismatch between the kind of rights movement that is being supplied and the kind that would be in demand if it were on offer.

The first common refrain is that human rights rhetoric is Western talk that fails to resonate in non-Western contexts. Rights ideas are presented in a way that is mainly secular, but the societies where rights abuse is worst are often religious. Moreover, NGO rights rhetoric individualizes rights, victims, and violators in societies where all three are commonly assessed in communal terms.

While these mismatches are real, they exaggerate the gap. Kathryn Sikkink's *Justice Cascade* points out the role of grass-roots groups in the developing world, such as Argentina's Mothers of the Disappeared, in placing issues of individual criminal accountability on the global agenda.[18] Sally Engle Merry points out that universalistic talk about rights accountability is a double-edged sword in the developing world. It can play into the hands of those promoting an anti-imperialist backlash, as in Kenyan Presidential candidate Uhuru Kenyatta's successful

[14] Judith M Brown, *Gandhi's Rise to Power: Indian Politics, 1915–1922* (Cambridge: Cambridge University Press, 1972).

[15] Doug McAdam, *Political Process and the Development of Black Insurgency, 1930–1970* (Chicago: University of Chicago Press, 1982).

[16] Stephen Hopgood, *The Endtimes of Human Rights* (Ithaca: Cornell University Press, 2013), ch. 2.

[17] Kenneth Roth, "Defending Economic, Social and Cultural Rights: Practical Issues Faced by an International Human Rights Organization," *Human Rights Quarterly* 26 (February 2004): 63–74, at 72.

[18] Kathryn Sikkink, *The Justice Cascade* (New York: Norton, 2011), ch. 3.

exploitation of his indictment by the International Criminal Court as a campaign rallying cry. But at the same time, some disempowered groups, cultural minorities, women, gays, and oppressed classes may be enthralled by the notion that the most powerful, most successful societies on earth articulate universal arguments that can be applied to their own plight.[19] In earlier times, such people were attracted to Christianity or to Marxism for the same reason: the Christians say I don't have to bind my feet. Hallelujah!

A second common charge is that human rights claims engage the enthusiasm of developing societies only to the extent that they are seen as contributing to economic development and a broad agenda of social justice, but the international human rights organizations that control the global rights agenda are concerned above all with civil and political rights. Except for justiciable violations such as those that involve discrimination based on race, ethnicity, or gender, the major international rights organizations tend to see many economic and social demands as matters for policy deliberation and political compromise rather than claimable rights.[20]

It is true that the developing world has been more eager than first-world international rights organizations to adopt the broad-ranging rhetoric of economic rights. Sometimes this puts local rights organizations at cross-purposes with international backers. Shareen Hertel shows, for example, how Mexican rights campaigners against pregnancy testing for factory workers tolerated the gender discrimination frame used by Human Rights Watch for international public relations, but for "backdoor" local mobilization they stressed the right to work and the needs of families, which resonated better with the concerns of existing local social movements that they sought to recruit. And in Bangladesh, Hertel recounts how local rights organizations blocked international labor's demands to shut down exporters using child labor, preferring to lobby for better working conditions and educational opportunities.[21] This kind of mismatch is chronic, if not necessarily fatal.

Third, and at the most general level, much classic social theory teaches that individual rights consciousness comes only with modernity, whereas rights problems are most intense in countries that are at best semi-modern.

[19] Peggy Levitt and Sally Merry, "Vernacularization on the Ground: Local Uses of Global Women's Rights in Peru, China, India, and the United States," *Global Networks* 9, no. 4 (2009): 441–61.
[20] Roth, "Defending Economic, Social and Cultural Rights"; Neier, *International Human Rights Movement*, ch. 3.
[21] Shareen Hertel, *Unexpected Power: Conflict and Change among Transnational Activists* (Ithaca: Cornell University Press, 2006), ch. 3 and 4.

Emile Durkheim claimed that individualism emerges as a by-product of the modern capitalist division of labor; Max Weber argued that impersonal, rule-based social relations arise with modern bureaucratic rationalization; Karl Marx asserted that liberal rights thinking is the ideology of the advanced capitalist mode of production. Insofar as any of these basic assumptions about social order are correct, rights-based social movements would seem to be a hard sell in traditional societies with patronage-based political economies.[22]

But this goes too far. James Ron's survey of attitudes in four developing countries shows that local human rights organizations are more trusted than the average institution in their society, always ahead of the country's politicians, but well behind the most trusted institution, which varies from country to country among business, the army, and the church.[23] Rights-based social movements can mobilize support in the developing world when they tailor appeals to local conditions and outlooks, as Gandhi did, as the indigenous movement has done in prioritizing land reform and education rights in Ecuador, and as the religion-based peasant movement has in Brazil.[24]

The fourth and final hypothesis is that the problem is mainly on the supply side: international human rights organizations, which control flows of resources and streams of legitimating rhetoric, simply do not want global human rights to be a mass movement, let alone a vernacularized one with religious rhetoric or an economic-rights agenda.[25] Neier worries that "partisans of social justice," which he equates with the redistribution of wealth and resources, "violate human rights when they have the power to do so." "As for mass mobilization," he continues, "it is often one of the means whereby proponents of social justice seek power. Of course, it does not necessarily follow that such power will be used

[22] Michael Mousseau, "The Social Market Roots of the Democratic Peace," *International Security* 33, no. 4 (Spring 2009): 52–86; Michael Mousseau, "Market Civilization and Its Clash with Terror," *International Security* 27, no. 3 (Winter 2002/3): 5–29.

[23] James Ron, Archana Pandya, and David Crow. "Universal Values, Foreign Money: Funding Local Human Rights Organizations in the Global South," *Review of International Political Economy* 23, no. 1 (2015): 29–64, available online at: http://james ron.com/wp-content/uploads/2016/02/Ron_Pandya_Crow_RIPE-2016.pdf; James Ron and David Crow, "Who Trusts Local Human Rights Organizations? Evidence from Three World Regions," *Human Rights Quarterly* 37, no. 1 (February 2015): 188–239, based on surveys in Colombia, India, Mexico, and Morocco.

[24] Donna Lee Van Cott, *From Movements to Parties in Latin America* (New York: Cambridge University Press, 2005), 107, 132; Miguel Carter, ed., *Challenging Social Inequality: The Landless Rural Workers Movement and Agrarian Reform in Brazil* (Durham: Duke University Press, 2014).

[25] R. Charli Carpenter, "Setting the Advocacy Agenda: Theorizing Issue Emergence and Nonemergence in Transnational Advocacy Networks," *International Studies Quarterly* 51, no. 1 (March 2007): 99–120.

abusively. Yet it sometimes happens. The methods traditionally used by HRW [Human Rights Watch] are less susceptible to abuses."[26]

Not all human rights luminaries share Neier's wariness about economic rights and mass social movements. Indeed, one branch of the human rights enterprise is the "rights-based approach to development."[27] Some NGOs organize product boycotts.[28] Others organize marches and public protests, though international NGO human rights funders typically shy away from supporting such overtly politicized events.

Even Neier understands that the future of the human rights movement will be largely determined by attitudes in the developing world, and he has a plan for co-opting them to his traditional vision. Under Neier's stewardship in 2010, the George Soros-funded Open Society Foundations gave Human Rights Watch $100 million, which was earmarked to "staff advocacy offices in key regional capitals around the world and to deepen its research presence on countries of concern," and "especially to increase its capacity to influence emerging powers in the global South to push a pro-human rights agenda."[29] Soros explained that "Human Rights Watch must be present in capitals around the globe, addressing local issues, allied with local rights groups and engaging with local government officials. In five years' time it aims to have as much as half its income and a majority of its board members come from outside the United States." The plan is not, however, to shift to a new global-South-driven rights agenda, but to attract local matching funds to Human Rights Watch's traditional agenda of naming and shaming. Kenneth Roth noted that "ending serious abuses requires generating pressure from any government with clout, including emerging powers in the global South."[30] If this vision succeeds, the human rights movement will remain a largely elite-steered, legalistic, professionalized enterprise rather than a mass social movement.

Drawing on several of these perspectives, I argue that the human rights movement can make substantial progress toward achieving its goals if – and only if – it does a better job of tapping into the latent power of mass civil society. It can do this only if it embeds legalistic, professionalized

[26] Aryeh Neier, "Misunderstanding Our Mission," *openGlobalRights*, July 23, 2013, at www .opendemocracy.net/openglobalrights/aryeh-neier/misunderstanding-our-mission.
[27] Peter Uvin, *Human Rights and Development* (Bloomfield: Kumarian Press, 2004), ch. 2, 17–38.
[28] Hertel, *Unexpected Power*, 26–7, 36, 43–50; Gay W. Seidman, *Beyond the Boycott* (New York: Russell Sage, 2009).
[29] "George Soros to Give $100 Million to Human Rights Watch," September 7, 2010, at www.hrw.org/news/2010/09/07/global-challenge.
[30] Both quoted in "George Soros to Give $100 Million to Human Rights Watch," September 7, 2010.

advocacy work in broad-based mass movements, including ones animated by religious and local cultural themes, and coordinates with broad-
based reformist political parties. In making this case, I will first discuss
research showing the limitations of the current advocacy strategy, and
then discuss research on the complementarity and frictions among different organizational forms and strategies for advancing progressive
causes, including rights.

Effectiveness of Rights Movement Strategies and the Centrality of Democracy

The limited effort to mobilize a mass-based global rights movement might
not matter much if the prevailing elite-based strategy were working well.
Some scholars say it is succeeding; others say it has stalled out, while
many agree that its successes are highly dependent on the fit between its
tactics and facilitating circumstances.

Critics of the prevailing tactics of the rights movement claim that efforts
to measure human rights progress show little change over the past two
decades. They say that the movement's tactics are based on a superficial
understanding of what causes rights abuse and are hampered by the
limited resonance of its one-size-fits-all rhetoric.[31] But defenders of mainstream approaches argue that this criticism reflects a measurement error:
greater scrutiny and stricter standards are turning up abuses that would
have previously been overlooked.[32] In qualitative analyses, case studies of
success stories vie with skeptical accounts showing that compliance with
norms of accountability is often opportunistic or just for show.[33]

---

[31] Emilie Hafner-Burton, *Making Human Rights a Reality* (Princeton: Princeton University
Press, 2013), chs. 1–3; Emilie Hafner-Burton and James Ron, "Seeing Double: Human
Rights Impact through Qualitative and Quantitative Eyes," *World Politics* 61, no. 2 (April
2009): 360–401.

[32] Ann Marie Clark and Kathryn Sikkink, "Information Effects and Human Rights Data:
Is the Good News about Increased Human Rights Information Bad News for Human
Rights Measures?" *Human Rights Quarterly* 35, no. 3 (August 2013): pp. 539–68; Ann
Marie Clark, "The Normative Context of Human Rights Criticism: Treaty Ratification
and UN Mechanisms," in Thomas Risse, Stephen C. Ropp, and Kathryn Sikkink, eds.,
The Persistent Power of Human Rights (Cambridge University Press, 2013), 125–44;
Christopher J. Fariss, "Respect for Human Rights Has Improved Over Time,"
American Political Science Review 108, no. 2 (May 2014): 297–318.

[33] Compare Sikkink, *Justice Cascade*, and Thomas Risse, Stephen C. Ropp, and
Kathryn Sikkink, eds., *The Power of Human Rights* (New York: Cambridge University
Press, 1999), to Kate Cronin-Furman, "Managing Expectations: International Criminal
Trials and the Prospects for Deterrence of Mass Atrocity," *International Journal of
Transitional Justice* 7, no. 3 (2013): 434–54; Jelena Subotic, *Hijacked Justice: Dealing
with the Past in the Balkans* (Ithaca: Cornell University Press, 2009), and Monika Nalepa,
Skeletons in the Closet: Transitional Justice in Post-Communist Europe (New York:
Cambridge University Press, 2010).

Practitioners themselves, not surprisingly, tend to err on the upbeat side. For example, Neier, writing a few months into the Arab Spring, was far too optimistic about the contribution that the human rights movement, conducting its business as usual, was making to the success of progressive change in the Middle East.[34] That said, NGOs are sometimes quite blunt in assessing the shortfalls of the tactics they use (for example, whether truth commissions as actually constituted contribute to peace and reconciliation), even if they rarely challenge the basic assumptions of the enterprise.[35]

Qualitative and quantitative studies increasingly agree that the success of traditional tactics based on treaty law, monitoring, shaming, and the threat of sanctions is highly sensitive to scope conditions. These methods are often effective in what might be called the easier cases, where the country is at peace, is relatively far along in its transition toward democracy, has relatively independent courts, allows some freedom for civil society groups to operate, has a functioning state administration, and is vulnerable to international pressures.[36] The effectiveness of mainstream rights tactics in the absence of these facilitating conditions is generally agreed to be considerably lower. While some studies address the vibrancy of civil society groups as a factor in successful rights promotion, quantitative studies normally measure this as the number of (or, more rarely, membership in) local or international non-governmental organizations or as the number of protest actions, not as the sustained organization of mass social movements.[37]

The linchpin of these scope conditions for rights is democracy. Statistically, the conditions that correlate with better rights are either causes of democracy, such as relatively high per capita income, or consequences of consolidated democracy, such as civil peace or democracy itself.[38] Although measures of a country's level of democracy do not track

---

[34] Neier, *International Human Rights Movement*, 319–20, 333–4.

[35] International Center for Transitional Justice and the Kofi Annan Foundation, *Challenging the Conventional: Can Truth Commissions Strengthen Peace Processes?* (New York: ICTJ, June 2014), at www.ictj.org/challenging-conventional-truth-commissions-peace/docs/ICTJ-Report-KAF-TruthCommPeace-2014.pdf.

[36] Beth Simmons, *Mobilizing for Human Rights* (New York: Cambridge University Press, 2009), esp. 31–6; Risse, Ropp, and Sikkink, eds., *The Persistent Power of Human Rights*.

[37] Simmons finds, for example, that independent courts matter for some issues but not others. For exploration of various scope conditions for success, including popular protests and civil society activism, see Amanda Murdie and David R. Davis, "Shaming and Blaming: Using Event Data to Assess the Impact of Human Rights INGOs," *International Studies Quarterly* 56, no. 1 (2012): 1–16.

[38] Steven C. Poe, Neal Tate, and Linda Camp Keith, "Repression of the Human Right to Personal Integrity Revisited: A Global Cross-National Study Covering the Years 1976–1993." *International Studies Quarterly* 43, no. 2 (1999): 291–313.

perfectly with measures of its civil liberties, in most cases they run closely parallel.

Some kind of mass social movement or mass political party is necessary to make this marriage of democracy and rights work. Studies of transitions to democracy find that "imposed" democratic transitions managed by dominant elites without a prominent role played by organized popular groups are likely to lead to sham liberalization. They are unstable and easily reversed. Successful democratic transitions tend to be based on alliances between reformist elite factions and popular groups that are newly included in official political processes.[39] Democratic consolidation typically depends on mobilizing mass middle-class and working-class groups, preferably in alliance with each other, around socially inclusive policies and liberal rights commitments.[40] Statistical studies show that ruling coalitions of parties on the left of the political spectrum are more likely to have good human rights records.[41] The historical development of rights, and of movements promoting them, supports this conclusion, which has profound implications for how to advance rights successfully.

Rights Movements: Political Contexts and Organizational Strategies

Historically, the key to the development of civil and human rights has been the evolution of effective organizational forms of collective action to push for and sustain them. Where reformist social movements and political parties lacked sustainable mass organization, efforts to broaden rights were ephemeral. In early modern Europe, contentious popular collective actions began as one-off outbursts demanding the alleviation of some specific, immediate grievance – food shortages, onerous taxation, or arbitrary justice procedures. They flared up and then were over, leaving no institutionalized trace. But by the late eighteenth century in Britain and France, Charles Tilly's research shows that people began to organize not just for immediate redress, but with an eye toward sustained action to reform basic social and political institutions.

As the modern state increasingly imposed costs of war and taxation on its subjects, they came to understand that their welfare depended on

---

[39] Juan J. Linz and Alfred Stepan, *Problems of Democratic Transition and Consolidation* (Baltimore: Johns Hopkins University Press, 1996), 55–65; Scott Mainwaring, *Democracies and Dictatorships in Latin America: Emergence, Survival, and Fall* (New York: Cambridge University Press, 2013), ch. 2.

[40] Dietrich Rueschemeyer, Evelyne Huber Stephens, and John D. Stephens, *Capitalist Development and Democracy* (Chicago: University of Chicago Press, 1992).

[41] Poe, Tate, and Keith, "Repression of the Human Right to Personal Integrity Revisited."

gaining influence in the organs of state power through pressure on ruling elites, alliances of convenience with capitalists and wealthy landowners, and changes in the rules of political representation. Popular groups developed ideologies to justify the worthiness of their claims and rituals of mass collective action to demonstrate their unity, numbers, and commitment to bear sustained costs. In this way, modern social movements were born, making general claims to civil rights and political power.[42] But legal-sounding pronouncements guaranteeing "the rights of man," as in the French Revolution, were not enough. What really counted was sustained mass organization.

Sometimes, the mass organization that spearheaded democratic advances has been a mass political party, such as the Jacksonian Democrats who expanded direct election of officials and reduced property qualifications for voting. Sometimes, though, reform parties in democratizing circumstances have remained fairly elitist for a time, but have aligned with mass social movements of voters. An example is the alliance between Britain's Whig party and its mass movements demanding parliamentary reform, opposing slavery, and advocating diverse social reforms that swept into power the political coalition that passed the Great Reform Bill of 1832.[43] In 1846 a similar coalition of reform-minded political elites, capitalist employers, and urban workers mobilized in the streets and in parliament to repeal tariffs on imported grain, simultaneously advancing their economic interests and addressing the humanitarian crisis caused by the failure of the Irish potato crop.[44]

Comparing Britain and France in the nineteenth century, Tilly emphasizes that the British were far ahead in institutionalizing parliamentary politics and in developing the full panoply of social movement repertoires, including demonstrations, public meetings, petition drives, press statements, symbols of personal affiliation, and the emergence of specialized associations sustaining activism around particular social causes. The French, in contrast, remained stuck in a more primitive phase of contentious politics, featuring mass demonstrations but few institutionalized activities tied to parliamentary or other sustained political processes. As an underlying factor, Tilly notes France's slower pace

---

[42] Charles Tilly and Lesley J. Wood, *Social Movements, 1768–2012*, 2nd edn. (Boulder: Paradigm Publishers, 2009), 3–5, 25–9, 33, 35–7.

[43] Chaim Kaufmann and Robert Pape, "Explaining Costly International Moral Action: Britain's Sixty-year Campaign against the Atlantic Slave Trade," *International Organization* 53, no. 4 (Autumn 1999): 654–7.

[44] Jack Snyder, *Myths of Empire* (Ithaca: Cornell University Press, 1991), 192–7; Lucy Brown, *The Board of Trade and the Free Trade Movement* (Oxford: Oxford University Press, 1958), 57–60.

of industrialization, making for weaker constituencies for democratic reform and popular rights.[45]

Building on Tilly's insights, Kurt Weyland has compared the processes of rapid copycat diffusion during the revolutions of 1848 and the Arab Spring, contrasting them with the evolutionary development of more successful democratic reforms in Latin America during the 1980s.[46] He argues that the inchoate public spheres in the earlier revolutions led to an uncritical boom-and-bust spread of popular ideas, whereas the better institutionalized social movements and political organizations of the Latin American cases encouraged a more measured and enduring pattern of gradual transitions based on political pacts among elite and mass factions. Consistent with this view, Carew Boulding's impressive statistical study of civic action and democratization in Latin America finds that that an individual's contact with NGOs increases their likelihood of voting in countries where democratic political institutions are reasonably well developed, whereas it increases their likelihood of participating in collective protest actions, including violent protest, in poorly institutionalized political systems.[47]

In a similar vein, Daniel Schlozman shows how parties and social movements have worked together inextricably to shape rights outcomes in the United States, for example, in the early Republican Party and the anti-slavery movement. While some movements remain at arm's length from parties, those that align with a party shape its ideological development, and over the long term nudge it away from policies aimed at the median voter. At the same time, movements entering into a long-term alliance with a party "lose their early zeal, radicalism, and naïveté, instead accepting the strategies and compromises of ordinary politics."[48] Working through brokers with deep ties to both the party and the social movement, these parties and movements enter into "multilevel bargains that sprawled across campaigns, appointments, and policies."[49] These ties are especially valuable in giving party politicians access to better information about the attitudes of their crucial vote bases. In return, "when constitutional claims of social movements are placed before courts, it matters a great deal whether the movement's

---

[45] Charles Tilly, *Contentious Performances* (New York: Cambridge University Press, 2008), 72, 87.

[46] Kurt Weyland, *Making Waves: Democratic Contention in Europe and Latin America since the Revolutions of 1848* (New York: Cambridge University Press, 2014).

[47] Carew Boulding, *NGOs, Political Protest, and Civil Society* (New York: Cambridge University Press, 2014), 110–17.

[48] Daniel Schlozman, *When Movements Anchor Parties: Electoral Alignments in American History* (Princeton: Princeton University Press, 2015), 242–3.

[49] Schlozman, *When Movements Anchor Parties*, 5–9, quotation at 9.

representatives have the benefit of friends in high places."[50] Schlozman applies this model to both progressive and conservative movements and parties.

In modern democratic transitions, the insulation of reforming elites from mass politics cannot last long.[51] If progressive mass coalitions do not form quickly, populist coalitions based on traditional, exclusionary social identities will coalesce around illiberal elites. During the era of decolonization, for example, Britain often tried to hand power to a multiethnic, elite power-sharing coalition, as in Sri Lanka and Malaysia, but more populist parties quickly moved to mobilize the grass-roots along ethnically exclusionary lines.[52] For democracy to prevail, inclusionary, liberal parties and mass movements need to be more numerous, cohesive, and motivated than illiberal ones. Any rights promotion strategy needs to plan around this elementary fact.

Forms of Organization for Progressive Politics

Popular movements for rights exist in a variety of organizational forms that include political reform parties, various kinds of mass and elite pressure groups, and violent popular insurgencies. Each of these forms of organization tends to have its distinctive modes of strategic operation, which brings with it characteristic advantages and disadvantages. These diverse organizational forms work best to advance rights when they converge on compatible conceptual frames and coordinate their efforts in complementary ways. However, their different inclinations with respect to principles, expedient compromise, and support coalitions sometimes create stumbling blocks for rights promotion. Tilly speculated, for example, that the increasingly professionalized rights movement led by elite-run NGOs might tame and narrow the scope of mobilization for social reform.[53]

These differences across progressive organizational forms affect even the definition of "civil society" used by rights advocates. Some definitions rule out political parties as "political (hence, not civil) society" and exclude reformist labor unions or business lobbies as self-interested (hence, not principled) economic organizations. Neier makes much of the fact that Quaker anti-slavery activists of the late eighteenth century

---

[50] Schlozman, *When Movements Anchor Parties*, 248, quoting Jack M. Balkin, "How Social Movements Change (or Fail to Change) the Constitution: The Case of the New Departure," *Suffolk University Law Review* 39 (2005): 57–8.
[51] Tilly and Wood, *Social Movements, 1768–2008*, 2d ed., 56–8.
[52] Jack Snyder, *From Voting to Violence* (New York: Norton, 2001), 273–287.
[53] Tilly and Wood, *Social Movements, 1768–2008*, 153–7.

constituted the first altruistic rights movement that concerned itself with the rights of others.[54] Keck and Sikkink stress the role of *principled* transnational activist groups, and other commentators on civil society distinguish it from "uncivil society" – i.e., social movements whose principles the authors do not like.[55]

These definitional efforts come at the cost of diverting attention from the historically necessary connections between rights activism and the group's striving for political power and economic self-interest. Tilly includes the legitimation of a movement's "worthiness" as one of its four generic tasks, but he shows that claims of worthiness do not require forsaking power or self-interest. Indeed, any basic textbook on the history of rights will include chapters showing that the expansion of rights from aristocratic privileges through the protection of bourgeois property rights and personal liberties to labor rights tracked closely the rise in social clout and the self-interest of these social strata.[56] Understanding how rights get established requires studying their relation to power and self-interest, not defining that relationship away. One intriguing theoretical path is offered by Miguel Carter's study of the Brazilian peasant rights movement that was fostered by Catholic liberation theology. Drawing on Max Weber's concept of "value rationality," Carter demonstrates the importance to the rights project of social movements that are grounded in justifiable group self-interest, but focus on normatively internalized long-term goals rather than short-term, instrumental strategies.[57]

Parties, mass and elite pressure groups, and revolutionary insurgencies are each tools that have strengths and limitations that make them appropriate to particular tasks and circumstances (or, as they say in the social movements literature, "opportunity structures").[58] Sometimes the prominence of each organizational tool varies over time in the evolution of a rights struggle. Sometimes multiple tools come into play simultaneously in complementary ways, yet they may also work at cross-purposes if their goals, discursive styles, and strategies are misaligned.

---

[54] Neier, *The International Human Rights Movement*, ch. 2.

[55] J. R. Goody, "Civil Society in an Extra-European Perspective," in Kaviraj, ed., *Civil Society*, 149.

[56] Micheline R. Ishay, *The History of Human Rights* (Berkeley: University of California Press, 2004).

[57] Miguel Carter, *Ideal Interest Mobilization: Explaining the Formation of Brazil's Landless Social Movement* (Columbia University dissertation, 2002), ch. 1, p. 43.

[58] Sidney Tarrow, *Power in Movement: Social Movements and Contentious Politics*, 3rd edn. (New York: Cambridge University Press, 2011), ch. 8.

Reformist Political Parties

Ultimately, the goal of any successful, across-the-board, rights-promoting movement must be the creation of a strong reform party that is capable of ruling through democratic control of the state apparatus. Without that, rights rest on a shaky foundation. How to accomplish that over the long run is the basic strategic task of a rights movement in countries where a strong reform party is lacking.

When conditions allow, the most direct strategy – forming a mass-based reform party to contend for power through elections – is best. For example, when the rather elitist US Whig party collapsed in the face of the Democrats' pro-slavery Jacksonian populism, Northern ex-Whigs such as Abraham Lincoln constituted a catch-all Northern anti-slavery party. They took advantage of the favorable opportunities provided by demographic and economic growth of the Northern states, democratic constitutional rules, historic Jeffersonian libertarian discursive themes, and widespread Northern dismay over what was seen as the arrogance of "the Slave Power" in the wake of "bleeding Kansas" and the Dred Scott decision. In this situation, the Republican Party functioned as a mass social movement for rights reform as well as a conventional political party.

But often the opportunity to create a dominant reform party is lacking and needs to be created. This is the case when democratic rules of the game are entirely absent or, as in Tory Britain in the eighteenth and early nineteenth century, when restrictions on the franchise, rules of representation, or electoral competition allow a reform-resisting oligarchy to rule. It is also the case when the majority rejects the claims of a rights-deprived minority, as in the Jim Crow system. Indeed, one of the criticisms of taking the political party route to reform is that some principled objectives, such as protection of the rights of the weak and of minorities, may be jettisoned in the process of making the expedient compromises that are needed to forge a ruling coalition. Among scholars, Frances Fox Piven has forcefully (if not always convincingly) argued that elites always sell out "poor people's movements" in the end, and the movements' leaders get co-opted and professionalized.[59]

It is important, however, to distinguish sell-outs from tactical compromises that strengthen rights in the long run. For example, the uncompromising rhetoric and counterproductive tactics of hard-core abolitionists often frustrated Lincoln. "Slavery is founded on both injustice and bad

---

[59] Frances Fox Piven and Richard A. Cloward, *Poor People's Movements: Why They Succeed, How They Fail* (New York: Vintage, 1979); on the decline of the civil rights movement, see McAdam, *Political Process*, ch. 8.

policy," he said, "but the promulgation of abolition doctrines tends rather to increase than to abate its evils."[60] Abolitionist talk scared off moderates, and Lincoln wanted to avoid alienating the Northern Democrats and border states.[61] The most uncompromising forms of abolitionism were impatient with constitutional niceties, and Lincoln explicitly disavowed William Lloyd Garrison's "higher law" doctrine, which he saw as undercutting the legal basis for anti-slavery.[62] Lincoln believed that even the more moderate, political abolitionists harmed their own cause by splitting the anti-slavery vote. Lincoln argued that the defection to the Liberty Party of anti-slavery "conscience Whigs" in the religiously obsessed "burned-over district" of upstate New York had cost Henry Clay and the Whigs the election of 1844, having the unintended consequence of electing the pro-slavery expansionist Democrat James K. Polk as President and thus setting the stage for the Mexican War and the destruction of the Missouri Compromise. "By the fruit the tree is to be known," Lincoln said.[63]

A key task for reform parties is to press for institutional changes that will help guarantee effective representation for groups whose rights are at risk. Sometimes this requires pressure from outside the formal political system to overcome resistance to change within it.

Mass Social Movements and Professionalized Civil Society Organizations

When access to power through political parties is blocked or rights issues are stalemated in the party system, the mobilization of mass social movements in civil society may be needed to break the stalemate. These groups may use tactics such as mass protests, strikes, boycotts, picketing, and sit-ins to demand general changes in the rules for the allocation of political power and the freedom of public discourse, or to demand recognition of specific rights to non-discrimination, union organization, marriage equality, and the like. Mass social movements may also provide organizational means for direct action on the issues of concern to its support community, providing social services and economic support networks, "crowdsourcing" information on abuses, and facilitating decentralized discussion and recruitment of participants. Depending on the context, they can

---

[60] Stewart Winger, *Lincoln, Religion, and Romantic Cultural Politics* (DeKalb: Northern Illinois University, 2003), 185, quote from the year 1837.

[61] John Burt, *Lincoln's Tragic Pragmatism: Lincoln, Douglas, and Moral Conflict* (Cambridge, MA: Harvard Belknap, 2013), 225, 401, 403, 405–7.

[62] Richard J. Carwardine, *Lincoln: Profiles in Power* (Harlow: Pearson Longman, 2003), 104.

[63] Winger, *Lincoln, Religion, and Romantic Cultural Politics*, 192.

also provide an organized basis for group self-defense or the coercive use of force. Unlike episodic protests and riots, social movements capable of sustained effort require a centralized leadership cadre to develop an ideology, articulate a common framing discourse, formulate strategy, recruit existing groups and individuals to join the movement, and organize coordinated sequences of action.[64]

Professionalized organizations, such as NGOs, provide another way of organizing civil society to promote rights.[65] Typically, they have a professional staff funded by foundations, private donors, governments, or international organizations, and occasionally also have a public membership that plays a limited role in core organizational activities. Rather than organizing mass protests or directly coercive actions such as civil disobedience, rights NGOs advocate for the adoption of rights norms, collect information about the violation of existing rights norms and laws, demand compliance, comment on or occasionally participate in legal actions to enforce rights, and lobby governments and other powerful actors to sanction or shun rights violators. Allied organizations may deliver services to rights-deprived populations, as in the rights-based approach to development or humanitarian assistance. They may mount grass-roots efforts to persuade local communities to abandon abusive cultural practices such as female genital cutting. Thus, they do some of the same tasks as mass social movements, especially framing issues and formulating strategies for publicity, but the most prominent human rights NGOs mainly lobby others to take direct action rather than organizing it themselves.

Parties, Movements, and NGOs Working Together – or Not

Since it is possible to have mass social movements, NGOs, and political parties pressing simultaneously for rights, asking which gets better results is not necessarily the right question. They can be complementary, good at distinctive but additive tasks. That said, it is worth considering what their distinctive tendencies, strengths, weaknesses, and points of mutual friction might be.

A key task for social movements, NGOs, and reform parties is to define rights objectives and strategies, which must be framed in ways that resonate for key audiences. While it is possible that in a given instance

---

[64] McAdam, *Political Process*, 45.
[65] Donatella Della Porta and Mario Diani, *Social Movements: An Introduction*, 2nd edn. (Oxford: Blackwell, 2006), 145.

these different kinds of organizations might converge on the same priorities, they nonetheless tend to have characteristic biases that stem from differences in the constituencies to which they are accountable and the inclinations and skills of their professional staffs. Social movements are likely to prioritize goals that make life tangibly better for the grass-roots participants that they seek to mobilize. Often these will have an economic dimension. In contrast, elite, professionalized NGOs, often staffed with lawyers and other experts, are more likely to prioritize legal objectives. Finally, party politicians are likely to prioritize whatever rights goals can be achieved through the coalition partnerships that might be available.

A telling example is the arc of the US Civil Rights movement from the 1940s to the late 1960s. As Risa Goluboff recounts the story, grass-roots protest by African Americans during World War II and the immediate postwar period were substantially focused on economic issues, especially "the right to work without discrimination."[66] This issue posed problems for the elite lawyers who dominated strategic planning at the NAACP, which was at the time attempting to forge an alliance with the US labor movement, which included segregated unions. Their legal strategy targeted not employment issues, but state-mandated discrimination, as in *Plessy* v. *Ferguson*. They feared that venturing a broad "right to work" interpretation of the equal protection clause of the Fourteenth Amendment would alienate organized labor and endanger the narrower interpretation that eventually led to the *Brown* v. *Board of Education* decision.[67] Party politicians were even keener to compromise – for example, allowing Southern senators to water down Lyndon Johnson's 1958 civil rights bill, cutting out the voting rights provisions. With the party system and thus also legal remedies for Jim Crow largely stalemated, a mass social movement was needed to overwhelm opposition in Southern states and to mobilize the potentially sympathetic Northern electorate. Martin Luther King and especially the grass-roots Student Non-Violent Coordinating Committee mobilized existing church networks in the North and South to engage in directly coercive action, framing issues around integration and civic equality.[68] As Piven notes, President Kennedy's decisive speech announcing his support for a far-reaching civil rights bill was triggered when non-violent confrontation using methods of civil disobedience was fast degenerating into violent repression and rioting.[69] The passage of the bill, however, took some of the steam out of the movement and diverted its cadres to implementing

---

[66] Risa L. Goluboff, *The Lost Promise of Civil Rights* (Cambridge, MA: Harvard University Press, 2007), 37.
[67] Goluboff, *Lost Promise*, 223–30, 251.   [68] McAdam, *Political Process*, 129–33, 152.
[69] Piven, *Poor People's Movements*, 240.

the voting rights act, never to return to a full-bore mass effort centered on economic rights.[70]

One of the key tasks for any of these organizational types is framing the issue under contention. Sidney Tarrow, the dean of social movements theory, stresses that resonant frames reflect or create a common identity among participants. They tap into emotion, especially by making a connection between the personal and the political through symbols, practices, and rituals.[71] Thus, social movements work in much the same way that religious movements do, so it is not surprising that many social movements for rights and economic justice, such as the liberation theology movement in Latin America, recruit from religious organizations and are animated by religious ideas. In contrast, political coalitions are contingent and instrumental, so their legitimating frames are less likely to produce a personal sense of belonging and a common future.[72]

Frames selected by professional NGOs often strive to connect the personal to the political for their target audience, especially donors, and for their own cadres.[73] However, the heavily legal framing of much NGO work can sometimes limit resonance.[74] Reminiscent of Hertel's study of framing maneuvers over pregnancy testing in Mexico, Catherine MacKinnon's framing of workplace sexual harassment as an economic discrimination issue did not gain traction in Europe, where the strong labor movement framed the problem as a "violation of worker's dignity." In France, where less social stigma was attached to on-the-job flirting, the issue of a "hostile work environment" was dropped, instead framing the problem as arising mainly in the case of a demand for a sexual quid pro quo.[75] Indeed, sometimes framing an issue as rights per se is considered a barrier to progressive collective action: "rights framing individualizes the struggle at work" and thus undermines the preferred labor solidarity frame.[76]

---

[70] Piven, *Poor People's Movements*, 252; McAdam, *Political Process*.

[71] Della Porta and Diani, *Social Movements: Introduction*, 28, 107; John D'Emilio, "The Gay Liberation Movement," in Jeff Goodwin and J. Jasper, eds., *The Social Movements Reader*, 2nd edn. (Oxford: Blackwell, 2009), 38, reprinted from D'Emilio, *Sexual Politics, Sexual Communities* (Chicago: University of Chicago Press, 1998).

[72] Della Porta and Diani, *Social Movements*, 24.

[73] Clifford Bob, *The Marketing of Rebellion* (New York: Cambridge University Press, 2005), 27–28.

[74] Tarrow, *Power in Movement*, 3rd edn., 248.

[75] Conny Roggeband, "Transnational Networks and Institutions: How Diffusion Shaped the Politicization of Sexual Harassment in Europe," in Givan, Roberts, and Soule, eds., *The Diffusion of Social Movements*, 23–30.

[76] Lance Compa, "Framing Labor's New Human Rights Movement," in Givan, Roberts, and Soule, eds., *Diffusion of Social Movements*, 71, citing labor lawyer Jay Youngdahl, "Solidarity First: Labor Rights Are Not the Same as Human Rights," *New Labor Forum* 18 (2009): 31–37.

Another criticism of rights NGO framing habits is the "silent victim advocacy model."[77] In its harshest variant, critics charge that rights NGOs' overall discourse features first-world saviors of third-world victims who suffer at the hands of savage third-world abusers.[78] If so, that imagery might resonate extremely well with self-congratulatory, privileged, progressive audiences, as bestseller fiction and Hollywood have repeatedly demonstrated with narratives such as *To Kill a Mockingbird* and *The Help*. However, if Lynn Hunt's theory of *Inventing Human Rights* through narrative is correct, victims need to show pluck, not passive victimhood, in order to elicit empathy and outrage at rights deprivation rather than mere pity and charity from readers.[79]

Different forms of civil society organization might have different substantive consequences, which might not be intended, and trade-offs among them might not be explicitly considered. For example, the Czech gay rights movement initially comprised a legislation-oriented lobbying wing as well as a grass-roots component. The lobbying effort proved so successful that the country soon boasted of an internationally cutting-edge set of legal protections of gay liberty and equality. As an unintended consequence, the steam went out of the grass-roots social movement, and public discourse about gay life evaporated, leaving the change in Czech cultural attitudes incomplete, in the view of some.[80]

Various scholars portray a mixed bag of tendencies, strengths, and weaknesses associated with different organizational forms. Measured against armed insurgencies, non-violent social movements attract more participants, according to the research of Erica Chenoweth.[81] Measured against political parties, Herbert Kitschelt argues that social movements are constitutionally set up to extract unilateral concessions, not to bargain (the same might be said of NGOs), which might be good or bad at

---

[77] Cathy Albisa, "Drawing Lines in the Sand: Building Economic and Social Rights Norms in the United States," in Shareen Hertel and Kathryn Libal, eds. *Human Rights in the United States: Beyond Exceptionalism* (Cambridge University Press, 2011), 68–88, at 85.

[78] Makau Mutua, "Savages, Victims, and Saviors: The Metaphor of Human Rights," *Harvard International Law Journal* 42, no. 1 (Winter 2001): 201–45.

[79] Lynn Hunt, *Inventing Human Rights* (New York: Norton, 2007). To be fair, one of the victims in *The Help* shows a great deal of pluck, even if the white aspiring journalist is still her voice to the outside world.

[80] Conor O'Dwyer, "From NGOs to Naught: The Rise and Fall of the Czech Gay Rights Movement," in Kerstin Jacobsson and Steven Saxonberg, eds., *Beyond NGO-ization: The Development of Social Movements in Central and Eastern Europe* (Burlington: Ashgate, 2013), 117–38.

[81] Erica Chenoweth and Maria J. Stephan, *Why Civil Resistance Works: The Strategic Logic of Nonviolent Conflict* (New York: Columbia University Press, 2011), 55.

different moments.[82] Partly for that reason, protest activity around a rights issue has been found to matter most in agenda-setting, as measured, for example, by spurring Congressional hearings, while having little effect on the endgame of policy change.[83] Kitschelt also argues that social movements are better than more transitory political coalitions at sustaining the organizational development that is needed for ongoing struggle for social change.[84] Neier makes a similar point about rights NGOs, noting that one-shot mobilizations in response to historical events such as "the Bulgarian atrocities" failed to sustain a rights movement, which happened only after the movement began to make its claims in universalistic terms, such that there would *always* be a burning rights issue to keep the movement in perpetual motion.[85] The National Organization for Women, a legally oriented elite organization without a mass component, is held to be very good at getting publicity, but not good at getting policy results.[86] Mary Kaldor argues that "NGOization" erodes traditional grass-roots "mutual benefit" organizations in local communities.[87] Judged in terms of Tilly's effectiveness criteria for social movements, NGOs are good at establishing *worthiness*, sometimes good at achieving *unity* among NGOs, weak in demonstrating *numbers* of popular supporters, and extremely good at demonstrating *commitment*, but only their own.

A final tactical trade-off is whether human rights advocacy should hold itself at arm's length from democracy promotion. On the one hand, human rights organizations like to present themselves as apolitical, pressing for legal accountability to universal civic norms but usually not actively promoting democratic regime change per se. In part, this reflects a pragmatic calculation of what is required to maintain the NGO's operations in a non-democratic country. It also reflects a rhetorical strategy of holding all countries accountable for rights violations, whether they are democracies or not. NGOs that explicitly engage in democracy promotion are distinct from human rights NGOs in mounting programs that

[82] Herbert Kitschelt, "Landscapes of Political Interest Intermediation: Social Movements, Interest Groups, and Parties in the Early Twenty-First Century," in Pedro Ibarra, ed., *Social Movements and Democracy* (New York: Palgrave, 2003), 84.

[83] Brayden G. King, Keith G. Bentele, and Sarah Anne Soule, "Protest and Policymaking: Explaining Fluctuation in Congressional Attention to Rights Issues, 1960–1986," *Social Forces* 86, no. 1 (September 2007): 137–63.

[84] Kitschelt, "Landscapes of Political Interest Intermediation," 84.

[85] Neier, *International Human Rights Movement*, 42.

[86] Jo Freeman, "The Women's Movement," in Goodwin and Jasper, eds., *Social Movements Reader*, 2nd edn., 29, reprinted from Freeman, "The Origins of the Women's Liberation Movement," *American Journal of Sociology* 78, no. 4 (January 1973), 792–811.

[87] Mary Kaldor, *Global Civil Society: An Answer to War* (Cambridge, UK: Polity, 2003), 92.

seek to strengthen institutions of democratic participation, such as training the staffs of political parties.[88] On the other hand, human rights NGOs do acknowledge that democracy and rights are mutually reinforcing. The aspirational Universal Declaration of Human Rights says that "the will of the people shall be the basis of the authority of government; this will shall be expressed in periodic and genuine elections which shall be by universal and equal suffrage."[89] Rights NGOs' somewhat coy, arm's-length treatment of democracy makes some tactical sense, but this rhetorical positioning may inadvertently create a mindset that hinders developing long-term strategies that fully integrate the necessarily linked goals of democracy and rights.

Overall, it seems reasonable to conclude that the best results come when strategists of rights-based progressive change prepare a full menu of complementary organizational tools, including reform parties as well as social movements and elite civil society organizations. These organizations work best when they converge on a common (or at least complementary) frame that resonates with mass audiences, and also allows for legal follow-through and the political flexibility to close deals within a capacious reform coalition.

A Tall Order?

That sounds like a tall order, and it is. Some claim that the mainstream human rights movement's more modest vision is better in part because it is more feasible. The problem is that this claim is mostly untrue outside of societies that already have relatively favorable facilitating conditions for the promotion of rights through legal remedies and universalistic shaming tactics. Elsewhere, those scope conditions need to be created through economic development, peace making, and the gradual, expedient strengthening of reform coalitions and social movements. There are no magic shortcuts that get directly to rights through law and moralism by taking a detour around politics.[90]

A second criticism of the mass politics approach is better founded: as Aryeh Neier says, there is no guarantee that mass social movements will respect rights rather than abuse them. The Nazis and the Italian Fascists were, after all, social movement regimes that emerged from electoral

---

[88] Sarah E. Mendelson and John K. Glenn, eds., *The Power and Limits of NGOs* (New York: Columbia University Press, 2003).

[89] Of course, even Stalin's Soviet Union was able to sign on this general statement.

[90] Jack Snyder and Leslie Vinjamuri, "Trials and Errors: Principle and Pragmatism in International Justice," *International Security* 28, no. 3 (Winter 2003–4): 5–44.

competition.[91] But this is not a reason to set aside mass politics and stay focused on principled legalism and moralism, especially when nationalists, anti-imperialists, and cultural nativists can exploit universalistic rhetoric on rights to mobilize resistance to liberal rights ideas. Instead, the danger of illiberal social movements is a reason to take the effect of advocacy tactics on mass politics into account when crafting human rights strategies.[92]

A third objection might be that my analysis of reform parties and progressive social movements is based just as much on easy cases as is the mainstream rights approach. It is true that the favorably aligned British case provides a starting point for my thinking about the components of an effective rights strategy, but it also provides a basis for identifying what is missing in harder cases.

Human rights activists and scholars look to the anti-slavery movement in Britain as the earliest model of a true human rights movement, and a highly effective one. Often this is taken to be a model that validates contemporary NGOs' operational style of mobilizing civil society through moral rhetoric and the uncompromising use of publicity to shame perpetrators and those who fail to sanction them.[93] The very first book explaining the success of the British campaign to ban the slave trade, written by one of its main protagonists, Thomas Clarkson, makes this kind of argument. Clarkson claimed that the self-evidently true teachings of prominent Christian authorities – Methodists, Quakers, Anglicans, and others – gradually persuaded Englishmen over the last third of the eighteenth century that slavery was sinfully incompatible with the basic precepts of Christian charity and love.[94]

This is a superficial view. A better-rounded interpretation of the case should also highlight the embedding of the anti-slavery issue in a broader movement for democratization, rights, and social reform. This was a mass social movement in which religion played a central role in motivating participants and legitimating their demands.[95] Its success stemmed from

---

[91] Douglas McAdam and Sidney Tarrow, "Social Movements and Elections: Toward a Broader Understanding of the Political Context of Contention," in Jacqueline van Stekelberg et al., eds., *The Future of Social Movement Research: Dynamics, Mechanisms, and Processes* (Minneapolis, University of Minnesota, 2013), 329.

[92] See Leslie Vinjamuri's chapter on backlash in this volume (Chapter 5).

[93] Neier, *International Human Rights Movement*, 33–7; Keck and Sikkink, *Activists Beyond Borders*, 41–51.

[94] For commentary, see Howard Temperley, "Anti-slavery as a Form of Cultural Imperialism," in Christine Bolt and Seymour Drescher, eds., *Anti-slavery, Religion, and Reform* (Hamden: Dawson. 1980), 338.

[95] Seymour Drescher, *Capitalism and Antislavery* (Oxford: Oxford University Press, 1987), ch. 4, 6; David Turley, *The Culture of English Antislavery, 1780–1860* (London: Routledge, 1991), ch. 3, 5; Edith Hurwitz, *The Politics of Public Conscience: Slave*

the development of a unified frame for reform that joined together the twin themes of Christian ethics and English liberties.[96] The movement arose in a facilitating context of dynamic economic and social change that empowered the constituencies that favored reform. The anti-slavery effort made methodical progress through politically pragmatic bargaining between the leaders of the wider reform movement and elites who dominated political parties.[97]

It was not only Britain that followed this pattern. Many of the success cases of the "third wave" of democratization were given their impetus by inclusive mass movements, often with religious dimensions, and reformist political parties. In Poland, the key actors were Solidarity, at first a labor-based social movement and later a political party, and the Catholic Church.[98] In the Czech Velvet Revolution, human rights groups mobilizing around the Helsinki agreement's standards constituted the kernel around which a mass social movement and progressive party formed.[99] Spain, whose transition was stabilized by well-organized business, labor, and religious groups, provided a template for "pacted" transitions led by reform parties in South America.[100] In Brazil, social movements based on Catholic liberation theology and labor provided a push; slow-moving elite negotiations provided a stable political framework.[101] In Chile, the unions and the church played key roles, as did the institutional legacy of Chile's earlier democratic period. In South Africa, the UDF unified a well-organized movement of non-profit civic organizations in the 1980s, even before Nelson Mandela's ANC provided the final push to end apartheid.[102] The end of the Cold War removed some of apartheid's ideological cover, and the legacy of British political

Emancipation and the Abolitionist Movement in Britain (London: George Allen & Unwin, 1973), 23; Robin Blackburn, *The Overthrow of Colonial Slavery, 1776–1848* (London: Verso, 1988), 96, 102.

[96] Blackburn, *Overthrow*, ch. 2.

[97] Kaufmann and Pape, "Explaining Costly Moral Action," 651–7; Blackburn, *Overthrow*, 76–7, 307–15; Hurwitz, *Politics of Public Conscience*, 49–54; Brian Harrison, "A Genealogy of Reform," in Bolt and Drescher, Anti-slavery, Religion, and Reform, 119–48; G. M. Ditchfield, "Repeal, abolition, and reform: a study in the interaction of reforming movements in the parliament of 1790–96," in Bolt and Drescher, 101–18.

[98] John K. Glenn, *Framing Democracy: Civil Society and Civic Movements in Eastern Europe* (Stanford: Stanford University Press, 2001), ch. 3–4.

[99] Glenn, *Framing Democracy*, ch. 5–6.

[100] Víctor Pérez-Díaz, *The Return of Civil Society: The Emergence of Democratic Spain* (Cambridge: Harvard University Press, 1993); Linz and Stepan, *Problems of Democratic Transition*, ch. 6.

[101] Ruth Berins Collier, *Paths toward Democracy: The Working Class and Elites in Western Europe and South America* (New York: Cambridge University Press, 1999), 132–8; Linz and Stepan, *Problems of Democratic Transition*, ch. 11; Weyland, *Making Waves*, ch. 6.

[102] Elke Zuern, *The Politics of Necessity: Community Organizing and Democracy in South Africa* (Madison: University of Wisconsin Press, 2011), 30–1.

and legal institutions facilitated an orderly transition to majority rule. The cleric Desmond Tutu presided over the Truth and Reconciliation Commission that made the politically expedient amnesty seem ethical. Indonesia – in what many would consider a hard case because of its ethnically and religiously diverse makeup and history of a politicized military – negotiated a surprisingly smooth transition to democratic party politics in part because of the central parliamentary role played by Amin Rais's moderate, mass-based Islamic party.[103] All of these progressive transitions improved rights outcomes, but only in a few of them were elite-based, legalistic rights NGOs at the center of the action.

True, social movements pushing for political change have not always provided reliable backing for rights-promoting reform parties. The People Power movement that overthrew Ferdinand Marcos did too little to uproot the corrupt system that continues to trouble Philippine political life. Movement-based populist regimes in Venezuela, Bolivia, and Ecuador have not gone very far in institutionalizing liberal rights. Islamic popular movements in Iran, Egypt, and Turkey have not brought liberal rule of law. No less than mainstream approaches, a theory of rights promotion through popular social movements allied to reform parties needs to specify its scope conditions and what strategies are constructive when those conditions are not met. In general, the preferred strategy in that approach is two-fold: (1) the painstaking building of a progressive movement, and (2) expedient action to help put in place social and economic conditions that will facilitate progressive change in the long run.

Finally, it must be acknowledged that rights principles were compromised even in relatively successful cases of movement-driven democratic change. In Argentina, the Alfonsin regime decided it had to disappoint the maximalist demands for criminal accountability put forward by the Mothers of the Disappeared in order to stabilize the newly democratic regime in the face of threats from the military.[104] In Myanmar, Aun Sang Suu Kyi's National League for Democracy, a reform party with a strong base in ethnic Burmese Buddhist civil society, impressively co-opted elected support from all of Burma's rebellious ethnic religious minorities, though she has made no promises to deal with Myanmar's greatest human rights disaster, the subjugation of the unjustly reviled Rohingya Muslim minority. As critics point out, party politics is inescapably the politics of expediency, and social movements are inescapably shaped by

[103] Mirjam Künkler and Alfred Stepan, eds., *Democracy and Islam in Indonesia* (New York: Columbia University Press, 2013).

[104] Carlos Nino, *Radical Evil on Trial* (New Haven: Yale University Press, 1996), 116.

the prejudices of their constituencies as well as the tactical choices of their leaders.

These examples suggest that progressive rights reform can draw support from mass social movements, including religious ones, and can make common cause with the pragmatic political strategies of a reform party seeking to form a national ruling coalition. This does not mean that human rights NGOs' accustomed style of work cannot contribute to the overall reform goal, but rather that its angle of vision is far too narrow to be the central engine of progressive change, even in its own arena of human rights. Rights progress depends on far broader trends of socio-economic context, political coalition possibilities, and cultural modes of discourse about norms that govern social relations. Human rights activists and the scholars who study them should approach their work with that wider view.

5   Human Rights Backlash

Leslie Vinjamuri

Backlash against human rights is rampant. States that appeared to be liberalizing have retreated. In Russia, Turkey, and Egypt, governments have forced the departure of leading international human rights organizations and clamped down on individual freedoms. China has curtailed the independence of its lawyers even further. And, in Africa, where progress on human rights was given concrete form when no fewer than 34 states voluntarily signed up to be members of the International Criminal Court, several states have banded together to unsettle that emerging consensus and protest the International Criminal Court's attempts to investigate the crimes of sitting heads of states.

Often, scholars have treated human rights backlash as a problem confined to authoritarian states, or states in transition, especially those in the Global South. Today, the retreat from human rights is a problem not only for the rest, but also for "the West." In the United States, a new administration led by Donald Trump has attacked the media, abandoned human rights talk, and threatened to withdraw from the Human Rights Council. Within weeks of Trump's inauguration, the White House talked of extensive cuts to the United Nations system. In its 2017 survey, the Economist Intelligence Unit re-categorized the United States from a "full democracy" to a "flawed democracy" for the first time.[1] In the United Kingdom, Theresa May has threatened to abandon the 1998 Human Rights Act which incorporates provisions of the European Convention on Human Rights into UK law.

The immediate effects of human rights backlash may seem dramatic, but the long-term effects are harder to decipher. Backlash may even be a natural part of progress and entail no lasting setbacks. Those who try to restrict rights may simply find that their efforts fail. The agents of backlash may find that their moral authority has been irreparably eroded and, with this, their influence. In the United States,

---

[1] The Data Team, "Declining trust in government is denting democracy" *The Economist*, January 25, 2017. www.economist.com/blogs/graphicdetail/2017/01/daily-chart-20

Trump's attacks on Muslims, women, and the media generated a liberal (pro-rights) backlash when nearly four million people took to the street to join the Women's March within days of Trump's inauguration. Trump's travel ban, an Executive Order designed to halt immigration and refugees from several Muslim majority countries, was met by popular protest and a multitude of legal challenges, leading the White House to revise its plans and issue a scaled-down version that came under legal challenge and was blocked, first, by a federal judge in Hawaii. In South Africa, an attempt by the government to withdraw from the International Criminal Court was effectively challenged by the High Court in Pretoria.

But when backlash has a lasting and negative effect on human rights, this raises a fundamental problem for human rights advocacy. Elites in Kenya and Sudan have developed increasingly sophisticated strategies to push back against international justice for mass atrocities. President Al-Bashir responded to an ICC arrest warrant by forcing the exit of leading humanitarian organizations, abandoning his retirement plans, and successfully running for re-election.[2] In Kenya, elites targeted by international justice formed a new electoral alliance and proceeded to win national elections based in part on an anti-ICC platform. Some of these strategies may undermine the ICC's effectiveness, and also restrict the space for civil society activism.

Despite the pervasiveness of backlash against international justice, theorizing about this phenomenon has been cursory.[3] Scholarly research has evaluated the impact of investigations, indictments, trials, and ICC ratification on outcomes such as repression and civilian killings.[4] These stark measures create significant difficulties for empirical analysis and so are unlikely to generate much confidence in their findings.[5] More importantly, though, they have focused debate in a direction that may be counterproductive.

This chapter takes the phenomenon of backlash seriously. A focus on backlash shifts our attention toward the impact of elite and popular efforts

---

[2] Sarah Nouwen notes that President Bashir had been planning to retire from political office before the ICC arrest warrant was issued, but then changed his mind. Sarah Nouwen, *Complementarity in the Line of Fire: The Catalysing Effect of the International Criminal Court in Uganda and Sudan* (Cambridge: Cambridge University Press, 2013).

[3] One important exception to this is the work of Clifford Bob, especially, *The Global Right Wing and the Clash of World Politics* (New York: Cambridge University Press, 2012).

[4] Kathryn Sikkink, *The Justice Cascade: How Human Rights Prosecutions Are Changing World Politics* (New York: WW Norton & Company, 2011); Hyeran Jo and Beth Simmons, "Can the International Criminal Court Deter Atrocity," *International Organization*, Volume 70, Issue 3, pp. 443–75.

[5] Jack Snyder and Leslie Vinjamuri, "To prevent atrocities, count on politics first, law later," openGlobalRights, May 12, 2015, at: www.opendemocracy.net/openglobalrights/jack-snyder-leslie-vinjamuri/to-prevent-atrocities-count-on-politics-first-law-late.

to block or inhibit policies on the development of norms and institutions as well as on specific policy outcomes. This is a first step in clarifying concepts in the debate about backlash and its effects on human rights progress. The chapter offers a definition of backlash, differentiates between tactical and strategic backlash, and identifies various forms that backlash takes. Its primary empirical focus is on the backlash against international justice and accountability for mass atrocities. But theorizing about backlash and its consequences has significance for liberal backlash strategies also. The effects of backlash, in both its liberal and illiberal forms, are conditional on strategy and also political context, especially the strength of domestic institutions.

Backlash and Its Effects

The backlash against international justice shows little sign of abating. The fact that it is so widespread, and yet there have been significant advances in human rights, may explain why scholars disagree so vehemently about its importance. For some human rights scholars, backlash is even interpreted as an indicator of success, a natural by-product of normative change.[6]

Early scholarship on human rights norms identified backlash as a behavior commonly associated with early stages of the norms life cycle. In *The Power of Human Rights*, backlash is an integral part of the spiral model of norm diffusion.[7] In response to external pressure, Risse, Ropp, and Sikkink suggest that states may seek to appease human rights entrepreneurs by making tactical concessions. These concessions generate social mobilization. Backlash is a state response to this mobilization, a temporary setback that is part and parcel of the process of normative change. It underscores the salience of human rights and signifies a movement toward a deeper embrace of human rights norms.

When authoritarian regimes attempt to subvert human rights and accountability norms, they may unwittingly engage with human rights in ways that increase their salience. Human rights advocates cite protests against human rights oversight as an indicator that human rights matter, even to those who disregard them. When a UN Commission of Inquiry (COI) released a report documenting North Korea's atrocious human rights abuses, North Korea actively denounced its findings. Greg Scarlatiou, Executive Director of the Committee for Human Rights in

---

[6] Thomas Risse, Stephen Ropp, and Kathryn Sikkink, *The Power of Human Rights: International Norms and Domestic Change* (Cambridge: Cambridge University Press, 1999).

[7] Ibid.

North Korea, remarked on North Korea's response to international investigations of its human rights record, "The interesting thing, at least to me, is that this issue really seems to have bothered them this time," he said. "The reason they are conducting this investigation is because it goes directly to the North Korean regime's most vulnerable point; its legitimacy."[8]

North Korea also made efforts to counter the narrative by highlighting its positive human rights. In August 2014, North Korea announced that it would hold its own human rights investigation. Human Rights organizations at once denounced this as a sham, but many also argued that this represented a significant turn in North Korea's engagement with human rights and was in fact a good sign, suggesting that North Korea cared far more about its international legitimacy than it has in the past. Ken Kato, Director of Human Rights in Asia argued "[t]hat they have taken this step suggests to me that bad publicity is taking its toll on the regime and the international pressure is working."[9]

For some human rights scholars, and for many advocacy organizations, sustained international pressure has been embraced as the optimal response to human rights backlash.[10] The visibility of human rights campaigns sheds light on continued abuse and creates the possibility for civil society both locally and abroad to sustain pressure against rights violators.

In this volume, Geoff Dancy and Kathryn Sikkink suggest that backlash is a natural concomitant of human rights advocacy, much like automobile accidents are a natural concomitant of driving cars.[11] But in the automobile sector this correlation has not been dismissed as a necessary if unfortunate by-product of driving. Instead, research has probed the conditions that determine when automobile driving results in road accidents, and drawn on those findings to minimize the risk of accidents through safety-related innovations.

Human rights scholarship has in this sense integrated backlash as part of a general theoretical account of normative change. For many advocates, backlash against human rights reflects bad behavior but has little

---

[8] Quoted in "North Korea Report to Counter 'Lies and Fabrications,'" *supra* note 7.

[9] Ibid.

[10] Margaret Keck and Kathryn Sikkink, *Activists beyond Borders: Advocacy Networks in International Politics* (Ithaca: Cornell University Press, 1998); in their 2013 volume, Risse, Ropp, and Sikkink argue that under certain conditions, especially in areas of limited statehood, capacity building is more important than sustained advocacy in resolving problems of non-compliance. Thomas Risse, Stephen Ropp, and Kathryn Sikkink, *The Persistent Power of Human Rights: From Commitment to Compliance* (Cambridge: Cambridge University Press, 2013).

[11] See Chapter 2 by Geoff Dancy and Kathryn Sikkink in this volume.

bearing on questions about optimal advocacy strategies. Even in the most difficult contexts, justice advocates have continued to argue that international justice helps undermine support for elite war criminals and facilitates peace by removing perpetrators from the political scene.[12]

In some cases, backlash may be a step along the way toward engaging human rights violating states in peace building and human rights reform. But, not all backlash is inconsequential. For example, the liberal backlash in the United States provoked by Trump's first travel ban achieved many of its objectives. It achieved a stay on the ban. This stay was challenged by the Department of Justice, but subsequently upheld by a federal appeals court. More importantly, in the short term, the White House withdrew the first ban and scaled it back to meet several of the protesters criticisms: it removed Iraq from the list of countries banned, protected the rights of current visa holders, and also removed an exception for religious minorities to avoid charges of religious bias. Although this was widely viewed as a move designed to avoid further legal challenge while continuing to block immigration from several Muslim majority countries and reduce the inflow of refugees, it secured some of the goals sought by backlash activists.

The liberal backlash, in this case, succeeded by drawing on a range of tactics including mass protests, constitutional law, economic and business interests, and the federal and state courts. If a liberal backlash can achieve success in some cases, it should follow, logically, that illiberal backlash (the type that most human rights scholars focus on) should also be successful in many cases. The strength of domestic civil society, institutions, laws, and norms play a central role in facilitating or limiting the success of backlash. In democracies, courts matter and they draw on the mood of the public, as expressed in part through the vehicle of mass protest. Similarly, with illiberal backlash, strategies and tactics matter and have varying outcomes and effects.

The Formalization of the Justice Regime

Contemporary backlash against international justice is linked in part to changes in the institutional environment. The demand for truth and justice during the democratic transitions in Latin America had its origins in civil society activism. Many activist organizations were formed by family members of victims who disappeared.

---

[12] David Mendeloff, "Punish or Persuade? The Compellence Logic of International Criminal Court Intervention in Cases of Ongoing Civilian Violence," *International Studies Review*, forthcoming 2017.

The creation of ad hoc and mixed tribunals, and especially the International Criminal Court, has altered the context for justice and accountability.

First, with the creation of the ICC the perception of the threat that perpetrators of mass atrocities will come under the shadow of justice has risen markedly. The density of laws, tribunals, and public references to accountability for mass atrocities has risen dramatically in the past two decades. Those who threaten to spoil the peace have little confidence that they will be exempt from oversight, investigation, or the prospect of an actual trial.

Second, despite the increased prominence and significance of accountability for mass atrocities in international politics, enforcement remains very weak. This means that perpetrators of mass atrocities operate in a highly uncertain environment. In part, this is a reflection of the limited jurisdiction of the ICC. Not all perpetrators of mass atrocities easily or automatically come under the jurisdiction of an existing tribunal. The fact that the resources available to pursue justice are limited also contributes to the uncertainty that hovers over perpetrators of mass atrocities. The mechanisms for containing alleged perpetrators and delivering them to court are also inherently weak. More importantly, the promise of safe exit or even amnesty is now overshadowed by doubt as to its credibility. Powerful spoilers may doubt that even a persistent demand for their investigation will lead to their effective restraint, but they also cannot be sure that a promise of exemption from accountability is secure.

Third, externalization of the demand for accountability has reduced the efficacy of traditional tactics that government elites use to deflect human rights pressure. Coercive measures of the kind frequently used by authoritarian states to silence domestic civil society – from registration requirements, to the raiding of offices, to the disappearing of civil society workers – do not have the same utility for dealing with external pressures for accountability, nor are these instruments as palatable in states that are or aspire to be democratic. But, the externalization of the requirement for accountability and justice means that backlash strategies have an additional ideological resource to draw on, one that frames justice and accountability demands as a violation of national sovereignty and a form of imperialism. The availability of anti-imperial tropes in many societies has played into the hands of elites who seek to undermine the legitimacy of international accountability initiatives.

Taken together, these three factors have led to the apparent standardization and formalization of the justice regime, in the guise of new institutions, and more clearly articulated expectations, standards, and rules in accountability politics. Despite the fact that enforcement is often weak, the combined effect of a seeming legal rigidity in combination with ongoing uncertainty about enforcement has decreased the prospect for striking effective bargains and crafting transitional justice compromises tailor-made for specific contexts. This new context has contributed to a new politics of backlash and, paradoxically, undermined the stability of the accountability regime.

Defining Backlash

Backlash against international justice has been depicted as a violent reaction by targeted spoilers who respond to the threat of trials by digging in their heels and fighting to the death.[13] Samuel Huntington famously stressed the threat to a democratic transition posed by powerful military actors. For this reason, he anticipated that trials would be unlikely in negotiated transitions where the military remained powerful.[14] Realist scholars of civil wars and democratic transitions agree that the threat of a backlash from powerful spoilers presents a grave threat to the success of democratic transitions and civil war settlements.[15] Bargaining strategies that draw on the promise of carrots (even amnesties) as well as the threat of sticks (trials) to secure a transition create a stronger prospect for a rights-abiding transformation.[16]

Despite this seeming consensus, at least among realist scholars, most references to backlash are fairly casual. I propose the following definition for backlash: a behavioral response to the application or clear anticipation of a specific policy or institutional practice that is perceived to be in opposition to the interests or values of a particular actor or set of actors; it is character-ized by an attempt to alter, restrict, subvert, or otherwise resist this applica-tion of policy or practice. Tactical backlash may seek simply to restrict or block policies and may be short term in nature. Strategic backlash seeks to block international justice interventions, but goes much further. Its ambi-tion is to embed new rules, practices, or, sometimes, alternative sources of authority. Its practitioners adopt a number of tactics to achieve this goal, sometimes working within institutions but sometimes seeking to undermine the authority of existing institutions and replace them with new ones.

---

[13] For an apt, but classic statement of this, see Philippe Sands, "The ICC Arrest Warrants Will Make Colonel Gaddafi Dig in His Heels," *The Guardian*, May 4, 2011, at: www .theguardian.com/commentisfree/2011/may/04/icc-arrest-warrants-libya-gaddafi.

[14] Samuel Huntington, *The Third Wave: Democratization in the Late Twentieth Century* (Norman and London: University of Oklahoma Press, 1991).

[15] Stephen John Stedman, "Spoiler Problems in Peace Processes," *International Security* 22, no. 2 (October 1997): 5–53; Jack Snyder and Leslie Vinjamuri, "Trials and Errors: Principle and Pragmatism in Strategies of International Justice," *International Security* 28, no. 3 (Winter 2003/04): 5–44.

[16] Snyder and Vinjamuri, ibid.

There are several distinct features of backlash that distinguish it from other phenomenon such as contestation. Most importantly, backlash is reactive and seeks to undermine and block. It is a response to a specific policy or practice, or the anticipation of one. This reaction may be popular or elite led. As backlash becomes more strategic and less tactical, it often combines elite and popular elements. Popular references to backlash frequently assume that backlash is violent, but backlash may also take a nonviolent form.

Contestation is premised on a deeper engagement with and commitment to alternative norms, principles, or ideologies. Unlike backlash, contestation is not inherently reactive, but is interactive. Backlash differs from contestation in that it is essentially reactive and motivated by a desire to obstruct or push back against a particular intervention, policy, advocacy, or practice. When actors engage in backlash politics they may embrace an alternative set of ideas or principles to strengthen their ability to reject a policy or demand, but this is done as part of a blocking response to a specific practice. However, backlash may trigger contestation over basic principles, ideas, and expectations, in this case for rights, justice, and accountability.

Backlash varies significantly across cases, especially in duration and complexity and in the extent to which its practitioners attempt to create alternative policies or institutional mechanisms. At one end of the spectrum, tactical backlash may involve a rapid response that seeks to block or retaliate against a particular policy, often by inflicting punishment or restricting access. Outright refusal and obstructionism are highly visible backlash tactics that usually come rapidly on the heels of unwelcome rights advocacy. North Korea abandoned talks with the Europeans as a protest against the release of the Commission of Inquiry report documenting its human rights abuses. Immediately after the International Criminal Court announced that it was issuing an arrest warrant for President Al-Bashir of Sudan, the government of Sudan expelled leading humanitarian organizations from the country, claiming that they had been complicit in providing evidence of atrocities taken from refugee populations and passing these to the ICC.

States that have remained outside the ICC but have come under its jurisdiction against their will despite their wishes have rarely rejected the basic principle of justice or of human rights. Instead, they have challenged the legitimacy of international justice and stressed the fundamental value of state sovereignty. Sometimes they have drawn on rationales that stress the pragmatic reasons why international justice is unlikely to generate a positive outcome. China responded to calls for a referral of North Korea to the International Criminal Court by arguing that dialogue based on mutual respect and equality, not an ICC investigation or trial, was the optimal strategy for improving human rights in North Korea.[17] Although these classic blocking strategies elicit great condemnation from the international human rights community, they have not radically challenged the basic orientation of international justice, serving instead to slow its pace in areas where international justice was already very limited.

At the other end of the spectrum, strategic backlash is carefully constructed and deliberative, employing complex tactics designed collectively to wage a sustained attack on accountability, and, crucially, to create alternative norms, policies, or institutions that alter the locus of authority for making judgments about accountability. Strategic backlash seeks not only to displace existing rules and procedures but also to replace them with something different that alters current but also future practice.

Strategic backlash seeks to build coalitions around an agenda that embeds alternative rules and institutions. It varies in its embrace of legalism as a mode of justifying alternative rules and institutions. Transitional states that aspire to democracy have adopted multifaceted strategies of backlash, but have rarely rejected justice, accountability, and human rights outright. A driving force behind these efforts has been the ambition to control and also exercise authority over human rights and accountability claims. Transitional states often work within existing frameworks but seek to alter them in important ways. Kenya, for example, has worked through the ICC forum while spearheading a campaign to shift the locus of authority for crimes against humanity prosecutions away from the ICC to an African Court.

Democracies have also relied heavily on strategic forms of backlash that seek to adapt rather than replace existing institutions. Support for the creation or design of alternative collective institutions has been rare. Under the George W. Bush administration, the United States went to great lengths to secure safeguards to ensure that US citizens would not come under the ICC's jurisdiction. When Obama took office, the United States began to work far more closely with the Court, but remained a non-member and continued to actively safeguard its sovereignty from the Court's oversight. For example, the United States government insisted that a Security Council Resolution referring Libya to the ICC included explicit language exempting citizens of those nations such as the United States that are "non-party" to the Rome Statute from the Court's jurisdiction.

---

[17] "China Opposes Sending North Korea to International Court," *Washington Post*, October 23, 2014, at: www.washingtonpost.com/world/asia_pacific/china-opposes-sending-north-korea-to-intl-court/2014/10/23/edebc956-5a8e-11e4-9d6c-756a229d8b18_story.html.

Democracies have also relied on backdoor tactics designed to delay or even impede the work of international justice institutions when they fear that these institutions will undermine their peace and security strategies. Denying institutions critical resources is a classic strategy that democracies frequently adopt to obstruct justice.[18] This was a common strategy adopted by both the US and the UK governments in dealing with efforts to investigate and prosecute war criminals in the former Yugoslavia.[19]

Backlash Strategies

Violent Entrenchment

The most commonly discussed type of backlash against international justice is "violent entrenchment" – this is when a suspected perpetrator of mass atrocities responds to news of an impending arrest warrant or trial by escalating. Rather than ceding power, perpetrators commit more atrocities and dig in their heels, choosing to fight to the bitter end. Arrest warrants against individual perpetrators not only provoke further atrocities against civilians, but also against individuals or groups who agree to cooperate with international investigators and tribunal staff. When the prospect of arrest is credible but relies on the defeat of an alleged perpetrator, violent backlash strategies may be a rational, even dominant strategy for perpetrators who come under the radar of international justice.

Libya is a classic case of an elite perpetrator responding to international justice by adopting a strategy of violent entrenchment. Qaddafi's initial decision to fight was driven by its dynamics with the rebels, but Qaddaffi's fight intensified in response to NATO's air campaign. Once Qaddafi and his forces began to lose ground, evidence suggests that he was aware of the arrest warrant and felt he had no space to negotiate a peaceful end.[20] The presence of an ICC arrest warrant also created ambiguity for those involved in negotiating with Qaddafi, as they felt that their ability to offer Qaddafi a secure exit was constrained. The failure of the ICC to investigate rebel atrocities may also have intensified this strategy of entrenchment.[21]

---

[18] David Bosco, *Rough Justice: The International Criminal Court in a World of Power Politics* (New York: Oxford University Press, 2014).

[19] Author interview with Cherif Bassiouni, 1999.

[20] Priscilla Hayner, "Libya: The ICC Enters During War," *European Council on Foreign Relations*, project on International Justice and the Prevention of Atrocities, November 2013, at: www.ecfr.eu/page/-/IJP_Libya.pdf.

[21] Ibid.

Human rights advocates challenge the tendency to attribute responsibility for war to the International Criminal Court, which they say is wrongly blamed for being the enemy of peace.[22] During the conflict in Libya, advocates agreed that making deals with powerful spoilers may be an acceptable and pragmatic compromise, but they rejected any formal offer of amnesty for international crimes.[23]

Nonviolent Entrenchment

Entrenchment tactics are not always violent. Often, these take a nonviolent form. Leaders targeted by international tribunals have pursued a range of strategies to secure their power, in effect 'digging in their heels' but without resorting to violence. Electoral mobilization and the embrace of anti-imperial justice rhetoric is one increasingly common strategy embraced by elites that seek to enhance their personal security and authority by challenging the legitimacy of international justice. In Kenya, government elites leveraged arrest warrants to mobilize Kenyans around an anti-imperialist campaign that placed the ICC at the center of its attack. Kenyatta and Ruto formed an unlikely cross-ethnic coalition, the Jubilee Alliance, to mobilize voters on the basis of an anti-ICC platform. Once in office, they continued to pursue a range of strategies to block the advance of the ICC. Since Kenya was a member of the ICC, the success of this electoral strategy was crucial to a sustained critique of the ICC. Rather than challenging the ICC as a whole, Kenyatta slowly latched onto the critique that sitting heads of state should be immune from international prosecution. President Bashir of Sudan pursued a similar strategy, effectively using anti-ICC rhetoric to rally the electorate to support him.

Restrictions on access are another weapon in the arsenal of elite perpetrators that seek to entrench their power. Humanitarian organizations often hold firm to an ethical principle that assistance should be delivered neutrally and aid workers should refrain from engaging with human rights advocacy. By ignoring these distinctions,

---

[22] Paul Seils, "ICC's Intolerance of Impunity Does Not Make It an Enemy of Peace," *openGlobalRights*, November 17, 2014, at: www.opendemocracy.net/openglobalrights/paul-seils/intolerance-of-impunity-does-not-make-icc-enemy-of-peace.

[23] Even human rights advocates have recognized the power of deals. Aryeh Neier, former President of OSF, argued that "deals" could be made to secure the exit of leaders such as Qaddafi, so long as impunity is never formalized. A Neier on the Arab Revolutions, *European Council on Foreign Relations*, March 9, 2011, at: www.ecfr.edu/content/entry/europe_and_the_arab_revolutions.

authoritarians justify restrictive practices through the logic of guilt by association, claiming that humanitarian workers assist tribunal staff and may provide direct support to investigators or prosecutors. President Bashir of Sudan responded to an arrest warrant against him by immediately forcing the evacuation of several leading humanitarian organizations, claiming that humanitarian organizations had provided evidence to the ICC.[24] Access restrictions are not always so dramatic. They may fall short of evacuation but rely on tactics that restrict the activities and movements of international NGOs, including monitoring, policing, and harassment. During the war in Bosnia, war crimes investigators were routinely obstructed from pursuing their investigations.[25] Efforts to obstruct the work of investigators in Kenya almost immediately. Following the indictment of the so-called Ocampo Six, efforts to obstruct the work of court investigators were both swift and also pervasive.[26]

Entrenchment tactics are pervasive in the politics of international justice. These strategies have a direct effect on the diffusion of justice and the evolution of accountability. Rather than leading perpetrators to adopt a reformed position, or marginalizing them from national politics, entrenchment leaves international actors with a stark choice: use coercive measures to remove perpetrators from power, offer an amnesty that can be credibly enforced, or accept a stalemated situation and play the long game.

Forum Shopping

States engage in strategic rather than tactical backlash when they seek not merely to resist being targeted by international justice, but go further, working to mobilize coalitions and adapt existing rules and institutions or create new institutions that embed alternative rules, values, or norms. Strategic backlash entrepreneurs may seek to shift the locus of authority to an alternative institution, in a kind of 'forum shopping' that is designed to hold back international justice processes. Cooley and Schaaf argue in this volume that regional institution building is an authoritarian tool used to create space for counternorms and

---

[24] "Sudan Expels Aid Groups in Response to Warrant," *NBC News*, March 4, 2009, at: www.nbcnews.com/id/29492637/ns/world_news-africa/t/sudan-expels-aid-groups-response-warrant/.

[25] Author interview with Cherif Bassiouni, 1999.

[26] "ICC Kenya Probe 'Hampered by Intimidation,'" *Institute of War and Peace Reporting*, January 12, 2012, at: https://iwpr.net/global-voices/icc-kenya-probe-hampered-intimidation.

practices.[27] Authoritarian clubs engage in a 'democracy containment doctrine' that seeks to counter norms of democracy and human rights.[28] This type of aggressive regionalism has been designed to push back international norms rather than to ground them organically in regional values and traditions.

State entrepreneurs may seek to mobilize counter-rights coalitions, create new norms, or build new institutions that obstruct or displace international authority. This core motivation is common to other theories of normative adaptation. Sally Engle Merry's vernacularizing brokers sit at the interface of international and national politics. They adopt local languages and discourses and adapt international norms to fit local practices. Merry's brokers seek to make it work in a normative world by negotiating two worlds.[29] Acharya's localizers aim to give international norms domestic roots and greater traction.[30] The practice of "localization" involves "pruning" those parts of norms that are alien or incompatible with local custom, and "grafting," which involves linking new transnational norms with existing customs and practice.[31] Each of these strategies engages existing norms with the goal of grounding them in national and local sources of authority.

But, not all efforts to displace international authority entail a rejection of human rights principles. Vernacularization and localization reject international authority, but leave the door open for core human rights principles. Backdooring and subsidiarity may sometimes entail a more fundamental rejection of human rights, but this is not their core premise. Actors that seek to block international norms and bring their own distinct agenda through the "backdoor" will not necessarily embrace human rights.[32] Subsidiarity displaces international norms and the actors that promote them, replacing them with regional norms.

Strategic backlash goes further. It challenges fundamental aspects of core human rights principles by seeking to alter the balance between

---

[27] Cooley and Schaaf, Chapter 7 in this volume.

[28] Christopher Walker, "Authoritarian Regimes are Changing How the World Defines Democracy," *Washington Post*, June 13, 2014, at: www.washingtonpost.com/opinions/ch ristopher-walker-authoritarian-regimes-are-changing-how-the-world-defines-democracy/ 2014/06/12/d1328e3a-f0ee-11e3-bf76-447a5df6411f_story.html.

[29] Sally Engle Merry, "Transnational Human Rights and Local Activism: Mapping the Middle," *American Anthropologist* 108, no. 1 (March 2006): 38–51.

[30] Amitav Acharya, "How Ideas Spread: Whose Norms Matter? Norm Localization and Institutional Change in Asian Regionalism," *International Organization* 58, no. 2 (Spring 2004): 239–75.

[31] Amitav Acharya. "Norm Subsidiarity and Regional Orders: Sovereignty, Regionalism and Rule Making in the Third World," *International Studies Quarterly* 55, no. 1 (March 2011): 95–123.

[32] Shareen Hertel, *Unexpected Power: Conflict and Change among Transnational Activists* (Ithaca: Cornell University Press, 2006).

individual rights and national sovereignty. Spoilers' ability to engage in strategic backlash often depends on mobilizing sovereignty-based anti-rights discourse designed to empower illiberal forces and diminish the potential success of liberalizing ones while still adhering to basic tenets of liberalism and human rights. For example, the government of South Africa led by President Zuma exited the ICC primarily because it opposed the Court's targeting of sitting heads of state, not because it rejected the basic principle of accountability. The success of these initiatives depends on the extent to which pre-existing institutions have embedded a liberal rights-oriented culture. In South Africa, where a rights culture has taken root, the government's reluctance to cooperate in arresting a head of state was resisted by domestic courts. Backlash strategies that succeed in altering existing norms, institutions, and related practices also alter the course of future accountability practices by creating the conditions for new path-dependent decision making.

States have deployed different strategies to alter the course of accountability. In some cases, states have pressed for restrictions on existing laws or institutions that encroach on international accountability norms. But at other times, states have sought to displace existing structures and shift the locus of authority to new institutions. This allows them to exert greater control by shaping institutional rules, while still maintaining the legitimacy that is afforded by participating in collective initiatives that recognize a role for accountability.

Strategic Legalism

Democracies are not immune to human rights backlash. Under the GW Bush Administration, the United States pursued a strategic backlash campaign against international justice that included efforts to restrict universal jurisdiction laws, negotiate bilateral immunity agreements, and embed great-power restraint formally in the rules of international tribunals are prime examples of this. The United States successfully pressed smaller states to roll back universal jurisdiction laws, restricting these to cases where a direct link to territory or citizenship can be established. The United States responded aggressively when Spanish Judge Garzon threatened to pursue a trial against Bush administration officials for torture on the basis of universal jurisdiction laws.[33] In 2003, seven Iraqi families in Belgium requested an investigation

---

[33] Soeren Kern, "Spain Changes Tack on Universal Jurisdiction," *The Brussels Journal*, June 1, 2009, at: www.brusselsjournal.com/node/3945.

of former president George H. W. Bush and other members of his administration for their alleged crimes in the first Gulf War.[34] The United States initially threatened to remove NATO's headquarters from Brussels. Belgium responded by adapting its universal jurisdiction laws, inserting a requirement that universal jurisdiction trials in Belgium be linked to Belgium either through the citizenship of concerned individuals or their residence in Belgium.[35]

Amnesty laws are a second type of strategic backlash that are sometimes announced preemptively to hold back the threat of prosecution. The increased incidence of human rights trials has been associated with a rise in the use of amnesties. This is one of the most prominent legal mechanisms for deflecting justice and accountability measures.

The legality of amnesty for international crimes has come under increasing dispute.[36] The credibility of amnesty offers have also suffered with the creation of ad hoc tribunals and the ICC. This has led many international lawyers to argue that amnesty for international crimes is no longer legal. The credibility of amnesties has also suffered in the face of very real removal of amnesties, as in Argentina, or exile deals, as with Charles Taylor.[37] The majority of amnesties, though, have not been reversed, and amnesties remain in use in many high-profile conflicts, such as Afghanistan and Libya.[38] In the case of Libya, there is genuine disagreement about whether recent amnesties cover international crimes.[39] Often, even amnesties that state an exception for international crimes have become de facto amnesties for all crimes.

Amnesties that are passed through a legitimate process, especially one that is voted by a legislative body, or agreed through a legal process (rather than a self-amnesty) will increase the costs that external actors face when they consider reversing these policies. Even if an amnesty is eventually

---

[34] Stewart M. Patrick and Claire Schachter, "Spain's Welcome Retreat on Universal Jurisdiction," *Council on Foreign Relations*, February 14, 2014, at: http://blogs.cfr.org/patrick/2014/02/14/spains-welcome-retreat-on-universal-jurisdiction/.

[35] "Belgium: Universal Jurisdiction Law Repealed," *Human Rights Watch*, August 1, 2003, at: www.hrw.org/news/2003/08/01/belgium-universal-jurisdiction-law-repealed; "Belgium to Curb War Crimes Law," *Global Policy Forum*, June 23, 2003, at: www.globalpolicy.org/component/content/article/163/29400.html.

[36] Mark Freeman, *Necessary Evils: Amnesties and the Search for Justice* (New York: Cambridge University Press, 2009).

[37] Priscilla Hayner, "Negotiating Peace in Liberia: Preserving the Possibility for Justice," *Centre for Humanitarian Dialogue*, November 2007, at: www.ictj.org/sites/default/files/ICTJ-Liberia-Negotiating-Peace-2007-English_0.pdf.

[38] Mark Kersten, "Impunity Rules: Libya Passes Controversial Amnesty Law," *Justice in Conflict*, May 8, 2012, at: http://justiceinconflict.org/2012/05/08/impunity-rules-libya-passes-controversial-amnesty-law/.

[39] Confidential author interview, DAG meetings.

retracted, an agreed amnesty will allow perpetrators to buy additional time to regroup and make plans.

Amnesty has not always been embraced as an ideal strategy for evading justice.[40] In peace talks, parties have sometimes been reluctant to accept an amnesty because doing so is perceived to signal an acknowledgment of guilt.[41] Given its historical and varied use, and the complex set of motivations that drive amnesty laws, careful process tracing is crucial in discerning whether an amnesty has been designed to fend off justice. Louise Mallinder notes that the use of amnesties increased during the 1990s, and remained steady for several years after this. After 2007, the enactment of amnesty laws declined somewhat, but existing datasets have not yet analyzed whether associated changes in patterns of atrocities account for this, or whether this is the product of the perceived illegality of amnesties.[42] In select cases, mobilization around demands for amnesty has been linked to a specific threat of prosecution. In Afghanistan, amnesty demands came several years after the Bonn Agreement (which left the issue of accountability off the table, offering no formal guarantees against prosecution but also making no formal provisions for trials). These amnesty demands reflected increased activism internationally around an anti-impunity agenda in Afghanistan.[43]

Regionalism

In one of the most marked episodes of strategic backlash, Kenya spearheaded a campaign by several African states under the cover of the African Union. This emerged initially as part of Kenyatta and Ruto's anti-ICC campaign, but gradually took on greater significance as it developed into a region-wide effort to reassert sovereign authority and especially to claw back protections for sovereign immunity. Rather than rejecting the ICC outright, Kenyatta sought to win in Presidential elections at home, but also turned to the African Union as a shield against the Court. Collective legitimacy

---

[40] Freeman, *supra* note 30.   [41] Hayner, *supra* note 31.

[42] Louise Mallinder. "Amnesties' Challenge to the Global Accountability Norm? Interpreting Regional and International Trends in Amnesty Enactment," in Francesca Lessa and Leigh A. Payne, *Amnesty in the Age of Human Rights Accountability* (New York: Cambridge University Press, 2012), 69–96; Tricia D. Olsen, Leigh A. Payne, and Andrew G. Reiter, *Transitional Justice in Balance: Comparing Processes, Weighing Efficacy* (Washington, DC: United States Institute of Peace Press, 2010).

[43] Author interview; "Afghanistan: Repeal Amnesty Law," *Human Rights Watch*, March 10, 2010, at: www.hrw.org/news/2010/03/10/afghanistan-repeal-amnesty-law.

under the veneer of African regionalism, not simply Kenyan sovereignty, was marshaled to give legitimacy to Kenya's protests.

This campaign developed in trial-and-error fashion. After attempting to garner support for a collective withdrawal from the ICC, Kenya downgraded its ambitions. Kenya failed to gain support from a majority of African Union members for a collective withdraw from the ICC. Many African Union member states preferred to maintain their membership of the ICC. Its second best position was instead to amass a majority behind a proposal that demanded immunity for heads of state. As part of this counter-ICC strategy, it has also worked to invigorate an African court still in its infancy, the African Court of Human and People's Rights as a forum for prosecuting crimes against humanity.

This initiative has been spearheaded by Kenya but pursued in partnership with a broad coalition of authoritarian, semi-authoritarian, and democratic states. African states have cast their mobilization against the ICC by referring to the inherent legitimacy of alternative rules. They also sought reforms that would restrict the ICC's authority and assert the primacy of regional institutions with more palatable rules.

Elite mobilization around this anti-ICC coalition has created barriers to civil society activists in Kenya who seek to advance an accountability agenda at home. According to one prominent activist, civil society in Africa is besieged by a social climate infused with an anti-ICC discourse that portrays the Court as an instrument of Western imperialism.[44]

In July 2014, the African Union voted to grant immunity from prosecution in the African Court of Justice and Human Rights to sitting heads of state.[45] Kenya's efforts to work through the African Union to transfer authority for justice and accountability in Africa to the African Human Rights and People's Courts underscore a highly strategic and potentially consequential backlash strategy. But even these states have sought to balance a strategy of playing by the rules while also breaking them, as witnessed by Kenya's antics before the ICC.

These efforts stand in marked contrast to Latin America's regionalism. The Inter-American Court of Human Rights is frequently viewed as a force for human rights. In 2010, the Inter-American Court ruled against Brazil's amnesty for the military.[46] Civil society has increasingly turned to

---

[44] Confidential author interview, October 2014.

[45] "Africa: AU Grants Sitting Leaders Immunity to African Court," *All Africa*, July 2, 2014, at: http://allafrica.com/view/group/main/main/id/00031144.html.

[46] Alexei Barrionuevo, "Amnesty for Brazil Dictatorship is Challenged," *New York Times*, December 16, 2010, at: www.nytimes.com/2010/12/16/world/americas/16brazil.html?_r=0.

the Inter-American Court for support in pushing its own governments in the direction of greater accountability.

In contrast to the regional strategies that Cooley and Schaaf identify that seek to embed counternorms, regionalism in Africa represents a multi-vocal and also multi-pronged response that is presented as having a regional authenticity but that explicitly seeks to be norm-compliant rather than norm-subversive.[47] This does not mean, however, that these strategies are simply evidence of the success of human rights norm diffusion. In fact, they suggest the prospect that accountability in Africa may follow a different trajectory than it has in Latin America or in Europe.

Containing Backlash

Why is backlash present but not always prevalent? In some cases, there is a conspicuous absence of backlash. This is instructive. When those pressing for more human rights and justice or greater accountability anticipate a backlash, they have often effectively warded off its more pernicious or lasting effects by anticipating and exercising restraint. Anticipated restraint is defined by an exercise of deliberation, caution, and moderation in the face of an expectation that a more decisive strategy will produce a negative reaction. The expectation that a failure of restraint will undermine the longer-term prospects for an ideal policy often factor quite heavily in this type of decision making.[48]

Sometimes this takes the form of actively negotiating compromises, or deals, that ward off interventions by international tribunals. In 2015, the government of Colombia announced that it has agreed a peace deal with the FARC designed to secure the goodwill of all sides. Despite protests by Human Rights Watch that arrangements for a negotiated justice were tantamount to impunity, its initial success was contingent on pragmatic compromises.[49] When the peace deal was put to a public referendum, it became the source of inter-elite political antics and mobilization, which, combined with low voter turnout in regions where voters supported the deal, led to its rejection. Subsequent efforts succeeded by negotiating a series of pragmatic compromises to ensure the deal would be approved by Colombia's Congress.

---

[47] Cooley and Schaaf, Chapter 7 in this volume.

[48] Jack Snyder and Leslie Vinjamuri, "Trials and Errors: Principle and Pragmatism in Strategies of International Justice," *International Security* 28, no. 3 (Winter 2003/ 04): 5–44.

[49] "Colombia: Dealing Away Justice," *Human Rights Watch*, 28 September 2015, at: www .hrw.org/news/2015/09/28/colombia-dealing-away-justice.

A recent study of the ICC suggests that the Prosecutor has often accommodated the political interests of great powers.[50] Court officials are rarely oblivious to state power, either internationally or domestically. In most cases that have been referred to it by state parties, the ICC has only pursued rebel crimes. Unsurprisingly, the prospect of a violent backlash is sharply reduced in these circumstances.

In the Balkans, both tribunal and state officials exercised restraint in the pursuit of justice. Restraint was exercised by states that created, assisted, and financed the tribunal (which was often crippled due to this lack of support). This has been a pervasive feature historically. Leaders in liberal states have often refrained from pursuing international justice during war for fear it would generate a backlash against their prisoners of war.[51] In the Second World War, British leaders feared a possible backlash by Germany against their POWs.[52] In Argentina, the decision to bring a premature halt to human rights trials during the early stages of transition was born of a fear that pushing forward with justice would provoke a backlash.[53]

The anticipation of backlash has also led many small states to tread with a very light foot. In East Timor, leaders lacked any mechanism to restrain Indonesia. Instead, they chose not to support trials out of a fear that doing so would sour relations with neighboring Indonesia. The Indonesians faced little if any limits on their own autonomy and manipulated their justice proceedings to recast the narrative of post-referendum violence in Timor, blaming local militias and absolving their own generals.

Coercive capacity has also mitigated backlash in many cases. Military force has paved the path for peace settlements and facilitated or impeded the pursuit of international justice. In the absence of force, the reaction to international justice would have been very different. In Sierra Leone, British intervention paved the path for the Special Court for Sierra Leone. The failure of an amnesty plus truth strategy that was the basis of the 1999 Lome Peace Accords in Sierra Leone was the result of an inability to contain Foday Sankoh, leader of the Revolutionary United Front, and, in light of this, a failure to remove him from power. A subsequent British military intervention in Sierra Leone and the defeat of the RUF was a crucial step that paved the way for prosecutions. In Liberia, the growing

---

[50] David Bosco, *Rough Justice: The International Criminal Court in a World of Power Politics* (New York: Oxford University Press, 2014).

[51] Gary J. Bass, *Stay the Hand of Vengeance: The Politics of War Crimes Tribunals* (Princeton: Princeton University Press, 2002).

[52] Ibid.

[53] Carlos Nino, *Radical Evil on Trial* (New Haven: Yale University Press, 1998).

success and military effectiveness of the rebels substantially mitigated any threat to peace that may have been posed by a backlash against the indictment of Charles Taylor by the Special Court. The absence of more widespread trials against parties to these peace talks that took the form during peace negotiations of "silence plus truth" was an important part of getting to "yes" in these talks.[54]

Conclusion

Violent outbursts, leaders digging in their heels, and angry mobs are the images that immediately come to mind in discussions about backlash and its consequences. Spoiler entrenchment, even when it takes a nonviolent form, has a negative impact on the prospect for human rights progress. But backlash is more likely to have a lasting and consequential impact when it succeeds in its ambition to alter institutions or create new norms and even laws.

This chapter calls for further research on the dynamics of backlash that takes several factors into consideration. First, backlash strategies differ markedly in the extent to which they reject basic norms and normative frameworks. Outright rejection of basic human rights, justice, and accountability norms has garnered an inordinate amount of attention among civil society activists. When leaders openly denigrate the rights of individuals based on gender, religion, or race, there is good reason to protest. But strategies that pay some heed to existing norms and institutional frameworks can be equally or even more subversive and may be harder to block in part because they do not always garner the same public outrage.

Second, strategic backlash may present a greater risk to the stability of existing accountability norms and institutions than an outright refusal to cooperate. Strategic backlash attempts to alter the existing institutional framework of international justice by reformulating the relationship between individual accountability, state sovereignty, and regional autonomy may have more far reaching consequences, even though they directly engage with legal norms and practices. It does this by creating new domestic coalitions, limiting the space for civil society mobilization, and placing limits on institutional frameworks. This not only threatens to alter the balance between sovereignty claims and individual rights but also to create a new path-dependent direction with lasting effects on justice,

---

[54] Priscilla Hayner, "Negotiating Peace in Liberia: Preserving the Possibility for Justice," *Centre for Humanitarian Dialogue*, November 2007, at: www.ictj.org/sites/default/files/ICTJ-Liberia-Negotiating-Peace-2007-English_0.pdf.

accountability, and human rights. Elite efforts to whip up anti-Western and anti-human rights discourses have been enabled, in part, by the growing assertiveness of justice advocates. In many places, elite efforts to whip up anti-Western and anti-human rights discourses have been enabled, unwittingly, by the growing assertiveness of justice advocates. When strategic backlash succeeds, it may be more consequential than tactical and even violent backlash precisely because it creates a new normative framework and sets in motion a new path dependence.

In theory, proposals by the African Union to hold investigations or trials at the regional level with rules that diverge in minor rather than radical ways from international standards but embrace the fundamental principle of criminal accountability for mass atrocities contain the possibility of a progressive outcome. In practice, were it to succeed, a regional court that rejected accountability for sitting heads of state at the level of doctrine would mark a radical qualification of human rights norms, one that strengthened national sovereignty at the expense of individual rights.

Finally, transitional and democratic states often seek to adapt rather than to reject existing institutional frameworks. Strategic backlash differs from counter-norming when it seeks to modify rather than reject the rule of law and recognizes the value of human rights and international justice. The United States and Kenya both sought to alter the ICC's rules in order to restrain the Court's authority over their territory and citizens. Smaller states, like Kenya, see regionalism as a strategy for balancing against international institutions.

Backlash may sometimes be a natural concomitant to progress. Often, though, backlash poses a more serious threat. Understanding the conditions under which either of these outcomes is more likely is crucial in developing a pragmatic justice strategy that will strengthen the prospect for human rights.

6   Human Rights in Areas of Limited Statehood:
     From the Spiral Model to Localization and
     Translation

Thomas Risse

This chapter addresses a common blind spot in human rights research shared by most quantitative as well as qualitative work, including the so-called "mainstream," as the editors to this volume put it (see Introduction).[1] Most studies assume fully functioning Weberian states that enjoy a monopoly over the means of violence and/or the capacity to implement and enforce central decisions. I claim that this idealized picture neither represents the contemporary international system nor has been valid from a historical perspective. Rather, most countries are characterized by "areas of limited statehood" which pose particular challenges for international human rights – whether political and civil rights or economic and social rights. Areas of limited statehood lack domestic sovereignty – that is, the ability of central authorities to implement and enforce decisions and/or to control the means of violence.

Yet, areas of limited statehood are neither ungoverned nor ungovernable.[2] We find huge variation in the degree to which public services are provided, and this variation includes human rights performance. Many areas of limited statehood perform reasonably well with regard to civil and political rights – mostly in democratizing or democratic states – even though central governments lack the capacity to protect them. This chapter explores why and under which conditions this is the case.

Theoretically, I take what is often called the "mainstream" in human rights research as my point of departure (see the editors' Introduction and

---

[1] I thank the editors of this volume for their very helpful and thoughtful criticisms and suggestions for this chapter. Much of the research reported below about human rights in areas of limited statehood has been carried out in the framework of the Collaborative Research Center "Governance in Areas of Limited Statehood" at the Freie Universität Berlin, Germany. Funding by the German Research Foundation (*Deutsche Forschungsgemeinschaft*) is gratefully acknowledged.
[2] Stephen D. Krasner and Thomas Risse, External Actors, State-Building, and Service Provision in Areas of Limited Statehood: Introduction. *Governance* 27 (4) (2014): 545–67.

Conclusion, this volume).[3] Most recently, this "mainstream" has paid more attention to scope conditions for human rights change, instead of focusing solely on processes and mechanisms such as the "boomerang effect" or the "spiral model." I discuss two scope conditions to explain the variation in human rights performance in areas of limited statehood, namely regime type and the material as well as social vulnerability of local rulers or "strongmen" in areas of limited statehood. I argue that localization and vernacularization[4] as well as translation approaches[5] complement rather than substitute the socialization approaches and their emphasis on persuasion as theorized by the spiral model. Together, these approaches account for the variation in human rights compliance in areas of limited statehood.

The chapter starts with a short summary of the "mainstream" in human rights research, as exemplified by the *Power of Human Rights* (PoHR)[6] and the *Persistent Power of Human Rights* (PPoHR)[7] volumes. I then move on to define the concept of limited statehood, followed by an overview of the human rights performance in areas of limited statehood. The third section of the chapter reviews various attempts at explaining the (non-)compliance with human rights in areas of limited statehood. Fourth, I introduce the localization and translation perspectives as complementing the socialization mechanisms emphasized by the spiral model. I discuss how localization and translation shed

---

[3] E.g., Alison Brysk, *The Politics of Human Rights in Argentina: Protest, Change, and Democratization* (Stanford: Stanford University Press, 1994), Alison Brysk, *Globalization and Human Rights* (Berkeley: University of California Press, 2002); Anne Marie Clark, *Diplomacy of Conscience: Amnesty International and Changing Human Rights Norms* (Princeton: Princeton University Press, 2001); Margaret E. Keck and Kathryn Sikkink, *Activists Beyond Borders. Advocacy Networks in International Politics* (Ithaca: Cornell University Press, 1998); Kathryn Sikkink, *The Justice Cascade: Human Rights Prosecutions and World Politics* (New York: W. W. Norton, 2011); Thomas Risse, Stephen C. Ropp, and Kathryn Sikkink, eds., *The Power of Human Rights: International Norms and Domestic Change* (Cambridge: Cambridge University Press, 1999), Thomas Risse, Stephen C. Ropp, and Kathryn Sikkink, eds., *The Persistent Power of Human Rights. From Commitment to Compliance* (Cambridge: Cambridge University Press, 2013); Beth A. Simmons, *Mobilizing for Human Rights. International Law in Domestic Politics* (Cambridge: Cambridge University Press, 2009).

[4] Peggy Levitt and Sally Merry, "Vernacularization on the Ground: Local Uses of Global Women's Rights in Peru, China, India, and the United States," *Global Networks* 9, no. 4 (2009): 441–61; Amitav Acharya, "How Ideas Spread: Whose Norms Matter? Norm Localization and Institutional Change in Asian Regionalism," *International Organization* 58, no. 2 (2004): 239–75.

[5] Doris Bachmann-Medick, "Meanings of Translation in Cultural Anthropology," in *Translating Others*, ed. Theo Hermans (Manchester: St. Jerome, 2006), 33–42; Doris Bachmann-Medick, ed., *The Trans/National Study of Culture. A Translational Perspective* (Berlin: De Gruyter, 2014); Lawrence Venuti, *The Translation Studies Reader*, 2nd edn. (New York: Routledge, 2004).

[6] Risse et al., *Power of Human Rights*.   [7] Risse et al., *Persistent Power of Human Rights*.

light on the variation in human rights performance in areas of limited statehood and how these mechanisms interact with two scope conditions for human rights change – namely, regime type and material, as well as social vulnerability of local authorities and other actors. I illustrate my argument with examples of human rights research in various areas of limited statehood. The concluding section summarizes my points.

Theorizing Human Rights Change: Boomerang Effects, Spiral Models, and Scope Conditions

The "spiral model" of human rights change that we developed in PoHR built upon work on the "boomerang effect" that had previously been done by Keck and Sikkink.[8] Both concepts were meant to explain the domestic implementation of and compliance with international human rights norms (or lack thereof) through a dynamic and complex interplay of global transnational and domestic as well as local processes involving mainly non-state actors. The spiral model developed five stages in a socialization process sequentially involving instrumental adaptation, argumentation and persuasion, and – last but not least – habitualization. We tried to operationalize these phases and concepts in such ways that they could be evaluated and tested empirically.

While PoHR developed the original model, PPoHR tried to push the argument further through three moves. First, we concentrated on later phases in the process, namely "prescriptive status" and "rule-consistent behavior." The original spiral model had underspecified these processes. This had invited widespread criticism that the spiral model somehow assumed an automaticity between states ratifying international treaties and compliance with these rules. As particularly quantitative work on human rights change pointed out,[9] treaty ratification as such does not lead to better compliance. Moreover, commitment with international human rights law no longer appears to be the main problem in the twenty-first century, since each and every state in the

---

[8] Keck and Sikkink, *Activists Beyond Borders*. This part summarizes Thomas Risse and Stephen C. Ropp, "Introduction and Overview," in Risse et al., *Persistent Power of Human Rights*, 3–25.

[9] E.g., Oona A. Hathaway, "Do Human Rights Treaties Make a Difference?," *The Yale Law Journal* 111, no. 8 (2002): 1942–2042; Linda Camp Keith, "The United Nations International Covenant on Civil and Political Rights: Does It Make a Difference in Human Rights Behavior?," *Journal of Peace Research* 36, no. 1 (1999): 95–118; Emilie M. Hafner-Burton and James Ron, "Seeing Double: Human Rights Impact Through Qualitative and Quantitative Eyes," *World Politics* 61, no. 2 (2009): 360–401.

contemporary system is treaty partner of at least one international human rights regime.[10]

The second move of PPoHR has been empirical. We demonstrated that the increasingly quantitative literature on international human rights is fully compatible with and complementary to the spiral model, which had originally been developed using comparative case studies.[11] Moreover, we extended the analysis to different types of rights (including economic, social, and gender),[12] and to non-state actors such as companies, as well as rebel groups.[13] Finally, we also examined powerful states in the international systems accused of human rights violations, namely the United States and China.[14]

Finally, PPoHR specifies more clearly the scope conditions under which we would expect these four social mechanisms to induce compliance by both state and non-state actors with international human rights law (see also the editors' conclusions on preconditions). This move replied to criticism of the original spiral model, namely that it emphasized social mechanisms over causal factors. We identified the following factors:

1) regime type, i.e., democratic vs. authoritarian regimes,[15] with a focus on electoral participation by citizens and competition for executive office so as to avoid endogeneity problems;

2) centralized vs. decentralized rule implementation, i.e., whether central authorities are in charge of compliance directly or whether rule addressees (those who commit) are also rule targets (who have to comply) or not (see also chapter by Dancy and Sikkink, Chapter 2, this volume);

[10] Andrea Liese, *Staaten am Pranger. Zur Wirkung internationaler Regime auf innerstaatliche Menschenrechtspolitik* (Wiesbaden: VS Verlag für Sozialwissenschaften, 2006).

[11] See particularly Beth A. Simmons, "From Ratification to Compliance: Quantitative Evidence on the Spiral Model," in Risse et al., *Persistent Power of Human Rights*, 43–59; Xinyuan Dai, "The 'Compliance Gap' and the Efficacy of International Human Rights Institutions," ibid., 85–102; Ann Marie Clark, "The Normative Context of Human Rights Criticism: Treaty Ratification and UN Mechanisms," ibid., 125–44.

[12] On the latter, see Alison Brysk, "Changing Hearts and Minds: Sexual Politics and Human Rights," ibid., 259–274; see also Hertel, Chapter 10, this volume.

[13] Wagaki Mwangi, Lothar Rieth, and Hans Peter Schmitz, "Encouraging Greater Compliance: Local Networks and the United Nations Global Compact," in Risse et al., *Persistent Power of Human Rights*, 203–21; Nicole Deitelhoff and Klaus Dieter Wolf, "Business and Human Rights: How Corporate Norm Violators Become Norm Entrepreneurs," ibid., 222–38; Hyeran Jo and Katherine Bryant, "Taming of the Warlords: Commitment and Compliance By Armed Opposition Groups in Civil Wars," ibid., 239–74.

[14] Kathryn Sikkink, "The United States and Torture: Does the Spiral Model Work?," ibid., 145–63; Katrin Kinzelbach, "Resisting the Power of Human Rights: The People's Republic of China," ibid., 164–81.

[15] See, e.g., Simmons, *Mobilizing for Human Rights*.

3) material as well as social vulnerability of rule targets to external pressures.

We also added consolidated vs. limited statehood as another scope condition. However, as I argue below, while consolidated statehood plus democracy correlate strongly with human rights compliance, limited statehood per se does not lead to human rights violations. In addition, as the editors point out in the Introduction (this volume), peace (or at least the absence of war) might be another scope condition. I am less convinced about per capita income, since the quantitative evidence on this finding is not particularly robust.[16]

PPoHR also contained a chapter on human rights issues in areas of limited statehood as a neglected problem of human rights commitment and compliance. The following section of this chapter deals with human rights issues in areas of limited statehood in a more systematic way.

Areas of Limited Statehood and Human Rights

Most human rights scholarship contains implicit assumptions about states and statehood.[17] First, no matter whether states violate or respect human rights, they are conceptualized as enjoying both the monopoly over the means for violence and the ability to make, implement, and enforce central political decisions. As the editors point out in the Introduction, a strong institutional capacity of the state seems to be a prerequisite for human rights compliance – but also for state repression, one might add. Second, most work on human rights assumes that states, e.g., illiberal regimes, violate human rights intentionally – that is, because they want to, not because they lack the capacity to comply with international norms.

In other words, human rights scholarship usually expects that states are fully capable of complying with international human rights norms if they only want to or are forced to by transnational mobilization through mechanisms such as the "boomerang effect."[18] The original spiral model took it for granted that states would be able to enforce the law. The underlying theory of compliance is one of deliberate or voluntary

---

[16] The most comprehensive quantitative study on human rights commitment and compliance, Simmons' *Mobilizing for Human Rights*, does not provide much evidence for a linear correlation of GDP pc and human rights improvements.

[17] The following builds upon Tanja A. Börzel and Thomas Risse, "Human Rights in Areas of Limited Statehood: The New Agenda," in Risse et al., *Persistent Power of Human Rights.*, 63–84.

[18] For a recent exception see Wade M. Cole, "Mind the Gap: State Capacity and the Implementation of Human Rights Treaties," *International Organization* 69, no. 02 (2015): 405–41.

non-compliance.[19] Autocratic regimes violate human rights, e.g., because they want to stay in power.

But what if governments commit to international human rights through ratification of the relevant treaties, appear willing to comply, but cannot do so for a variety of reasons? The literature calls this "involuntary defection"[20] or "involuntary non-compliance."[21] What if governments do not have sufficient capacity to enforce the law to which they have committed? What if central decision-making authorities lack the institutional means to control, e.g., their military or their police forces, let alone non-state actors violating human rights? These considerations lead to a discussion of "limited statehood."

Conceptualizing Limited Statehood

But what is "limited statehood?" I start with Max Weber's conceptualization of statehood as an institutionalized authority structure with the ability to steer hierarchically and to legitimately control the means of violence.[22] While no state governs hierarchically all the time, consolidated states at least possess the ability to authoritatively make, implement, and enforce central decisions for a collectivity. In other words, they command what Stephen Krasner called "domestic sovereignty" – i.e., "the formal organization of political authority within the state and the ability of public authorities to exercise effective control within the borders of their own polity."[23] This understanding allows us to distinguish between *statehood* as an institutional structure of authority, on the one hand, and the kind of *governance* services it provides, on the other hand. The latter is an empirical not a definitional question. The ability to effectively make, implement, or enforce decisions constitutes statehood. Whether this enforcement capacity is exercised within the boundaries of the rule of law and through the respect for basic human rights or not, concerns the quality of governance, but not the definition of statehood.

---

[19] Kal Raustiala and Anne-Marie Slaughter, "International Law, International Relations, and Compliance," in *Handbook of International Relations*, ed. Walter Carlsnaes, Beth Simmons, and Thomas Risse (London et al.: Sage, 2002), 538–58.

[20] Robert Putnam, "Diplomacy and Domestic Politics. The Logic of Two-Level Games," *International Organization* 42, no. 2 (1988): 427–60.

[21] Abram Chayes and Antonia Handler Chayes, "On Compliance," *International Organization*, 47 (1993): 175–205, Abram Chayes and Antonia Handler Chayes, *The New Sovereignty. Compliance with International Regulatory Agreements* (Cambridge, MA: Harvard University Press, 1995).

[22] Max Weber, *Wirtschaft und Gesellschaft*, 5th edn. (Tübingen: J. C. B. Mohr, 1921/1980).

[23] Stephen D. Krasner, *Sovereignty. Organized Hypocrisy* (Princeton: Princeton University Press, 1999), 4.

One can now define more precisely the concept of "areas of limited statehood." While areas of limited statehood belong to internationally recognized states, it is their domestic sovereignty which is circumscribed. Areas of limited statehood concern those parts of a country in which central authorities (usually governments) lack the ability to implement and/or enforce rules and decisions and/or in which the legitimate monopoly over the means of violence is lacking. The ability to enforce rules or to control the means of violence can be restricted along various dimensions: (1) territorial, i.e., concerning parts of the territory; (2) sectoral, i.e., with regard to specific policy areas; and (3) social, i.e., with regard to specific parts of the population. As a result, we can distinguish different configurations of limited statehood.

Areas of limited statehood are a ubiquitous phenomenon in the contemporary international system, but also in historical comparison. After all, the state monopoly over the means of violence has only been around for a little more than two hundred years. Most states in the contemporary international system contain "areas of limited statehood" in the sense that central authorities do not control the entire territory, do not completely enjoy the monopoly over the means of violence, and/or have limited capacities to enforce and implement decisions, at least in some policy areas or with regard to large parts of the population.

The concept of "limited statehood" needs to be distinguished from "failing" and "failed" statehood. Most typologies in the literature and datasets on fragile states, "states at risk," etc., reveal a normative orientation toward highly developed and democratic statehood and, thus, toward the Western model.[24] The benchmark is usually the democratic and capitalist state governed by the rule of law. This is problematic on both normative and analytical grounds. It is normatively questionable, because it reveals a bias toward Western statehood and Euro-centrism. It is analytically problematic, because it tends to conflate definitional issues and research questions. If we define states as political entities that provide certain services and public goods, such as security, the rule of law, and welfare, many "states" in the international system do not qualify as such.

Moreover, failed and failing states comprise only a small percentage of the world's areas of limited statehood. Almost all countries, but certainly most developing and transition countries, contain areas of limited statehood insofar as they only partially control the means of violence and are

---

[24] See, e.g., Robert I. Rotberg, ed., *State Failure and State Weakness in a Time of Terror* (Washington: Brookings Institution Press, 2003), Rotberg, ed., *When States Fail. Causes and Consequences* (Princeton: Princeton University Press, 2004).

often unable to enforce collectively binding decisions, mainly for reasons of insufficient political and administrative capacities.[25] Brazil and Mexico, on the one hand, and Somalia and Sudan, on the other, constitute the opposite ends of a continuum of states containing areas of limited statehood. Moreover, I do not talk about "states of limited statehood," but about areas – i.e., territorial or functional spaces within otherwise functioning states in which the latter have lost their ability to govern. While the Pakistan state enjoys a monopoly over the use of force in some parts of its territory, the so-called tribal areas in the country's Northeast are beyond the control of the central government.

In sum, areas of limited statehood are not some sort of aberration in world history to be overcome by the relentless forces of (Western) modernity, but the default condition in the contemporary international system. In this sense, Ghana, Mexico, and Indonesia are more typical for statehood than, say, Canada or Denmark.

Measuring limited statehood is no easy task, however, because of endogeneity issues whereby weak state capacity results from deliberate choices by political, economic, and social elites.[26] On the one hand, there are "neoliberal" states which have voluntarily withdrawn from regulating particular policy areas (e.g., capital flows) or from providing particular public services (e.g., telecommunications) and thus have ceased to maintain the institutional capacity in these issue areas. These are mostly consolidated and democratic states in the global North which are not of concern here, since they mostly respect human rights. On the other hand, there are the so-called cunning states,[27] wherein political and social elites deliberately keep state institutions weak in order to reap economic and political benefits or to increase their rents. Randeria, for example, has argued that India represents such a state in that its elites keep the state deliberately weak in order to remain unaccountable to the citizens domestically and to retain as much foreign aid as possible. Reno makes a similar argument about the state in Sub-Saharan Africa, wherein state

[25] This is not to argue that limited statehood is confined to developing countries. Southern Italy, for example, contains areas of limited statehood insofar as the Italian central state authorities are incapable of enforcing the law vis-à-vis those parts of the population who are directly or indirectly involved with the mafia. The same holds true for the drug business in many parts of the world's major cities, including New York, London, Paris, and Berlin.
[26] I thank the editors of this volume for alerting me to this point.
[27] Shalini Randeria, "Cunning States and Unaccountable International Institutions: Legal Plurality, Social Movements and Rights of Local Communities to Common Property Resources," *European Journal of Sociology / Archives Européennes de Sociologie* 44, no. 01 (2003b): 27–60.

institutions are captured by rent-seeking warlords to feed their clientelistic networks.[28]

Whether limited statehood results from lack of capacity or lack of willingness of ruling elites is ultimately an empirical question. Moreover, it is necessary to clarify what is endogenous to what. In the case of the "neoliberal" state, keeping the state out of certain parts of the economy has little to do with weak state institutions in general. The "neoliberal" US or UK states are perfectly capable of enforcing the law with regard to national security issues and command enormous resources in this regard. With regard to "cunning states," however, I would argue that elite choices to keep the state weak are endogenous to limited statehood and not the other way round. African or Indian clientelistic networks are only capable of capturing state institutions and preventing the development of institutional capacities because these states were weak to begin with, thereby enabling state capture by corrupt elites. Moreover, past deliberate choices by elites might then lead to institutional weakness in the sense of limited statehood later on.

Yet, areas of limited statehood are not ungoverned or ungovernable spaces where chaos and anarchy prevail. The literature on fragile or failed states mostly assumes that state failure automatically implies governance failure. This is wrong.[29] Instead, we encounter a huge variation with regard to areas of limited statehood and their governability.[30] Even some failed states (such as Somalia) contain well-governed areas (such as the province Somaliland) where service provision reaches rather decent standards.[31] The same holds true for human rights.

Limited Statehood and Human Rights Performance

Human rights are not that different from other policy areas. There is no linear correlation between degrees of statehood, on the one hand, and the

---

[28] William Reno, *Warlord Politics and African States* (Boulder: Lynne Rienner Publ., 1998), William Reno, *Warfare in Independent Africa* (Cambridge: Cambridge University Press, 2011); Gero Erdmann, "Neopatrimonialism and Political Regimes," in *Routledge Handbook of African Politics*, ed. Nic Cheeseman and Dave Anderson (London/New York: Routledge, 2013), 59–69; Robert H. Bates, *When Things Fall Apart. State Failure in Late-Century Africa* (Cambridge: Cambridge University Press, 2008); Catherine Boone, *Political Topographies of the African State. Territorial Authority and Institutional Choice* (Cambridge: Cambridge University Press, 2003).

[29] Krasner and Risse, "External Actors, State-Building, and Service Provision in Areas of Limited Statehood: Introduction."

[30] Melissa Lee, Gregor Walter-Drop, and John Wiesel, "Taking the State (Back) Out? A Macro-Quantitative Analysis of Statehood and the Delivery of Collective Goods and Services," ibid.: 635–54.

[31] On public health in Somalia, see Marco Schäferhoff, "External Actors and the Provision of Public Health Services in Somalia – Task Complexity Matters," *Governance* 27, no. 4 (2014): 675–95.

144   *Thomas Risse*

degree to which human rights – whether political and civil or social and economic rights – are secured, on the other. While a strong institutional capacity of the state including a Weberian impartial bureaucracy certainly helps to secure human rights (see the editors' Introduction to this volume), it does not seem to be a necessary condition. Take Sub-Saharan Africa, for example, probably the region of the world with the highest concentration of both failing and failed states and areas of limited statehood. Citizens of Benin, Botswana, Ghana, Lesotho, Namibia, and Senegal enjoy relatively high levels of political rights and civil liberties. At the other end of the spectrum are Angola, Cameroon, Chad, Ethiopia, South Sudan, and Zimbabwe, where political and civil rights are systematically violated. Many other African countries are located in between.[32] While regime type highly correlates with levels of human rights (non-) compliance in general, degrees of statehood do not. Sub-Saharan Africa is no exception.

However, limited statehood can mitigate the positive effect of democracy on human rights.[33] Many transition countries on a path to democratization have committed themselves to international human rights and have ratified the respective treaties to lock in their regime change. But human rights are nevertheless violated because of limited statehood. Human rights violations in areas of limited statehood are often committed because of two interconnected phenomena. First, weak central governments – even those committed to human rights – cannot protect them in areas of limited statehood, e.g., because they do not control their own enforcement agencies, such as the police or the military. In such cases, human rights are violated by state agents outside the reach of central authorities. Second, lack of enforcement capacity also means that non-state actors such as warlords, private militias, (multinational) companies, or transnational criminal organizations become perpetrators of rights violations in areas of limited statehood. In other words, limited statehood and decentralized rule implementation interact.

At the same time, we find a number of countries whose domestic institutions lack both democratic quality and effective statehood, yet which nevertheless are *not* human rights violators. These double findings of norms-violating democratic transition countries, on the one hand, and norms-respecting weak states, on the other, suggest a rather complex

[32] Data according to Freedom House, 2013 Report: www.freedomhouse.org/sites/default/files/FIW%202013%20Charts%20and%20Graphs%20for%20Web_0.pdf.
[33] Simmons, *Mobilizing for Human Rights*, 82; Simmons, "From Ratification to Compliance: Quantitative Evidence on the Spiral Model"; Andrew Moravcsik, "The Origins of Human Rights Regimes: Democratic Delegation in Postwar Europe," *International Organization* 54, no. 2 (2000): 217–52.

Configurations of Statehood Regime Type	Limited Statehood	Consolidated Statehood
Democratic Regimes	Human rights violations due to lack of capacity	Mostly Human Rights Compliance
Authoritarian Regimes	Human rights violations due to lack of willingness and capacity	Human rights violations due to lack of willingness

Figure 6.1: Human Rights by Regime Type and Degree of Statehood.

(Taken from Börzel and Risse, "Human Rights in Areas of Limited Statehood: The New Agenda," 69.)

interaction between democracy, degrees of statehood, and human rights performance.

Figure 6.1 conceptualizes human rights problems according to degrees of statehood and regime type (for the sake of the argument, both dimensions are treated here as dichotomous, which is, of course, overly simplistic).

As argued above, most human rights scholarship, including PoHR, implicitly assumed consolidated statehood (the Eastern cells of Figure 6.1). Human rights are mostly complied with in democratic consolidated states (Northeastern cell of Figure 6.1) and violated by authoritarian regimes (Southeastern cell of Figure 6.1). Since the latter are supposed to be able to enforce the law (consolidated statehood), compliance is a question of willingness. The spiral model theorized under which conditions local as well as transnational social mobilization would move countries from the Southeastern to the Northeastern cell of Figure 6.1.[34] To put it in terms of the various compliance theories,[35] most of the human rights literature incorporates compliance mechanisms theorized by enforcement and legitimacy approaches. Enforcement

---

[34] Risse et al., *Power of Human Rights*; Risse et al., *Persistent Power of Human Rights*.
[35] E.g., Raustiala and Slaughter, "International Law, International Relations, and Compliance"; Ian Hurd, "Legitimacy and Authority in International Politics," *International Organization* 53, no. 2 (1999): 379–408.

approaches focus on sanctions as well as positive incentives to change the cost–benefit calculations of actors, thereby inducing compliance. The legitimacy school concentrates on persuasion and learning to induce actors "to do the right thing" and thereby comply with costly rules.

But the Eastern cells of Figure 6.1 only cover a small part of the world's population of states. Most countries in the real world – whether democracies or autocracies and, thus, irrespective of regime type – populate the Western cells of Figure 6.1. The world is full of authoritarian as well as democratic regimes that try to govern areas of limited statehood. Almost all Sub-Saharan African states mentioned above fall into this category. The Southwestern cell of Figure 6.1 is populated by authoritarian and semi-authoritarian regimes in countries with areas of limited statehood where human rights are violated, because central governments lack both the willingness *and* the capacity to enforce compliance. The Northwestern cell of Figure 6.1 contains democratic or democratizing regimes with areas of limited statehood. For example, India, the world's largest democracy, belongs in this category. If we assume that democracies are willing to commit to and comply with human rights at least in principle, rights violations in countries populating the Northwestern cell of Figure 6.1 occur mainly because a state is not in full control of parts of its territory or with regard to parts of the police forces or the military. In other words, the compliance problem is a capacity issue in these cases.

Let me now look at some data concerning the human rights performance in areas of limited statehood. The following two figures use a similar layout as Figure 6.1, wherein the y-axis depicts degrees of democracy and the x-axis degrees of statehood. Figure 6.2 depicts the above-average human rights performers ("rights protecting states"; using civil and political rights performance as indicators), while Figure 6.3 shows the below-average performers ("rights-violating states").[36]

A comparison of Figures 6.2 and 6.3 yields the following insights: First, the figures confirm the correlation between democracy and rights

---

[36] Each dot represents the human rights performance of one state. Human rights data are taken from Amnesty International/Political Terror Scale measuring civil and political rights on a five-point scale, with 1 connoting the best and 5 connoting the worst performers. HR protecting states reach points 1 and 2 on the scale, HR violating states 3–5 points. Degrees of democracy are measured using both Freedom House and Polity 2 data. Average of Freedom House (fh_pr and fh_cl) is transformed to a scale 0–10 and Polity (p_polity2) is transformed to a scale 0–10. These variables are averaged into fh_polity2. The imputed version has imputed values for countries where data on Polity is missing by regressing Polity on the average Freedom House measure. Degrees of limited statehood are measured using combined indicators for the monopoly of force and for bureaucratic quality. Statehood data comes from Stollenwerk, Eric/Jan Opper 2017: The Governance and Limited Statehood Dataset, version March17. Freie Universität Berlin, SFB 700 available at http://www.sfb-governance.de/publikationen/daten/index.html. I thank Eric Stollenwerk and Jan Opper for their help producing and collecting these data.

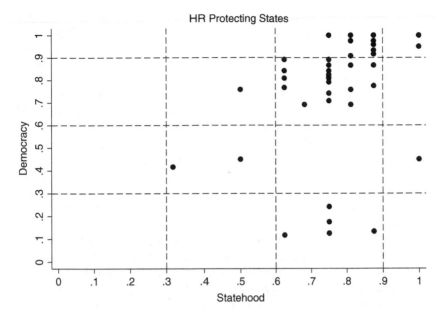

Figure 6.2: Human Rights Protecting States and Areas of Limited Statehood.

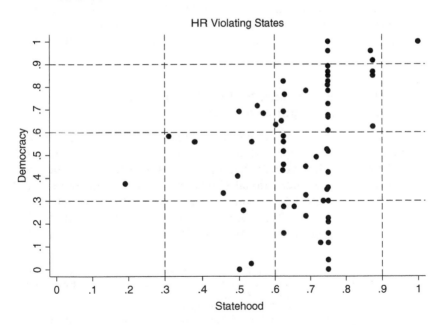

Figure 6.3: Human Rights Violating States and Areas of Limited Statehood.

protection, at least with regard to civil and political rights.[37] Civil rights protecting states are mostly located in the upper half of Figure 6.2. Second, however, rights violating states cover the entire range of regime type, from the bottom of Figure 6.3 (autocracies) all the way up to the top (stable democracies).

Third, with regard to degrees of limited statehood, most rights-protecting states contain some areas of limited statehood (0.6–0.85 points on the statehood scale) or exhibit strong state institutions (0.9–1.0 on the statehood scale). There is not a single rights-protecting failed state in Figure 6.2, suggesting that a minimum degree of statehood is necessary for the protection of political and civil rights.[38] However, there is quite a number of fragile states with rather low statehood scores (0.7 and below)[39] that protect human rights. These outliers deserve special attention.

Fourth, as Figure 6.3 reveals, rights-violating states can be found all over the map with regard to (limited) statehood. Rights violations and statehood do not seem to correlate at all, even if one controls for degrees of democracy. However, there are few rights-violating consolidated states (with statehood degrees of 0.85 and above), while most rights violators can be found with degrees of statehood of 0.8 and below. Thus, on average, lack of domestic sovereignty or limited statehood significantly contributes to the violation of human rights. This confirms the argument that most rights-violating states in the international system suffer from both a lack of willingness *and* a lack of capacity to comply with these norms.

Explaining Human Rights (Non-)Compliance in Areas of Limited Statehood

So, what explains (non-)compliance with human rights in areas of limited statehood, and why do we find the variation documented in Figures 6.2 and 6.3? At this point, we must distinguish between socioeconomic rights as enshrined in the International Covenant on Social, Economic, and Cultural Rights (ICSECR), on the one hand, and political as well as civil rights as covered by the International Covenant on Civil and Political Rights (ICCPR), on the other. As to the ICSECR, there are quite a few

---

[37] Note that using economic and social rights as indicators for human rights would yield a rather different picture. In fact, the variation would actually be even greater; see Lee et al., "Taking the State (Back) Out?"

[38] See also Cole, "Mind the Gap," for similar findings.

[39] Anything below 0.6 in Figures 6.2 and 6.3 constitutes failed statehood given the way in which the index was built.

reasons why their protection might be easier on average in areas of limited statehood than securing civil and political rights.[40]

First, protecting many social and economic rights requires the provision of public goods and services, which can be done by actors other than the state in areas of limited statehood. For example, companies can secure the right to work irrespective of whether the central state institutions are weak or not. Whether or not labor and environmental rights are protected in areas of limited statehood depends as much on successful transnational mobilization in the global North against (multinational) corporations with a brand name to defend as on efforts by weak states. Here, we observe similar mechanisms at work as the "boomerang effect" or the "spiral model" have demonstrated with regard to states.[41] In addition, asset specificity matters, too – that is, whether companies can easily relocate without losing important investments.[42] This is the difference between extractive industries and automobile companies, on the one hand, and the global textile industry, on the other.[43]

Second, external actors such as foreign aid agencies, international organizations, transnational public–private partnerships as well as (I)NGOs are often the main providers of public goods and services in areas of limited statehood which then secure basic economic and social rights.[44]

Third, many autocratic and semi-authoritarian governments use the little state capacity left in areas of limited statehood to help secure socioeconomic rights. The reason is simple: Effectively providing basic public goods and services is likely to increase the "output legitimacy" of (semi-) authoritarian states as one of the few sources of legitimacy available to

---

[40] See Stephen D. Krasner and Thomas Risse, eds., *External Actors, State-Building, and Service Provision in Areas of Limited Statehood*; Krasner and Risse, "External Actors, State-Building, and Service Provision in Areas of Limited Statehood: Introduction," ibid., 545–67, for the following.

[41] Deitelhoff and Wolf, "Business and Human Rights: How Corporate Norm Violators Become Norm Entrepreneurs"; Annegret Flohr et al., *The Role of Business in Global Governance. Corporations as Norm-Entrepreneurs* (Houndmills: Palgrave Macmillan, 2010).

[42] For details, see Christian R. Thauer, *The Managerial Sources of Corporate Social Responsibility. The Spread of Global Standards* (Cambridge: Cambridge University Press, 2015).

[43] Tanja A. Börzel and Christian Thauer, eds., *Business and Governance in South Africa* (Houndmills: Palgrave Macmillan, 2013).

[44] Marianne Beisheim and Andrea Liese, eds., *Transnational Partnerships. Effectively Providing for Sustainable Development?* (Houndmills: Palgrave Macmillan, 2014); Amanda Murdie and Alexander Hicks, "Can International Nongovernmental Organizations Boost Government Services? The Case of Health," *International Organization* 67, no. 3 (2013): 541–73.

them.[45] China is the quintessential example of a state with rather weak institutions in many policy areas (such as the environment) that has taken millions of citizens out of poverty, thereby securing the ("output") legitimacy of state authorities and the Communist party.

Protecting political and civil rights in areas of limited statehood appears to be more complicated. First, securing these human rights constitutes rather complex tasks and, thus, necessitates highly institutionalized governance structures, state or non-state.[46] Second, the protection of political and civil rights requires at least some rudimentary rule of law and a functioning court system, be it on the domestic or the international level.[47] In that sense, some state capacity – on the domestic level or provided by external actors – appears to be necessary for the protection of civil and political rights.[48] A lot has been written recently on non-state court systems and their ability to protect citizens in cases in which state courts are thoroughly corrupt.[49] Yet, it remains questionable whether a full-fledged and effective rule of law system can be maintained in a sustainable way in cases of complete state failure.

But Figures 6.2 and 6.3 also reveal variation with regard to civil and political rights protection in countries with areas of limited statehood. How can this be explained? First, the enforcement perspective in compliance research mentioned above is of little help under these circumstances. By definition, central state institutions are too weak to hierarchically enforce human rights or to cast a credible "shadow of hierarchy"[50] in areas of limited statehood. Alternatively, the ability of external authorities to interfere hierarchically in the "Westphalian/Vattelian" sovereignty of

---

[45] On the distinction between "input" and "output" legitimacy, see Fritz W. Scharpf, *Governing in Europe. Effective and Democratic?* (Oxford: Oxford University Press, 1999).

[46] Krasner and Risse, "External Actors, State-Building, and Service Provision in Areas of Limited Statehood: Introduction."

[47] Sikkink, *The Justice Cascade.*

[48] See Cole, "Mind the Gap: State Capacity and the Implementation of Human Rights Treaties," for a quantitative analysis.

[49] Milli Lake, "Organizing Hypocrisy: Providing Legal Accountability for Human Rights Violations in Areas of Limited Statehood," *International Studies Quarterly* 58 (2014): 515–26; Matthias Kötter and Gunnar Folke Schuppert, eds., *Normative Pluralität ordnen. Rechtsbegriffe, Normenkollisionen und Rule of Law in Kontexten dies- und jenseits des Staates* (Baden-Baden: Nomos, 2009); Matthias Kötter et al., eds., *Non-State Justice Institutions and the Law. Decision-Making at the Interface of Tradition, Religion and the State* (Houndmills: Palgrave Macmillan, 2015). Shalini Randeria, "Glocalization of Law: Environmental Justice, World Bank, NGOs and the Cunning State in India," *Current Sociology* 51, no. 3–4 (2003a): 305–28; Tobias Berger, *Global Norms and Local Courts. Translating the Rule of Law in Bangladesh* (Oxford: Oxford University Press, forthcoming).

[50] Fritz W. Scharpf, *Games Real Actors Play. Actor-Centered Institutionalism in Policy Research* (Boulder: Westview, 1997).

states[51] and to protect political and civil rights demonstrates a mixed record at best: While Bosnia and Herzegovina, Kosovo, and Timor Leste are rated "partly free" by Freedom House, Afghanistan and Iraq are in the "not free" category.[52]

Second, an emphasis on human rights violations resulting from limited statehood directs our attention toward the "management school" in compliance research.[53] This group has argued that non-compliance with international regulations results from weak institutions, lack of resources, and resulting problems of involuntary defection rather than lack of willingness by governments. Interestingly enough, many international organizations have long understood that capacity building and assistance in building up sustainable institutions goes a long way in the promotion of human rights and democracy and have acted accordingly. Most of the resources spent on democracy promotion by donors such as the United States and the EU focus on capacity building through financial and technical assistance.[54] But there is a catch: Helping to build state capacity from the outside is only likely to improve the human rights record of democratizing states, while increasing administrative capacity of (semi-)authoritarian states will only make them more effective in repressing the citizens.

Third, the legitimacy perspective in compliance research[55] might also be helpful in these cases. The more particular norms are considered appropriate and legitimate in a given collectivity, the more compliance with costly rules is likely. This could explain why (imperfect) democracy and civil rights protection go together even in countries with areas of limited statehood (see Figure 6.2). The more democratic values are considered legitimate by the citizens, the more political and civil rights might be secured even in the absence of functioning law enforcement institutions. As research on external democracy promotion has shown, it is more effective, the more it can rely on local liberal elites – also under conditions of limited statehood.[56]

---

[51] Krasner, *Sovereignty. Organized Hypocrisy.*

[52] See Freedom House, 2013 Report: www.freedomhouse.org/sites/default/files/FIW%20 2013%20Charts%20and%20Graphs%20for%20Web_0.pdf

[53] Particularly Chayes and Chayes, "On Compliance"; Chayes and Chayes, *The New Sovereignty. Compliance with International Regulatory Agreements.*

[54] Amichai Magen, Thomas Risse, and Michael McFaul, eds., *Promoting Democracy and the Rule of Law. American and European Strategies* (Houndmills: Palgrave Macmillan, 2009).

[55] E.g., Hurd, "Legitimacy and Authority in International Politics."

[56] Tanja A. Börzel and Vera Van Hüllen, "State-Building and the European Union's Fight against Corruption in the Southern Caucasus: Why Legitimacy Matters," *Governance* 27, no. 4 (2014): 613–34; Nelli Babayan and Thomas Risse, eds., *Democracy Promotion and the Challenges of Illiberal Regional Powers.* Special Issue of *Democratization*, 22, no. 3, 2015.

Last but not least, if local communities cherish political and civil rights and consider them normatively appropriate, they can be protected under extremely adverse conditions. Moreover, as Lake shows with regard to the Democratic Republic of Congo and Berger with regard to Bangladesh, non-state justice institutions in areas of limited statehood work particularly well if and when local or transnational NGOs can mobilize around them to protect citizens' rights.[57] These findings point to the importance of vibrant civil society organizations to foster human rights change in areas of limited statehood. In other words, state weakness can be compensated for by civil society organizations and human rights NGOs, at least partially.[58] In this context, the localization and vernacularization perspective discussed in the Introduction to this volume becomes particularly relevant. As I argue below, it nicely complements the emphasis on socialization and persuasion emphasized by the spiral model and other approaches to human rights change.

Localization and Translation of Human Rights in Areas of Limited Statehood

The spiral model was meant to systematically link processes on the global, transnational, and regional levels with those on the ground, be it national or local, to explain domestic human rights change at the behavioral level. However, the socialization perspective gave rise to the suspicion that this was essentially a "top down" perspective. International human rights norms enshrined in legal conventions would be simply "downloaded" in various domestic contexts, and the targets of socialization were passive containers who had to be persuaded of the prescriptive status of human rights. Indeed, if one takes the standard definition of socialization as "a process of inducting actors into the norms and rules of a given community,"[59] one could misunderstand this as a unidirectional movement from norms (international human rights in this case) to targets of socialization.

Yet, both "type 1" (role-playing: actors know the rules and behave accordingly) and "type 2" (normative persuasion: actors accept the validity of the rule and behave accordingly)[60] socialization processes imply active

---

[57] Lake, "Organizing Hypocrisy: Providing Legal Accountability for Human Rights Violations in Areas of Limited Statehood"; Berger, "Global Norms and Local Courts."

[58] This is, of course, consistent with Keck and Sikkink, *Activists Beyond Borders*, and Risse et al., *Power of Human Rights*.

[59] Jeffrey T. Checkel, "International Institutions and Socialization in Europe: Introduction and Framework," *International Organization* 59, no. 4 (2005): 801–26, 804.

[60] For these distinctions, see ibid.

processes of acquiring knowledge (types 1 and 2) and normative convictions (type 2). Normative discourses and persuasion, in a Habermasian sense, are equally active processes and not unidirectional as if socializers talk and socializees listen.

Understanding and interpreting norms are, thus, active processes. As a result, understandings of what a particular norm means in a given domestic or local context might change. Focusing on these processes of active acquisition and interpretation of international norms, vernacularization and localization approaches take explicit "bottom up" perspectives to theorize how local domestic actors relate to, acquire, or reject international norms.[61] Far from being passive recipients of international norms, local groups develop their own understandings and interpretations of rights agendas. In addition, cultural brokers work as "translators" – i.e., they adapt and adjust international norms to local contexts.[62] In the process, norms do not remain stable containers of some given content, but they acquire different meanings.

The localization and vernacularization perspectives complement rather than contradict the spiral model and similar approaches. These concepts remind us that universal norms need to become part of the domestic context and to be localized in order to result in behavioral consequences. These approaches also emphasize that the wholesale adoption of international human rights in domestic practices is only one possible outcome of norm diffusion.[63] Active localization and adaptation of international norms to local contexts is likely to improve compliance rather than lead to non-compliance.

Moreover, it makes little sense theoretically to give either the international/global or the local/domestic prime of place. First, doing so overlooks

---

[61] On localization, see Acharya, "How Ideas Spread: Whose Norms Matter? Norm Localization and Institutional Change in Asian Regionalism"; Amitav Acharya, *Whose Ideas Matter? Agency and Power in Asian Regionalism* (Ithaca: Cornell University Press, 2009); on vernacularization in a human rights context, see Peggy Levitt and Sally Merry, "Vernacularization on the Ground: Local Uses of Global Women's Rights in Peru, China, India, and the United States," *Global Networks* 9, no. 4 (2009): 441–61; Peggy Levitt and Sally E. Merry, "Making Women's Human Rights in the Vernacular: Navigating the Culture/Rights Divide," in *Gender and Culture at the Limits of Rights*, ed. Dorothy Hodgson (Philadelphia: University of Philadelphia Press, 2010), 81–100.

[62] Acharya calls this "grafting"; see Acharya, "How Ideas Spread: Whose Norms Matter?"

[63] On diffusion processes in general, see Fabrizio Gilardi, "Transnational Diffusion: Norms, Ideas, and Policies," in *Handbook of International Relations. Second Edition*, ed. Walter Carlsnaes, Thomas Risse, and Beth Simmons (London: Sage, 2013), 453–77; Etel Solingen, "Of Dominoes and Firewalls: The Domestic, Regional, and Global Politics of International Diffusion," *International Studies Quarterly* 56 (2012): 631–44.

what historians have termed "entangled histories."[64] This essentially means that global processes and local ones have been intermingled for centuries in every corner of the world and that it makes no sense to conceptualize the local as cultural containers not affected by any inter- or transnational processes. Take the human rights discourse: The language of rights has permeated every part of the world, even though it has been translated and appropriated very differently according to various religious, philosophical, and cultural traditions.[65] At the same time, local grievances and repression have been added to and have changed the global rights discourse – take the rights of indigenous peoples as an example. In this sense, localization has affected globalization and vice versa. It makes no sense to analytically privilege one level over the other.

Second, the localization perspective in particular is in danger of emphasizing continuity rather than change.[66] Prioritizing the local over the global risks overlooking the possibility of change when the two meet. When international norms are translated into and adapted to local contexts and practices, these practices do not remain the same. The translation perspective in cultural studies is all about the transformation of local practices.[67] This must not necessarily conform to some given – let alone Western – understandings and interpretations of human rights. But adapting and translating international human rights into local contexts inevitably changes these contexts, too. The change might be minimal when repressive practices prevail despite some tactical concessions, to use the language of the spiral model. But it might also be transformative and change the local practices for good. Our task as social scientists is to specify the conditions and the causal mechanisms in order to account for this variation.

But what do these considerations have to do with areas of limited statehood? Localization and translation practices become particularly relevant under these circumstances, when central state authorities are

---

[64] Sebastian Conrad and Shalini Randeria, eds., *Jenseits des Eurozentrismus. Postkoloniale Perspektiven in den Geschichts- und Kulturwissenschaften* (Frankfurt/Main: Campus, 2002); Michael Werner and Bénédicte Zimmermann, "Penser l'histoire croisée: entre empirie et réflexivité," *Annales Histoire, Sciences Sociales* 58, no. 1 (2003): 7–36, Werner and Zimmermann, "Beyond Comparison: 'Histoire Croisée' and the Challenge of Reflexivity," *History & Theory* 45, no. 1 (2006): 30–50.

[65] David P. Forsythe, *Human Rights in International Relations* (Cambridge, UK: Cambridge University Press, 2000).

[66] I owe the following thoughts to Tobias Berger. See Berger, "Global Norms and Local Courts. Translating the Rule of Law in Bangladesh."

[67] See, e.g., Bachmann-Medick, "Meanings of Translation in Cultural Anthropology"; Bachmann-Medick, "Introduction: The Translational Turn," *Translation Studies* 2, no. 1 (2009): 2–16; Lawrence Venuti, *The Translator's Invisibility: A History of Translation*, 2nd edn. (New York: Routledge, 2008).

too weak or too unwilling to enforce human rights standards. Let me now discuss how two of the scope conditions emphasized by PPoHR – regime type and material, as well as social vulnerability of the local rulers – affect localization and translation practices for human rights in areas of limited statehood.

With regard to regime type, the good news is that repressive governments have fewer means at their disposal to commit human rights violations under these circumstances, because areas of limited statehood are simply out of their reach. This opens up space for activists – local as well as transnational – as cultural brokers translating international human rights norms into local contexts and adapting them to these circumstances, as Lake argues with regard to remote areas of the DRC.[68] In the context of authoritarian regimes, limited statehood might be a blessing for human rights promotion since it allows other actors to circumvent the (repressive) state. As argued above, external actors such as IOs or foreign governments could foster translation processes in areas of limited statehood of repressive states.

With regard to liberal or liberalizing regimes, central governments lack the capacity to enforce human rights standards in areas of limited statehood, of course. However, they can still use their limited capacity and their legitimacy as democratic rulers to foster human rights change as socializing agents and to assume a broker role in localization attempts. This is precisely what the "post-Arabellion" Tunisian government has been doing, and what external actors such as the EU have been supporting.[69]

The bad news for areas of limited statehood – irrespective of regime type – is that human rights violations are likely to be committed by non-state actors, be it warlords, rebel groups, (multinational) companies, or even (I)NGOs (see above). As a result, local conditions and the local balance of power in conjunction with transnational forces become even more relevant for human rights practices in areas of limited statehood. Therefore, the second scope condition – material and social vulnerability – comes into play here, but it has to be adapted to refer to the vulnerability of local rulers and the local power structure rather than the central government, as in the original formula.[70]

---

[68] Lake, "Organizing Hypocrisy: Providing Legal Accountability for Human Rights Violations in Areas of Limited Statehood."

[69] Vera Van Hüllen, "The 'Arab Spring' and the Spiral Model: Tunisia and Morocco," in Risse et al., *Persistent Power of Human Rights*, 182–99; Assem Dandashly, "The EU Response to Regime Change in the Wake of the Arab Revolt: Differential Implementation," *Journal of European Integration* 37, no. 1 (2015): 37–56.

[70] For a related argument concerning the conditions under which rebel groups conform to human rights, see Hyeran Jo, *Compliant Rebels. Rebel Groups and International Law in World Politics* (Cambridge: Cambridge University Press, 2015).

Relating the local power balance to the argument about localization and translation would then yield a simple rational choice proposition, according to which the discourse of the powerful is also the most powerful discourse: The more the local power balance favors repressive rulers, including non-state actors (warlords, tribal leaders, and so forth), the less localization of international human rights is likely to occur and to lead to behavioral change. This is the sad situation in many remote areas of limited statehood where repression is no longer exercised by the central state, but by powerful local actors including (multinational) private companies. Think South Sudan, for example.

Yet, local power balances are rarely static, and local activists linked up with transnational networks might be able to change the local rights discourse. Moreover, even materially powerful local actors are rarely invulnerable socially, since their rule often depends on being trusted by the local communities. Here, agentic constructivism, in Sikkink's terms, can be combined with a Habermasian perspective on critical discourse attempting to change the behavior and the preferences of actors.[71] My point is that one can apply the "boomerang effect" model[72] to areas of limited statehood targeting local rulers and "big men" rather than central governments. In other words, alignments between local activists working as cultural brokers or translators, on the one hand, and transnational advocacy networks, on the other, can bring about change under these circumstances.

Tobias Berger's work about local justice and gender rights in rural Bangladesh serves as a powerful illustration of this argument.[73] In light of the thorough corruption of the state court system in Bangladesh, even international donors trying to promote the rule of law became increasingly aware that they needed to include non-state justice systems to further their goals. The EU, for example, instituted a program – "Activating the Village Courts" – which used a particular non-state court system in rural Bangladesh to further rights and the rule of law, thereby transforming the state justice system through the village courts. By acknowledging the role of non-state courts in Bangladesh, the EU already tried to localize its understanding of the rule of law and to adapt it to the local context. However, the local translation and implementation of the program transformed it once again. Rather than aligning village courts with the state court system, local implementation transformed them into

---

[71] See Dancy and Sikkink, Chapter 2, this volume; Sikkink, *The Justice Cascade*; Jürgen Habermas, *Faktizität und Geltung. Beiträge zur Diskurstheorie des Rechts und des demokratischen Rechtsstaats* (Frankfurt/Main: Suhrkamp, 1992).
[72] Keck and Sikkink, *Activists Beyond Borders*.
[73] See Berger, "Global Norms and Local Courts," for the following.

another non-state justice system, namely Shalish courts adjudicating according to Islamic legal traditions. Yet, as Berger shows in his study, gender rights were indeed enforced through village-courts-turned-shalish once one condition was met: When local NGOs linking up with the international implementation agency of the EU program mobilized around the village courts, they effectively provided social justice to poor rural women. When such NGOs as "local translators" were not present, village courts simply reproduced the local power structure or were not "activated" at all.

In sum, when local NGOs in Bangladesh translated international gen-der-rights norms into a local context, they grafted these norms onto understandings of Islamic law – thereby transforming the interpretation of Sharia law and greatly improving the accessibility of local informal courts to poor women. The example serves to illustrate the explanatory power of the spiral model in conjunction with a localization and transla-tion perspective to account for human rights change under adverse con-ditions of extremely limited statehood in rural Bangladesh. In this case, social vulnerability of local rulers and power brokers was the scope con-dition enabling discursive change to work and to lead to behavioral transformation.

As the example illustrates, compliance with human rights is possible even under rather adverse conditions of limited statehood where central authorities are unable or unwilling to enforce the law. The mechanisms of the spiral model amended by the localization/translation perspective apply – provided that the local power structure is not too deeply entrenched, that rulers must maintain social trust, and that they are therefore socially vulnerable to local-cum-transnational pressure.

Conclusions

This chapter has made the following points:
1) Human rights research – irrespective of the particular approach – has so far largely ignored the context of limited statehood that is the default condition in the contemporary international system. Scholars and human rights activists alike assumed fully functioning states were capable of enforcing the law. As a result, compliance with human rights norms has been mostly theorized as a question of willingness rather than capacity.
2) Areas of limited statehood are ubiquitous in the international system. However, there is strong variation in areas of limited statehood with regard to human rights protection. While democratizing and demo-cratic states tend to respect (political and civil) rights even in areas of

limited statehood, there is variation among semi-authoritarian states. The puzzle remains why human rights can be protected under conditions of limited statehood even if central state authorities are too weak to enforce compliance.

3) With regard to economic and social rights, actors other than the state often step in to secure them and to provide the respective public services under certain conditions. This includes external actors such as international organizations and foreign aid agencies, but also multinational companies and (I)NGOs.

4) It is more difficult to protect civil and political rights in areas of limited statehood since these are complex tasks. Explaining the puzzle requires looking at scope conditions and mechanisms of human rights change. With regard to scope conditions, regime type and target vulnerability (of local rulers and other potentially rights-violating [non-state] actors) matter. The localization and translation perspectives are particularly useful to account for human rights change even under rather adverse conditions of limited statehood, since they emphasize the crucial role of local as well as transnational brokers linking the local with the global. These approaches nicely complement the socialization mechanisms emphasized by the spiral model, including a Habermasian account of persuasion and arguing.

My discussion of human rights change under conditions of limited statehood aimed to illustrate essentially one major point: The differences between various approaches in human rights research – whether quantitative or qualitative, whether "mainstream" or "critical" – should not be overdone. Localization emphasizes that international norms must resonate with local conditions and understandings in order to shape behavior. However, neither localization nor socialization approaches have sufficiently theorized the role of "translators" or cultural brokers between the global and the local. The major take-home message is that as a result of these translations, both the meanings of international human rights norms and the local context change. Neither the global nor the local can claim pride of place.

7 Grounding the Backlash: Regional Security Treaties, Counternorms, and Human Rights in Eurasia

Alexander Cooley and Matthew Schaaf

Introduction: The Backlash Against Human Rights Promotion in Eurasia

After the dissolution of the Soviet Union, the 1990s provided a brief window of optimism for policymakers and scholars regarding the potential of the Eurasian successor states to adopt liberal norms and international human rights standards. From Minsk to Dushanbe, Eurasian governments signed and ratified the major human rights protocols and committed themselves to upholding these new standards. They joined new regional organizations with Western counterparts and framed their state-building and political challenges in terms of pursuing post-Communist reforms and transitions. At the time, the international system seemed conducive to such pro-liberal transformation and human rights norm diffusion – Western-backed non-governmental organizations freely operated throughout the former Soviet space, regional groups such as the Organization of Security and Cooperation in Europe (OSCE) and the Council of Europe (COE) emphasized democracy and human rights as unquestioned "values dimensions,"[1] and liberal principles went unchallenged as the main normative framework through which the Eurasian states would, at their own pace, integrate with the international system's institutions and standards.

Yet, by the late 1990s, it had become evident that most of the Eurasian states were not meeting these expectations for reform and that the group of East European and post-Soviet states that had begun negotiations to join the European Union were much further down a path of political

An earlier draft of this paper was presented at the 2013 Annual Convention of the International Studies Association, San Francisco. The arguments and opinions expressed in this paper are those of the authors and do not necessarily represent the views of their affiliated organizations.
[1] See Rick Fawn, *International Organizations and Internal Conditionality: Making Norms Matter* (London: Palgrave Macmillan, 2013), 20–56.

reform than those outside of the EU orbit.[2] Eurasian rulers had built up their security services, consolidated control over key economic assets, eliminated or exiled political opponents, and built new states that only gave lip-service to liberal norms and maintaining their international human rights commitments.[3] During the 2000s, the Global War on Terror, as with other parts of the world, led to a securitization of the political and human rights sphere. In addition, the onset of the Color Revolutions in Georgia (2003), Ukraine (2004), and Kyrgyzstan (2005), in which long-time rulers were overthrown on election day following street protests, signaled that to Eurasian rulers, and most importantly the Kremlin, that the West would fund and back democracy and human rights monitors in a bid to destabilize governments and topple regimes.[4]

Thus, from about the mid-2000s, Eurasian elites and authoritarians have been at the forefront of a public backlash against the actors and norms involved in Western human rights and democracy promotion.[5] The countertactics have included placing increasing restrictions on the activities of foreign-sponsored NGOs, challenging the appropriateness of liberal norms by introducing new counternorms of sovereignty and stability, and actively pushing back against the promotion of the Western values agenda within regional organizations such as the OSCE and the COE. During this time, the human rights monitor Freedom House has noted a consistent and unabated decline in its measures of political freedoms and rights in Eurasia and a growth in authoritarianism across the region.[6]

This chapter examines one part of this backlash – the formation of new regional treaties, laws, and counternorms to institutionalize or ground the local pushback against the encroachment of liberal norms. The chapter focuses on the region of Eurasia, but the institutions, processes, and techniques that we identify are rapidly being adopted elsewhere, including across the Middle East, Africa, and Latin America, making Eurasia a bellwether region for understanding the emerging theoretical and practical challenges faced by external human rights promoters and defenders.

---

[2] See Thomas Carothers, "The End of the Transition Paradigm," *Journal of Democracy* 13:1 (2002): 5–21.

[3] See Steven Levitsky and Lucan Way, "The Rise of Competitive Authoritarianism," *Journal of Democracy* 13.2 (2002): 51–65.

[4] See Mark R. Beissinger, "Structure and Example in Modular Political Phenomena: The Diffusion of Bulldozer/Rose/Orange/Tulip Revolutions," *Perspectives on Politics* 2 (2007): 259–276; Lincoln Mitchell, *The Color Revolutions* (Philadelphia: University of Pennsylvania Press, 2012).

[5] Thomas Carothers, "The Backlash against Democracy Promotion," *Foreign Affairs* 85 (2006): 55–68.

[6] Freedom House, *Nations in Transit 2015* (New York: Freedom House, 2015).

In this chapter we focus on the new legal and normative frameworks established in two Eurasian regional treaties – the Shanghai Cooperation Organization and its 2009 Anti-Terror Treaty, and the Minsk Convention (1994) of the Commonwealth of Independent States.

Though signed at different times with different original purposes in mind, both have come to constitute important new fabric for authoritarian rulers to violate international human rights norms and practices as well as consolidate their control over their people. In 2009, the six members of the Shanghai Cooperation Organization (SCO) – China, Russia, Kazakhstan, Kyrgyzstan, Uzbekistan, and Tajikistan– signed a new Anti-Terror agreement at the treaty level.[7] The treaty, ratified soon after by all members, institutionalized a number of forms of extra-territorial cooperation in law enforcement and security, including accepting each other's designation of "terrorists and extremists," allowing member states to conduct investigations on each other's territory, and allowing countries to turn suspects over without a national extradition hearing. Not surprisingly, international human rights groups have sharply criticized the agreement, with one watchdog referring to it as a "vehicle for human rights violations."[8]

The Commonwealth of Independent States (CIS), another grouping of Eurasian states, codified similar norms for legal cooperation among members in its Minsk Convention (formally the Convention on Legal Assistance and Legal Relations in Civil, Family, and Criminal Cases). Ratified by Armenia, Belarus, Kazakhstan, Kyrgyzstan, Moldova, Russia, Tajikistan, Turkmenistan, Uzbekistan, and Ukraine in 1994, the Minsk Convention provides for extra-territorial implementation of member states' laws and court rulings, and expedited extradition.[9] But its use as a legal tool, cited by states to justify extra-territorial cooperation, has increased over the same time period, as has the SCO convention.

The use of the SCO Anti-Terror Treaty and the CIS Minsk Convention by member governments begs the simple theoretical question: Why would Eurasia's authoritarian rulers actually codify this extra-territorial

---

[7] Shanghai Cooperation Organization. "The Convention Against Terrorism of the Shanghai Cooperation Organization," June 16, 2009. Unofficial translation from Russian published by the International Federation for Human Rights, www.fidh.org/The-Convention-Against-Terrorism.

[8] *Shanghai Cooperation Organization: A Vehicle for Human Rights Violations* (Paris: International Federation for Human Rights, 2012).

[9] Commonwealth of Independent States, "Convention on Legal Assistance and Legal Relations in Civil, Family, and Criminal Cases," January 22, 1993. http://base.consul tant.ru/cons/cgi/online.cgi?req=doc;base=LAW;n=5942. Ukraine and Turkmenistan have not formally ratified the CIS charter, but they are participants/associates of the CIS. Ukraine has ratified the Minsk Convention.

cooperation at the treaty level? After all, authoritarians and their security services face few, if any, constraints on their actions. Even if these modes of cooperation were useful, why would authoritarians, who so zealously guard their sovereignty and autonomy, institutionalize them in a treaty that formally confers rights and obligations to other states? Further, human rights scholars have persuasively documented the reverse logic: that authoritarians tend to sign human rights commitments in order to formally appear to comply with international or regional expectations, even if in practice they regularly violate them.[10]

Drawing upon recent evidence from Eurasia, we develop a set of arguments about the political, transactional, and normative advantages that such regional frameworks bestow on authoritarian states – or, more precisely, on groups of authoritarian states. These regional frameworks are now critical weapons in the emerging backlash against liberal values and human rights promotion. Specifically, we argue that these new regional treaties:

1) Enhance executive or regime power by facilitating the targeting of political opponents residing abroad;
2) Reduce the transactions costs of cooperation among security services through the twin processes of blacklisting and logrolling; and
3) Generate counternorms and legal frameworks at the regional level that serve to erode the clarity of these states' international human rights commitments and treaty obligations.

Taken together, these mechanisms have created a new space for authoritarian pushback to international human rights regimes that merits more sustained attention from scholars and practitioners alike.

We begin by briefly reviewing what are usually viewed as the unrelated literatures on the rise of regionalism in world politics and the relationship between formal treaty ratification and human rights compliance. We provide a different perspective on the noted practice of "norm localization" by showing how Eurasian authoritarians are embedding new counternorms and illiberal practices within these new regional frameworks. We then review the relevant legal articles of the SCO and the CIS Minsk Convention that facilitate transnational authoritarian cooperation, and note their specific tensions with existing international human rights obligations and norms. Next, drawing upon both strategic and constructivist logics, we present the three mechanisms through which the regional treaty process benefits autocrats. For each of these mechanisms we provide an

---

[10] See Beth Simmons, *Mobilizing for Human Rights: International Law in Domestic Politics* (New York: Cambridge University Press, 2009); Emilie M. Hafner-Burton et al., "International Human Rights Law and the Politics of Legitimation Repressive States and Human Rights Treaties," *International Sociology* 23 (2008): 115–41.

illustrative case study from the Eurasian region: we compare and contrast the different legal justifications for extraordinary renditions in Eurasia and their impact on the practices of Russia, China and the United States in the region; we examine the effect of blacklisting regional "extremist and terrorist" groups onto a unified SCO list; and we chart how Ukraine steadily eroded its commitments to uphold its treaty obligations under the previous regime by cooperating with the security services of other CIS states, such as Russia and Uzbekistan. In conclusion, we offer some suggestions for broadening this emerging research agenda.

Theory: Regionalism, Treaty Commitments, and Authoritarian Logics

The study of formal inter-authoritarian cooperation within Eurasia and beyond can be instructively situated at the intersection of literatures on the rise of regionalism and international treaty compliance.

Regionalism as a Trend Post-9/11

Regions in world politics are more than geographical groupings – they define categories of social groups and political networks, while varying in their architectures, forms of institutionalization, and external penetration.[11] Rick Fawn observes[12] that the process of coordination and collaboration among actors in an area defines a region as a political entity. He notes that shared values and definitions of security, as well as the more traditionally studied density of economic relations, can define both a region's internal characteristics and its interactions with other actors in the international system. In the security sphere, the so-called Copenhagen School notes how regions themselves can become sites of joint member securitization against a common external threat, or where members, through identifying security concerns, mutually recognize and constitute each other's social identities.[13]

Similarly, as Amitav Acharya's work has shown,[14] regional organizations, especially security organizations, can also serve as sites of mediation

---

[11] Peter J. Katzenstein, *A World of Regions: Asia and Europe in the American Imperium* (Ithaca: Cornell University Press, 2005).

[12] Rick Fawn, "'Regions' and their Study: Where from, What for and Where to?," *Review of International Studies* 35 (2009): 5–34.

[13] Barry Buzan and Ole Waever. *Regions and Powers: The Structure of International Security* New York: Cambridge University Press, 2003).

[14] See Amitav Acharya, *Constructing a Security Community in Southeast Asia* (New York: Routledge, 2009); Amitav Acharya, "How Ideas Spread: Whose Norms Matter? Norm Localization and Institutional Change in Asian Regionalism," *International Organization* 58 (2004): 239–75.

between international norms and more locally based identities and practices. The practice of "localization," according to Acharya, involves both the practices of "pruning" (trimming aspects of norms that are alien or incompatible with local custom) and "grafting" (the process of linking new transnational norms with existing customs and local practice). These pathways and practices for norm diffusion are especially important in non-Western regions as liberal norms and norm diffusers will be rejected if local populations perceive them as alien, moralizing, or incompatible with local practices, values, and beliefs. Thus, norm localization is not only a distinct pathway of norm diffusion – in many cases, it sets the parameters within which certain Western principles can be accepted and gain enduring legitimacy at the regional level.

Regionally, Eurasia has emerged as both a "regional security complex" and a space that mediates the diffusion of, and backlash against, these international norms. Since the 2000s, the region has become embedded within several new regional security governance structures, including the Russian-led Collective Security Treaty Organization and the Chinese-led SCO. Since 2001, it has also become a critical staging area for US and NATO operations in Afghanistan, making it a crossroads of a number of externally driven new security systems.[15] As a result, Central Asia has served as an arena for the US, Russian, and Chinese strategic and normative engagement; meanwhile, the other post-Soviet states have been subjected to the competing push and pulls exerted by the European Union and NATO on the one hand, and Russia on the other.[16] In the Central Asian case, the outcome of these competing influences appears to have been a steady erosion of Western norms, particularly commitments to democracy, and a greater emphasis on state sovereignty, non-interference in domestic affairs, territorial integrity, and counterterrorism, as more formally embodied in the doctrines of the SCO and CSTO.[17]

One good test case for the normative trajectory of Eurasia has been the evolution of the OSCE. Founded as a direct successor to the CSCE, with a strong mandate to promote the "human dimension" and inform its security-related mandate with "Helsinki-style" commitments to

[15] Alexander Cooley, *Great Games, Local Rules: The New Great Power Contest in Central Asia* (New York: Oxford University Press, 2012).

[16] See Roy Allison, "Virtual Regionalism, Regional Structures and Regime Security in Central Asia," *Central Asian Survey* 27 (2008): 185–202; Roy Allison, "Regionalism, Regional Structures and Security Management in Central Asia," *International Affairs* 80 (2004): 463–83.

[17] Stephen Aris. *Eurasian Regionalism: The Shanghai Cooperation Organisation* (London: Palgrave Macmillan, 2011); and Thomas Ambrosio, "Catching the 'Shanghai spirit': How the Shanghai Cooperation Organization Promotes Authoritarian Norms in Central Asia." *Europe-Asia Studies* 60 (2008): 1321–44.

democratic governance and human rights, the organization's "values agenda" has been slowly picked apart and now nearly curtailed, leading some scholars to question whether the organization itself was more a site of anti-Western normative diffusion than a socializing actor in its own right.[18] The organization's mandate to promote democratic rights and practices endure formally, but the efforts of certain Eurasian countries to erode its commitments and implementation infrastructure have had palpable effects.

The Authoritarian Politics of Regime Survival and Regional Treaties

Eurasia's regional practices have also been driven by a clear political logic of authoritarianism and the pursuit of regime survival.[19] From this perspective, Eurasian governments have been quick to use regional security cooperation to both advance their political standing and to shield themselves from international political pressures. As a result, Eurasia's regimes have conflated internal political opposition and external security threats in their understanding and formulation of regional security challenges.

So far, theoretical accounts of the impact of international human rights law have focused mostly on the question of whether international treaty obligations actually constrain authoritarians or lead to any demonstrable human rights improvements. While some scholars find that the ratification of human rights treaties may precipitate marginal improvements in democracies with strong civil societies[20] and in transitioning countries,[21] most studies strongly suggest that human rights treaties do not improve the behavior of authoritarians, and might even encourage worse practices.[22] Hafner-Burton, Tsutsui, and Meyer argue that international treaties provide low-cost opportunities to signal compliance with international norms, even when authoritarians have no intention of complying with their provisions. Simmons speculates that authoritarians in the same region tend to cluster their ratifications, creating a "social camouflage" dynamic where no state can be singled out as a formal outlier to international human rights obligations. Avdeyeva is more cautiously optimistic

---

[18] David Lewis, "Who's Socialising Whom? Regional Organisations and Contested Norms in Central Asia," *Europe-Asia Studies* 64 (2012): 1219–37.

[19] Bueno De Mesquita, Bruce et al., *The Logic of Political Survival* (Cambridge: The MIT Press, 2005).

[20] Eric Neumayer, "Do International Human Rights Treaties Improve Respect for Human Rights?" *Journal of Conflict Resolution* 496 (2005): 925–53.

[21] Simmons, Mobilizing for Human Rights: International Law in Domestic Politics, 64–7.

[22] Hafner-Burton, Tsutsui, and Meyer, "International Human Rights Law and the Politics of Legitimation Repressive States and Human Rights Treaties."

in her examination of post-Communist compliance with international treaties that regulate domestic violence,[23] though the social pressure she notes as important in exerting pressure on governments is clearly lacking in the Central Asian states where the NGO sector and civil society partners are weaker. These are all important findings, but the actual strategies that authoritarians in Eurasia are deploying to push-back against human rights commitments extend well beyond just non-compliance.

Rather, what we see in the Eurasian case is that rulers are actively creating new bodies of law, at the regional level, to institutionalize and justify their illiberal practices and human rights violations. Certain forms of supranationalism, as embodied within regional security organizations and treaties, can provide tools to more effectively clamp down on political opponents, muddy their international legal obligations, and provide an alternative legal framework to justify their actions. As such, and contra Acharya's view that localization translates international norms into local idioms, the regional level now offers an important new international source of counternorms and practices to actually shield governments against international criticism and to ground this backlash in these regional legal and normative frameworks.

The SCO and the Minsk Conventions: Extraterritoriality and Clashes with Human International Rights Standards and Practices

The SCO's Counterterrorism Treaty of 2009 is the latest in a number of new agreements reached by the organization that have established legal frameworks for both regional security cooperation and the construction of an alternative normative fabric. The organization itself was founded on the principle of "non-interference" in members' domestic affairs, often referred to as the "Shanghai Spirit."[24] The organization's charter is also filled with references to celebrating the diversity of civilizations, rejecting unipolarity, and promoting the "democratization of international relations" – all jibes at the Western-led world order and the practice of Western imposed political and economic conditionality.[25] In parallel to its foundational treaty in 2001, the SCO adopted a security convention dedicated to combatting the "three

---

[23] Olga Avdeyeva, "When Do States Comply with International Treaties? Policies on Violence against Women in Post-Communist Countries," *International Studies Quarterly* 51 (2007): 877–900.

[24] Ambrosio, "Catching the 'Shanghai Spirit.'"

[25] Cooley, *Great Games, Local Rules*, 74–5.

evils" of terrorism, separatism, and extremism, a clear reference to China's own domestic security doctrine.[26]

The organization itself emerged out of a group known as the "Shanghai Five" in the 1990s that was tasked with concluding Soviet-era border negotiations between the Central Asian states and China.[27] Officially, the spirit of cooperation was so positive that the forum also was used for discussions on how to promote regional security against transnational threats, especially terrorists and separatists, with Beijing especially concerned about the activities of Uighur groups operating out of Central Asia. The SCO was founded in June 2001, but the subsequent US-led War on Terror gave the group renewed impetus and in 2002 it concluded an agreement to institutionalize security cooperation in a common anti-terrorism center. Opened in Tashkent in 2004, the Regional Anti-Terrorism Structure (RATS) coordinates the efforts of member countries' security services that, by treaty, enjoy full diplomatic immunity, and keeps a common database of regional individuals and organizations accused of terrorism or extremism.[28]

Formalized in the 2005 Cooperation Concept agreement, the main principle of RATS is the commitment to "reciprocal recognition of a terrorist, separatist, or extremist act regardless of whether the legislation of SCO member states includes a corresponding act in the same category of crimes or whether the act is described using the very same terms."[29] Accordingly, the reciprocity of the RATS framework encourages designation of a threat regardless of the threshold of evidence produced or a host country's legislation, including whether the act is even a crime in a host country.

The 2009 Counterterrorism Convention formalizes the extraterritoriality of the principle in a number of important legal ways. Article 10 obliges members to recognize another state's designation of an individual or organization as "terrorist" when they engage in "the planning, organization, preparation, and commission of actions" of "even one of the offenses," regardless of whether the specific elements of the crime, burden of proof or

[26] See Michael Clarke. "Widening the Net: China's Anti-terror Laws and Human Rights in the Xinjiang Uyghur Autonomous Region." *The International Journal of Human Rights* 14 (2010): 542–58; and Shanghai Cooperation Organization, "The Shanghai Convention on Combating Terrorism, Separatism and Extremism." June 15, 2001.

[27] For a critical perspective, see George Gavrilis, *The Dynamics of Interstate Boundaries* (New York: Cambridge University Press, 2008), 121–23.

[28] Shanghai Cooperation Organization, "Protocol on Amendments to the Agreement Between Member States of the Shanghai Cooperation Organization on the Regional Anti- Terrorist Structure," August 16, 2007.

[29] Shanghai Cooperation Organization, "Concept of Cooperation Between SCO Member States in Combating Terrorism, Separatism, and Extremism", June 5, 2005, Principle 3.

standards of evidence meet national law. Article 18 allows members of one country to "dispatch its personnel to the territory" of another member in order to participate in operations and criminal investigations, and Article 14 obliges requests for extraditions to be responded to in the expedited period of just 30 days.

Taken together, these measures clearly conflict with a number of international human rights norms, including standards for considering political asylum, UN recommendations about safeguarding human rights in counterterrorism listings, and the non-refoulement provisions (prohibition of the return of a person to a country where s/he may be at risk to be tortured) of the Convention Against Torture, as well as any safeguards in domestic extradition procedures.[30] These same SCO provisions, when invoked in individual human rights cases, have been criticized or denounced in by the UN Committee Against Torture, the UN Committee on the Elimination of Racial Discrimination, and the Human Rights Committee.[31]

The CIS was created in the ashes of the Soviet Union to serve as the glue that bound what had essentially been regions within a highly centralized state. Over the years the CIS sought to tackle various issues of social, political, and economic relations. Grand plans to replace the Soviet Union with a CIS common economic space, however, have never solidified.[32] Much like the documents underpinning the SCO, the 1993 CIS charter lays out the organization's primary goals, among them facilitating economic, political, and humanitarian cooperation; providing for rights and fundamental freedoms in conformity with generally recognized principles and international law; and mutual legal assistance and cooperation. These goals are to be achieved while recognizing the CIS's guiding principles of, inter alia, sovereignty and independence, territorial integrity, non-interference in internal and external affairs, and ensuring human rights.

Created in the early 1990s when the Soviet Union's monolithic structure had just collapsed, and prior to the emergence of the rainbow of regional economic, political, and security linkages and projects in Eurasia, the CIS reaffirmed the only accepted institutionalized norms still standing at the time. Unlike the SCO, the CIS explicitly draws

[30] See *Shanghai Cooperation Organization: A Vehicle for Human Rights Violations* (Paris: International Federation for Human Rights, 2012); *Counterterrorism and Human Rights: The Impact of the Shanghai Cooperation Organization* (New York: Human Rights in China, 2011).
[31] *Shanghai Cooperation Organization: A Vehicle for Human Rights Violations*, 11.
[32] Martha Brill Olcott, Anders Åslund, and Sherman W. Garnett, *Getting It Wrong: Regional Cooperation and the Commonwealth of Independent States* (Washington, DC: Carnegie Endowment for International Peace, 1999).

inspiration from the Helsinki Final Act and the CSCE and later the OSCE.

Despite these affirmations of shared values embodied by OSCE and UN commitments, the region's values and practices began to reassume their own unique structure and institutionalization through the emergence of counternorms and entities such as those dealing with elections and interstate legal cooperation. The 1994 CIS Minsk Convention governs legal cooperation among CIS members and the legal status and rights of citizens of CIS countries when within the CIS bloc, including in mundane areas such equal access to the law and judicial bodies.

The Minsk Convention also provides for the extra-territorial implementation of procedural norms of one CIS member by the authorities of another CIS member. According to the Convention's Article 8, a country may apply its own domestic procedural norms or the norms of a CIS country seeking legal cooperation, provided the foreign country's norms do not violate domestic law. In effect, the authorities in Ukraine or Belarus could forfeit their own legal norms and procedures in favor of those of Uzbekistan or Turkmenistan when considering civil and criminal legal issues. It is not hard to see how the extra-territorial implementation of legal norms and decisions of a country such as Uzbekistan, infamous for widespread and violent repression, could lead to violations of fundamental due process and other rights in areas such as extradition. Thus, both the Minsk Convention and the SCO provide for extra-territorial implementation of second country laws in the sphere of immigration and extradition and both have been invoked by Eurasian governments to justify forced transfers and the bypassing of domestic extradition procedures.

Regional Mechanism #1: Extra-Territorial Cooperation as Expanding Executive Discretion

Given that the overwhelming political imperative of authoritarians is regime survival, the post-9/11 environment has provided opportunities to executives worldwide to formally open up spaces for "freedom of action" under the pretext of counterterrorism. Routine measures of asserting executive control have included elevating the status of terrorism to a special category crime in national law, monitoring terrorist financing and creating new agencies, increasing surveillance and monitoring domestically, and restricting asylum cases and refugee claims.[33] The

---

[33] Kim Lane Scheppele, "The Migration of Anti-constitutional Ideas: The Post-9/11 Globalization of Public Law and the International State of Emergency," in *Migration of Constitutional Ideas*, ed. Sujit Choudhry (Cambridge: Cambridge University Press, 2006), 347–73.

spread of these new "anti-constitutional" ideas has been rapid and far-reaching, creating a new body: "global security law."

In turn, these changes have networked executives and security services at the transnational level, though this new cooperation has not been accompanied by a corresponding networking of civil society or set of transnational watchdogs to monitor these practices for their effectiveness or abuse. Kim Lane Scheppele sums up:

> Transnational links among national executives, national militaries, national police and national security agencies have been strengthened with the anti-terrorism campaign and links between national executives and their own domestic parliaments and courts have been attenuated. In short, so many countries have complied so quickly with the new international security law because the very national executives who have pushed along these changes also have a strong interest in gaining the power that this new legal regime gives them relative to the other players in their own domestic space.[34]

In turn, this quick adoption of executive-empowering counternorms points to a critical twist in the norm diffusion process from that outlined by Acharya and other scholars of non-Western norm adoption. Though Eurasian rulers have indeed proven reluctant to embrace liberal cosmopolitan norms and human rights values, the Global War on Terror actually provided an overarching framework, originating in the West, from which they readily justified illiberal policies and practices and placed them into a new global normative context. Such an expedient use of norms suggests that the process of "norm grafting" is not so much a matching or translation of global norms into local ones, but a more cynical and practical deployment of both global and local norms to justify executive actions such as increased surveillance, arbitrary detentions, and the clampdown on all "destabilizing" forms of independent political protest and rights monitoring.

Case Study: Executive Power and Extraordinary Renditions – Comparing Russia, China, and the United States

Perhaps the most acute abuse of executive power has been the growing practice of forced abduction and transfer of suspects across borders without due process – a process termed "extraordinary rendition." Since the early 2000s, dozens of accused terrorists and extremists have been forcibly transferred within and out of Eurasia by signatories of the SCO treaty and Minsk conventions. In the SCO case, it appears that the two main vectors of transfers have taken suspected Central Asians from

---

[34] Scheppele, "The Migration of Anti-constitutional Ideas," 5.

Russia back to their home countries, mostly in Uzbekistan, and Uighurs from Russia and Central Asia to China.

Prominent Chinese rendition cases include those of Celil Huseyn, an ethnic Uighur granted Canadian citizenship in 2001, who was abducted in 2006 while visiting relatives in Uzbekistan and then sentenced to life in prison in China. More recently, in May 2011 Kazakhstan extradited Arshadin Israil, a Uighur refugee and journalist who had covered the 2009 Urumqi riots, back to China under the SCO accord, despite Israil having been granted political asylum status by UNCHR in Almaty and accepted for resettlement by Sweden.[35]

Of the Russian cases, most appear clearly motivated as requests by Central Asian governments to seize and detain political opponents. The European Court of Human Rights (ECHR), the court responsible for applying the European Convention of Human Rights, has considered 18 such cases since 2007, most of them involving citizens of Uzbekistan or Tajikistan abducted or otherwise forcibly transferred from Russian territory to Central Asia. The most well known of these is the case of Mahmadruzi Iskandarov, leader of the Democratic Party of Tajikistan and outspoken critic of Tajikistan's President Rahmon, who was abducted on April 15, 2005, from outside his home in exile in Moscow. Iskandarov was forcibly detained for two days without being shown an arrest or detention order, before being forcibly transported by plane from Moscow to Dushanbe, where he entered the country under an alias. At the airport he was met by officials from the Tajik Ministry of Interior, taken directly into custody, and then sentenced to 23 years in prison. Iskandarov had been wanted by Tajik authorities on a long list of charges, including terrorism, fraud, and embezzlement of property.[36]

Strikingly, the abduction took place just days after a Russian prosecutor had refused a formal extradition request by Tajikistan, for lack of evidence, as well as just after a high-level meeting between the Tajik president and Russian Defense Minister Sergei Ivanov. Though Russian officials deny any knowledge or involvement in the episode, Tajik officials, in a communication to the ECHR, stated that the transfer involved official cooperation between the two governments consistent with their international counterterrorism treaties.[37]

Russian and Ukrainian human rights groups have tracked and studied secret renditions by special services across the region, and especially from Russia, to countries in Central Asia such as the case of Iskandarov noted

---

[35] "Kazakhstan Extradites Uygur Journalist," RFE/RL, June 7, 2011.

[36] Andrei Soldatov and Irina Borogan, *The New Nobility: The Restoration of Russia's Security State and the Enduring Legacy of the KGB* (New York: PublicAffairs, 2010), 219–220.

[37] Soldatov and Borogan, *The New Nobility*; and Cooley, *Great Games, Local Rules*, 106.

above. Following the case of Leonid Razvozzhaev, who was abducted from Kiev and transported to Moscow, one noted how "these disappearances occur when a person is needed in a neighboring country but the chances of receiving that person through legal procedures is small."[38]

The trajectory of these renditions and abductions, facilitated by the SCO and Minsk Convention, can be instructively compared with the renditions carried out by the United States in the immediate post 9/11 period. According to Dick Marty, special investigator for the COE, the CIA operated at least 1,245 rendition flights through European airspace.[39] Tashkent seemed to be a critical destination from these European locations, with one author of a comprehensive study terming it "a vital hub," and noting that "no other destination east of Jordan had received so many flights from the CIA fleet."[40] Other news reports published accounts of the frequent flights, usually undertaken by defense contractors such as Blackwater, which transported detainees between Afghanistan and Uzbekistan.[41] These accounts were further corroborated by a global inventory of renditions and black site detention centers carried out by the Open Society Justice Initiative.[42]

But there was a major legal distinction between these US renditions and their Russian and Chinese counterparts. Unlike Russia and China, which have justified renditions as part of obligations to regional and international anti-terror treaties, US officials initially sanctioned these flights as part of the executive's expanded new powers in the Global War on Terror. According to Margaret Satterthwaite,[43] much like its legal approach to the torture debate, Bush administration officials tried to place the conduct of renditions in a legal space "free of the constraints placed on it of human rights and humanitarian law."

This attempt to legally locate the rendition program beyond the law has arguably curtailed its broad sustainability. Unlike the extra-territorial use of Guantanamo Bay, whose legal justification dates back to a number of

---

[38] Aleksandr Artemev and Ekaterina Vinokurova, "Sojuz nezavisimyh pohititelej," [Union of Independent Kidnappers], *Gazeta.ru*, October 25, 2012. www.gazeta.ru/politics/2012/10/25_a_4824453.shtml.
[39] Dick Marty, "Secret Detentions and Illegal Transfers of Detainees Involving Council of Europe Member States: Second Report." Council of Europe Doc. 11302 (June 7, 2007).
[40] Stephen Grey. *Ghost Plane: The True Story of the CIA Torture Program.* New York: Macmillan, 2006, 181.
[41] Jeremy Scahill, *Blackwater: The Rise of the World's Most Powerful Mercenary Army* (New York: Nation Books, 2007), 309–10.
[42] Amrit Singh, *Globalizing Torture: CIA Secret Detention and Extraordinary Rendition* (New York: Open Society Foundations Justice Initiative, 2013).
[43] Margaret L. Satterthwaite, "Rendered Meaningless: Extraordinary Rendition and the Rule of Law," *The George Washington Law Review* 75, no. 5–6 (2006): 1333–420.

pre 9/11 cases,[44] the media scrutiny surrounding renditions and possible "torture flights" has now limited their use. By Executive Order in January 2009, the Obama administration announced that it would close its "black site" overseas detention facilities and order an investigation into rendition practices. It has not disavowed the practice, but it appears its use as a standard tool has been greatly cut back (though not eliminated). As the Open Society Justice Initiative report notes, the courts have failed to hold the executive accountable for any abuses, while not a single case brought by a rendition victim has made it passed the merits stage at a US court.[45]

In contrast, the fact that rendition practices were embedded now within SCO and the Minsk Convention seem to have contributed to their sustainability. Indeed, there seems to have been no significant drop off in the number of reports of possible forced abductions and renditions, even though the ECHR seems increasingly concerned by such cases. In February 2012 the ECHR sent Russia a letter of concern about the plight of a group of Central Asian applicants who allegedly had been rendered to their host countries from Russia. Referred to as the "Garabayev list," named after a political dissident who was extradited to Turkmenistan, the group comprises 18 cases brought to the court from 2007 to 2011, most of them citizens from Uzbekistan and Tajikistan who were forcibly abducted. According to another report, between August 2011 and October 2012 at least 7 foreigners in Russia were secretly deported.[46]

Though it is still very early to reach any definitive judgment, so far the embedding of renditions and abductions within the SCO and Minsk Convention frameworks has both empowered executive discretion and sustained these practices, making them more durable than the similar practices carried out in the early years of the Bush administration.

Regional Mechanism #2: Reducing Transaction Costs – The SCO Consolidated List and Logrolling

Second, embedding authoritarian relations within treaties and permanent institutions may increase cooperation by reducing transaction costs. Neoliberal institutionalists have long noted that international institutions and regimes, even when assuming self-interested states, may be advantageous to states by providing monitoring mechanisms, increasing iteration,

---

[44] Jonathan M. Hansen, "A History of Legal Impunity at Guantánamo Bay," *Diplomatic History* 35 (2011): 905–8.

[45] Singh, *Globalizing Torture: CIA Secret Detention and Extraordinary Rendition*, 21.

[46] Artemev and Vinokurova, "Union of Independent Kidnappers."

pooling information, and facilitating issue-linkage among states.[47] Such instrumental reasoning about the functions of institutions is usually made in reference to institutions that govern economic areas such as trade, finance, and development assistance.

Yet, reducing transaction costs may also be of great benefit to authoritarian states that choose to cooperate on security matters through regional institutions. We have already observed how the principle of reciprocity – a key mechanism of cooperation for regime theorists[48] – in the form of mutual recognition of regime threats is the founding principle of extra-territorial cooperation within the SCO. But the organization has also created common databases of security threats (either perceived or politically motivated), common monitoring procedures, and forums for exchanging information, all valuable for anticipating and targeting regime threats. Institutionalizing these practices in a permanent organization that can, in turn, foster issue-linkage among the different concerns of cooperating authoritarians is also potentially valuable. Analytically, authoritarians may find that international regimes and institutions provide many of the benefits that states get from participating in public goods or economic regimes, the difference being that benefits in the authoritarian case will flow directly to the executive and its security services rather than the state as whole.

One of the most common tools of international counterterrorism that has proliferated over the last decade is the blacklist. De Goede estimates that there are 214 blacklists of terrorist groups and individuals worldwide, including the UN Security Council 1267 Sanctions List, the US Office of Foreign Asset Control (OFAC) Blacklisting and discrepancies, the EU list, and then numerous other regional and national lists.[49] In practice, blacklisting can be used in extradition procedures, to justify international criminal warrants, and as a basis for targeting the assets and finances of individuals and groups.

In terms of its human rights implications, listing is itself fraught, because of both the tricky and politicized definitional issues of what constitutes a terrorist group, and the need to ensure procedural safeguards for groups and individuals that have been mistakenly listed to appeal their designation. Most listing organizations do not have

---

[47] Robert O. Keohane, *After Hegemony: Cooperation and Discord in the World Political Economy* (Princeton: Princeton University Press, 1984).

[48] See Robert Axelrod, "The Emergence of Cooperation among Egoists," *The American Political Science Review* 75 (1981): 306–18; Kenneth Oye, *Cooperation under Anarchy* (Princeton: Princeton University Press, 1986).

[49] Marieke De Goede, "Blacklisting and the Ban: Contesting Targeted Sanctions in Europe," *Security Dialogue* 42 (2011): 499–15.

mechanisms for judicial oversight and lack clear evidentiary standards in listing procedures.[50] Listing organizations comprised of authoritarian states or aggregating information from such states would be especially likely to omit such human rights and judicial safeguards. Similar criticisms have been made of authoritarian states' abuse of Interpol's "red flag" system, with one study singling out several Eurasian states for using the system to pursue political opponents.[51]

Case Study: The SCO-RATS Consolidated List

The evolution of the SCO's Consolidated list of "terrorists and extremists," under the institutional auspices of the group's Regional Anti-Terror Structure (RATS), suggests both increasing cooperation and clear violations of international standards in listing procedures and oversight. RATS, based in Tashkent, emerged out of a 2002 Counterterrorism initiative signed in Saint Petersburg and involved the creation of a permanent institutional structure where the security and intelligence services of the member states could institutionalize their cooperation. Organizationally, RATS officials report directly to their respective Ministries of Interior, not the SCO's Secretariat in Beijing, while the foundational agreement also provides diplomatic immunity for RATS officials in other member states.

The RATS consolidated list features individuals and organizations deemed to pose a threat to regional security or embody one of the "three evils" – terrorism, separatism, and extremism. The list appears to be generating horse-trading or "logrolling" among member states, as each country lists its own threats in exchange for agreeing to other countries doing the same. In 2006, the first RATS Council placed 15 organizations and 400 individuals on the list. The next year, the consolidated list had exploded to 42 organizations and 944 individuals. Then, at an April 2010 meeting, the RATS Director Dhzenisbek Dzhumanbekov revealed that the database listed 42 organizations and 1,100 individuals sought in connection with "terrorist and extremist activities."[52] RATS has not followed through on its earlier pledges that promised to make the members of the list public information.

---

[50] Gavin Sullivan and Ben Hayes, *Blacklisted: Targeted Sanctions, Preemptive Security and Fundamental Rights* (Berlin: European Center for Constitutional and Human Rights, 2011).

[51] Libby Lewis, "Interpol's Red Notices used by some to pursue political dissenters, opponents." ICIJ, www.icij.org/project/interpols-red-flag/interpols-red-notices-used-some-pursue-political-dissenters-opponents.

[52] *Counterterrorism and Human Rights: The Impact of the Shanghai Cooperation Organization*, 86.

By allowing each authoritarian regime the definitional flexibility to designate its particular threat and place it on the list, RATS has seemingly fostered reciprocity and issue-linkage, without any accompanying protections or concern for the rights of the listed. In 2009, the United Nations Special Rapporteur on Counterterrorism and Human Rights, Martin Scheinin, expressed "serious concerns" about SCO data-sharing practices and listing procedures, noting that "this sharing of data and information is not subject to any meaningful form of oversight and there are no human rights safeguards attached to data and information sharing."[53]

In turn, the logrolling and reciprocity promoted by RATS-SCO appear to have led to a number of changes in actual policy by countries. For example, the Islamic group Hizb ut Tahrir (HuT) was only placed on the Russian nationalist of terrorist organizations in 2005, while just a year later, at a RATS meeting, Russia's FSB director confirmed that Russia had transferred 19 terror suspects to Uzbekistan, all of them accused of being members of HuT.[54]

Regional Mechanism #3: Muddying the Waters: Creating Regional Counternorms to Erode International Legal Commitments

Third, institutionalizing authoritarian cooperation at the regional level has the potential to generate broader counternorms that, over time, can erode longer-standing universal commitments. Rather than just shielding their activities from international scrutiny, creating new regional law provides autocrats with new norms that qualify, exempt, and justify actions that otherwise might constitute clear violations of international commitments. Counternorms, in other words, need not be broadly accepted as legitimate or sanctioned by international bodies. Rather, if they can be strategically deployed to "muddy the legal waters," they provide useful legal and normative cover for autocrats.

Regional treaties offer ideal vehicles for this purpose, precisely because they have grown to occupy a growing mediating space between national practices and international legal commitments, especially in the post 9/11 world. Take the issue of election monitoring and international observation that has emerged as an international norm even in authoritarian

---

[53] Martin Scheinin, *Report of the Special Rapporteur on the Promotion and Protection of Human Rights and Fundamental Freedoms While Countering Terrorism* (December 28, 2009), UN Doc. A/HRC/13/37.

[54] See Soldatov and Borogan, *The New Nobility*.

states.[55] Both the SCO and the CIS have established their own "election observers" missions, mostly as a response to the consistent criticism that Central Asian elections received from the OSCE's established monitoring missions run by its Office for Democratic Initiatives and Human Rights (ODIHR). These bodies seemingly seek to emulate the form, but not the substance, of the ODIHR in an effort to contest its authority and critical findings.[56] Their assessments of Central Asian elections are strikingly positive compared to the ODHIR's. Neither regional body has adopted the United Nations Code of Conduct for International Election Observation. Yet, as Judith Kelley points out,[57] their presence erodes the authority and clarity of the more established observer, especially when they are given media coverage by authoritarian governments. For example, while in December 2007 the ODHIR sharply criticized the conduct of the Kyrgyz parliamentary elections that were orchestrated by President Kurmanbek Bakiyev to consolidate his grip on power, both CIS and SCO monitors certified the legitimacy and legality of the poll.[58]

In recent years, the deployment of shadow or "zombie" observers by authoritarians appears to have become a critical part of their local legitimization strategies and an important counter against Western criticism that polls have not met international standards. For example, of more than 40 election observation missions that monitored the 2013 Azerbaijani Presidential election – which re-elected President Ilham Aliyev with 85 percent of the vote – only the ODHIR issued a critical assessment, while first-time monitoring outfits from the United States, the Caribbean, and Latin America all certified the vote as "transparent" and "free and fair."[59] And in the elections organized by separatists in October 2014 in the Donbass region of Ukraine, local officials made it a point to invite "international observers" that were mostly drawn from European far-right and far-left parties.[60] Despite the EU and the OSCE condemning the vote as "illegal," one observation mission self-identified as the Agency for Security and Cooperation in Europe (ASCE), a clear

[55] Susan D. Hyde, *The Pseudo-Democrat's Dilemma: Why Election Monitoring Became an International Norm* (Ithaca: Cornell University Press, 2011).

[56] Rick Fawn. "Battle over the Box: International Election Observation Missions, Political Competition and Retrenchment in the Post-Soviet Space." *International Affairs* 82 (2006): 1133–53.

[57] Judith Kelley, "The More the Merrier? The Effects of Having Multiple International Election Monitoring Organizations," *Perspectives on Politics* 7 (2009): 59–64.

[58] Alexander Cooley, "The League of Authoritarian Gentlemen," *Foreign Policy*, January 30, 2013.

[59] Christopher Walker and Alexander Cooley, "Vote of the Living Dead," *Foreign Policy*, October 31, 2013.

[60] Anton Shkehotsov, "Fake Monitors 'Observe' Fake Lections in Donbass," *The Interpreter*, November 2, 2014.

attempt to mimic the OSCE. Indeed, further confusion prevailed when Russian media started conflating the ASCE's presence at the separatist poll with the OSCE, a charge that prompted vigorous denials from OSCE officials.

Similarly, in the realm of counterterrorism, Scheppele notes that the diffusion of counter-constitutional ideas has often spread via regional organizations that have been tasked to formulate their own counterterrorism procedures, ideas, and standards.[61] But the exact normative struggles have varied significantly. While some organizations, such as the EU, ASEAN, and the African Union, have struggled to craft and revise regional standards, the Eurasian groups have been more ready to, in Acharya's formulation, "graft" the emerging norm of counterterrorism onto clusters of different groups, organizations, and behaviors, all of which are political targets for one or more of the member state regimes.[62] China's attempt to link Uighur groups with Al-Qaeda immediately following 9/11 is just one noteworthy example.

Practically, regional treaties help autocrats to justify bypassing institutional checks and constraints, such as domestic extradition procedures, political asylum hearings, and the protection of international human rights law (such as the Convention Against Torture). They might even be used to revoke national citizenship or used to justify arbitrary detention. The latter seems especially important for justifying cooperation within a cluster of authoritarian countries which, by having signed treaties such as the Convention Against Torture, might in all cases be subject to international sanction over violations of the non-refoulement provision that mandates that a "State party cannot return an individual if a risk of torture exists in the receiving State."

There are growing signs that Central Asian officials are now actively invoking both the SCO and the Minsk obligations as justification for returning suspects to countries in violation of this provision. For example, in June 2010, Kazakhstan extradited 29 political asylum seekers to Uzbekistan. Kazakhstani prosecutors justified the extradition under both the Minsk and SCO accords, stating that the complainants were involved in "illegal organizations" and accused of "attempts to overthrow the constitutional order"; however, a subsequent letter from the UN CAT asserted forcefully that Kazakh authorities had still violated the non-refoulement obligation.[63]

---

[61] Scheppele, "The Migration of Anti-constitutional Ideas: The Post-9/11 Globalization of Public Law and the International State of Emergency."
[62] Ambrosio, "Catching the 'Shanghai Spirit.'"
[63] Alexander Cooley, "The League of Authoritarian Gentlemen," *Foreign Policy*, January 30, 2013.

More recently, the watchdog Human Rights Watch, in its attempt to clarify the actual legal hierarchy of commitments, while discussing the proposed extradition to Uzbekistan of Khabibullo Sulaimanov from Kyrgyzstan, noted that international treaty obligations took precedent over these emerging regional commitments:

> these international obligations [international human rights law treaties] prevail over Kyrgyzstan's obligations under bilateral and regional agreements relating to extradition, such as the Convention on Legal Assistance and Conflicts of Law in Matters of Civil, Family and Criminal Law (The Minsk Convention), or agreements between members of the Shanghai Cooperation Organization (SCO). Extraditing Mr. Sulaimanov would constitute a serious breach of Kyrgyzstan's obligations under international law and call into question Kyrgyzstan's willingness to respect its international commitments.[64]

Case Study: Ukraine's Increasingly Muddied Legal Practices

To illustrate this dynamic, we turn to a brief assessment of Ukraine and its fluid legal practices under previous regimes. Under successive administrations, Ukraine has regularly cooperated with authoritarian and democratic governments and is party to the main institutions on both sides: the Minsk Convention on the one hand; and the main UN human rights instruments, the Helsinki Final Act and associated OSCE agreements, and the European Convention on Human Rights on the other. Ukraine's steps to adopt apparently contradictory normative law likely reflects tumultuous domestic political jockeying such as occurred during the Orange Revolution and the Euromaidan events, and frequent efforts to influence Ukrainian internal and external affairs from neighboring countries such as Russia to the East and members of the European Union to the West. Ukraine's constant position on a geographical and political fulcrum, sometimes moving in one direction and other times moving in the other, provides some instructive cases to consider the nature and effect of extraterritoriality.

In 2006, Ukraine was widely condemned for returning to Uzbekistan 10 Uzbek political refugees who were actively seeking asylum in Ukraine. The 10 political refugees were among a larger group of several hundred Uzbekistani citizens who fled the country following the 2005 violent government crackdown in the city of Andijon. The Uzbeks who fled to Ukraine, and many of the others who fled elsewhere, were accused in

---

[64] Human Rights Watch, Letter to the Prosecutor General of the Kyrgyz Republic, February 1, 2013. www.hrw.org/news/2013/02/01/human-rights-watch-letter-prosecutor-general-kyrgyzstan.

connection with the Andijon case. Of the 10 returned, 9 had already filed for asylum status and one was preparing to do so.

Up until the 2006 case, Ukraine was widely perceived as a safe country for those fleeing political persecution in other countries of the Former Soviet Union. The decision to return the 10 refugees was roundly criticized by Ukraine's European neighbors and representatives of international organizations as being illegal. The Belgian OSCE Chairman-in-Office at the time called the forcible repatriation of asylum seekers "a serious violation of the principle of non-refoulement and of international commitments undertaken by Ukraine, namely the 1951 UN Refugee Convention and the 1984 Convention Against Torture to both of which Ukraine is signatory."[65] The return also likely violated Ukraine's obligations under Article 3 of the European Convention on Human Rights, which is interpreted to prohibit refoulement. Reports indicate that upon their return, all 10 were convicted on trumped-up charges and sentenced to terms ranging from 3 to 13 years.[66]

Through 2010, extraditions in Ukraine were governed exclusively by the Minsk Convention and bilateral agreements,[67] which are conspicuously inconsistent with the above-mentioned treaties and their restrictions on refoulement. Reforms introduced in 2010 and 2011 somewhat clarified domestic procedures and rules for considering extradition requests and strengthened protections. Under the Minsk Convention's Articles 56–71, signatories are generally obligated to accept the court rulings and other judgments of other signatory countries by carrying out extraditions based on simple requests in cases where the person is wanted or convicted on criminal charges. While the Minsk Convention allows signatories to reject extradition requests in limited circumstances, it does not pertain to cases where there are concerns that the charges are politically motivated or if it is likely that the person would be abused or tortured if extradited.[68] While under the SCO, extra-territorial cooperation is

---

[65] OSCE, "OSCE Chairman Expresses Consternation at Ukraine's Decision to Return Uzbek Asylum Seekers" February 17, 2006. www.osce.org/cio/47117.

[66] No Borders Project, "Pjataja godovshhina prinuditel'nogo vydvorenija 11 uzbekskih bezhencev – povtoritsja li ih istorija opjat'?" [Fifth Anniversary of Forced Deportation of 11 Uzbek Refugees – Will History Repeat Itself?], February 15, 2011. http://noborders.org.ua/ru/o-nas/novosti/pyataya-hodovschyna-prynudytelnoho-vyidvorenyya-11-uzbekskyh-bezhentsev-%E2%80%93-povtorytsya-ly-yh-ystoryya-opyat. [Original link expired, now found at: https://webcache.googleusercontent.com/search?q=cache:FNhsjLiKJ1QJ:helsinki.org.ua/index.php%3Fid%3D1297772627±&cd=1&hl=en&ct=clnk].

[67] No Borders Project, "Bezhency v Ukraine – bez prava na ubezhishhe." [Refugees in Ukraine – without a right to protection], 2012. http://noborders.org.ua/ru/files/2012/01/Refugees-in-Ukraine_short-overview.pdf.

[68] Commonwealth of Independent States, Convention on Legal Assistance and Legal Relations in Civil, Family, and Criminal Cases.

required regardless of national law, the Minsk Convention extradition procedures apply only to persons accused of acts that are considered crimes in both countries. A politically motivated conviction for terrorism, however, or any other crime recognized in both countries could spark extradition regardless of the veracity of the allegations or quality of the process.

As was the case with the 10 Uzbeks who were returned in 2006, acceptance of court decisions and rulings of other countries has conspired with weak protections and governance in Ukraine to lead to the extradition of numerous people who were likely to suffer persecution or abuse upon return, in clear violation of international law. In most cases, however, due to a lack of transparency, the authorities generally do not state publicly which procedures are being followed in an extradition case. In fact, in 2007, the UN High Commission for Refugees expressed concern "over the state of general respect for human rights and refugee protection in line with international standards," highlighting inadequate domestic procedural safeguards, inadequate inclusion of international obligations into domestic law, "manifestly unfounded clauses by the Migration Services and the lack of respect for due process of court procedures."[69]

Despite numerous amendments to immigration statutes, including amendments to the criminal procedure code bringing them into line with international standards on refugee return, the Ukrainian authorities in 2012 extradited a Russian and an Uzbek citizen "recognized as refugees by the United Nations High Commissioner for Refugees (UNHCR) who faced a clear risk of torture" upon return.[70] Commenting on the case of the Russian asylum seeker who was returned in August 2012, the UNHCR said that "10 years after Ukraine acceded to the 1951 Refugee Convention, refugees still cannot enjoy protection from persecution in Ukraine," and that "we continue to observe the practice of deliberate violation of provisions of both national and international law." The UNHCR representative further reiterated that "the obligation to respect the principle of non-refoulement as provided for under international refugee and human rights law takes precedence over any duty to extradite on the basis of a bilateral or multilateral extradition agreement,"[71] such as the Minsk Convention. Much like RATS, by generally accepting

[69] UNHCR, "UNHCR Position on the Situation of Asylum in Ukraine in the Context of Return of Asylum-Seekers," October 2007. www.unhcr.org/refworld/docid/472f43162.html.

[70] *World Report 2013: Ukraine* (New York: Human Rights Watch, 2013). www.hrw.org/world-report/2013/country-chapters/ukraine.

[71] UNHCR, "The UN Refugee Agency condemns refoulement of a refugee to Russian Federation," August 17, 2012. www.unhcr.org/502e576c9.html.

decisions, rulings, and norms of other CIS countries, the Minsk Convention gives countries seeking the extradition of an individual the flexibility to designate criminals and seek their extradition.

Two more recent high-profile cases further illustrate how the Ukrainian government has, based on unverified claims of its authoritarian neighbors and partners, willfully ignored its other international obligations to protect people from torture. In one case, a former prime minister of Tajikistan and internationally recognized refugee was detained upon arriving at the airport in Kyiv in February 2013 on an extradition request from the Tajik government. Abdumalik Abdulladjanov was traveling on a US-issued travel document with a valid Ukrainian visa. In a statement, the UNHCR noted that "since Mr. Abdoulladjanov's return to his country of origin would violate both international and domestic law, his continued detention for extradition purposes lacks a legitimate purpose."[72] Abdulladjanov, an opponent of President Rahmon in Tajikistan's 1994 presidential elections and, like Mahmadruzi Iskandarov, a critic of President Rahmon, is wanted in Tajikistan on allegations that are widely believed to be politically motivated. While eventually released by the Ukrainian authorities before he was returned to Tajikistan, Abdulladjanov's detention shows how even clearly problematic extradition requests are given the benefit of the doubt by the Ukrainian authorities.

The case of Leonid Razvozzhaev hints at deeper and less transparent modes of extra-territorial cooperation among governments in Eurasia, and could even point to the operation of one country's security services in the territory of another country, with or without the second country's knowledge. Razvozzhaev, a Russian political activist and assistant to a member of Russia's Duma (parliament), had fled Russia in 2012 to escape charges of organizing mass disorder in connection with a demonstration that took place in Moscow in May 2012. Razvozzhaev is one of many accused in the so-called Bolotnoe case. Razvozzhaev was apparently forcibly returned to Russia after officially seeking asylum in Ukraine, a status which should preclude his return until the request is considered by the competent authorities. While taking a break during a meeting with legal advisers that work with the UNHCR in Kyiv, Razvozzhaev disappeared in an especially brazen affront to international human rights law. Days later, he reappeared in Russia claiming that he had been captured in Ukraine and forcibly returned to Russia, where he allegedly suffered severe psychological abuse. Razvozzhaev was sentenced to 4.5 years in a

---

[72] UNHCR, "UNHCR asks Ukraine to free detained refugee, decline extradition request," March 20, 2013. www.unhcr.org/5149c9cb6.html.

penal colony by a Russian court in July 2014.[73] It is unclear if Razvozzhaev's story is accurate, and, if it is, who detained and deported him to Russia. A spokesperson for the Ukrainian Ministry of Internal Affairs said that "it wasn't criminals [who kidnapped him], or terrorists, it was a foreign special operation on Ukrainian territory." The spokesperson also hinted that Russia's Federal Security Service (or FSB) was responsible.[74] It is unclear what role the Ukrainian authorities played in Razvozzhaev's capture and deportation, but it is well known that Russia's security services do operate in neighboring countries.[75]

Whereas we noted earlier how extra-territorial cooperation could in fact expand executive discretion and reduce transaction costs, it is unclear why Ukraine's various governments with their differing political orientations regularly circumvent national and international law to extradite persons wanted in other countries. Ukraine's extraditions to Uzbekistan and Tajikistan are unlikely to be practically reciprocated as those countries are not locations where Ukrainians fleeing persecution typically seek refuge.

Perceptions that Ukraine was economically and politically beholden to Russia prior to the Euromaidan events may hint at why the Ukrainian government extended Russian extraterritoriality to Ukrainian soil and even allowed Russian agents to operate in its territory. With another new government in Ukraine, however, one with an official orientation toward European institutions and democratic governance, we should expect a new approach. With former Ukrainian officials implicated in crimes and human rights abuses, chief among them former President Yanukovich, seeking refuge in Russia, Ukraine has tellingly turned to Interpol, an institution that adheres to some procedural and due-process guarantees but has itself been accused of facilitating politically motivated extraditions, to seek their extradition. Indeed, in January 2015, Interpol issued a "red notice" warrant for several former Ukrainian officials.[76] While hundreds of thousands of Ukrainians fled to Russia in 2014, including former President Yanukovich and his associates, Russia is

---

[73] Andrew Roth, "Russia: 2 Activists Sent to Prison Colony," *New York Times*, July 24, 2014. www.nytimes.com/2014/07/25/world/europe/russia-2-activists-sent-to-prison-colony.html.

[74] Aleksandr Artemev and Ekaterina Vinokurova, "Sojuz nezavisimyh pohititelej," [Union of Independent Kidnappers], *Gazeta.ru*, October 25, 2012. www.gazeta.ru/politics/2012/10/25_a_4824453.shtml.

[75] Andrei Soldatov, "The FSB Opens a New Foreign Front," *The Moscow Times*, March 18, 2013. www.themoscowtimes.com/opinion/article/the-fsb-opens-a-new-foreign-front/477005.html.

[76] Maxim Tucker, "Interpol rejects Ukrainian murder charges against ex-officials," *The Kyiv Post*, January 12, 2015. www.kyivpost.com/content/kyiv-post-plus/interpol-rejects-ukrainian-murder-charges-against-ex-officials-377233.html.

unlikely to return any of them, seeing them as a political club to batter the Ukrainian government and the West. As a result, seeking extradition through Interpol as opposed to under the Minsk Convention or a bilateral agreement with Russia is likely Ukraine's only hope for the extradition of former President Yanukovich and his associates should they decide to travel to a country that will act upon the Interpol warrant.

Conclusions

This chapter has explored the theoretical and practical underpinnings of how regional treaties are providing new legal, institutional, and normative frameworks for Eurasia's backlash against liberal norms and Western human rights promotion. The Eurasian cases suggest that the extraterritoriality institutionalized in SCO and CIS agreements are increasingly being invoked by authoritarians to expand their executive power, facilitate internal security cooperation, and generate counternorms that erode their standing commitments to international human rights conventions. Authoritarians are not just refusing to comply with their international legal and normative commitments – they are actively constructing new frameworks, at the regional level, to ground their violations, counternorms, and backlash against the human rights project. Contra arguments about how regional organizations can help to translate and hence localize prevailing international norms, these new regional frameworks both oppose and erode the influence of the international human rights monitoring architecture.

Whether such regional bodies can generate a widely accepted set of counternorms that actually substitutes for major Western human rights principles remains to be seen. Here, some interesting differences characterize the respective approaches of Russia and China. For Moscow, its set of counternorms is increasingly emphasizing the importance of traditional values, religion, and a strong anti-LGBT agenda to push back against the encroachment of perceived "Western moral decay" in the Eurasia region.[77] Indeed, in an international normative battle over Kyrgyzstan, the small Central Asian state alarmed civil society members and global LGBT advocates by passing a law in October 2014, copying a Russian version, that introduced criminal punishments for "popularizing homosexual relations" and "propaganda of a homosexual way of life."[78]

[77] Alexander Lukin, "What the Kremlin is Thinking: Putin's Vision for Eurasia." *Foreign Affairs* 93, no. 4 (July-August 2014) 85–93.
[78] Olga Dzyubenko, "U.S. Raps Kyrgyzstan for Proposed Gay Propaganda Law," *Reuters*, October 13, 2014. www.reuters.com/article/us-rights-kyrgyzstan-gay-idUSKCN0I20HR 20141013.

For Beijing, the antithesis of liberal values seems to be more in the lines of the SCO's principles of "civilizational diversity" and non-interference.

This analysis has focused on Eurasia, but the underlying logic of regional treaties and the networking of authoritarians could apply to other areas as well. Intriguingly, the recent signing of a Security Pact by the members of the Gulf Cooperation Council (GCC) suggests that many of the same extra-territorial, listing, and data-sharing measures enabled by the SCO and Minsk treaties have also been institutionalized among the GCC states. Similarly, Sabatini's observations[79] that Latin American states are increasingly engaged in "meaningless multilateralism" points to their use of regional organizations to champion national sovereignty and pushback against the encroachment of US hegemony and international norms on human rights and democracy. In these cases, as with Eurasia, the lines between "norm localization" and "norm displacement" are increasingly being blurred.

One noteworthy theoretical and practical observation that emerges from the study of this "new regionalism" is that of lack of regional leadership on these normative issues. Regional powers, or so-called swing states, appear to be deferring to members on so-called values questions precisely because they do not wish to be perceived as representatives of the West or moralizing regional hegemons. Whether it is Kazakhstan in Central Asia, Qatar in the Gulf, Turkey in the Middle East, Brazil in Latin America, or South Africa in Africa, these "swing states" seem eager to be perceived as regional leaders, but are unwilling to publicly speak on behalf of international norms and standards or to explicitly criticize the values practices of their neighbors and fellow regional organization members. If this is the case, then the emerging regional challenge to the international human rights institutional and normative framework may be even more potent than scholars and policymakers have initially considered.

References

Allison, Roy. "Regionalism, Regional Structures and Security Management in Central Asia." *International Affairs* 80 (2004): 463–83.
"Virtual Regionalism, Regional Structures and Regime Security in Central Asia." *Central Asian Survey* 27 (2008): 185–202.
Acharya, Amitav. *Constructing a Security Community in Southeast Asia*. New York: Routledge, 2009.

---

[79] Christopher Sabatini, "Meaningless Multilateralism," *Foreign Affairs*, August 8, 2014.

"How Ideas Spread: Whose Norms Matter? Norm Localization and Institutional Change in Asian Regionalism." *International Organization* 58 (2004): 239–75.

Ambrosio, Thomas. "Catching the 'Shanghai Spirit': How the Shanghai Cooperation Organization Promotes Authoritarian Norms in Central Asia." *Europe-Asia Studies* 60 (2008): 1321–44.

Aris, Stephen. *Eurasian Regionalism: The Shanghai Cooperation Organisation.* London: Palgrave Macmillan, 2011.

Avdeyeva, Olga. "When Do States Comply with International Treaties? Policies on Violence against Women in Post-Communist Countries." *International Studies Quarterly* 51 (2007): 877–900.

Axelrod, Robert. "The Emergence of Cooperation among Egoists." *The American Political Science Review* 75 (1981): 306–18.

Beissinger, Mark R. "Structure and Example in Modular Political Phenomena: The Diffusion of Bulldozer/Rose/Orange/Tulip Revolutions." *Perspectives on Politics* 2 (2007):259–76.

Bueno De Mesquita, Bruce, Alastair Smith, Randolph M. Siverson, and James D. Morrow. *The Logic of Political Survival.* Cambridge: The MIT Press, 2005.

Buzan, Barry and Ole Weaver. *Regions and Powers: The Structure of International Security.* New York: Cambridge University Press, 2003.

Carothers, Thomas. "The Backlash against Democracy Promotion." *Foreign Affairs* 85 (2006): 55–68.

"The End of the Transition Paradigm." *Journal of Democracy* 13:1 (2002): 5–21.

Cooley, Alexander. 2009. Cooperation Gets Shanghaied: Russia, China and the SCO. *Foreign Affairs Online.* December 14, 2009.

2012. *Great Games, Local Rules: The New Great Power Contest in Central Asia.* New York: Oxford University Press.

Cooley, Alexander. "The League of Authoritarian Gentlemen." *Foreign Policy.* January 30, 2013. https://foreignpolicy.com/2013/01/30/the-league-of-auth oritarian-gentlemen.

De Goede, Marieke. "Blacklisting and the Ban: Contesting Targeted Sanctions in Europe." *Security Dialogue* 42 (2011): 499–515.

Fawn, Rick. "Battle over the Box: International Election Observation Missions, Political Competition and Retrenchment in the Post-Soviet Space." *International Affairs* 82 (2006): 1133–53.

International Organizations and Internal Conditionality: Making Norms Matter. London: Palgrave Macmillan, 2013.

"'Regions' and Their Study: Where from, What for and Where to?" *Review of International Studies* 35 (2009): 5–34.

FIDH. *Shanghai Cooperation Organization: A Vehicle for Human Rights Violations.* Paris: International Federation for Human Rights, 2012. www.fidh.org/en/ region/europe-central-asia/Publication-of-a-report-Shanghai-12031.

Foot, Rosemary. "Human Rights and Counterterrorism in Global Governance: Reputation and Resistance." *Global Governance: A Review of Multilateralism and International Organizations* 11 (2005): 291–310.

Gavrilis, George. *The Dynamics of Interstate Boundaries.* New York: Cambridge University Press, 2008.

Hafner-Burton, Emilie M., and Kiyoteru Tsutsui. "Human Rights in a Globalizing World: The Paradox of Empty Promises." *American Journal of Sociology* 110 (2005): 1373–411.

Hafner-Burton, Emilie M., Kiyoteru Tsutsui, and John W. Meyer. "International Human Rights Law and the Politics of Legitimation Repressive States and Human Rights Treaties." *International Sociology* 23 (2008): 115–41.

Hansen, Jonathan M. "A History of Legal Impunity at Guantánamo Bay." *Diplomatic History* 35 (2011): 905–8.

Counterterrorism and Human Rights: The Impact of the Shanghai Cooperation Organization. New York: Human Rights in China, 2011. www.hrichina.org/sites/default/files/publication_pdfs/2011-hric-sco-whitepaper-full.pdf.

Hyde, Susan D. *The Pseudo-Democrat's Dilemma: Why Election Monitoring Became an International Norm.* Ithaca: Cornell University Press, 2011.

Katzenstein, Peter J. *A World of Regions: Asia and Europe in the American Imperium.* Ithaca: Cornell University Press, 2005.

Kelley, Judith. "The More the Merrier? The Effects of Having Multiple International Election Monitoring Organizations." *Perspectives on Politics* 7 (2009): 59–64.

Kelley, Judith Green. *Monitoring Democracy: When International Election Observation Works, and Why It Often Fails.* Princeton: Princeton University Press, 2012.

Keohane, Robert O. *After Hegemony: Cooperation and Discord in the World Political Economy.* Princeton: Princeton University Press, 1984.

Levitsky, Steven, and Lucan Way. "The Rise of Competitive Authoritarianism." *Journal of Democracy* 13.2 (2002): 51–65.

Lewis, David. "Security Sector Reform in Authoritarian Regimes: The OSCE Experience of Police Assistance Programming in Central Asia." *Security and Human Rights* 22 (2011): 103–17.

"Who's Socialising Whom? Regional Organisations and Contested Norms in Central Asia." *Europe-Asia Studies* 64 (2012): 1219–37.

Lukin, Alexander. "What the Kremlin Is Thinking: Putin's Vision for Eurasia." *Foreign Affairs* 93, No. 4 (July-August 2014): 85–93.

Memorial, *Fabrication of "Islamic Extremism" Criminal Cases in Russia: Campaign Continues.* Moscow: Memorial Human Rights Centre, 2007. www.memo.ru/2008/09/04/0409082.htm.

Mitchell, Lincoln. *The Color Revolutions.* Philadelphia: University of Pennsylvania Press, 2012.

Neumayer, Eric. "Do International Human Rights Treaties Improve Respect for Human Rights?" *Journal of Conflict Resolution* 496 (2005): 925–53.

Olcott, Martha Brill, Anders Åslund, and Sherman W. Garnett. *Getting it Wrong: Regional Cooperation and the Commonwealth of Independent States.* Washington, DC: Carnegie Endowment for International Peace, 1999.

Oye, Kenneth A. *Cooperation under Anarchy.* Princeton: Princeton University Press, 1986.

Sabatini, Christopher. "Meaningless Multilateralism." *Foreign Affairs*, August 8, 2014. www.foreignaffairs.com/articles/south-america/2014-08-08/meaning less-multilateralism.

Satterthwaite, Margaret L. "Rendered Meaningless: Extraordinary Rendition and the Rule of Law." *The George Washington Law Review* 75, no. 5–6 (2006): 1333–420.

Scahill, Jeremy. *Blackwater: The Rise of the World's Most Powerful Mercenary Army.* New York: Nation Books, 2007.

Scheinin, Martin. *Report of the Special Rapporteur on the Promotion and Protection of Human Rights and Fundamental Freedoms While Countering Terrorism* (December 28, 2009). UN Doc. A/HRC/13/37.

Scheppele, Kim Lane. "International Standardization of National Security Law." *The Journal of National Security, Law & Policy* 4 (2010): 437–53.

"The Migration of Anti-constitutional Ideas: The Post-9/11 Globalization of Public Law and the International State of Emergency." In *Migration of Constitutional Ideas*, ed. Sujit Choudhry Cambridge: Cambridge University Press, 2006: 347–73.

Shkolnikov, Vladimir. "Missing the Big Picture? Retrospective on OSCE Strategic Thinking on Central Asia." *Security and Human Rights* 20 (2009): 294–306.

Simmons, Beth. *Mobilizing for Human Rights: International Law in Domestic Politics.* New York: Cambridge University Press, 2009.

Singh, Amrit. *Globalizing Torture: CIA Secret Detention and Extraordinary Rendition.* New York: Open Society Justice Initiative, 2013. www.opensocie tyfoundations.org/reports/globalizing-torture-cia-secret-detention-and-extr aordinary-rendition.

Soldatov, Andrei, and Irina Borogan. *The New Nobility: The Restoration of Russia's Security State and the Enduring Legacy of the KGB.* New York: PublicAffairs, 2010.

Sullivan, Gavin, and Ben Hayes. *Blacklisted: Targeted Sanctions, Preemptive Security and Fundamental Rights.* Berlin: European Center for Constitutional and Human Rights, 2011. www.ecchr.eu/en/documents/pub lications/ecchr-publications/studies-and-reports/articles/blacklisted-targe ted-sanctions-preemptive-security-and-fundamental-rights.html.

Walker, Christopher and Alexander Cooley. "Vote of the Living Dead." *Foreign Policy*, October 31, 2013. https://foreignpolicy.com/2013/10/31/vote-of-the-living-dead.

8   Governing Religion as Right

Elizabeth Shakman Hurd

1   Three Approaches to Religion and Rights

Today, all states, including secular states, regulate religious affairs.[1] There is no religion without government involvement in some form.[2] While the comparative study of state religious governance is well established,[3] the role of transnational forms of governance in relation to religious lives and practices is less well understood. This is especially the case when it comes to international human rights. There are two prominent approaches to religion and international human rights, described here as the curatorial model and the foundations model. They are not mutually exclusive. The former is characterized by a sense that international rights advocacy – though embedded in power and never neutral – does its own thing, separate from religion. In Benjamin Berger's felicitous phrasing, law is seen as the curator,

---

[1] "State secularism does not imply the withdrawal of the state from religious matters, but on the contrary it consists of the state assuming the role of the ultimate regulator of religious affiliations and arbiter of religious claims": Nandini Chatterjee, "English Law, Brahmo Marriage, and the Problem of Religious Difference: Civil Marriage Laws in Britain and India," *Comparative Studies in Society & History* 52, no. 3 (2010): 524–52, 537.

[2] Even the Stasi Commission, an investigative body created by the French National Assembly to debate the principle of *laïcité*, observed that, "the secular state . . . cannot be content with withdrawing from all religious and spiritual matters." Quoted in Talal Asad, "Trying to Understand French Secularism," in *Political Theologies: Public Religions in a Post-Secular World*, edited by Hent de Vries and Lawrence E. Sullivan (New York: Fordham University Press, 2006): 494–526, 524, n80.

[3] Winnifred Fallers Sullivan and Lori G. Beaman, eds. *Varieties of Religious Establishment* (London: Ashgate, 2013); Vincent Goossaert and David A. Palmer, The Religious Question in Modern China (Chicago: University of Chicago Press, 2012); Markus Dressler, *Writing Religion: The Making of Turkish Alevi Islam* (Oxford: Oxford University Press, 2013); Nandini Chatterjee, *The Making of Indian Secularism: Empire, Law and Christianity 1830–1960* (New York: Palgrave Macmillan, 2011); Hussein Ali Agrama, *Questioning Secularism: Islam, Sovereignty, and the Rule of Law in Modern Egypt* (Chicago: University of Chicago Press, 2012); Joan W. Scott, *Politics of the Veil* (Princeton: Princeton University Press, 2007); Linell E. Cady and Elizabeth Shakman Hurd, eds., *Comparative Secularisms in a Global Age* (New York: Palgrave MacMillan, 2013).

and not a component, of cultural pluralism.[4] Law, including human rights law, stands above the fray of cultural difference. This curatorial perspective on religion and rights is appealing to many liberal internationalists. Human rights and religion, in this view, are like oil and water. Their respective practitioners are engaged in different normative discourses and live in different worlds. In curatorial discourse, the right to religious freedom takes its place in an array of universal rights that are seen as pragmatic global norms of human solidarity and extensions of the tradition of liberal theorizing summed up in Rawls' famous dictum, "political, not metaphysical."[5] Human rights and religion are presumed to operate in separate spheres, reflecting and re-instantiating what Robert A. Yelle has referred to as the "charter myth of modern law." As Yelle explains, this myth

describes a progressive growth of freedom, above all freedom of and from religion, following the European wars of religion in the sixteenth and seventeenth centuries. Despite periodic relapses into barbarism, this narrative affirms an irreversible progress. Never again will we return to the evil old days, when religion oppressed the individual conscience and became the cause of violence and war.[6]

Though Yelle and others have shown persuasively that the myth of modern law's freedom from religion is itself the product of particular historical, political, and theological developments, the curatorial model nonetheless retains its allure, particularly in international law and political science debates and among human rights advocates. At the international level it is associated with a powerful consensus surrounding the need for legal protections for religious freedom, guarantees for religious minority rights, and adherence to international legal standards embodied in the International Covenant on Civil and Political Rights and the Universal Declaration of Human Rights (UDHR).[7] Talal Asad captures the

---

[4] Benjamin L. Berger, "The Cultural Limits of Legal Tolerance," in *After Pluralism: Reimagining Religious Engagement*, eds. Pamela E. Klassen and Courtney Bender (New York: Columbia University Press, 2010): 98–123, 100.

[5] "By avoiding comprehensive doctrines [i.e., basic religious and metaphysical systems], we try to bypass religion and philosophy's profoundest controversies so as to have some hope of uncovering a stable overlapping consensus." John Rawls, Political Liberalism (Cambridge: Harvard University Press): 151–2.

[6] Robert A. Yelle, "Moses' Veil: Secularization as Christian Myth," in Winnifred Fallers Sullivan, Robert A. Yelle, and Mateo Taussig-Rubbo, eds., *After Secular Law* (Stanford: Stanford University Press, 2011): 23–42, 23.

[7] This consensus is reflected in the activities and reports of the UN Office of the Special Rapporteur for Freedom of Religion or Belief, which focuses on ensuring state compliance with international and regional human rights conventions including the 1948 Universal Declaration of Human Rights (Article 18), the European and American human rights conventions of 1950 and 1978, the two human rights conventions of 1976, the 1981 UN Declaration on the Elimination of All Forms of Intolerance and of Discrimination Based on

sweeping power of this discourse in his discussion of the UDHR, suggesting that in this case *"the rule called law* in effect usurps the entire universe of moral discourse."* It does so by privileging the state's (or associations thereof) norm-defining function, "thereby encouraging the thought that the authority of norms corresponds to the political force that supports them as law."[8] In presuming a direct convergence between the rule of law and social justice, the curatorial model effaces the distinction between them.

In a second approach to religion and rights, the foundations model, different religious traditions are seen as complementing or, more strongly, serving as the source or foundation of the modern rights tradition. As in the curatorial model, there are many approaches in this vein and they are not necessarily compatible.[9] An example is a project housed at the Berkley Center at Georgetown, entitled "Christianity and Freedom: Historical and Contemporary Perspectives," which builds on a long history of attempts to cement and to celebrate a foundational connection among Christianity, human rights, pluralism, and freedom.[10] Charles Malik, a Lebanese philosopher, diplomat, and one of the authors of the UDHR, was among the earlier and more influential representatives of this view on religion and rights. In 1968 he observed that

there is nothing that has been proclaimed about human rights in our age, nothing, for instance, in our Universal Declaration of Human Rights, which cannot be traced to the great Christian religious matrix ... Even those in our own day who carry on a non-religious or even on an anti-religious basis the burden of human rights with such evident passion and sincerity ... owe their impulse, knowingly or unknowingly, to the original inspiration of this tradition.[11]

This conviction is carried forward not only in the Berkley Center's project and others like it, but also among theologians such as Max

---

Religion or Belief, and regional human rights instruments such as the 1986 African Charter on Human and Peoples Rights and the 1990 Cairo Declaration on Human Rights in Islam.

[8] Talal Asad, "Redeeming the 'Human' in Human Rights," in *Formations of the Secular: Christianity, Islam, Modernity* (Stanford: Stanford University Press, 2003): 138 (emphasis in original).

[9] Abdullahi An-Naim, for instance, has attempted to establish the compatibility of Islamic law and tradition with international human rights; see his *Islam and Human Rights (Collected Essays in Law)*, Mashood A. Baderin and Abd Allah Ahman Naim, eds. (London: Ashgate, 2010). See also the essays collected in Thomas Banchoff and Robert Wuthnow, eds., *Religion and the Global Politics of Human Rights* (Oxford: Oxford University Press, 2011) and John Witte and M. Christian Green, eds., *Religion and Human Rights: An Introduction* (Oxford: Oxford University Press, 2012).

[10] http://berkleycenter.georgetown.edu/rfp/themes/christianity-freedom-historical-and-con temporary-perspectives.

[11] Cited in Samuel Moyn, *The Last Utopia: Human Rights in History* (Cambridge: Belknap Press, 2010): 127.

Stackhouse, for whom human rights cannot survive absent a religious foundation. In his words, universalizing values "are likely to fade over time if they are not anchored in a universal, context-transcending, metaphysical reality."[12] Melani McAlister has contextualized this claim, observing that, "according to Stackhouse, history showed that Christianity was more likely than other religions to encourage plural-ism. On this logic, then, political support for Christianity – even for Christian dominance – was actually support for both human rights and religious freedom for all."[13] Like the curatorial approach, the founda-tions approach is also influential in contemporary international political and public policy discussions. The founding document of American evangelical activism in the mid-1990s, the "Statement of Conscience of the National Association of Evangelicals Concerning Worldwide Religious Persecution," draws on a variation of it in describing religious freedom as a God-given human right that occupies a privileged position above other rights claims. In the words of the NAE, which led the campaign for the passage of the International Religious Freedom Act of 1998,[14] it is "our responsibility, and that of the government that repre-sents us, to do everything we can to secure the blessings of religious liberty to all those suffering religious persecution."[15]

Both the curatorial and foundations approaches to religion and rights are well represented in contemporary governmental and non-governmental international religious freedom advocacy. Their combined strength helps to explain the power and persuasion of a political move-ment that, while largely spearheaded by the United States, is increasingly

[12] Max Stackhouse, "Why Human Rights Needs God: A Christian Perspective," in *Does Human Rights Need God?*, eds. Elizabeth M. Bucar and Barbra Barnett (Grand Rapids: William B. Eerdmans, 2005): 39 (25–40), quoted in Melani McAlister, "US Evangelicals and the Politics of Slave Redemption as Religious Freedom in Sudan," *South Atlantic Quarterly* vol. 113, no. 1 (Winter 2014): 87–108, 93.

[13] McAlister, "US Evangelicals and the Politics of Slave Redemption as Religious Freedom in Sudan," 93.

[14] IRFA authorizes American attempts to sanction and cultivate forms of religion, religious subjects, and forms of state religious administration that align with US political, eco-nomic, and strategic interests. The legislation established an Office on International Religious Freedom in the State Department headed by an Ambassador-at-Large for International Religious Freedom, which prepares an annual report on the status of religious freedom in every country in the world with the exception of the United States. It also created an independent watchdog agency, the US Commission on International Religious Freedom (USCIRF), to oversee implementation of the Act, and a Special Adviser to the President on International Religious Freedom at the National Security Council. *International Religious Freedom Act of 1998*, HR 2431, 105th Cong., 2nd Sess. (1998).

[15] Quoted in Elizabeth A. Castelli, "Theologizing Human Rights: Christian Activism and the Limits of Religious Freedom," in *Non-Governmental Politics*, eds. Michel Feher with Gaëlle Krikorian and Yates McKee (New York: Zone Books, 2007), 675 (673–87).

globalized, as discussed in my book *Beyond Religious Freedom*.[16] Both approaches depict religious freedom as a stable and fundamental human right that can be measured and achieved by all political collectivities, no matter how reluctant or recalcitrant they may be initially.[17] It is a matter of persuading peoples and governments to understand and comply with a universal norm.[18] States and societies are positioned on a spectrum of progress, either inclined toward the achievement of religious freedom or slipping backward into religious persecution and violence.[19]

My work adopts a different starting point on the relation between religion and rights. Far from occupying an autonomous sphere independent of religious affairs, or representing the historical realization of any particular tradition, human rights advocacy is a particular mode of governing social difference that, like other social forms, implicates religion in complex and variable ways. Religious rights are a form of religious governance. This is what I call the "governance approach" to religion and rights. Rather than a stable and universal norm that stands above the fray, the deployment of religious rights is a technique of governance that authorizes particular forms of politics and regulates the spaces in which people live out their religion in specific ways.[20] It is a particular mode of governing social difference through (religious) rights.[21]

This form of governance impacts both politics and religion. Governing social difference through religious rights singles out individuals and groups for legal protection as religious individuals and faith communities. The discourse of religious rights and freedoms describes, defines, and governs individuals and groups in religious or sectarian terms rather

---

[16] Parts of this chapter are adapted from *Beyond Religious Freedom: The New Global Politics of Religion* by Elizabeth Shakman Hurd. © 2015, Princeton University Press. Reprinted by permission. For an introduction to the institutionalization of international religious freedom advocacy see E.S. Hurd, "Religious Freedom, American-style," *Quaderni di Diritto e Politica Ecclesiastica*, no. 1 (April 2014): 231–42.

[17] H. Knox Thames, Chris Seiple and Amy Rowe, *International Religious Freedom Advocacy: A Guide to Organizations, Law, and NGOs* (Waco: Baylor University Press, 2009).

[18] Thomas F. Farr, "Religious Freedom Abroad," *First Things* (March 2012): 21–3.

[19] Reflecting this logic, the IRFA legislation attributes a failure to achieve religious freedom to a lack of social and cultural maturity: "In many nations where severe violations of religious freedom occur ... there is not sufficient cultural and social understanding of international norms of religious freedom," *International Religious Freedom Act of 1998*, Sec. 501.

[20] Pamela Slotte, "The Religious and the Secular in European Human Rights Discourse," *Finnish Yearbook of International Law* 21 (2010): 1–56, 54. See also Saba Mahmood and Peter G. Danchin, "Immunity or Regulation? Antinomies of Religious Freedom," *South Atlantic Quarterly* Vol. 113, no. 1 (2014): 129–59.

[21] This argument is adapted from *Beyond Religious Freedom: The New Global Politics of Religion* by Elizabeth Shakman Hurd. © 2015 New Jersey: Princeton University Press. Reprinted by permission.

than on the basis of other affinities and relations – for example, as groups based on political leanings, geographical ties, neighborhood affiliations, kinship networks, generational ties, or socioeconomic status. In positing religion as prior to these other identities and affiliations, the religious rights model heightens the sociopolitical salience of whatever the national or international authorities designate as religion. This accentuates religious–religious and religious–secular divisions, leading to what the historian Sarah Shields describes as a particular "ecology of affiliation"[22] organized around and articulated through religious difference.

Governing social difference through religious rights also shapes how states and other political authorities distinguish groups from each other, often in law. This shapes both political and religious practice. Politically, advocacy for religious rights singles out groups and authorities as "religions" and locates them on a playing field in which they are presumed to represent a common type – religious groups – and to operate as equals. It also shapes religious possibilities, consecrating groups as discrete faith communities with identifiable leaders and neatly bounded orthodoxies. Those groups are both presupposed and produced as static bodies of tradition and convention that lend themselves to becoming objects of state and transnational legal regulation, and government engagement and reform. Official spokespersons are called forth to represent these faith communities, strengthening leaders that enjoy friendly relations with the political authorities and empowering groups that "look like" religions to those in power. In a religious landscape populated by faith communities, not only are particular hierarchies and orthodoxies reinforced, but dissenters, doubters, those who practice multiple traditions, and those on the margins of community are made illegible or invisible. On a political landscape governed through religious rights and freedoms, many violations of human dignity and justice fail to register at all, languishing beneath the threshold of national and international recognition as limited resources are devoted to rescuing persecuted religionists and defending faith communities that have achieved legal and political legibility and legitimacy. These selection dynamics inhere in the process and the politics of enforcing a right to religious freedom and cannot be remedied through a more sophisticated understanding of religion or religious community. Certain questions recur: Which religions to protect? Which leaders to engage?

This chapter elaborates on various aspects of these claims to develop a case for a governance perspective on the relation between religion and

[22] Sarah Shields, "Mosul, the Ottoman Legacy, and the League of Nations," *International Journal of Contemporary Iraqi Studies* Vol. 3, no. 2 (2009): 217–30, 218.

rights. It does so through a combination of empirical illustrations and theoretical discussion. Two criteria govern the selection of the empirical focal points. The first is the extent to which the lives of individuals and groups have been, and continue to be, shaped by the social, political, and religious possibilities and realities that are produced through efforts to globalize and legalize a right to religious freedom. The second, as discussed in detail in *Beyond Religious Freedom*, is the degree to which a particular case illustrates the analytical salience of distinguishing between discourses on religion as authorized by those in power and a broader field of social and religious practice and modes of coexistence. The first section, on the global political production of religious difference, draws on an extended discussion of the predicament of the Rohingya of Myanmar. The second section, on the creation of a landscape populated by faith communities and the effects on those excluded from such designations, draws on examples from the Central African Republic, Guatemala, India, and South Sudan. Throughout, I operate on the assumption that neither religion nor religious freedom is a stable, fixed quantity that can be used as either a dependent or independent variable. Stabilizing a definition of "religion" or "religious" for the purposes of assigning causal significance and drawing generalizable conclusions is impossible. Instead, the questions to be addressed include: What is accomplished in specific contexts when social difference is conceived and governed by those in positions of authority through religious rights and freedoms? What does it entail to govern religion as right? What political practices, social relations, and religious possibilities are enabled, and disabled, through such an approach? Exploring these questions leads me to join those contributors to this volume who have expressed skepticism about the project and promise of universalizing human rights. The promotion of religious rights, I argue, naturalizes the very lines of difference it is meant to soften or transcend, creating, in the process, new forms of social friction defined by and through religious difference.

2   The Religious Rights Imperative

Legal guarantees for religious rights are mechanisms of global governance that shape the religious and political fields in which they are deployed in at least three ways. First, lodged within a religious rights regime is the imperative to define identity in religious terms: "Are you *this* or are you *that*?" You need to know what you are to know how you fit in. Individuals with multiple affiliations or mixed backgrounds and dissenters from protected religions are uneasily accommodated in the rubrics of strict religious–secular identity and difference demanded by the logic of religious rights. Those who do not identify with orthodox versions of protected religions or beliefs fall between the cracks. Families that include multiple traditions under the same roof must choose a side. Such "in between" individuals and groups find themselves in an impossible position: either they must make political claims on religious grounds, or they have no ground from which to speak.[23] This occurred in Bosnia in the 1990s, when individuals who described themselves as atheists before the war woke up to find themselves identified – and divided – publically and politically, by a newly salient religious identity.[24]

Second, governing religion as right creates a social ecology of affiliation that presupposes and produces hard-and-fast religious identities that trump other modes of being and belonging. Singling out religion from among the many different given and chosen human ties naturalizes and normalizes religious–religious and religious–secular divides. Individuals and groups are identified publically and politically along those divides, rather than on the basis of other ties that bind, whether socioeconomic, geographic, familial, professional, or generational. To posit discrete religious communities as the defining features on the political landscape lends agency and authenticity to groups that are designated as religions, helping to create the world that religious rights discourse purports merely to describe. These groups come to occupy what Elizabeth Castelli describes as "the full terrain of the thinkable vis-à-vis freedom."[25] Governing citizens as Christians, Muslims, or Hindus conjures a collective imagining of fixed, stable categories of religious affiliation and confers upon them social and political currency. To the extent that individuals who had been marked by many affinities come to be identified by and through these particular categories of law and public discourse, the possibility of cross-cutting, nonsectarian forms of politics diminishes. Religions are transformed or remodeled into tractable, alienable commodities, in the sense described by Jean and John Comaroff in their work on the commodification of ethnicity and Samuli Schielke in his critique of world religions as entities with agency.[26]

Third, governing through religious rights reduces complex social, historical, and political histories and inequalities to a problem of

---

[23] Castelli, "Theologizing Human Rights," 684.

[24] David Campbell, *National Deconstruction: Violence, Identity and Justice in Bosnia* (Minneapolis: University of Minnesota Press, 1998).

[25] Castelli, "Theologizing Human Rights," 684.

[26] For the Comaroffs the commodification of ethnicity "has the curious capacity to conjure a collective imagining and to confer upon it social, political, and material currency – not to mention 'authenticity,' the spectre that haunts the commodification of culture everywhere." John L. Comaroff and Jean Comaroff, *Ethnicity, Inc.* (Chicago: University of Chicago Press, 2009), 10; Samuli Schielke, "Second Thoughts about the Anthropology of Islam." ZMO Working Papers 2 (2010): 4–5.

religion. As Michael Peletz has argued in reference to the concept of Islamization, this "discourages recognition of the complexity of the phenomena to which it is purportedly relevant."[27] The logic of religious rights and freedoms collapses social, economic, historical, political, and geographical factors into an emphasis on religion, obscuring other causes of discrimination and social tension and deflecting attention away from caste, class, colonial history, economic justice, land rights, and other factors.

The international response to the crisis involving the Rohingya in Myanmar illustrates the complex dynamics that follow the invocation of religious rights as a mode of international legal governance. A population of roughly 1,000,000 people living primarily in Northwestern Burma bordering Bangladesh, the Rohingya claim Burmese citizenship but are effectively stateless, having been denied citizenship by the Burmese state, classified by the government as "Bengali immigrants," and subjected to "persecution, discrimination and intrusive restriction on their rights to marry and have families."[28] Though many have lived in Rakhine (formerly Arakan) state for generations,[29] the Burmese state does not recognize them as one of the country's 135 ethnic groups, and the Rohingya have suffered a long history of exclusion and government-sponsored oppression. As journalist Kate Hodal explains, "Large-scale Burmese government crackdowns on the Rohingya – including Operation Dragon King in 1978, and Operation Clean and Beautiful Nation in 1991 – forced hundreds of thousands to flee to Bangladesh. Thousands of others have left for Thailand, Malaysia, and Indonesia, many of them by boat."[30] State-sanctioned violence has worsened in recent years, with many Rohingya driven out of their villages, separated from their families, and confined to squalid refugee camps. Those who remain in their villages cannot leave, even to go to the hospital.[31] The capital of Rakhine state,

---

[27] Michael Peletz, "Malaysia's Syariah Judiciary as Global Assemblage: Islamization, Corporatization, and Other Transformations in Context," *Comparative Studies in Society and History* 55, no. 3 (2013): 603–33, 626.

[28] Sophia Akram, "Cutting Borders: Ethnic Tensions and Burmese Refugees," *Fair Observer*, September 19, 2013, www.fairobserver.com/article/cutting-borders-ethnic-tensions-and-burmese-refugees.

[29] A document on Burmese languages dating to 1799 refers to "Rooinga as 'natives of Arakan [Rakhine],' but it is widely believed that most Rohingya came over from Bangladesh around 1821, when Britain annexed Myanmar as a province of British India and brought over migrant Muslim laborers." Kate Hodal, "Trapped Inside Burma's Refugee Camps, the Rohingya People Call for Recognition," *The Guardian*, December 20, 2012, www.guardian.co.uk/world/2012/dec/20/burma-rohingya-muslim-refugee-camps.

[30] Ibid.

[31] Jonathan Head, "The Unending Plight of Burma's Unwanted Rohingyas," BBC News, June 30, 2013, www.bbc.co.uk/news/world-asia-23077537.

Sittwe, had a population of about 73,000 Rohingya, which as of 2014 had dwindled to 5,000 confined in one heavily guarded neighborhood. According to anthropologist Elliott Prasse-Freeman, referring to the Rakhine (or Arakanese) majority population in Rakhine state, "local media, citizen bloggers, Buddhist monks all rallied around the Rakhine. Or more accurately, rallied *against* the Rohingya," describing them as illegal immigrants, a threat to Buddhism, a threat to security, and "simply aesthetically unpleasant." A refrain heard often from Prasse-Freeman's Burmese acquaintances was "'they are not like us; we cannot accept them.'"[32]

Most international commentators describe the Rohingya as a persecuted Muslim minority and call for the protection of Burmese Muslims.[33] In 2012, the US Commission for International Religious Freedom called for religious freedom for the Rohingya and identified them as persecuted Muslims. Many journalists and academics also rely on a religious persecution narrative to describe their plight. The Rohingya, it is said, lack religious rights. However, the Rohingya are not excluded from Burmese society exclusively with religious slurs, but also with racist and other dehumanizing terms. Prominent monks leading the charge to democratize Myanmar have turned against the Rohingya, blocking humanitarian assistance and calling for their social and political exclusion along the lines of what some have compared to apartheid in South Africa or racial segregation in the Southern United States.[34] A leaflet distributed by a monks' organization described the Rohingya as "cruel by nature." Ko Ko Gyi, a democracy activist and former political prisoner, has stated that the Rohingya are not Burmese. A loosely organized Buddhist activist group composed of monks and laity called "969," and its most prominent spokesperson, a Mandalay-based monk named U Wirathu, call for the social and economic exclusion of the Rohingya from Burmese society.[35] Claiming to work on behalf of the

---

[32] Elliott Prasse-Freeman, "Scapegoating in Burma," *Anthropology Today* Vol. 29, no. 4 (August 2013): 2–3, 2.

[33] "As Myanmar has liberalized, outsiders who had called for the US to overthrow the military dictatorship and install Aung San Suu Kyi have turned their attention to the plight of the Muslims, especially the Rohingya. They castigate Myanmar's current government and insist on making protection of Muslims a condition for better relations with the West." David I. Steinberg, "Myanmar: Buddhist-Muslim Tensions," *Sightings*, July 24, 2014, https://divinity.uchicago.edu/sightings/myanmar-buddhist-muslim-tensions-%E2%80%94-david-i-steinberg.

[34] Head, "The Unending Plight."

[35] In an interview, Wirathu explained that in his organization's name, 969, "the first 9 stands for the nine special attributes of the Lord Buddha and the 6 for the six special attributes of his Dhamma, or Buddhist Teachings, and the last 9 represents the nine special attributes of Buddhist Sanga [monks]. Those special attributes are the three Gems of the Buddha. In the past, the Buddha, Sangha, Dhamma and the wheel of Dhamma were Buddhists' sign. And the same goes for 969; it is another Buddhist sign." "Interview:

"religious rights and freedoms" of the majority Buddhist population of Myanmar, 969 reportedly "enjoys support from senior government officials, establishment monks and even some members of the opposition National League for Democracy (NLD), the political party of Nobel peace laureate Aung San Suu Kyi."[36] A representative of the Burmese Muslim Association compared the movement to the Ku Klux Klan.[37] Another 969 affiliate, the Organization for the Protection of Nation, Race and Religion – or, in the Burmese acronym, Ma Ba Tha, is also led by well-known Buddhist monks and oriented around pro-Buddhist, pro-Burman activism.

Discrimination against the Rohingya is complex and multifaceted: it is ethnic, racial, economic, political, religious postcolonial, and statist.[38] It is impossible to isolate any one of these factors as the definitive cause of a particular act of violence or discrimination. To identify the Rohingya as a persecuted religious minority suggests that a lack of religious rights is the main obstacle standing in the way of equality for the Rohingya. It singles out religion from the web of discriminatory forces in which the Rohingya are suspended. Identifying religious difference as uniquely motivating the violence against them – and, implicitly, religious rights as the solution to it – diverts attention from their comprehensive exclusion from Burmese state and society, historically and in the present. It masks the economic and political interests that profit from the Rohingya's subordination and repression. It subordinates to religious difference the state-sponsored violence, political and economic disagreements among the governing elite concerning the speed and content of proposed reforms, anti-immigrant and xenophobic basis of the discrimination, and economic insecurities and regional power dynamics accompanying Burma's tentative opening to global trade and foreign investment.

But the problem runs deeper. When international human rights advocates depict the violence in Myanmar as fundamentally religious in nature, and call for religious rights as the legal remedy, this reinforces 969's narrative, which insists that *these* lines of religious difference are indeed

Nationalist Monk U Wirathu Denies Role in Anti-Muslim Violence," *The Irrawaddy*, April 2, 2013, www.irrawaddy.org/interview/nationalist-monk-u-wirathu-denies-role-in -anti-muslim-unrest.html.

[36] According to one account, "the 969 movement is controlled by disgruntled hardliners from the previous junta, who are fomenting unrest to derail the reforms and foil an election landslide by Suu Kyi's NLD." Andrew R.C. Marshall, "Myanmar Gives Official Blessing to Anti-Muslim Monks," *Reuters*, June 27, 2013, www.reuters.com/art icle/2013/06/27/us-myanmar-969-specialreport-idUSBRE95Q04720130627.

[37] Cited in ibid.

[38] For a more comprehensive account of the many factors contributing to the Rohingya's exclusion from Burmese society, see the discussion in chapter 3 of *Beyond Religious Freedom*.

the most salient aspect of this profound societal and human crisis. In this case, promoting religious rights effectively strengthens the hand of a violently exclusionary set of nationalist movements that depend for their existence on perpetuating the perception of hard-and-fast lines of Muslim–Buddhist difference and immutable ties among majoritarian constructions of Buddhism, race, and Burmese national identity. In these circumstances, the logic of governing through religious rights fortifies those most committed to excluding the Rohingya from Burmese society and polity, and forfeits their chances of achieving equality. For their opponents, the Rohingya are subhuman. As Prasse-Freeman notes, "those who are killed are arguably not even killed *as* an identity group, but rather as so much detritus falling outside of a group, and hence outside of the political community entirely."[39] By reinforcing their status as *Muslims* rather than as Burmese citizens or as human beings, international efforts to govern religion as right in these circumstances make it less likely that the Burmese government – or the democratizing monks – will include the Rohingya in Burmese state and society as citizens and humans, rather than as Muslims.

In a 2013 lecture at the Council on Foreign Relations, former US ambassador to Nigeria John Campbell urged his audience not to describe recent violence in Nigeria as religious violence: "Are people [in Nigeria] being killed because they're Muslim, herders, or Hausa? It is often very hard to say."[40] Are the Rohingya being killed because they're Muslim, because they're immigrants, or because they're perceived as an economic or political threat to the former junta or other national or regional economic interests? Are Syrians being killed because they are Christian, regime supporters, or had been employed by or are related to a particular leader of the resistance? It's hard to say. Many factors lead to discrimination and violence: local histories, class disparities, disputes over natural resources, immigration status, urban–rural tensions, family grievances, oppressive governance, outside interventions, colonial legacies, land disputes, and economic rivalries. When social tension, discrimination, and violence are reduced to a problem of religious intolerance or religious persecution – and well-intentioned legal and political remedies subsequently reproduce and retrench those very lines of difference – the complex and multidimensional tapestry of human sociality and history is lost from sight. The multifaceted problems faced by persecuted groups become more difficult to address.

---

[39] Prasse-Freeman, "Scapegoating in Burma," 3.
[40] Ambassador John Campbell, Africa Update Panel Presentation, *Seventh Annual Religion and Foreign Policy Summer Workshop*, New York, June 25, 2013.

In the case of the Rohingya and other imperiled groups, governing through religious rights heightens the sociopolitical salience of whatever the authorities designate as religion: in this case, a hierarchical reading of entrenched Buddhist–Muslim difference. Rather than defanging 969 and its allies, this intensifies religious divisions while deferring and subduing the potential of alternative, cross-cutting movements that may be in a position to challenge the entrenched political and economic interests that profit most from the Rohingya's exclusion.

Governing religion as right shapes politics. Though the dynamics vary depending on context,[41] religious rights presuppose and produce lines of difference between religions, and between religion and non-religion, eclipsing other axes of being and belonging, and, in some cases, contributing to the very tensions these strategies are meant to tame or mitigate. Governing religion as right also shapes religion and religious possibilities. The rise to international prominence of a global religious rights mandate is transforming the experiences and self-understandings of groups around the world who are increasingly pressured to constitute themselves legally as discrete faith communities with clear boundaries, identifiable leaders, and neatly defined orthodoxies.[42] These aspects of governance, and in particular the political productivity of governing religion as right, are obscured from view in analyses which take for granted either the assumption of a distanced neutrality, which underlays the curatorial model, or the assumption of fixed and stable religious "traditions" that exist outside of politics and law, as in the foundations model. Exploring a second aspect of governing religion as right, the next section turns to the dynamics of empowerment and exclusion that shape the experiences of those who are subject to these legal distinctions and designations.

3   Empowerment and Exclusion

Under a regime of religious rights, becoming and being a "religion" bestows political benefits. Governing religion as right funnels individuals into discrete faith communities, empowers those communities and their spokespersons, and marginalizes other modes of solidarity. It hones in on religious identity as stable and singular, compelling those who identify

---

[41] For a discussion of several of these contexts, and an effort to unsettle the assumption that religious freedom is a singular achievement and that the problem lies in its incomplete realization, see the essays collected in Winnifred Fallers Sullivan, Elizabeth Shakman Hurd, Saba Mahmood, and Peter G. Danchin, eds., *Politics of Religious Freedom* (Chicago: University of Chicago Press, 2015).

[42] On the implications of the global religious rights imperative for Alevi communities in Turkey see my article "Alevis under Law: The Politics of Religious Freedom in Turkey," *Journal of Law and Religion* 29, no. 3 (September/October 2014): 416–35.

with several traditions to choose one above the others. Boundaries solidify. Lines between groups become more salient – a process described by the political theorist William Connolly as a modern drive to overcode the boundaries between groups.[43] Governing through religious rights overcodes the boundaries between religions, and also between religion and non-religion.[44] It produces discrete faith communities, perpetuating the notion that such communities are, in Martin Stringer's words, "coherent enough that individuals and leaders within [them] could more easily influence others within the community than those outside." It endows these communities with agency and authenticity. As Stringer explains, the "assumption of strong boundaries and clear identities within the community" means that "rather than breaking down these boundaries the policy aims to work within them and to build on the assumed solidarity of the community itself."[45]

Under a religious rights regime, established faith communities require representatives and spokespersons. A religious rights framework elicits individuals authorized by themselves or others to speak in the name of these communities. Their representatives meet with governments, nongovernmental organizations, international organizations, and other power brokers, becoming the objects of religious engagement and outreach. Governments and other authorities expect and encourage leaders to step forward. As recent US and UK foreign religious outreach activities illustrate, these dynamics contribute to shaping a broader political field in which some religious groups are empowered and others are excluded. The USAID Program Guide on Religion, Conflict and Peacebuilding informs practitioners:

Engagement with top religious leadership is critical to engagement at the local level. Without buy-in at this level, leaders at the local level may be reluctant to participate in the program even if they are interested and personally supportive of the program. As a result, organizing at the community level requires a great deal of groundwork and relationship building with senior leaders.[46]

The United States relies on religious leaders to secure access to local populations and to garner support for American strategic objectives in

---

[43] William E. Connolly, *The Ethos of Pluralization* (Minneapolis: University of Minnesota Press, 1995), 167.
[44] On the concept of "non-religion" see the work of the Nonreligion and Secularity Research Network at http://nsrn.net.
[45] Martin D. Stringer, *Discourses on Religious Diversity: Explorations in an Urban Ecology.* Farnham: Ashgate, 2013, 137.
[46] United States Agency for International Development, "Religion, Conflict and Peacebuilding: An Introductory Program Guide," Office of Conflict Management and Mitigation, Bureau for Democracy, Conflict, and Humanitarian Assistance (Washington, DC: 2009): 11.

conflict and post-conflict situations. In 2005, a Pentagon contractor paid Sunni religious scholars in Iraq $144,000 to assist in its public relations campaign. The contractor, "the Lincoln Group," was paid to "identify religious leaders who could help produce messages that would persuade Sunnis in violence ridden Anbar Province to participate in national elections and reject the insurgency."[47] Such programs would likely violate the Establishment Clause if undertaken domestically in the United States because they are sect-preferential.[48] As Jessica Hayden explains, "these programs are differentiated from domestic faith-based initiatives in that beneficiaries of US funds are not chosen in spite of their religious affiliations, but rather *because* of their ties to a specific religious group."[49] The British Foreign & Commonwealth Office (FCO) also pursues religious outreach as part of its external religious freedom programming, encouraging its 270 diplomatic posts to "consult local religious leaders" to determine whether "religious believers [are] able to publicise their religious information and promotional materials without unreasonable interference by the authorities."[50]

The point is neither to condemn nor to celebrate these activities, but rather to understand the assumptions about religion, religious community, and religious authority that underlie them. In this case, as Stringer points out, religions are presumed to be entities with agency, strong boundaries, and clear identities within the community, reflecting the assumptions of what I call the foundations approach to religion and rights, and occluding the processes through which particular authorities and groups become publically and politically recognizable as "religions." In an interesting reversal of these selection dynamics, governing religion as right also results in a politics of *non*-recognition for individuals and groups that fail to qualify as religions. While empowering those who qualify as faith communities and their spokespersons, governing through religious rights renders politically invisible less established religions, collective ways of life, and modes of belonging that do not qualify as religious. Non-traditional religions, unprotected religions, and non-religions are pushed into the wings. Violations of

---

[47] David S. Cloud and Jeff Gerth, "Muslim Scholars Were Paid to Aid US Propaganda," *New York Times*, January 2, 2006, www.nytimes.com/2006/01/02/politics/02propaganda.html?_r=0.

[48] Although, of course, in practice, and despite the official First Amendment jurisprudence, there is a long history of cooperation and collaboration between law enforcement officials and religious authorities in the United States, as is occurring at the time of this writing in Ferguson, Missouri.

[49] Jessica Powley Hayden, "Mullahs on a Bus: The Establishment Clause and US Foreign Aid," *The Georgetown Law Journal*, Vol. 95 (2006): 171–206.

[50] UK Foreign and Commonwealth Office. "Freedom of Religion or Belief – How the FCO Can Help Promote Respect for This Human Right." June 2010. www.gov.uk/government/uploads/system/uploads/attachment_data/file/35443/freedom-toolkit.pdf, 17.

human dignity that fail to register as religious infringements languish beneath the threshold of national and international recognition as the international community dedicates limited resources to rescuing persecuted religionists. To see these exclusionary dynamics requires expanding the field of vision beyond the curatorial and foundational constructions of (what counts as) religion, religious rights, and religious freedom to encompass a broader field of religiosities, histories, and forms of sociality. It requires apprehending local practices and histories on their own terms, particularly to the extent that they appear as unintelligible or illegible from within the normative understandings of religion that underlie the curatorial and foundations approaches and dominate UN and other international discussions and debates on international human rights.[51]

The K'iche', a Maya ethnic group living in the Western highlands of Guatemala, represent a case in point. Perhaps the most well-known K'iche' is indigenous rights activist Rigoberta Menchú, who won the Nobel Peace Prize in 1992. Tensions between the K'iche' community and the Guatemalan state have increased in recent years as 87 Maya communities in the department of El Quiché, represented by the K'iche' People's Council (KPC), unanimously rejected the mining and hydroelectric projects proposed for Guatemala in the wake of the North American Free Trade Agreement and other treaties. Foreign commercial companies responded to those rejections with offers to reward the KPC with a higher percentage of profits, failing to understand that, as Dianne Post observes, "the reason these projects were rejected is not monetary but is linked to the refusal to allow destruction of the earth for religious and cultural reasons."[52] The KPC's refusal to acquiesce in these projects has led to discrimination and violence, including massive violations of K'iche' cultural heritage and land rights facilitated by collusion among multinational mining corporations, the police, and the Guatemalan state.

The K'iche' are unable to portray these abuses as violations of religious rights or freedoms. As described by scholars of indigenous religion in other contexts,[53] K'iche' attachment to the land does not register legally as religious, making it difficult (and perhaps impossible) for them to avail

---

[51] For an analysis of the decontextualized treatment of religion in the monitoring practices of five UN human rights treaty bodies between 1993 and 2010 and the tensions between those practices and various domestic legal frameworks, see Helge Årsheim, *Legal Forms of the Religious Life*, PhD Dissertation, Faculty of Theology, University of Oslo, 2014.

[52] Dianne Post, "Land, Life, and Honor: Guatemala's Women in Resistance," *Fair Observer*, October 5, 2013, www.fairobserver.com/article/land-life-honor-guatemala-women-resistance.

[53] Greg Johnson, *Sacred Claims: Repatriation and Living Tradition* (Charlottesville: University of Virginia Press, 2007).

themselves of national or international legal protections for religion, religious rights, or religious freedom. Their claims are invisible to organizations, actors, and legal instruments focused on the legal realization of religious rights and freedom, because, in an important sense, they are perceived as having no (recognizable) religion.[54] The 2012 State Department International Religious Freedom Report for Guatemala confirms that there were "no reports of abuses of religious freedom" in the country. When cast in terms of religion as right (to believe or not to believe), violations of K'iche' religio-cultural heritage fall below the threshold of political and juridical legibility.

Similar dynamics have emerged in the Central African Republic (CAR) where, in 2010, the US State Department's Religious Freedom Report observed that as many as 60 percent of the imprisoned women in the country had been charged with "witchcraft," which is considered a criminal offense by the government. The State Department's report concluded that the CAR government "generally respected religious freedom in practice," and gave the CAR a good ranking overall. Discrimination against African traditional religion does not count as religious discrimination. Women imprisoned for witchcraft cannot suffer from violations of religious freedom because, in the eyes of the government and the authors of the religious freedom report, they have no religion. Like the K'iche', the imprisoned women in the CAR fail to appear on the persecuted religious minority radar screen because abuses of their cultural practices do not count as violations of the right to believe or not to believe protected by international instruments and advocates for religious freedom.

Individuals who identify with multiple religions also find themselves in a legally precarious position under legal regimes that govern religion as right. While the new state of South Sudan guarantees a list of religious rights for its minority citizens, including its Muslim population, the government has struggled with the question of religious representation because there, as elsewhere, it is often difficult to classify citizens as believers or non-believers as part of a single faith tradition.[55] As is the case in a lot of African countries, many South Sudanese practice both African traditional religions and Christianity or Islam, and do not distinguish sharply between these and other traditional practices. As Noah

---

[54] Tisa Wenger, *We Have a Religion: The 1920s Pueblo Indian Dance Controversy and American Religious Freedom* (Chapel Hill: The University of North Carolina Press, 2009).

[55] Noah Salomon and Jeremy F. Walton, "Religious Criticism, Secular Criticism, and the 'Critical Study of Religion': Lessons from the Study of Islam," in *The Cambridge Companion to Religious Studies*, ed. Robert A. Orsi (Cambridge: Cambridge University Press, 2012), 403–20, 406.

Salomon explains, "to think of such 'traditional' practices as distinct confessions does not represent the reality of South Sudanese who may identify as Christians and at the same time see no contradiction in maintaining these rites and rituals."[56] Under a regime of religious rights, those who identify with several traditions either are compelled to choose between (now, suddenly different and discrete) religious traditions and their appointed faith leaders or are rendered religiously invisible – even as officially recognized religions gain newfound political standing. This contributes to a striated political field organized by and governed through particular forms of religious difference. The South Sudanese government's Bureau of Religious Affairs, for example, which registers faith-based organizations, rejects Christian organizations whose constitutions "do not line up with Biblical chapters or verses," according to one inspector in the bureau interviewed by Salomon. In these circumstances, as Rosalind Hackett explains, "African indigenous or traditional religions are hampered by being part of a generalized and heterogeneous category with no clear designation or centralized leadership." Moreover, though indigenous religions are what Hackett aptly describes as "religious freedom misfits," it is not possible to simply assimilate them into international protections because, as she explains, "recent moves to grant institutional, protective space to indigenous expressions of 'spirituality' not only essentialize and objectify traditional forms of belief and practice but also translate and recast them to appeal to cultural outsiders who formally or informally adjudge these rights' claims."[57]

As C. S. Adcock has shown in her work on early twentieth-century India, and as Hackett's research also suggests, translating particular actions and forms of political struggle into the language of religion, religious rights, and religious freedom is not costless. It silences alternative social, political, and religious projects and possibilities. In *The Limits of Tolerance*, Adcock explores the history and politics of *shuddhi*, a ritual form of purification in India that was treated as religious but signified more broadly within a ritual politics of caste. Broadening the canvas, she demonstrates that the identification of shuddhi as religious proselytizing and conversion was not inevitable and carried significant implications for the politics of caste. By delinking debates over Indian secularism from the

---

[56] Noah Salomon, "Freeing Religion at the Birth of South Sudan," The *Immanent Frame*, April 12, 2012. http://blogs.ssrc.org/tif/2012/04/12/freeing-religion-at-the-birth-of-south-sudan/.

[57] Rosalind I. J. Hackett, "Traditional, African, Religious, Freedom?" in Sullivan et al., *Politics of Religious Freedom*, 90–1, 96. See also David Chidester, *Wild Religion: Tracking the Sacred in South Africa* (Berkeley and Los Angeles: University of California Press, 2012) and Makau Mutua, *Human Rights: A Political and Cultural Critique* (Philadelphia: University of Pennsylvania Press, 2008).

politics of caste, the translation of shuddhi into the language of religion deflected attention from its central role in the struggle against the micro-politics of exclusion by low caste groups of all religious backgrounds. Designating shuddhi as religious conversion, or as "making Hindus," thus effaced the complex politics of caste, erased the political complicity of the Gandhian ideal of Tolerance in these forms of exclusion, and, in deflecting attention away from the uncertainties surrounding Untouchables' religious identity, helped to establish a representative politics structured around a Hindu constitutional "majority" and Muslim "minority," laying the groundwork for current tensions.[58]

Like other human rights guarantees, religious rights are a particular and contextually variable technique of governance located firmly within and not outside of history. Governing religion as right requires the authorities, such as religious studies scholars, constitutional experts, and government officials,[59] to make determinations about what constitutes religion and non-religion, who counts as a legitimate religious subject or association, and who is authorized to represent these communities. These processes entrench religious–religious and religious–secular lines of difference and division by enforcing the interests and identities of groups that are defined in religious terms. They strengthen those in a position to determine what counts as religion, and whose religion counts most. They participate in what the ReligioWest project research team describe as the "formatting" of religion.[60] States and other authorities mold religions into static bodies of tradition and convention, transforming them into objects of national and international legal regulation and reform. Practices that fall outside of or that defy the tradition as defined by the religious-freedom-defining authorities are pushed aside.[61] Forms of popular religion that have "little

---

[58] Adcock, *Limits of Tolerance*, 14, 20, 121, 145, 163. As Adcock concludes, "Tolerance supported a 'secular majoritarianism' that served to disempower and minoritize non-caste-Hindus by a combined strategy of encompassment and exclusion." Ibid., 168. Ussama Makdisi has argued along related lines that the discourse of sectarianism under the Ottomans in late nineteenth-century Mount Lebanon "masked a final restoration of an elitist social order in Mount Lebanon and marked the end of a genuinely popular, if always ambivalent, participation in politics." Ussama Makdisi, *The Culture of Sectarianism: Community, History, and Violence in Nineteenth-Century Ottoman Lebanon* (Berkeley: University of California Press, 2000), 147.

[59] For an analysis of the role of Japanese political theorists, constitutional scholars, and scholars of religion in the construction of new theories of religious freedom as a human right in US-occupied Japan, see Jolyon Thomas, *Japan's Preoccupation with Religious Freedom*, PhD thesis, Department of Religion, Princeton University, 2014.

[60] The ReligioWest research project was directed by Olivier Roy and based at the European University Institute in Fiesole. www.eui.eu/Projects/ReligioWest/Home.aspx.

[61] An example is the tense relationship between the Catholic Church and the Southern Italian popular religion of Italian Harlem's Catholic community, as described by Robert Orsi, who observes that the Church's "cultural distaste for the immigrants amounted to

to do with the Church," do not "look like religion," or are deemed politically undesirable or unorthodox for whatever reason (e.g., because they challenge caste hierarchies, threaten entrenched material interests, or cast doubt on the legitimacy of social order in new ways) are cast out as "pagan and primitive."[62] Those who do not choose to speak or act as Christians, as Hindus, as Jews, or as unbelievers are rendered inaudible. Amahl Bishara comes close to making this argument when she writes that to identify Christian Palestinians *as* Christians is "not inviting to those Christian Palestinians who do not choose to speak or act as Christians."[63]

These dynamics of empowerment and exclusion inhere in the logic and practice of governing through religious rights nationally or internationally. They cannot be mitigated or transcended through the adoption of a more informed understanding of religion or a more effective regime of rights implementation. Critics of the politics of multicultural recognition have developed these insights in other contexts.[64] Patchen Markell diagnoses the binding quality of recognition and challenges its equation with justice, asserting that the conception of justice employed by recognition obscures the dynamics of subordination.[65] The politics of recognizing faith communities and their leaders correspondingly contributes to fixing particular politically authorized religious differences while subduing alternative forms of subjectivity and agency. Analyzing the legal and affective practices and social effects of liberal multiculturalism in Australian indigenous communities, Elizabeth Povinelli has shown that the liberal insistence, in the name of cultural or religious diversity, that colonized subjects identify not with the colonizer but with authentic traditional culture serves to reinforce liberal regimes of governance rather than opening them up to difference.[66] In the case at hand, individuals and groups who resist or subvert the secular–religious and religious–religious taxonomies and hierarchies instantiated through religious rights are sidelined. In a discussion of the politics of international attempts to protect

---

an existential rejection of their whole value system." Robert A. Orsi, *The Madonna of 115th Street: Faith and Community in Italian Harlem, 1880–1950*, 3rd edition. (New Haven: Yale University Press, 2010), 189.

[62] "The people knew, of course, that the leaders of the American church downtown frowned upon their devotion, upon this public display of a Catholicism that was viewed as pagan and primitive." Ibid., 220–1.

[63] Amahl Bishara, "Covering the Christians of the Holy Land," *Middle East Report* 267 (Summer 2013): 7–14, 14.

[64] On recognition as a political good, see the classic statement by Charles Taylor, *Multiculturalism and "The Politics of Recognition": An Essay with Commentary* (Princeton: Princeton University Press, 1992).

[65] Patchen Markell, *Bound by Recognition* (Princeton: Princeton University Press, 2003).

[66] Elizabeth Povinelli, *The Cunning of Recognition: Indigenous Alterities and the Making of Australian Multiculturalism* (Durham: Duke University Press, 2002).

the rights of sexual minorities, Joseph Massad has shown that the "Gay International"[67] reifies boundaries and risks imposing Western sexual ontologies and categorizations in diverse contexts.[68] Adapting Massad's terms, one could say that governing religion as right conjures and grants legal personality to "religions" while sidelining diverse and multiform practices that cannot or refuse to be assimilated into this normative frame.

4   Religion and Politics After Religious Rights?

National and international efforts to govern religion as right are often defended as the answer to how to co-exist peacefully, prosper economically, and thrive politically.[69] Celebrated as the key to emancipating individuals and minority communities from violence, poverty, and oppression, religious rights are heralded as the solution to political and economic backwardness, the tyranny of immoderate and archaic forms of religion, and the violence and despair associated with societal ills from women's oppression to economic desperation to environmental degradation. Communities around the world are seen as in need of transformative social engineering to create the conditions in which secular states and their religious subjects become tolerant, believing or non-believing consumers of free religion, willing practitioners of faith-based solutions to collective problems, and, more often than not, compliant defenders of American and/or international security.[70] Guarantees for religious rights are said to ensure an ideal balance between allegiance to the state and to (reformed) religion under law.

Today, scholars and practitioners working in the intersections between religion, law, human rights, and international relations are subject to considerable pressure to offer a prescription for how to live together peacefully with social and religious difference. For many, the discourse

---

[67] "It is these missionary tasks, the discourse that produces them, and the organizations that represent them that constitute what I call the *Gay International.*" Joseph A. Massad, "Re-Orienting Desire: The Gay International and the Arab World," *Public Culture*, Vol. 14, no. 2 (Spring 2002): 361–85, 362.

[68] "In contradistinction to the liberatory claims made by the Gay International in relation to what it posits as an always already homosexualized population, I argue that it is the discourse of the Gay International that both produces homosexuals, as well as gays and lesbians, where they do not exist, and represses same-sex desires and practices that refuse to be assimilated into its sexual epistemology." Ibid., 363.

[69] There are many examples. See, for instance, Thomas F. Farr, *World of Faith and Freedom: Why International Religious Liberty Is Vital to American National Security* (Oxford: Oxford University Press, 2008).

[70] William Inboden, "Religious Freedom and National Security," Hoover Institution Policy Review, no. 175 (October/November 2012), www.hoover.org/publications/policy-review/article/129086.

of religious rights and freedoms has persuasively presented itself as the solution. Powerful forces, including the law, incentivize individuals and groups to articulate demands for justice, equality, and dignity in the languages of religious rights and freedoms. It is understandable that some perceive that they have no alternative but to seek protections on these grounds. If being or becoming a persecuted religionist makes it more likely that development aid will be forthcoming or asylum will be granted, then it should not be surprising to see a rise in persecuted religionists.

In exploring the politics of governing religion as right, my intention is neither to judge those individuals or groups who find themselves in difficult circumstances nor to undermine those who are working to assist them. It is, rather, to insist on the importance of pulling back from the immediate situation to tell a larger story about the politics of governing religion as right. To return to the questions posed in the Introduction, governing through religious rights presupposes and elicits an emphasis on religion and religious difference as exceptionally threatening forms of social difference that need to be kept in check by the authorities (the logic of sectarianism) while obscuring complex social, economic, and political histories and inequalities, as well as alternative religiosities. It elevates established voices and institutions of protected groups that enjoy good relations with state and transnational authorities, while marginalizing individuals and groups that fall into the gray areas between contemporary formations of the secular and the religious (the logic of empowering faith communities). As I discuss elsewhere, it privileges and protects a particular understanding of religion as the right to choose and enact one's belief or non-belief (the logic of the free religious marketplace).[71] Before concluding that religious persecution is the culprit – and that legal guarantees for religious rights is the solution – it is worth weighing the costs of locking into a narrative that protects religion in law, posits religion as a stable and coherent category in legal and policy analysis, and privileges religion as a basis for protecting human flourishing.

One might object that the governance perspective on religious rights raises more questions than it answers. Is it not the case that any legal or political practice that invokes a categorical group distinction, whether gender, racial, linguistic, ethnic, or national, will re-inscribe the very markers of difference that it is intended to moderate or transcend? In what sense is this dilemma of recognition unique to the category of religion? There are resemblances between some of the dynamics

---

[71] See my essay "Believing in Religious Freedom" in *Politics of Religious Freedom.*

associated with the category of religion and other markers of identity. Yet different categories invoke different histories and shape sociopolitical landscapes in distinctive ways. Religion is not just any category. It has a history. To invoke religious rights is to invoke this history, including a long and complex genealogy emerging in the contentious and often violent history of church-state religions in Europe at the time of the founding of the modern state system, and forged through the histories of colonialism and other forces of capitalist modernity, as David Chidester, Nandini Chatterjee, Jean and John Comaroff, and many others have shown.[72] The history and politics of governing religion as right are hidden from sight in both the curatorial and foundations approaches to religion and rights. In assuming a position of neutrality above the cultural fray, the former fails to acknowledge the ways in which rights advocacy actively shapes and transforms the fields of religious and political practice and possibility in which it is deployed. In presuming the stability and boundedness of particular religious traditions, the latter fails to acknowledge the dynamic, shifting, and exclusionary political pressures and processes through which particular communities and orthodoxies are designated as "religions," and particular leaders authorized to speak on their behalf.

There are no authorities in contemporary international relations that are equipped to declare what is or is not "religion" with such a degree of certainty as to permit the enactment of international laws and regulations that discriminate among people and groups on that basis.[73] There are no shared criteria that enable one to identify and delimit the sphere of religion in a manner neutral to all religions.[74] Inventing a more inclusive mechanism of international legal protection by increasing the number or diversity of groups represented, or by exchanging a focus on religion as belief for a more inclusive model of religion as communal practice or ethics, does not offer a solution. A new and improved "International Religious Freedom 2.0" will repeat and re-instantiate a modified version of the same exclusionary logic.

---

[72] See Chatterjee, "English Law, Brahmo Marriage, and the Problem of Religious Difference: Civil Marriage Laws in Britain and India;" David Chidester, *Savage Systems: Colonialism and Comparative Religion in Southern Africa* (Charlottesville: University of Virginia Press, 1996); Jean and John Comaroff, *Of Revelation and Revolution: Christianity, Colonialism, and Consciousness in South Africa*, Vol. 1 (Chicago: University of Chicago Press, 1991).

[73] Winnifred Fallers Sullivan, "The Ambassador of Religious Freedoms," *The Sunday Edition with Michael Enright*, CBC Radio, February 24, 2013, www.cbc.ca/thesundayedi tion/shows/2013/02/24/ambassador-of-religious-freedoms/

[74] Jakob de Roover, "Secular Law and the Realm of False Religion," in *After Secular Law*, 43 (43–61).

There is no single policy prescription that emerges from this discussion of the politics of governing religion as right. This diagnosis may not sit well with many liberal internationalists and others for whom human rights have come to represent the last best hope for humankind. Different versions of both the curatorial and foundations models are likely to retain their appeal for some time across the political spectrum, particularly among legal scholars and practitioners, political scientists, and human rights advocates. Those interested in thinking more critically about the politics of international human rights can attempt to inform and enrich policy discussions, or, perhaps, try to convince political scientists and others to think more expansively about social freedom and the complex histories of human rights. A different, but arguably no less important, ambition is to avoid reproducing, in the guise of protecting human flourishing, the very normative distinctions and discourses that are most in need of interrogation and politicization. Religious rights fall in this category. Governing social difference through religious rights authorizes particular understandings of what it means to be religious, and what it means for religion to be free. Naturalizing the lines of difference they are intended to manage or tame, these projects risk exacerbating the very social tensions, forms of discrimination, and inter-communal discord they claim to be uniquely equipped to transcend. Far from a settled norm and achievable social fact that tames violence and mitigates insecurity, to govern religion as right is a historically specific and contextually variable mode of managing social difference. Other approaches will yield different results.[75] None will be perfect.

---

[75] For a "bottom up" history of the improvised arrangements through which early modern Europeans sometimes coexisted peacefully across lines of difference, see Benjamin J. Kaplan, *Divided by Faith: Religious Conflict and the Practice of Toleration in Early Modern Europe* (Cambridge: Belknap, 2007).

9   The Vernacularization of Women's Human Rights

Sally Engle Merry and Peggy Levitt

How do human rights travel around the world? They are created through diverse social movements in many parts of the world and crystallized into a form of symbolically universal law under the supervision of the UN and its human rights organizations. This law-like form is then reappropriated by myriad civil society organizations and translated into terms that make sense in their local communities. This is the process of vernacularization: the extraction of ideas and practices from the universal sphere of international organizations, and their translation into ideas and practices that resonate with the values and ways of doing things in local contexts. Local places are not empty, of course, but rich with other understandings of rights, the state, and justice. Some of the most important actors in this process are women's non-governmental organizations (NGOs) that translate human rights ideas into terms that make sense to them. This article explores the way NGOs vernacularize women's human rights discourse in four cities. Human rights constitute a valuable political resource in many of these situations, although their adoption is influenced by unequal North/South resources. This is an empirical study of an existing social process, not one of advocacy, but advocates adopt the strategies we are describing.[1]

The process of vernacularization converts universalistic human rights into local understandings of social justice. While considerable scholarship on human rights sees universalism and relativism as oppositional,

[1] This research was supported by the National Science Foundation Law and Social Sciences Program for support for this research, #SES-0417730 and the Wellesley College Faculty Research Fund. We appreciate the research of Liu Meng N. Rajaram, M. Rosa Alayza, Mercedes Crisóstomo, Vaishali Zararia, M. Liu, Y.H. Hu, M.L. Liao, Diana Yoon, and Mihaela Serban, as well as the work of Wasim Rahman, Sarah Alvord, and Jessica Hejtmanek on the project. Audiences at Cornell University, New York University School of Law, Wellesley Centers for Women, University of Connecticut, University of California/Irvine, Yale University, University of Michigan, Harvard University, Suffolk Law School, and the Canadian Institute for Advanced Research Successful Societies Program all provided good insights and comments on the article, for which we are grateful.

vernacularization bridges this divide.[2] A focus on this process follows the trend in the anthropology of law to examine human rights in practice, exploring how they circulate, how they are adopted and used, and what forms of resistance and opposition they encounter when they come into contact with other national or religious ideologies of social justice.[3] In contrast to scholarship on the dissemination of human rights in other disciplines, anthropology offers insights into the transformation of meanings and practices within small social settings, highlighting aspects of its circulation and use that can be obscured by the focus on the state in international relations and legal scholarship.[4] Although in this chapter we emphasize the way local actors appropriate global discourses, it is also clear that local actors shape the global system, raising issues, generating public support, and constituting the social movements that convert problems into human rights issues, such as occurred with violence against women.[5]

NGOs are critical actors in the circulation and localization of women's human rights. They translate global human rights ideas into terms that resonate with local understandings of social life. But an organization that defines itself as a women's human rights NGO and uses this language

[2] For discussion, see: Abdullahi An-Na'im, "Toward a Cross-Cultural Approach to Defining International Standards of Human Rights: The Meaning of Cruel, Inhuman, or Degrading Treatment or Punishment," in *Human Rights in Cross-Cultural Perspectives: A Quest for Consensus*, Abdullahi Ahmed An-Na'im, ed. (Philadelphia: University of Pennsylvania Press, 1992); Henry J. Steiner, Philip Alston, and Ryan Goodman, *International Human Rights in Context: Law, Politics, Morals*, 3rd edn. (Oxford and New York: Oxford University Press, 2007).

[3] Ellen Messer, "Anthropology and Human Rights," *Annual Review of Anthropology* 22 (1993):221–49; Ellen Messer, "Pluralist Approaches to Human Rights," *Journal of Anthropological Research* 53 (1997):293–317; Richard A. Wilson, "Introduction: Human Rights, Culture and Context," in Richard A. Wilson, ed., *Human Rights, Culture and Context: Anthropological Perspectives* (London: Pluto Press, 1996); Jane K. Cowan, Marie-Benedict Dembour, and Richard Wilson, eds., *Culture and Rights* (Cambridge: Cambridge University Press, 2000); Sally Engle Merry, *Human Rights and Gender Violence: Translating International Law into Local Justice* (Chicago: University of Chicago Press, 2006); Mark Goodale, "Toward a Critical Anthropology of Human Rights," *Current Anthropology* 47 (2009):485–511, and "In Focus: Anthropology Human Rights in a New Key," *American Anthropologist* 108 (2006):1–271; Mark Goodale and Sally Engle Merry, eds., *The Practice of Human Rights: Tracking Law between the Local and the Global* (Cambridge, UK: Cambridge University Press, 2007); Kamari Clarke, *The International Criminal Court* (Cambridge, UK: Cambridge University Press, 2008).

[4] Margaret E. Keck and Kathryn Sikkink, *Activists Beyond Borders: Advocacy Networks in International Politics* (Ithaca: Cornell University Press, 1998); Thomas Risse, Stephen C. Ropp, and Kathryn Sikkink, eds., *The Power of Human Rights: International Norms and Domestic Change* (Cambridge: Cambridge University Press, 1999); Sanjeev Khagram, James V. Riker, and Kathryn Sikkink, eds., *Restructuring World Politics: Transnational Social Movements, Networks, and Norms* (Minneapolis: University of Minnesota Press, 2002).

[5] Merry, *Human Rights and Gender Violence*.

extensively for its international funders and national and international audiences may make little reference to human rights in its day-to-day work. It may talk about civil rights rather than human rights, or teach women to stand up for themselves in their families rather than to claim their human rights. Our research found that with the exception of a small number of true believers, most activists in these organizations take a fairly strategic view of the use of human rights language and use it in limited ways.

This article explores how ideas and practices concerning women's human rights are vernacularized by two women's organizations in each of four large cities that vary by region, religion, and history of human rights activism: Baroda in India, Beijing in China, Lima in Peru, and New York City in the USA.[6] All the organizations are committed to using a human rights approach to help women. However, they carry out this mission quite differently. Each selects a set of issues and strategies from those promoted by local and national women's movements, national traditions of human rights, and the texts and practices of human rights law. As actors and organizations move across local, national, and international fields of power and meaning, they forge moral and instrumental strategies to promote their organizational goals within the constraints of funding, community support, and North/South power relations. They remake international human rights in the vernacular.

Human rights vernacularization is a process of translation within context. How various ideas are redefined or rejected varies across countries and settings. NGOs select how to use women's human rights according to their funders' preferences, their allies' interests, and their clients' support. They adapt them to local meanings of human rights, formed by the political and historical experience with human rights in the country. Where human rights ideas are central to political movements and have a long history, as in Peru,[7] framing women's claims to equality or freedom from violence in rights terms evokes greater public support than where human rights seem to be new and threatening, as in China. In general, enthusiasm for human rights discourse depends on its historical and cultural resonance in particular locales.

---

[6] Peggy Levitt and Sally Engle Merry, "Vernacularization on the Ground: Local Uses of Global Women's Rights in Peru, China, India, and the United States," *Global Networks* 9 (2009):441–61; Peggy Levitt and Sally Engle Merry, "Making Women's Human Rights in the Vernacular: Navigating the Culture/Rights Divide," in *Gender and Culture at the Limits of Rights*, ed. Dorothy Hodgson (Philadelphia: University of Pennsylvania Press, 2011).

[7] See: Peggy Levitt, Sally Engle Merry, Rosa Alayza, and Mercedes Crisóstomo Meza, "Doing Vernacularization: The Encounter between Global and Local Ideas of Women's Rights in Peru," in *Feminist Strategies in International Governance*, Gulay Caglar, Elisabeth Prugl, and Susanne Zwingel, eds. (New York: Routledge, 2013).

Activists appropriating ideas of women's human rights for local problems face what we call a "resonance dilemma." The more extensively a human rights issue is transformed to be concordant with existing cultural frameworks, the more readily it will be adopted but the less likely it is to challenge existing modes of thinking. The less extensively the human rights idea is vernacularized, the less likely it is be adopted but the more likely it is to challenge existing social structures. For example, one NGO we studied in India focused on familiar women's issues such as female infanticide and domestic violence and had widespread support, while another sought to improve the rights of LGBT individuals, a far more radical idea in the mid-2000s, and had limited uptake from individuals or other women's organizations. As this chapter shows, the extent to which any translator, particularly those embedded in NGOs, can promote new ideas that are only somewhat resonant with local issues depends on organizational autonomy and funding sources.

Although human rights ideas are often generated by local and national social movements, they exist in tandem with national civil rights. What distinguishes human rights ideas is that they refer to the international system for authority. Women's human rights ideas emerged from national women's movements, which pressured the international human rights system to incorporate women's rights as human rights. The 1993 Vienna Conference on Human Rights marked the first substantial recognition of women's rights by the UN human rights system. This idea was accepted only after a massive mobilization by women's groups around the world. Throughout the 1990s, leaders of national women's movements worked to establish women's rights as human rights by attending UN conferences, drafting documents, and demanding media attention, building on networks and ideologies that local activists had already put into place.[8] These global institutions were reshaped by the pressures of local and national social movements.[9] Thus, women's human rights came out of local social movements, were formalized in the international system, and subsequently traveled back from the global North to the global South.

From 2005 to 2009, we studied the circulation and localization of women's human rights ideas and practices in collaboration with professors Liu Meng at the Department of Social Work, National Women's

---

[8] Elisabeth Friedman, "Women's Human Rights: The Emergence of a Movement," in *Women's Rights, Human Rights: International Feminist Perspectives,* Julie Peters and Andrea Wolper, eds. (New York: Routledge, 1995); Merry, *Human Rights and Gender Violence.*

[9] Balakrishnan Rajagopal, *International Law from Below: Development, Social Movements, and Third World Resistance* (Cambridge: Cambridge University Press, 2003).

University in Beijing; N. Rajaram at the Department of Sociology, Maharaja Sayajirao University of Baroda in India; M. Rosa Alayza at the Escuela de Graduados, Pontífica Universidad Católica del Perú in Lima, Peru; and Sally Engle Merry in New York. In each site, we compared two or three NGOs working to implement women's human rights to see how they translated global concepts into local terms. We asked what women's human rights look like in the day-to-day work of these organizations and why organizations translate these concepts in different ways.

Each university collaborator hired and supervised a graduate student to carry out intensive ethnographic research on two to three organizations over a one to two year period: Mercedes Crisóstomo in Peru; Vaishali Zararia in India; M. Liu, Y. H. HU, and M.L. Liao in China; and Diana Yoon and Mihaela Serban in the USA. Each team wrote their own analysis. Merry was the primary supervisor for the New York City team and Levitt worked more intensively with the Peru team. Levitt and Merry developed the overarching research questions and raised the funds from NSF, but the detailed research strategies and questions for each site emerged through collaborative discussions. We traveled twice to each study site, and organized two conferences which were attended by all of the members of the research teams as well as by other regional experts, ensuring an active intellectual exchange among all of the researchers. Thus, this research is itself an international collaboration in which we all learned from one another. We worked to translate ideas about research, about the questions we asked, and about the meanings of our results from one national context to another.[10]

In each country, we compared two women's NGOs. All were selected because they had an explicit commitment to women's human rights. Each team interviewed the leaders of each organization, its trustees, and its staff members, observed staff/client interactions, determined caseload information, and traced the history of the organization. They each did ethnographic work in the organizations. There are clearly differences in how each team carried out this process, despite collective work on questions and issues for investigation. Although Merry and Levitt visited the sites, interviewed the leaders, and met the staff, we relied on the language skills, background knowledge, and analytic insights of each team.

In each site, NGOs cobbled together a collection of discourses and approaches to implementing women's human rights. Each NGO focused

---

[10] Peggy Levitt and Sally Engle Merry. *Global Networks: A Journal of Transnational Affairs* 9 (2009): 441–554; Sally Engle Merry, Peggy Levitt, Mihaela Serban Rosen, and Diana H. Yoon. "Law from Below: Women's Human Rights and Social Movements in New York City." *Law and Society Review* 44(1) (2010): 101–28.

on particular issues and kinds of services, such as providing legal aid to battered women or advocating for better treatment in court for battered women seeking custody of their children. Each adopted a communication technology to get out a message about gender equality and women's rights. Some used conventional practices such as street plays while others turned to techniques such as personal testimonials. All shared, to varying degrees, what we call the global values package of women's human rights.[11] This package is premised on ideas of equality and freedom from discrimination, as articulated in CEDAW (the Convention on the Elimination of all Forms of Discrimination Against Women), the major women's human rights convention. Article 1 of CEDAW defines discrimination against women as "any distinction, exclusion or restriction made on the basis of sex which has the effect or purpose of impairing or nullifying the recognition, enjoyment or exercise by women, irrespective of their marital status, on a basis of equality of men and women, of human rights and fundamental freedoms in the political, economic, social, cultural, civil, or any other field." This global values package, premised on an essentialized woman,[12] was shaped by worldwide events such as the end of the Cold War, the decline of socialism and communism, the rise of neoliberalism, and the promotion of democracy and the rule of law. When elite women lawyers in China adopt this values package, however, they use it differently than do neighborhood leaders in Peru with a tradition of liberation theology.

Overall, the work of these NGOs is deeply influenced by unequal global resources. The power of rich donors over poor recipients and the need to tailor and frame work in ways that elicit donations was dramatic, although it varied significantly among NGOs and countries. Some organizations refused to take foreign funds or speak English and resisted participating in global events. They drew on national and local agendas for women's reform, often explicitly rejecting international frameworks. Others relied heavily on international funding and ideological support, forcing them to conform to the agendas of their funders.

In order to understand how and when these organizations translated women's human rights into terms relevant to their work, we examined the issues each organization tackled, the way it communicated its ideas, and

---

[11] Amrita Basu, ed., with the assistance of C. Elizabeth McGrory, *The Challenge of Local Feminisms: Women's Movements in Global Perspective* (Boulder: Westview Press, 1995).

[12] See: Inderpal Grewal, "On the New Global Feminism and the Family of Nations: Dilemmas of Transnational Feminist Practice," in *Talking Visions: Multicultural Feminism in a Transnational Age*, Ella Shohat, ed. (New York: New Museum of Contemporary Art, 1998); Inderpal Grewal, "Review: Postcoloniality, Globalization, and Feminist Critique," *American Anthropologist* 110 (2008):517–20.

its modes of organization and funding. The importance of human rights in the choice of issues and communication strategies varied a good deal, depending on how receptive the local community was to human rights ideas, the value that a human rights frame added to working on local issues, and the extent of external funding that valued human rights.

1) *Issues* – The NGOs we studied selected some of the issues they tackled from the core values package, others from national and local women's movement issues, and still others from international human rights activism. Some issues are already well established in national social movements, such as domestic violence, while others are newer, such as sexual rights, and rely more extensively on international support and the human rights framework.

2) *Communications technologies* – Organizations may seek to convey their messages by using well-established local practices or new ones drawn from international models, such as citing international human rights conventions.

3) *Modes of organization and work* – Some groups had largely local leadership and funding, while others relied more extensively on donors, both national and international. Groups also differed in whether they provided more or less routine social services such as answering letters of complaint or providing legal aid or sought to promote systemic change by passing a new law or transforming ideas about rights.

The next section provides the empirical basis for this analysis. We acknowledge, from the outset, that the breadth of our comparison makes it quite difficult to capture fully the complexities of each case. The first two cases are presented in greater detail.

Vernacularizing Women's Human Rights: Four Case Studies

Baroda, India

Baroda is a city of more than 1.5 million people in Gujarat State, an economically industrialized region of Western India famous for trade and commerce. It is both economically progressive and the homeland of many who have migrated around the world and sent back financial and social remittances.[13] It is also socially conservative, a stronghold of the Hindu right and its political party, the BJP. Gujarat is deeply influenced by its native son, Gandhi, by labor movements, and by socialism, although the power of these ideologies is diminishing. Long a center of industrial

---

[13] Peggy Levitt, *God Needs No Passport* (New York: New Press, 2007).

activity, in the last few decades the region has experienced deindustriali-
zation leading to the impoverishment of former factory workers,
a decline in working-class labor solidarity, and a resurgence of communal
conflict.[14] The rise of the Hindutva movement has exacerbated violence
against Muslims, most recently in 2002. Like other parts of India,
Gujarat has a vibrant women's movement, originating in part in the
struggles against rape in police custody and dowry murders.[15] Maharaja
Sayajiarao University in Baroda was early in developing a women's studies program. Gujarat is home to the prominent women's NGO SEWA
(the Self-Employed Women's Association), a Gandhian-socialist organization that originated in the 1970s as a trade union for self-employed
women workers and expanded into the provision of microcredit activities.
There is a strong emphasis on families remaining together. Most women
do not work outside their homes and it is difficult for women to live
outside the context of a family.

The research team studied two NGOs in Baroda, both committed to
women's human rights. Both began with a focus on Marxism but are now
more clearly aligned with feminism. Both groups built on a strong presence of human rights ideas in public discourse, coupled with ideas about
Gandhian socialism and women's empowerment as developed by the
Indian women's movement. Over the last 40 years, the women's movement has worked on issues such as dowry murders, rape in custody,
violence in the family, sex selection, and female infanticide/foeticide.[16]
While both NGOs talked about using human rights to help women, they
took on different issues, embraced different ideologies, and relied on
different funding streams.

The more locally oriented organization we studied, Sahiyar, offers legal
aid and counseling for poor women. Sahiyar is located in a poor neighborhood in a small and unprepossessing office. It was founded in 1984 by
leaders who were influenced by the national women's movement and
Marxism. The key leader is a Trotskyite who attended university in
Baroda and belongs to the dominant caste in Baroda. All of the organization's trustees belong to the same caste and come from the surrounding
region. The leaders and staff deliberately speak the local language rather

[14] Jan Breman, "Communal Upheaval as a Resurgence of Social Darwinism," *Economic and Political Weekly*, 37 (2002):1485–8.

[15] Radha Kumar, *A History of Doing: An Illustrated Account of Movements for Women's Rights and Feminism in India, 1800–1990* (New Delhi: Zubaan, for Kali for Women, 1993); Radha Kumar, "From Chipko to Sati: The Contemporary Indian Women's Movement," in *The Challenge of Local Feminisms: Women's Movements in Global Perspective*, Amrita Basu, ed., with the assistance of C. Elizabeth McGrory (Boulder: Westview, 1995), reprinted in Delhi: Kali for Women, 1999.

[16] Kumar, *A History of Doing*; Kumar, "From Chipko to Sati."

than English, although the leaders are fluent in English. The staff members are primarily lower-middle-class young women who live in the immediate area. Their parents consider it a safe place to gain work experience. They receive a small honorarium rather than a salary because the work is considered a movement, not a job. They do not attend international conferences. Until recently, the organization refused to accept foreign funds. Its small budget comes from local sympathizers and organizations such as Hindu and Muslim charities.

The major issues tackled by this program are domestic violence, sex selection, advocacy for slum dwellers, and communal (Hindu/Muslim) violence. These are all core issues of the Indian women's movement. The program claims to support women who face violence, sexual exploitation, injustice and/or discrimination in the family, at their workplace or in society at large by providing counseling, moral and emotional support, legal help, and other practical assistance. It offers free legal advice through a lawyer who volunteers her time, and counseling through two regular staff members who are trustee-employees of Sahiyar. Many of the women who come to Sahiyar seek help for problems of domestic violence or divorce. During 2005/6, Sahiyar registered 51 cases, according to its annual report, more than half of which (28) concerned domestic violence. Sahiyar's report says that it settled the problems of 18 women without going to court, 8 cases are pending in court, and 24 cases are still in counseling and negotiation.

From March 2005 to November 2005, Rajaram and Zararia observed 47 persons coming to seek help, including 4 men. The women varied widely in caste, educational level, and income. Although most wanted legal advice, many required psychological counseling as well. Many women come just to see what their options are. One-third of the clients came to the office only once. Sahiyar often tries to bring parties together and help them reach a settlement. For example, in 2005 a woman came for help to claim her inheritance from her deceased husband's family. The family was willing to provide some support for her children but insisted that she pay a portion of an old family debt. The staff of Sahiyar met with both sides, offering legal advice and trying to persuade them to negotiate a compromise. In this and other cases, there was considerable discussion of the alternative of going to court. Human rights were rarely invoked but provided a backdrop for the intervention. For example, the lawyer at Sahiyar pressed the family to increase its contribution to the widow and her children.

Sahiyar also works on forging better Hindu/Muslim relationships and carries out public campaigns to combat widely recognized problems such as sex selection and dowry murders. The group uses traditional

communication technologies to convey its messages, such as making and
selling kites with messages on them (traditionally done during kite flying
festivals such as *Uttarayan*). One project involved hiring poor Muslim
women in the neighborhoods to make kites that highlighted the problems
of sex selection for a kite festival in January. Program staff and volunteers
sold the kites to repay the workers and to spread the message, dropped
from the sky as kites fell to the ground.

The program also stages street plays using familiar narrative forms.
These plays take traditional folk tales and rewrite them to expose social
problems such as domestic violence. For example, a street play called
Bandar Khel (Monkey Show) uses conventional characters, songs, and
performance to address the problem of dowry violence and murder.
It features a snake charmer (Kallu Madari), a male monkey (Ballu
Bandar), and a female monkey (Banno Bandariya). Our research team
translated the play, of which we provide a segment.

SNAKE CHARMER: See brother, they both fall in love with each other. Now if they
are in love, then we will have to get them married. But marriage is not a play
like among children! In that, we need our elders! So brother you become
a father of this heroine and you her mother and decide their marriage.
(The theater is so arranged that Sahiyar members sitting amidst – and thus
part of – the audience will become father and mother).
FATHER: We like the boy, but which religion does he belong to?
MOTHER: We like the girl, but what is her caste?
SNAKE CHARMER: Oh! religion and caste prevail among human beings. These are
petty animals. How would they know all these mental issues? At last, if groom
and bride are ready, then what will the father do!
So Ballu (male) and Banno (female) get married. Let us see what happens in their
house.

> Banno cooks the food, Ballu eats the food
> Banno washes the clothes, Ballu wears the clothes
> Banno remains at home, Ballu goes to work and earn

Oh! Today why is Ballu so upset? What happened? (Ballu says something in the
ears of snake charmer and he conveys it to audience). Listen, he says that he
suffered from a loss in his business. He is in need of money. You don't even
know from where the money will come? (Snake charmer to audience) Tell
me, will any one of you give him money? No one is ready. What is so big in
that? At last, the only solution is that ... Go and tell your wife to go to her
father's house and bring money from there.
(She refuses).
SNAKE CHARMER: Is she denying? What kind of a "man" are you! Can't you
convince your wife on such a small matter? Go and tell her again and if then
she is still not ready, slap her two or four times. Then she will definitely be
ready.

(Monkey beats the she-monkey; but the she-monkey refuses to go and ask for the money)

SNAKE CHARMER: Now what happened? What kind of a "hero'" you are! This guy needs to be taught everything. Go and buy kerosene from the market and burn her. Then there will be second marriage and you will get enough dowry.

(Monkey is scared and refuses to consider the idea)

SNAKE CHARMER: Oh! Why are you so scared? Nothing will happen to you. Don't you read newspapers every day? Burned; killed; but has any one been punished?

(Monkey looks at audience and says something in sign language to snake charmer)

SNAKE CHARMER: Are you afraid of society? People will forget in two or four days. Even her own sister will be ready to get married to you!

(Monkey goes back, says something to she-monkey and comes back again and whispers something in the ears of snake charmer)

SNAKE CHARMER (TO AUDIENCE): Do you know what this he-monkey and she-monkey told me? They told me that to burn and to kill your own wife is such a lowly and cowardly deed that we monkeys do not do that even in a "show" [theater]. Only a man can do such a thing.

Thus, Sahiyar tackles issues that are fundamental to the Indian women's movement through communication technologies that rely on established styles of performance and presentation. Their approaches to helping women through counseling and legal aid are common among NGOs in urban India. Sahiyar's leaders are closely tied to Baroda's women's movement, frequently collaborating with other groups with whom they share a pragmatic and Gandhian orientation. The leaders of Sahiyar talk about human rights, but there is not much discussion about it among the staff or with clients. Staff members frame the problems clients face in moralistic terms instead, in conformity with local understandings. For instance, after the communal riots of 2002 in which Muslim homes and businesses were attacked, staff members asked if it is *just* to attack innocent women from the minority community or if it is *fair* to hold women in the dominant community responsible for the wrong acts of their menfolk in carrying out these attacks. The organization is deeply embedded in Baroda society through its leadership, funding, staff, and client population, and uses human rights only as an incidental addition.

The second group, Vikalp, is far more national and transnational in its organization, leadership, funding, and issues. Although it promotes women's human rights and has been influenced by Marxism, it foregrounds different concerns and techniques. The program began in 1999 as a workers' rights organization. Now it works with an agricultural development program, supports women's courts or *nari adalats*, and works on HIV/AIDS issues. It has spun off a new group, Parma, which works on lesbian rights, a radical issue in this part of India. The leaders were raised and studied in other parts of India and abroad and are not Gujarati. They speak Hindi and English, are well-versed in national and international feminist debates, and are embedded in international activist networks. In the past, several of the leaders worked for the *Mahila Samakhya*, a feminist national women's organization. They travel widely and have recruited a board of trustees made up of like-minded, internationally oriented activists. Staff are encouraged to attend international conferences. The organization receives substantial support from the Ford Foundation and other international foundations which allows it to rent a fairly spacious office in a newer, middle-class area of the city.

Vikalp uses human rights discourse at the national and international levels, and to secure grants from funding agencies. At first it framed issues for staff and clients in terms of justice and morality, but it has started using the human rights framework for its staff as well and is pressing them to use it in their interactions with clients. During the two years of our study, leaders' references to staff about human rights increased. Some campaigns were framed in human rights language. For example, in 2005, during a period of floods, Vikalp sought to prevent the demolition of houses of the poor living on "encroached" land along a storm water drain. Rich encroachers succeeded in regularizing their land seizures, but the poor lacked the resources to do so. Vikalp collected allies, got media attention for the problem, and persuaded a well-known human rights lawyer to take this issue to the state high court as a human rights violation. The lawyer got an injunction saying that the poor should not be moved until alternative housing areas had been identified by the authorities. Vikalp also used rights language in a 2005 meeting on World Consumer Day when they sought to sell booklets and educate villagers about their consumer rights. At a rally on International Women's Day in 2005, Vikalp leaders distributed leaflets and talked about women's rights, issues of *dakan* (witch accusations), providing education for the girl child, delaying the age of marriage, gender discrimination, domestic violence, and alcoholism.

The leaders of Vikalp also used human rights in their campaign for acceptance of alternative sexualities. They found relatively little support from Indian women's NGOs for lesbian rights, so turned to the international community and started using the global language of "women's rights are human rights," CEDAW, and the Declaration on the Elimination of Violence Against Women. Other groups collaborate with them on issues such as housing rights for slum dwellers, but not on alternative sexuality. In 2006, they extended support to two lesbian girls from a small town near Baroda. After they ran away together, the parent of one of the girls and her brother were arrested by the police to force the girl and her partner to surrender. The leaders of Vikalp intervened to get the relatives released. After the girls were found, the local court issued an order saying that these two girls were free to go anywhere since they were adults.

Vikalp adopted novel modes of communication to present this issue to the public. At the Gujarat World Social Forum, Vikalp helped to sponsor a presentation by a gay and lesbian group featuring dance and testimonials about the difficulties of living as a gay person in this community. In 2006, one of the leaders appeared on a national TV channel in a discussion program about gays and lesbians. In the same year, she published a book about the lives of working-class lesbians in India that garnered national attention.[17] New approaches include a drop-in center for lesbians. The national and international sexual rights movement is an important source of inspiration for the work of this organization. A poster developed by the program exemplifies its use of national and international symbols for the lesbian rights movement (see Figure 9.1).[18] In this poster, traditional Indian religious figures are reconfigured to represent equally sized males and females and adorned with the Indian flag and the pink triangle as the poster announces that lesbian rights are human rights.

The impact of international human rights ideas is greater in Vikalp than in Sahiyar. It actively appropriates ideas and strategies from abroad and combines them with locally recognizable approaches to address new issues. This organization has international funding and its leaders are connected to national and international social networks. In contrast, Sahiyar is more Gujarat-oriented and uses locally appropriate repertoires, funds, and language to address women's concerns. The language of human rights is present when the leader talks about her work, but it is not actively incorporated and deployed in everyday practice. Both organizations advocate helping women to stand up for themselves, but Vikalp is more likely to refer to this as human rights and to locate this empowered subjectivity outside the home. For Vikalp, international human rights are particularly valuable for pursuing sexual rights, an issue that does not yet have broad support in the Indian women's movement. Thus, both groups translate parts of the global values package of women's human rights to support their activities, but, even though they work in the same city, they do so quite differently. The other three sites of the research showed similar patterns, in which forms of translation differed depending on

[17] Maya Sharma, *Loving Women – Being Lesbian in Unprivileged India* (New Delhi: Yoda Press, 2006).
[18] Figure reprinted here with permission of Vikalp.

Figure 9.1: Poster Created by Vikalp to Promote Lesbian Rights.

differences in funding and support, choice of issues, and local attitudes toward human rights.

New York City, USA

The two groups we studied in New York City work in an environment characterized by ambivalence toward using human rights to address domestic wrongs. The USA consistently denounces perceived human rights violations around the world, yet refuses to ratify several existing international human rights conventions. As in China, there is a sense that national institutions do a better job at protecting rights than their international counterparts. However, during the last ten years there has been a resurgence of interest in human rights by progressive groups. For example, some groups advocate seeing the victims of Hurricane Katrina as internally displaced people and adopting international standards to protect them.

We compared two NGOs in New York. One group, Voices of Women (VOW), works with women who have survived violence and now lobby for better treatment for battered women in the legal system. The other, the Human Rights Initiative (HRI), seeks to incorporate human rights principles into New York City law. Both groups talk about women's human rights and ways to apply them, but the second group has a far more explicit commitment to human rights. Its mission is to pass an ordinance in New York City implementing the human rights conventions on women and race (the Convention on the Elimination of all forms of Discrimination Against Women [CEDAW], and the Convention on the Elimination of Racial Discrimination [CERD]). There is more human rights talk here than at VOW.

The Voices of Women Organizing Project (VOW) of the Battered Women's Resource Center started in 2000 with the goal of enabling domestic violence survivors to become advocates on policy issues that affect battered women. In its recent report on the New York City family court, it describes itself as

[A] grassroots advocacy organization of survivors of domestic violence who are working to improve the many systems battered women and their children rely on for safety and justice. VOW members represent the diversity of New York City and include African American, Caribbean, Latina, white, Asian, immigrant, lesbian, disabled and formerly incarcerated women. Since 2000, VOW members have documented system failures and developed recommendations for change, and they have educated policy makers, elected officials, the public and each other through trainings, meetings, testimony, and most recently, with this report.[19]

Voices of Women is heavily influenced by the discourse and strategies of the battered women's movement. Members talk about being survivors. Human rights ideals are not a frequent topic of conversation, but are an additional political resource. For example, VOW's recent report on the family court argued that government accountability is a universal human rights norm and that institutions that provide public services should discharge their duties according to human rights principles such as accountability, transparency, and participation.[20] The organization mostly speaks the language of the feminist movement against domestic violence, but sees human rights as a valuable extra resource.

The organization runs with a small staff of director, associate director, and one part-time staff member, and a modest budget. It relies heavily on volunteers – formerly battered women who now do advocacy work in the courts and in the legislature. It is the only organization in New York with a mission to empower battered women in their transformation from

[19] Voices of Women Organizing Project, *Justice Denied: How Family Courts in New York City Endanger Battered Women and Children* (2008), p. 15: http://vowbwrc.org.
[20] Ibid.

victim to survivor to activist. The organization's focus on advocacy and activism renders it distinct from the service-delivery model of many other domestic violence organizations. The director has extensive experience in community organizing and leadership development and has worked with survivors of domestic violence for more than 25 years. The associate director came to VOW with expertise in direct services to battered women and advocacy on domestic violence policies. The organization's guiding principles and practices reflect the view that survivors' perspectives are an important source of authority and expertise. Interviews with members suggest that working with VOW involved a distinct process of politicization and transformation in consciousness. Thus, its political advocacy is deeply influenced by the battered women's movement, but some of VOW's work is also informed by human rights.

VOW members do not talk about how to use human rights or about specific international mechanisms such as treaty articles and institutions. However, staff and members have attended human rights trainings and use human rights technologies in their political activism. In 2003, the organization initiated the Battered Mothers' Justice Campaign in collaboration with the Urban Justice Center's Human Rights Project, the organization that promoted the Human Rights Initiative to pass an ordinance in New York City. In an effort to provide human rights documentation of the experiences of battered women in New York City family courts, VOW staff and the Human Rights Project trained 14 VOW members to interview survivors. In 2006, they interviewed 75 domestic violence survivors about their experiences in New York City family courts. Women talked about losing custody of children to their batterers despite histories of being the primary caretaker, about inadequate measures for safety in the court building, and about unprofessional conduct of judges and lawyers against women raising claims of domestic violence. The data provided the basis for a report, *Justice Denied: How Family Courts in New York City Endanger Battered Women and Children* that documented these problems and identified the articles of human rights conventions that the Family Courts violated.[21] It offered recommendations for change. The report was presented to city and state government officials and made available to the public on the web. VOW also planned to organize a tribunal, inspired by comfort women tribunals, for battered mothers and children to testify about these violations. These examples show how the organization adopted human rights technologies.

[21] Voices of Women Organizing Project, *Justice Denied: How Family Courts in New York City Endanger Battered Women and Children* (2008): www.leadershipcouncil.org/docs/VOW_JusticeDenied_sum.pdf

The Human Rights Initiative uses human rights far more explicitly. It has an ambitious agenda of promoting human rights in the USA. The project was born out of discussions among national and international activists at the world conference on racism in Durban, South Africa, in 2001. Building upon a successful effort in San Francisco, the leaders formed a coalition of organizations to draft and pass a new city ordinance in New York on women's human rights in the same year. Unlike the San Francisco ordinance, however, the law the HRI developed took an intersectional approach, prohibiting both gender and race discrimination. A coalition of three national groups – NOW Legal Defense Fund (now called Legal Momentum), Amnesty International USA, and the ACLU (including its local chapter) – and two New York groups – the Urban Justice Institute and the Women of Color Policy Network of NYU – worked on writing and promoting the ordinance. They formed a broader coalition of 160 New York City NGOs interested in using human rights, although the 15 we interviewed expressed a cautious commitment to human rights and were somewhat skeptical about its potential impact in the USA. After two years of work, the ordinance was sent to the city council, which substantially revised and weakened it. At the same time, after initial strong support by the better-funded national organizations, there was some drop-off in enthusiasm by these organizations and reluctance to devote further staff time to the project. The city organizations were left to carry it forward. When they failed to get funding, the initiative lost critical staffing and stalled.

The HRI explicitly used human rights law as the centerpiece of its work, building a coalition of supportive organizations behind the ordinance and providing them with human rights training. In contrast, VOW relied largely on the battered women's movement as its framework, but appropriated parts of human rights language and tactics in its documentation project. In contrast to HRI, which put human rights at the center of its strategy, VOW used human rights largely as a communications technology rather than as a way to define issues or focus its work. HRI relied on staff from well-funded national organizations and foundations, but lost steam when these sources of support disappeared. In contrast, VOW, with its volunteer advocates, was less reliant on substantial external funding. HRI emerged from a UN conference and an international network of human rights activists, while VOW was closely tied to the US battered women's movement. Thus, the differences in the way these organizations used human rights is closely connected to their choice of issues, mission, organization, leadership, and funding. Substantial funding enables a group to venture into less conventional areas of work, such as passing a municipal human rights ordinance, but makes that group vulnerable if the funding disappears.

Lima, Peru

In Lima, the use of human rights to promote social justice has a long and varied history. For nearly fifty years, progressive religious and lay leaders have worked actively with the urban poor, forming base-level communities and collective soup kitchens under the inspiration of liberation theology and the Catholic Church's commitment to serve the poor. During the Velasco Alvarado left-leaning military government (1968–75), the state dedicated major resources to improving conditions for the urban poor who had begun migrating to Lima en masse. Human rights ideas were later deployed by activists seeking to protect rural villagers from being forced to cooperate with the Maoist *Sendero Luminoso* (Shining Path) movement. They were subsequently used to challenge the oppressive policies put in place by the authoritarian Fujimori government in the 1980s and early 1990s to bring *Sendero* to its knees. The Catholic Church's opposition to abortion also inspired women's human rights activists to rally for reproductive freedom.

We studied two women's organizations working in the squatter settlements surrounding Lima. One, SEA (Servicios Educativos de El Agustino), was created by religious and lay leaders who embraced liberation theology. It began as a set of activities within the local parish and was spun off as an independent organization that maintains strong ties to the church. At the outset, one of SEA's principal activities was creating communal kitchens where neighborhood women pool their resources and cook together, thus feeding their families at a lower cost. Over time, the strong leaders that emerged from these activities tackled other issues, such as neighborhood improvement, education, and health care. The main international influence on this organization was religious, through contacts with like-minded progressive Catholic activists around the world. However, these imported ideas have deep Peruvian roots and resonate strongly with religious and social justice discourses already in place. Although its leaders say they are committed to human rights, human rights talk plays a very minor role in the operation of the program itself. Liberation theology is central to defining issues and work programs such as communal kitchens, but is quite compatible with aspects of women's human rights.

The other NGO we studied is more explicitly committed to a women's human rights framework. DEMUS (Estudio para la Defensa de los

Derechos Humanos de las Mujeres), based in Lima, is a national organization with strong ties to feminist organizations throughout Latin America. International funders support its programs. DEMUS runs a school for women leaders in a squatter settlement that served as one site for the research. This school brought international feminist ideas to the women living in this area, although not always in ways that were readily accepted by the community leaders who attended. For example, one exercise pointed out that women should be able to take leadership roles outside the home, yet most of the women in the class were already leaders in the communal kitchens and the neighborhood. Another promoted the right to sexual satisfaction, although the idea seemed quite unfamiliar and uncomfortable to many. Nevertheless, the women in the community were eager to take part in this leadership training program and signed up in substantial numbers. There was some discussion of human rights in the program, but most of it was framed by global feminist ideas. As in Baroda and New York, the more internationally focused and supported program was more explicit about human rights than the more locally grounded one.

Beijing, China

In contrast to Peru, China has resisted the idea of human rights. It has a rich tradition of women's rights dating from the creation of the People's Republic, and a mass political organization, the All China Women's Federation (ACWF), dedicated to protecting what it calls women's rights and interests. This government-backed mass organization for women seeks to help women who claim that their rights have been infringed. In 1992, China passed a national law defining women's rights and interests that articulates the principles of CEDAW for the Chinese context. A nation-wide network of offices for women's rights and interests responds to letters of complaint by contacting other government agencies or ACWF offices who can help women with violations of their rights and interests.

Of the two women's groups in Beijing we studied, both of which described themselves as using human rights to improve the lives of women, one emerged from these complaint bureaus. This experimental program, started about 2005, was funded by the government and a cosmetics company and headed by reliable party members. It offers counseling by university-trained social workers as well as legal assistance. The organization sorts complainants into those with "legal" problems who are helped through government administrative channels and those with "emotional" problems who are counseled by the social workers.

Their professional training includes a commitment to human rights, in the sense that every individual is equally worthy of receiving assistance. In general, the agency focuses on fixing individual problems rather than challenging the rules themselves. It addresses the same issues as the ACWF and follows similar procedures, although its use of social workers has added a new mode of intervention more compatible with human rights.

The second organization, established in 1995 and inspired by the Beijing Women's Conference in the same year, is a legal aid center that provides legal services to women, particularly those facing domestic violence. Increasingly, it works on model cases that challenge public policies. It is primarily interested in changing laws and policies through litigation, public education campaigns, and policy reform. For example, in one case, the agency challenged a policy prohibiting married women with children from attending the university. This organization receives a good deal of international financial and political support. Pictures of Madeleine Albright and Hillary Clinton adorn the walls of its office in a modern high-rise building. The organization is not led by a party member, but by a powerful board of directors that includes high-ranking officials who protect the organization from government critique. It is explicitly committed to promoting women's human rights. Its issues, communication strategies, and modes of intervention are drawn from international human rights activism.

The first organization uses human rights very indirectly. It is closely tied to the government and helps women within the context of existing laws. Leaders are connected to national government networks and well equipped to provide administrative solutions to women's grievances when they have had their rights infringed. However, the social workers, who are given the task of dealing with clients that the organization defines as emotionally suffering but without real claims, are in a relatively powerless position. Although they provide counseling that is inspired by human rights concepts, they can do little else to help their clients. The second organization looks to the international human rights framework, which emphasizes protection from discrimination and gender equality. It relies on international funding, its leaders travel internationally, and it often receives international visitors. Its goal is to promote social change and gender equality by changing laws and policies. Like the HRI in New York, it was a global conference, the 1995 World Conference on Women, that inspired the leaders. The organization still maintains connections to international funding and networks. As in the other examples, it appears that organizations that receive international funding and have leaders connected through international networks talk more explicitly about human rights and are able to tackle less conventional and less widely supported issues.

Conclusions

For all these organizations, human rights are an important aspect of the way they do their work. Civil rights defined by the nation, as well as other social justice ideologies such as liberation theology, are also important to these organizations, as are the ideas and issues raised by national women's movements. Human rights are only one set of ideas and approaches available to them. Some groups are deeply embedded in other justice ideologies, such as liberation theology or the feminist violence against women movement, and make only fleeting and indirect references to human rights. Sahiyar, Voices of Women, SEA, and the legal assistance bureau in Beijing all focus on core issues in their national women's movements and say relatively little about human rights within the organization. Other organizations are more explicitly committed to human rights and take on issues not so widely supported, such as Vikalp and its work on lesbian rights, the Human Rights Initiative and its intersectional approach to discrimination, and DEMUS's focus on women's reproductive rights. The Beijing legal aid program also tries to change policies that are discriminatory to women.

Funding is an important dimension of this variation. External funding, including international funding, offers more space to move into challenging issues and to engage in work that is relatively unsupported by local and national women's organizations and ideologies, such as lesbian rights in India or women's human rights in China. DEMUS's effort to impart regional and international feminism, the women's legal aid clinic in Beijing, Vikalp with its LGBT agenda, and the Human Rights Initiative's efforts to persuade New York City to pass human rights legislation all challenge conventional ways of thinking about women's rights. The funding allows them greater latitude to develop these campaigns, which are less resonant with local cultural understandings. On the other hand, this funding comes with strings attached. Organizations must respond to the agendas of their donors. Insofar as the donors wish to promote human rights, the organizations must take this approach. Groups that are less dependent on external funding tend to rely on ideologies and discourses grounded in national or local movements and domestic rights frameworks, such as socialism in the case of Sahiyar, the battered women's movement for Voices of Women, and liberation theology for SEA. These groups appropriate human rights in more limited and pragmatic ways. Their work is more resonant with local ideas.

What does the human rights framework offer in situations in which it does not have a strong resonance or a close fit with existing ideologies? It offers the legitimation of a transnational set of standards, the magic of a universal moral code, and technologies of building cases through reporting and documentation. But perhaps the most important contribution is access to allies outside the local community. By phrasing issues in the language of human rights, they become understandable to other organizations and individuals participating in this transnational ideological system. The human rights framework itself helps ideas travel. Groups that lack support from other women's groups in the area turn to international networks for information and support, as Vikalp does for lesbian rights and the Beijing legal aid clinic does for challenging gender discrimination. These international links provide political resources and ideas that challenge local ways of thinking and working. However, groups that rely on such international support are less in tune with national and local ways of framing problems. For example, DEMUS, a regional organization, failed to appreciate the leadership roles of the women in communal kitchens in their neighborhoods in its leadership training program.

Clearly, there is a connection between the organization of an NGO and the issues and strategies it adopts. Funding, leadership, and networks all make a difference. This is an iterative process as an organization seeks to establish itself, draw on the resources available to shape an agenda, and build the funds and infrastructure necessary to engage in social activist work. The interesting feature of this comparison is the variety of ways human rights, as a global discourse, is used under these different organizational and national constraints. It is clearly an open discourse, with multiple uses and appropriations. As it is vernacularized, it is reshaped so that its ideas and practices bear little resemblance to the original legal documents and political projects that put them into motion. The extent of transformation depends on the characteristics of the organization and the wider social context within which it works. Organizations funded by international donors tend to develop approaches at greater variance from local understandings but more similar to the human rights framework itself. They pose a greater challenge to local hierarchies but are more dependent on global funding and ideas. Locally supported organizations pick and choose segments of human rights ideas and practices more freely, but embed them within familiar issues and strategies.

Vernacularization is a process in which issues, communication technologies, and modes of organization and work are appropriated and translated, sometimes in fragmented and incoherent ways, at the interface of transnational, national, and local ideologies and practices. It is often a pragmatic strategy for mobilizing political, cultural, and financial resources. For some leaders, of course, human rights is a matter of faith and morality. Vernacularization is not a form of cultural homogenization since human rights ideas are substantially transformed by the organizations that use them. It is not a clash between universal principles and cultural relativist assertions of difference but a pragmatic process of negotiation and translation. When organizations talk little about human rights, this reflects a lack of political traction for human rights, not cultural relativist resistance. The process is a dimension of the partial, pragmatic, and unstable nature of the transnational circulation and adoption of ideas and practices that Tsing refers to as "friction," shaped by the structural conditions under which adoption and resistance take place.[22]

However, the need to vernacularize human rights in a way that is resonant with local cultural practices serves as a limitation on the transformative power of human rights. Our research shows a broad capacity on the part of human rights activists to tailor human rights ideas to local situations, which promotes adoption of these ideas, but possibly in a more attenuated form. Of course, the human rights system itself has no control over the way these ideas are appropriated, so the process of vernacularization can produce ideas and practices antithetical to human rights ideas themselves, yet legitimated by the aura of an international consensus on rights. For example, abortion debates can be framed as the opposition between the right to life and the right to choose, illustrating the malleability of human rights as a discourse of claims-making. From a pragmatic perspective, the risk of vernacularization that deviates from human rights principles is the price of vernacularization that makes them more appealing in particular cultural contexts.

Vernacularization captures the agency of intermediaries who remake transnational ideas and practices in the vernacular along with the structures that constrain agency. These include state policy, organizational leadership, and North/South inequalities in funding, along with cultural factors such as historical experiences and familiarity with ideas such as human rights. By focusing on organizations and actors that work across local, national, and international scales, we can begin to understand the dynamics of power and agency that shape the transnational circulation of ideas and practices such as human rights. Understanding the role of vernacularization in the human rights process highlights two dilemmas for human rights practitioners: the process of vernacularization may so attenuate the core principles of human rights that they no longer carry the

---

[22] Anna Tsing, *Friction: An Ethnography of Global Connection* (Princeton: Princeton University Press, 2005).

meaning that is embedded in the system as a whole. Moreover, human rights as a frame of reference can be appropriated in a variety of ways, including those that violate the core principles of the human rights system itself. Nevertheless, such active appropriation and redefinition of human rights is an inevitable dimension of the global circulation of ideas and practices.

10 Re-Framing Human Rights Advocacy: The Rise of Economic Rights

Shareen Hertel

Picture a gallery, with a long wall of paintings by "old masters." Now picture a wall studded with mosaic tiles in an abstract pattern. This chapter analyzes the evolution of human rights advocacy from roughly the 1990s onward, and argues that there are multiple and complex movements that animate the act of naming wrongs and claiming rights. To fully capture the nature of contemporary changes in human rights norms and modes of strategic interaction, we need to tune our eyes to "see" multiple forms of advocacy. The dominant international human rights movement (emanating out of industrialized states such as the United States or United Kingdom) is like the paintings by the "old masters." Its form and themes are readily identifiable to many observers. By contrast, there is a whole set of human rights movements (many localized in developing states or in marginalized communities within industrialized ones) that are less easily recognizable. They don't fit into the frames suited to the "old masters."

These alternative movements do not explicitly take their strategic aims from the dominant human rights movement. Nor do they necessarily operate in the same set of institutional arenas (i.e., at the transnational or international level). Rather, they operate strategically in the spaces (both discursive and physical) that are best suited to their varied and complex aims. Their goals are not necessarily antithetical to the mainstream human rights movement, but they are conceived of and executed largely independently of it. They are pieces of a more complex mosaic whose combined effects offer new ways of perceiving not only the act of rights claiming, but also the rights at stake themselves.

Within the mosaic, I focus on human rights activism animated around economic rights in order to demonstrate the role that such alternative human rights movements have played in the evolution of contemporary human rights norms, institutions, and advocacy. The growing wave of scholarship and advocacy on economic rights that has emerged since the early 2000s usefully complicates the standard picture of the human rights movement by revealing the contested nature of a broader range of human rights and the challenge of enforcing compliance with them. Economic rights-driven advocacy is not intent upon subverting the human rights canon or institutional framework per se. Rather, it advances a set of claims that extend beyond the civil and political rights frontiers that have defined the field in theory and practice for most of the latter twentieth century.

For economic rights advocates and others in the mosaic beyond the mainstream human rights movement, operating domestically and internationally are not necessarily opposed choices. Rather, these groups have made pragmatic decisions about whether to use international or domestic law (or some hybrid combination) as the normative baseline for naming wrongs and claiming rights. The have also been strategic in determining whether to work through domestic or international institutional frameworks (or both) for rights implementation. Rather than necessarily take their cues from external human rights organizations, these groups place a premium on being free to choose when and under what conditions international human rights norms will factor into domestic human rights campaigns and when domestic law will trump. In the process, they have developed a creative approach to legal and social mobilization and a creative array of vehicles for rights implementation.

My arguments in this chapter thus add to a broader stream in the human rights literature aimed at theorizing "bottom up" approaches to norms evolution. Political scientist Amitav Acharya[1] and anthropologist Sally Engle Merry[2] have offered seminal interpretations of how non-dominant actors influence norms evolution. Merry's notion of vernacularization and Acharya's notion of localization capture the process through which local actors render outside or "foreign" norms[3] acceptable, while Acharya's concept of subsidiarity explains how local actors outwardly project new normative constructs – in defiance of conventional norms – that can lead to wholly new interpretations of existing norms.[4]

---

[1] Amitav Acharya, "How Ideas Spread: Whose Norms Matter? Norm Localization and Institutional Change in Asian Regionalization," *International Organization* 58:2 (2004): 239–75; Amitav Acharya, "Norm Subsidiarity and Regional Orders: Sovereignty, Regionalism, and Rule-Making in the Third World," *International Studies Quarterly* 55:1 (2011): 95–123.

[2] Sally Engle Merry, "Legal Pluralism and Transnational Culture: The Ka Ho'okolokolonui Kanaka Maoli Tribunal, Hawai'i, 1993," in Richard A. Wilson ed., *Human Rights, Culture and Context: Anthropological Perspectives* (London: Pluto Press, 1997): 28–48; Sally Engle Merry, "Transnational Human Rights and Local Activism: Mapping the Middle," *American Anthropologist* 108:1 (2006): 38–51

[3] Acharya, "How Ideas Spread," 247, 251.

[4] Norms localization involves justifying international norms to local audiences but "does not require either a sense of exclusion or a perception of big power hypocrisy, or perception of dominance, neglect, violation, or abuse. The latter are triggers of norm subsidiarity" (see Acharya, "Norms Subsidiarity," 99). Over time, localization may or may not

My work echoes but is distinct from both Acharya's and Merry's in several respects. All of us are interested in subaltern dynamics of norms evolution. But localization, vernacularization, and subsidiarity emerge as part of an explicitly internationalized and conflict-ridden "response" to international norms. By contrast, the theoretical framework I develop in this chapter does not require either internationalized interaction or conflict. These are neither necessary nor sufficient conditions for the emergence of new norms from the bottom up.

Activists in non-dominant settings may forge new norms cognizant of what happens at the "center" but focused on waging more strategically important struggles at the local level that trump the need to craft strategy in reference to the "center." In the process, they go beyond localization/vernacularization or subsidiarity because they do more than legitimate or contest existing international norms. They can forge entirely new ones, or flesh out existing norms that have been underplayed or ignored by the center.

The chapter proceeds in three sections: first, it situates economic rights activism theoretically and practically as a central driver of change in human rights norms and advocacy. Second, using case examples from Mexico, Bangladesh, and India, it demonstrates that by recognizing the interplay between both the familiar and the less recognized forms of human rights advocacy, we gain a more comprehensive picture of why and how naming, shaming, and claiming in the name of rights take place. Third and finally, the chapter explores how this alternative picture of human rights advocacy opens a fuller view of potential future trends in the field of human rights.

Economic Rights as Drivers of Change in Human Rights Scholarship and Advocacy

Much of the pioneering literature on human rights advocacy has centered on civil and political rights concepts and case studies. The legal concepts, institutional analysis, and empirical cases central to the literature that informs many of the chapters in this edited volume – as well as Keck and Sikkink's classic *Activists Beyond Borders*[5] and Risse, Ropp and Sikkink's foundational work[6] – pivot around the idea that states are internally riven with and interconnected by networks through which state and non-state

---

"produce an incremental shift toward fundamental change or norm displacement" (see Acharya, "How Ideas Spread, 253).

[5] Margaret E. Keck and Kathryn Sikkink, *Activists Beyond Borders: Advocacy Networks in International Politics* (Ithaca: Cornell University Press, 1998).

[6] Thomas Risse, Stephen C. Ropp, and Kathryn Sikkink eds., *The Power of Human Rights: International Norms and Domestic Change* (New York: Cambridge University Press, 1999); Thomas Risse, Stephen C. Ropp, and Kathryn Sikkink eds., *The Persistent Power of Human Rights: From Commitment to Compliance* (New York: Cambridge University Press, 2013).

actors mediate persuasive as well as coercive incentives in the interest of enforcing compliance with human rights (typically civil and political rights).

In the exceptional cases in which this and other mainstream human rights literature has taken up economic rights cases, it has tended to analyze them in terms of violations – for example, flogging of workers in sweatshops or killing of unionists.[7] Or it has analyzed explicit discrimination in access to work or social services (health, education, etc.) based on ascriptive characteristics such as gender or race.[8] This literature mirrors trends on the ground among Northern-based human rights organizations. Aryeh Neier, founding director of Human Rights Watch, has argued consistently that groups like his should only take up the civil and political rights aspects of economic and social issues in situations "where violations, violators, and remedies can be clearly identified,"[9] such as in cases of clear discrimination in access to education or healthcare.[10]

Establishing responsibility for failure to fulfill a "minimum core" of economic rights is complex both substantively and temporally because economic rights are, by definition, "progressively realized" more fully over time.[11] This presents the challenge of a less direct or one-dimensional causal link between perpetrator and victim. Only cases of outright discrimination in access to economic rights fit the conventional standard of immediate realization.[12] Moreover, the risk of interruption, retrogression, and/or reinterpretation of economic rights looms larger than it does with

---

[7] Nicole Deitelhoff and Klaus Dieter Wolf, "Business and Human rights: How Corporate Norms Violates become Norms Entrepreneurs," in Risse, Ropp and Sikkink, *The Persistent Power of Human Rights*, 223, 230.

[8] Abuses such as flogging are more closely elided with physical integrity rights, the rights central to some of the most effective transnational human rights advocacy campaigns of the twentieth century, as discussed in Keck and Sikkink, *Activists Beyond Borders*. Flogging also involves a more direct link between perpetrator and victim than do cases of abuse stemming from denial of basic minimum guarantees of economic rights – such as insufficient state provisioning of the right to food.

[9] Aryeh Neier, *The International Human Rights Movement: A History* (Princeton: Princeton University Press, 2012), 80.

[10] Kenneth Roth, successor to Neier, has defended the organization's limited/strategic engagement with economic rights in a high-profile series of exchanges with other advocates across multiple issues of *Human Rights Quarterly*. For example, see Kenneth Roth, "Defending Economic, Social and Cultural Rights: Practical Issues Faced by an International Human Rights Organization," *Human Rights Quarterly* 26:1 (2004): 63–73.

[11] Clair Apodaca, "Measuring the Progressive Realization of Economic, Social and Cultural Rights," in Shareen Hertel and Lanse P. Minkler, eds., *Economic Rights: Conceptual, Measurement, and Policy Issues* (New York: Cambridge University Press, 2007): 165–81; Katherine G. Young, "The Minimum Core of Economic and Social Rights: A Concept in Search of Content," *The Yale Journal of International Law 33* (2008): 113–75; Shareen Hertel, "Why Bother? Measuring Economic Rights – The Research Agenda," *International Studies Perspectives* 7:3 (2006): 215–30.

[12] International law on economic rights – specifically, the 1976 International Covenant on Economic, Social and Cultural Rights (ICESCR) – requires states parties to the treaty to

regard to civil and political rights because of the progressively realized character of economic rights and their often debated baselines.[13]

Given the challenge of establishing evaluative baselines for economic rights fulfillment, a "violations approach"[14] to monitoring related state obligations initially took hold intellectually and was reinforced through UN practice from the late 1980s onward.[15] Mainstream human rights groups based in industrialized countries took up the violations approach extensively in the 1990s because it dovetailed with the prevailing legal and institutional frameworks not only within the UN but also at the national level in countries where "class standing" of poor people was non-existent (for purposes of legal redress) and civil and political rights guarantees were articulated constitutionally but not economic rights ones.[16]

Yet by the early 2000s, Chapman and other early proponents of the violations approach began to question its limits and urged a more comprehensive minimum core standard for assessing economic rights performance.[17] The minimum core approach was central to a burgeoning wave of creative legal advocacy in developing countries such as South Africa, India, and Brazil, all of which have constitutions that explicitly protect economic rights and ensure class-standing for poor people as plaintiffs of rights violations. Increasingly savvy local advocates used their own national or regional courts to demand redress of economic rights shortfalls in ways that outpaced activity either in the UN monitoring bodies themselves or in the courts of industrialized states.[18]

---

ensure that non-discrimination in access to economic rights is immediately actionable, whereas fulfillment of these rights can be realized progressively over time.

[13] Hertel, "Why Bother?,"224–27; see also Hertel and Minkler, *Economic Rights*, especially 14–20.

[14] Audrey Chapman, "A 'Violations Approach' for Monitoring the International Covenant on Economic, Social and Cultural Rights," *Human Rights Quarterly* 18:1 (1996): 23–66.

[15] The main documents used to interpret state obligations with the International Covenant on Economic, Social and Cultural Rights (ICESCR) are both anchored explicitly in a "violations" approach – namely, the 1987 Limburg Principles and the 1997 Maastricht Guidelines on Violations of Economic, Social & Cultural Rights. The Limburg and Maastrich documents have significantly informed the work of the UN committee responsible for monitoring the ICESCR.

[16] Roth, "Defending Economic, Social and Cultural Rights," 67–8.

[17] Audrey Chapman, "The Status of Efforts to Monitor Economic, Social & Cultural Rights," in Economic Rights: Conceptual, Measurement, and Policy Issues, Hertel and Minkler, eds., 143–64, see especially 155–6.

[18] Roberto Gargarella, Pilar Domingo, and Theunis Roux, *Courts and Social Transformation in New Democracies: An Institutional Voice for the Poor?* (Hampshire: Ashgate Publishing Ltd., 2006); Varun Gauri and Daniel M. Brinks, "Introduction: The Elements of Legalization and the Triangular Shape of Social and Economic Rights," in Varun Gauri and Daniel M. Brinks, eds., *Courting Social Justice: Judicial Enforcement of Social and Economic Rights in the Developing World* (New York/Cambridge UK: Cambridge University Press, 2008): 1–37; Heinz Klug, "Achieving Rights to Land, Water and Health in Post-Apartheid South Africa," in LaDawn Haglun and

Qualitative case-study-based literature, in turn, detailed the evolution of economic rights-based legal and social mobilization. This was complemented by a growing body of robust quantitative indicators for measuring state willingness to fulfill economic rights, including index-based measures such as the Economic and Social Rights Fulfillment (or SERF) Index that could be used to compare the relative willingness to fulfill economic rights on the part of state and sub-state entities.[19] The resulting synthesis has yielded a type of human rights scholarship and activism that is focused on shortfalls of fulfillment of economic rights, such as lack of sufficient access to food[20] or the right to development.[21] It substantively

Robin Stryker, eds., *Economic, Social and Cultural Rights: Emerging Possibilities for Social Transformation* (University of California Press, 2015): 199–218; Laura Birchfield and Jessica Corsi, "Between Starvation and Globalization: Realizing the Right to Food in India," *Michigan Journal of International Law* 31:4 (2010): 691–764; Young, "The Minimum Core of Economic and Social Rights"; Alicia Ely Yamin and Siri Gloppen, eds., *Litigating Health Rights: Can Courts Bring More Justice to Health?* (Cambridge: Harvard University Press, 2011); Danie Brand and Sage Russell, *Exploring the Content of Socioeconomic Rights: South African and International Perspectives* (Pretoria, South Africa: Protea Boekhuis, 2002).

[19] Developed by Fukuda-Parr, Lawson-Remer, and Randolph, the SERF index can be used to compare government willingness to fulfill economic rights by assessing how far different countries fall from an idea "achievement possibilities frontier" that captures what they could achieve in terms of fulfillment, given their own resource endowments and the performance of their peers; see Sakiko Fukuda-Parr, Terra Lawson-Remer, and Susan Randolph, "An Index of Economic and Social Rights Fulfillment: Concept and Methodology," *The Journal of Human Rights* 8, 3 (2009): 195–221. See also Susan Randolph, Sakiko Fukuda-Parr, and Terra Lawson-Remer, "Economic and Social Rights Fulfillment Index: Country Scores and Rankings," *The Journal of Human Rights* 9, 3 (2010): 230–61. The SERF index can be adapted to make subnational comparisons such as among states within the United States: see Susan Randolph, Michelle Prairie, and John Stewart, "Monitoring State Fulfillment of Economic and Social Rights Fulfillment in the United States," *Human Rights Review* 13, 2 (2012): 139–65. It can also be adapted for comparison across subnational units within India; see Susan Randolph and Shareen Hertel, "The Right to Food: A Global Perspective," in *The Right to Food in South Africa: New Directions for Economic and Social Policies*," Viviene Taylor and Sakiko Fukuda-Parr (Cape Town: University of Cape Town Press, 2016), 25–52, reprinted with permission from Cambridge University Press. Other quantitative indices for rating national-level performance on economic rights fulfillment have been developed by David Cingranelli and David Richards, "Measuring Government Effort to Respect Economic and Social Human Rights: A Peer Benchmark," in Hertel and Minkler, *Economic Rights*, 214–32, and by Mwangi S. Kimenyi, "Economic Rights, Human Development Effort, and Institutions," in Hertel and Minkler, *Economic Rights*, 182–213.

[20] Daniel Chong, *Freedom from Poverty: NGOs and Human Rights Praxis* (Philadelphia: University of Pennsylvania Press, 2010); Shareen Hertel, "Hungry for Justice: Social Mobilization on the Right to Food in India," *Development and Change*, 46, 1 (January 2015): 72–94.

[21] Paul J. Nelson and Ellen Dorsey, *New Rights Advocacy: Changing Strategies of Development and Human Rights NGOs* (Washington, DC: Georgetown University Press, 2008); LaDawn Haglund and Rimjhim Aggarwal, "Test of Our Progress: The Translation of Economic and Social Rights Norms into Practice," *The Journal of Human Rights* 10, 4 (2011): 494–520.

and procedurally changes the nature of claim-making from traditional approaches focused on civil and political rights. Rather than focusing principally on conventional "shaming and blaming" techniques, the new economic rights-based advocacy and scholarship takes a structural view of the generative forces of poverty and seeks to transform institutions, modes of interaction, and social hierarchies that give rise to inequality, as revealed in the case studies below.

Much of the intellectual heft undergirding this new work owes to the involvement of scholars and policy analysts from countries outside of the industrialized world. Some have partnered with academic and policy groups in the United States, Europe, and elsewhere to develop mixed qualitative and quantitative indicators-based frameworks for analyzing state compliance with economic rights obligations. For example, participatory budgeting pioneered in cities and states within Brazil from the late 1980s onward[22] sparked the parallel development of exhaustive academic assessments of the human rights impact of state budgeting in rich as well as poor countries.[23] Similarly, the evaluative framework developed by the New York-based Center on Economic and Social Rights that integrates analysis of "*outcomes, p*olicy *e*fforts and *r*esources" to produce an economic rights "*a*ssessment" of programs and policies (i.e., the OPERA framework) has been field-tested in Guatemala but can be applied internationally.[24]

Southern norms protagonists and scholars have thus played a central role in the emergence of economic rights as a central concern of the human rights field. To be fair, mainstream human rights scholarship does not wholly ignore the role of developing country-based activists as norms protagonists. Kathryn Sikkink, for example, argues that Argentine human rights activists were the catalysts for a global "justice cascade" around norms of universal jurisdiction and individual criminal accountability while acknowledging that other Southern actors can spur norms cascades in other settings.[25] But neither she nor others plumb the depths and complexity of the contemporary evolution of economic rights norms.

---

[22] Leonardo Avritzer, Leonardo. *Participatory Institutions in Democratic Brazil* (Baltimore: The Johns Hopkins University Press, 2009).

[23] Anja Rudiger and Benjamin Mason Meier, "A Rights-based Approach to Health Care Reform," in Elvira Beracochea, Corey Weinstein, and Dabney Evans, eds., *Rights-Based Approaches to Public Health* (New York: Springer Publishing, 2011), 69–86; Radhika Balakrishnan and Diane Elson, *Economic Policy and Human Rights: Holding Governments to Account* (London: Zed Books, 2011).

[24] Center for Economic and Social Rights, *The OPERA Framework: Assessing compliance with the obligation to fulfill economic, social, and cultural rights* (New York: CESR, not dated), 14–15, 26, 29.

[25] Kathryn Sikkink, *The Justice Cascade: How Human Rights Prosecutions Are Changing World Politics* (New York: WW Norton & Co., 2011), 90.

The research and advocacy explored in this chapter thus complicate the picture of who the drivers of human rights advocacy are and what their central aims may be. The following case studies analyze episodes of rights advocacy in which actors make strategic decisions to downplay, ignore, re-route, reject, or augment dominant human rights norms and traditional modes of advocacy and, in the process, expand the scope of claim-making and the nature of compliance.

Piecing the Mosaic Together: Rights Contestation in Practice

Much of the human rights literature central to the "old masters" school shares the overarching assumption that the mainstream human rights movement exercises a disproportionate influence over the normative frameworks, mobilization strategies, and vehicles for implementation central to human rights advocacy worldwide. Yet my research has consistently revealed that less powerful actors within networks can and do act in ways contrary to this assumption – regardless of whether their activism spans borders or takes place purely domestically.

Gaps or outright clashes in normative understandings complicate the traditional "boomerang" advocacy pattern laid out by Keck and Sikkink,[26] which presumes that activists in oppressive settings seek international support or solidarity abroad, in order to pressure their own states to stop abusing human rights. The boomerang pattern assumes a uniformity (or relative harmony) of human rights understandings across borders and within networks at the national level. In a similar fashion, the norms "life cycle" theory developed by Finnemore and Sikkink[27] explains changes in global human rights norms as a function of growing concord over time in human rights understandings. The "emergence" phase of norms evolution, in particular, assumes a high degree of normative uniformity among actors who are catalysts at the beginning of the norms life cycle.

But this chapter points us in another direction. Just as Acharya argues with respect to the emergence of new norms of regional security influenced by subsidiarity,[28] human rights norms do not necessarily emerge within centers of relative economic and political power and then move "out" toward comparably less powerful people in response to requests for help from local activists in oppressed settings. They may do

---

[26] Keck and Sikkink, ibid., 13.

[27] Martha Finnemore and Kathryn Sikkink. "International Norms Dynamics and Political Change," *International Organization* 52, 4 (1998): 887–917.

[28] Acharya, "Norm Subsidiarity."

so in some instances. But my research highlights instances in which ou
side actors may also thrust a campaign (and corresponding normati'
frame) onto people on the "receiving end" of transnational advoca_,
efforts, with little to no prior consultation. This can provoke a range of
responses on the receiving end – from downplaying, to ignoring, to re-
routing, to outright rejection of the outsiders' efforts.

Local actors can and often do put forward new forms of human rights
norms that are rooted not in international legal frameworks, but instead
are grounded in domestic constitutional law or localized social understandings. These new norms may or may not be compatible with international norms; the extent to which they are is dependent upon the nature
of interests and identities at the local level. While Merry has demonstrated
this in her analysis of cultural rights – specifically, with respect to the
vernacularization of women's rights[29] – my work reveals similar processes
at play in the evolution of economic rights and introduces two mechanisms to explain why and how new human rights norms emerge amid this
alternative set of processes.[30]

"Blocking" of outside norms can take place at the local level, followed
by intense negotiation, reinterpretation, and, ultimately, the export of
new norms from the receiving-end to the sending-end of the campaign
and beyond. Or activists outside the dominant human rights movement
may indirectly challenge and/or augment the normative framework of
a transnational campaign by introducing additional norms through the
"backdoor." In so doing, they can transform single-target campaigns into
dual target ones that seek to achieve both normative *and* material policy
change on multiple levels – not unlike Putnam's classic two-level game[31]
strategy, in which actors negotiate bargains in domestic and international
arenas simultaneously.

Blocking and backdoor moves are central to non-dominant activists'
efforts at downplaying, ignoring, re-routing, rejecting, or augmenting
norms that are not in sync with their interests. Two original case studies
in Bangladesh and Mexico demonstrate blocking and backdoor mechanisms in action.[32] Anti-child labor activists from the United States
launched a transnational advocacy campaign in the early 1990s aimed
at eliminating child labor from Bangladesh's burgeoning garment manu-
facturing export sector. Local Bangladeshi activists (irate that they had

---

[29] Merry, "Mapping the Middle."
[30] Shareen Hertel, *Unexpected Power: Conflict and Change Among Transnational Activists*
(Cornell University Press, 2006).
[31] Robert D. Putnam, "Diplomacy and Domestic Politics: The Logic of Two-Level
Games," *International Organization* 42:3 (1988): 427–60.
[32] Hertel, *Unexpected Power.*

not been consulted before the campaign to "help" them was launched) responded by blocking the US-driven campaign. Bangladeshis viewed the anti-child labor campaign as an assault on the rights of the very children the foreign activists intended to help. Blocking in this case eventually resulted in the emergence of a new normative framework for child labor that was sensitive to a wider and more complex set of child rights than US activists had originally envisioned – a more nuanced normative framework with relevance far beyond the Bangladesh case.

Notably, the dominant normative reference point for child labor prior to the 1990s was International Labour Orgnaization (ILO) Convention 138 on Minimum Age, which emphasized minimum age requirements but made no distinction between differing types of work children may perform. Bangladeshi activists feared the negative consequences of expelling tens of thousands of children from factory jobs with little to no plan in place for alternative economic sustenance. They pointed to the UN Convention on the Rights of the Child (CRC) as an alternative normative reference point, arguing that the CRC couches protections against exploitative forms of child work (Article 32) within a broader framework of children's overarching economic rights. The unexpected power resulting from Bangladeshi blocking ultimately resulted in the emergence of an international human rights standard – ILO Convention 182 (on the Worst Forms of Child Labor) – that transcended an overly simplistic US urge to ban child labor without distinguishing "worst forms" of child labor from acceptable forms of child work. The new standard (i.e., ILO 182) is not only more congruent with the CRC, but also offers a normative benchmark more palatable to a wider range of actors from states at differing levels of economic development than the narrower ILO 138.

Activists in Bangladesh argued that firing children in factories (the focus of the US campaign) without providing alternative means of income support would violate children's rights to food, shelter, and education – all of which are guaranteed in the CRC. It could also jeopardize their physical integrity rights if they moved into more dangerous occupations (such as the sex trade). Bangladeshi activists thus grounded the normative force of their appeal both in the recognition of the nonderogable rights of the person[33] and in the logic of progressive realization of economic rights. But these dynamics operated in reverse from the pattern anticipated by Keck and Sikkink's boomerang mechanism. The appeal for protection of nonderogable rights was used by local actors in Bangladesh to *reject* outside advocacy frames (by blocking them) until those frames shifted to

---

[33] Keck and Sikkink, ibid.

incorporate recognition of a broader range of children's economic rights – both normatively (through reference to the CRC, since 1LO 182 had not yet been drafted) and materially (through US support for a stipend program negotiated with international donors on behalf of children fired from work in garment factories).

A second transnational campaign in the 1990s illustrates backdoor moves in action. In this case, US-based activists sought to protect the rights of female workers in export factories (*maquiladoras*) along the US–Mexico border who were being forced to take pregnancy tests in a veiled attempt at screening them out of the labor force so that employers could avoid paying maternity leave benefits. Activists from the United States cultivated relationships with Mexican labor rights groups along the border and with feminist NGOs in Mexico City in an effort to launch a transnational campaign spotlighting the abuse.

There was mutual interest among all the players in using the labor side accord of the North American Free Trade Agreement (NAFTA) to shame and blame their respective governments into reform (i.e., to shame the Mexican government into enforcing domestic labor laws against gender-based discrimination; and to shame the US government into pressuring US companies not to allow discrimination in their off-shore operations in the *maquiladoras*). But the scope of reform that Mexican activists sought to achieve was broader than simple non-discrimination at work. Mexican activists also hoped to protect generous social welfare benefits for pregnant workers while at the same time main-taining the Mexican Constitution's commitment to promoting the right to work.

The aims of Mexican activists were thus well beyond the scope of the NAFTA side accord on labor (which addresses only a narrow set of workplace-based rights and labor standards, not broader social welfare or employment policy). In the interest of sustaining a mutually advantageous campaign but enlarging its scope, Mexicans inserted additional human rights claims into this campaign's agenda through the "backdoor." While US activists wanted to eliminate pregnancy discrimination because they argued it violated women's rights to non-discrimination in the workplace,[34] Mexican activists in communities along the US–Mexico

---

[34] US human rights advocates invoked the following as normative reference points: the UN Convention on the Elimination of All forms of Discrimination against Women (CEDAW); ILO Convention 111 (on Discrimination); the North American Agreement on Labor Cooperation (i.e., the labor side accord to the NAFTA); and Article 4 of Mexico's Constitution, which protects the right to freely determine the number and spacing of children. Conspicuously absent was reference to the International Covenant on Economic, Social & Cultural Rights – see Hertel, *Unexpected Power*, 72–5.

border adopted the rhetorical justification of non-discrimination – but simultaneously inserted a broader claim that the practice of pregnancy screening also violated women's right to work, guaranteed under the Mexican Constitution (Article 123), the American Convention on Human Rights, and Universal Declaration of Human Rights. These border-based groups helped US activists gather testimony from factory workers who had suffered pregnancy discrimination. But in articulating the rationale for the campaign at the grass-roots level, border-based activists focused not only on discrimination, but also on protecting the constitutionally-guaranteed right to work, which they argued would resonate more strongly at the local level.

Feminist activists in Mexico City adopted not only the overt non-discrimination frame of the main campaign, but also demanded state recognition of *reproduction as work*. Child-bearing, they argued, is an act of reproducing the state itself. Hence, it should be protected through the continued existence of social welfare guarantees under national law that safeguard paid maternity and lactation benefits for pregnant and nursing mothers. Such benefits are also integral to upholding Mexico's obligations under international law it has ratified, feminists argued, citing the UN Convention on the Elimination of all forms of Discrimination Against Women.

Maternity benefits had been threatened since the mid-1990s by Mexico's liberalization of its labor law and constitutional reforms undertaken in the context of the country's preparations for NAFTA accession, so Mexican feminists organized a parallel campaign focused on reproduction as work, which ran alongside the main non-discrimination campaign organized by US-based advocacy groups. In order to demonstrate that pregnancy screening was rampant throughout the Mexican economy, extending well beyond the maquiladora zones into other sectors of the economy (including government agencies and private sector firms), Mexican feminists invited a wide range of women to offer testimony at a public "tribunal on reconciling maternity and work."[35]

Simultaneous demands for non-discrimination, protection of the right to work, and recognition of reproduction as work were not easily reconciled in practice, however. Neither the US-based nor the Mexican activists expressed resounding satisfaction with the outcome of their efforts. Indeed, this case study could be argued to reveal "incoherent strategies that undermine both sets of goals," a possibility that Snyder,

[35] Hertel, *Unexpected Power*, 72–3.

Vinjamuri, and Hopgood have raised with respect to bargaining amid vernacularization.[36]

In part, this internal incoherence owed to the fact that the institutional framework of the NAFTA labor side accord was only suited to address discrimination-based claims (not broader claims related to shortfalls in economic rights fulfillment), so the non-discrimination frame in the main campaign trumped the "messaging" of this advocacy, even while alternative messages continued to circulate. In part, the difficulty of advancing multiple frames stemmed from longstanding hierarchies among Mexican groups themselves. Poorer, border-based groups of women workers resisted the "elite" feminist label of the Mexico City-driven parallel campaign and its more radical frame, and thus engaged minimally, if at all, with it (save for a few workers invited to travel from the border of Mexico to the capital to give testimony in the tribunal discussed above). In the end, the only concrete policy reform to result from either the US-driven campaign or the "backdoor" parallel efforts in Mexico was the outlawing of pregnancy screening among municipal employees in Mexico City by a leftist feminist mayor in the late 1990s.

This research on bargaining in economic rights advocacy yields two significant insights relevant to broader theorizing on strategic interaction in the human rights arena. First, these cases demonstrate the inherent complexity of advocating around economic rights issues given the standard of progressive realization. Second, they demonstrate how international norms are challenged and augmented at the local level in settings on the receiving end of advocacy, thus extending both Acharya's[37] and Merry's foundational work[38] by adding both blocking and backdoor mechanisms to the repertoire of local interpretation of norms. But there is an important distinction: whereas both Acharya and Merry assume that norms evolution necessarily occurs through dialogue among activists on one or the other side of a physical or normative border, I do not restrict blocking or backdoor moves to happening in transnationalized arenas. Though the mechanisms identified in the Bangladesh or Mexico cases emerged inductively through deeply ethnographic fieldwork in transnational human rights campaigns of the 1990s, they are evident in purely domestic campaigns as well.

---

[36] Jack Snyder, Leslie Vinjamuri, and Stephen Hopgood, memo to volume contributors, dated August 17, 2013, on file with author.

[37] Acharya, "How Ideas Spread."

[38] Merry, "Legal Pluralism and Transnational Culture"; see also Mark Goodale and Sally Engle Merry eds., *The Practice of Human Rights: Tracking Law Between the Global and Local* (Cambridge: Cambridge University Press, 2007).

Indeed, activity in the transnational arena is not essential to the emergence of blocking or backdoor moves. A number of factors are at play, including: how a campaign emerges; variation in levels of funding, media attention, or inter- and intra-group rivalry; audience receptivity to particular frames; institutional structures; and culture and ideology. These factors may be situated at the domestic or the international level. Within the United States, for example, backdoor moves were evident in the strategies of women of color in the US Civil Rights movement.[39] Both blocking and backdoor moves can also help explain the evolution of labor rights campaigns in the New York State agricultural sector – specifically, the power relations between Latino and Caribbean workers and Anglo advocates acting on their behalf vis-à-vis the New York State legislature and media.[40] Analysis of these and other domestic human rights campaigns within the United States reveals not only the tensions and hierarchies among activists, but also the broader challenges faced by advocacy groups facing the limits of US courts to address economic rights issues.[41]

Ongoing research in India on right-to-food advocacy in that country further reveals that vernacularization may take place without much (if any) reference to international treaty norms and without significant international engagement on the part of activists.[42] Yet the normative frames that result are wholly consonant with international human rights law. Since the mid-1990s, Indian activists have engaged in a series of popular campaigns at the national level, aimed at defending human rights through the use of Indian Constitutional and statutory law. The rights at stake have included core economic rights such as access to employment, land, and food as well as the right to information.[43] The claim-making in these campaigns has centered principally on strengthening Indian legal protections for such rights and enforcing compliance through bureaucratic

---

[39] Hertel, *Unexpected Power*, 109–10; Evelyn Simien and Danielle L. McGuire, "A Tribute to the Women: Rewriting History, Retelling Herstory in Civil Rights," *Politics & Gender* 10:3 (2014): 413–31.

[40] Margaret Gray and Shareen Hertel, "Immigrant Farmworker Advocacy: The Dynamics of Organizing," *Polity* 41:4 (2009): 409–35; for broader discussion of labor rights dynamics in US agriculture, see Margaret Gray, *Labor and Locavore: The making of a Comprehensive Food Ethic* (Berkeley: University of California Press, 2013).

[41] Cathy Albisa, "Drawing Lines in the Sand: Building Economic and Social Rights Norms in the United States," in Shareen Hertel and Kathryn Libal, eds., *Human Rights in the United States: Beyond Exceptionalism* (New York: Cambridge University Press, 2011), 68–88.

[42] Shareen Hertel, "Hungry for Justice," 77.

[43] Jayna Kothari, "Social Rights Litigation in India: Developments of the Last Decade," in Daphne Barak-Erez and Aeval M. Gross, eds., *Exploring Social Rights: Between Theory and Practice* (Oxford and Portland: Hart Publishing Limited, 2007), 171–92; Shylashri Shankar and Pratap Bhanu Mehta, "Courts and Socioeconomic Rights in India," in Gauri and Brinks, eds., Courting Social Justice, 146–82.

reform of existing public programs. While some recent human rights advocacy in India has indeed had transnational dimensions – particularly campaigns on the rights of Dalit or "untouchable" people,[44] and on the rights of Adivasi tribal peoples[45] – those campaigns tend to resonate with the emphasis on non-discrimination that is central to many Western human rights advocacy efforts.

By contrast, the high-profile Indian economic rights campaigns of the 1990s and early 2000s have taken place largely (if not exclusively) in the national sphere. In part, this is a function of the comparative strength of Indian Constitutional protections for economic rights vis-à-vis those in many Western constitutions.[46] In part, it is a function of the neoliberalization of India's economy since the 1980s, which has generated internal resistance among left-leaning academics and grass-roots advocates, who are wary of uniting forces with "outside" advocates lest they risk being tarred with the neoliberal or neocolonial brush.

All of these factors have played a role in the evolution of the Right to Food (RTF) campaign, which since 2001 has employed a three-pronged strategy of legal mobilization, grass-roots outreach, and parliamentary lobbying in an effort to strengthen protections for the right to food in Indian law and to improve the corresponding implementation of government feeding programs. India has one of the highest rates of childhood malnutrition in the world and nearly half its population is undernourished,[47] despite spending more than 2 percent of its GDP on core social safety net programs, of which food represents a significant portion.[48] Well over half – and, by some estimates, upward of 70 percent – of that food is lost to corruption or waste in delivery.[49] The RTF campaign has argued that hunger deaths and persistent under-nutrition are thus avoidable, and that the federal government and state governments

---

[44] Clifford Bob, *The Marketing of Rebellion: Insurgents, Media and International Activism* (New York: Cambridge University Press, 2005).

[45] Amita Baviskar, "Social Movements," in Niraja Gopal Jayal and Pratap Bahnu Mehta, eds., *The Oxford Companion to Politics in India* (Oxford/New York: Oxford University Press, 2010), 368.

[46] For comprehensive content analysis of the human rights provisions of constitutions worldwide and their respective mechanisms for implementation, see David S. Law and Mila Versteeg. "The Evolution of Global Constitutionalism," Washington University in St. Louis School of Law – Legal Studies Research Paper Series No. 10-10-01 (2010).

[47] Harsh Mander, *Ash in the Belly: India's Unfinished Battle Against Hunger* (New Delhi/New York: Pearson, 2012), 12, 18–21.

[48] Madhura Swaminathan, *Weakening Welfare: The Public Distribution of Food in India* (New Delhi: Left World/Naya Rasta Publishers, Ltd., 2000); The World Bank, *Social Protection for a Changing India: Volume 1* (Washington D.C., 2011), xii.

[49] World Bank, *Social Protection*, 16; Jim Yardley, "India Asks, Should Food Be a Right for the Poor?" *The New York Times*, August 8, 2010, www.nytimes.com/2010/08/09/world/asia/09food.html

are complicit in human rights violations if they do not act to reform public feeding programs.

The campaign has sought to transform the ordinariness of hunger in India into a source of national shame. Rather than advocate for generalized economic reforms, the campaign has focused on improving food delivery through existing public feeding programs. Members of the RTF campaign acknowledge problems in the global political economy of food, but have focused their advocacy on the more proximate solutions that can be achieved by ensuring that government-subsidized food actually reaches the people for whom it was intended.

In 2001, the RTF campaign filed a landmark public interest litigation (PIL) case with the Indian Supreme Court, in which it framed the right to food as integral to the right to life and demanded reform of key government social welfare programs in order to safeguard the lives of the people most vulnerable to hunger. The Supreme Court accepted this interpretation and issued the first of what would become a decade's worth of "interim orders" in the PUCL case, ordering state agencies to ensure adequate access to food through reform of public food distribution programs. Although the RTF campaign has acknowledged both the relevant international law on economic rights to which India is a signatory and the international dimensions of food insecurity, it has nevertheless legitimated its actions and sought to institutionalize its claims with reference to national-level norms and institutions. In part, this decision is a function of the difficulty of building a litigation strategy around international law, as explained by the Human Rights Law Network (a key player in the RTF campaign):

[H]olding the Indian Government accountable for not fulfilling their obligation to adhere to the international laws relating to food security is extremely difficult. Reasons for the sustained levels of hunger in India are multifaceted and one organisation or person cannot be held responsible ... A human rights-based approach is required in the measures taken in an attempt to abolish hunger as well as in the overall philosophy in attitudes to hunger and malnutrition.[50]

The human rights approach undertaken by the RTF campaign is far broader than the violations-based strategy advocated by Neier or Roth.[51]

---

[50] Human Rights Law Network (not dated), "Analysis of the Application of the International Human Rights Standards from the Perspective of Human Rights Practitioners: The Right to Food in India," 14–15, www.hrln.org/hrln/right-to-food/rep orts/296-analysis-of-the-application-of-the-international-human-rights-standards-from -the-perspective-of-human-rights-practitioners-the-right-to-food-in-india.html.

[51] Neier, *The International Human Rights Movement*; Roth, "Defending Economic, Social and Cultural Rights."

Again, the intent of activists here is not to overturn international norms. Rather, the aim is to frame economic rights and corresponding strategies for implementation in a way that stands to enhance the likelihood of compliance. Invoking national law may be a more effective strategy for ensuring compliance with economic rights over time (i.e., progressive realization) than invoking international law – particularly if the benchmarks for economic rights fulfillment are more clearly defined and/or higher in national law than in international law. Indian activists have thus opted for national implementation frameworks over international legal ones, largely in the interest of ensuring compliance with economic rights more expediently and with greater domestic social legitimacy[52] than by relying on translation of international norms or compliance through international institutions.

The decision to focus its efforts nationally is also a function of the Right to Food campaign's need to galvanize local mobilization around concepts and processes that are locally legible – again, a variant of vernacularization absent transnational exchanges. Capitalizing on the work of a contemporaneous "Right to Information" campaign that emerged in India in the late 1990s, RTF activists have demanded access to public records of feeding programs as well as the right to participate in social auditing of such programs. Public involvement in "naming and shaming" in this case takes place at the national level, rather than across borders as would be predicted by the boomerang mechanism. As an integral part of its strategy of popular mobilization at the grass-roots level, the RTF campaign has focused on shaming bureaucrats involved in domestic corruption while at the same time conducting public outreach and popular education on the right to food.[53]

The campaign has also lobbied political parties involved in parliamentary debates over an evolving National Food Security Bill (NFSB) from roughly 2009 onward. Since the campaign's inception, among its chief policy priorities have been: universal guarantees for access to public feeding programs (rather than targeted access based on above- and below-poverty-line distinctions); a broader range of publicly provided foodstuffs; more ample provisions for pregnant/nursing women and pre-school-aged children; and stronger monitoring provisions. The RTF campaign has also opposed cash transfers, which The World Bank and

---

[52] Sangeeta Kamat, *Development Hegemony: NGOs and the State in India* (New Delhi: Oxford University Press, 2002).

[53] Dipa Sinha, "Social Audit of Midday Meal Scheme in AP," *Economic & Political Weekly* 43:44 (2008): 57–61; Yamini Aiyar, Soumya Kapoor Mehta, and Salimah Samji, "A Guide to Conducting Social Audits: Learning from the Experience of Andhra Pradesh," Accountability Initiative working paper (not dated).

some prominent Indian economists, including Arvind Panagariya and Jagdish Baghwati, have recommended in lieu of direct provisioning of food.[54]

When it became apparent to the RTF campaign in late 2012 that a parliamentary standing committee would release a draft bill that fell far short of these goals, key segments of the campaign began to "block" the very bill they had pushed to have created, arguing that no bill was better than a bad bill.[55] Indian activists in the RTF campaign blocked not in response to foreign norms, but in response to what they perceived as unacceptable local interpretations of the right to food in principle and practice. In the RTF campaign, Indian activists are not "translating" international norms into the vernacular in order to justify their demands. Rather, they are demanding fulfillment of the right to food in keeping with the norms and standards for progressive realization articulated in their own Supreme Court's jurisprudence.

The experience of the RTF campaign thus holds important lessons for the analysis of compliance with economic rights. Harsh Mander, a longstanding protagonist in the RTF campaign and one of the Indian Supreme Court-appointed "Commissioners on the Right to Food" mandated to ensure implementation of related court orders, argues that a human rights approach "transforms people from passive recipients of State benevolence to *active agents* who claim and enjoy their legal and equal human rights *as citizens*."[56] For Mander, the RTF campaign's ability to translate Indian Constitutional protections of human rights into a normative imperative for public action hinges on galvanizing people at the grass-roots level, and Indian public opinion more generally, into recognizing hunger as a violation of rights and a source of national shame.[57] Shaming and blaming in this case is thus domestically driven in response to a largely nationally derived normative framework rooted in the Indian Constitution and local social practice. There is no need to downplay, ignore, re-route, or reject international norms in this case because domestic human rights norms are the principal focal point of campaign discourse.

Nevertheless, Indian norms protagonists' ideas about the nature of the right to food and strategies for ensuring its fulfillment may move outward into the wider human rights arena. For example, the Indian RTF campaign and other campaigns on social welfare reform in India since the 1990s have integrated the vehicle of local social auditing into their "repertoire of

---

[54] The World Bank, *Social* Protection, xviii, 15–16.
[55] Hertel, "Hungry for Justice," 87–8.
[56] Mander, *Ash in the Belly*, 232, emphasis added.   [57] Ibid.

contention."[58] State-level statutes mandating the creation of public works programs and public feeding programs throughout India include provisions for a participatory process of social auditing of economic rights guarantees. Not unlike the participatory budgeting pioneered in Brazil, the Indian experience with public auditing aims both at increasing grass-roots level participation in governing and at staunching the corruption that undercuts government efficiency and public justice. Activists in established social welfare democracies are taking note of these and other strategies as they promote reform of social welfare, education, and housing programs in the United States.[59]

Future Present?

The ascendance of economic rights has the potential to breathe new life into mainstream human rights scholarship. The more qualified reading of compliance central to Risse, Ropp, and Sikkink's 2013 book, for example, is rooted in the authors' growing awareness of the potential for "crowding out" of traditional human rights by rival discourses or unfavorable structuring conditions.[60] The millions of people involved in legal and social protests around the right to food, water, and health, for example, simply are not waiting for the "mainstream" human rights movement to lead on these issues. They don't have time to waste.

Orthodox human rights approaches can undercut or even sabotage substantive change if they fail to engage local people in fashioning solutions to their own problems – solutions that respond to domestic understandings of human rights and domestic constraints and opportunities. Some might argue that the emergence of economic rights advocacy is a risky business that could lead to concept stretching[61] or rights proliferation: if everything is a right, then nothing is. Yet in distancing himself intellectually and practically from economic rights and their protagonists, Neier leaves out a central swath of the present and future terrain of human rights advocacy. He acknowledges as much when he notes the contemporary human rights movement's "widespread" commitment to economic and social rights (albeit "to a large extent rhetorical") and recognizes that he and a "dwindling minority" of economic rights skeptics are "on the losing side of the argument."[62]

---

[58] Sidney Tarrow, "Social Movements and Contentious Politics: A Review Article," *American Political Science Review* 90, 4 (1996), 874–83.

[59] Albisa, "Drawing Lines in the Sand."

[60] Risse, Ropp, and Sikkink, *The Persistent Power of Human Rights*, 21–2.

[61] Giovanni Sartori, "Concept Misinformation in Comparative Politics," *American Science Review* 64:4 (1970), 1033–53.

[62] Neier, *The International Human Rights Movement*, 92.

As this chapter has demonstrated, actors central to the mosaic of campaigns discussed here could end up saving human rights from the increasingly rejectionist responses it provokes on the borders of consensus around the normative or institutional canon of the field. Fights over meaning and implementation of economic rights are at the heart of deep implementation struggles, because economic rights fulfillment entails not only changes in the immediate condition, but also transformation of the long-term position of people who suffer rights violations. As Hopgood, Snyder, and Vinjamuri argue in this volume (see Introduction), we need new concepts and modes of inquiry for understanding the agents at the heart of struggles over compliance with human rights. The constraints and opportunities people face at the micro-level, along with their choices of frame and venue for struggle, are critical to understanding when, under what conditions, and in what form compliance with human rights does (or does not) take place.

The campaigns analyzed in this chapter demonstrate the complexity of the bargains that activists strike in the interest of promoting economic rights. Their claim-making is not a cynical end-run around the principles and tenets of universal human rights. Rather, it represents some of the most creative contemporary attempts at ensuring compliance with even the thorniest types of rights. We would do well to watch and learn from efforts at bargaining economic rights back into the mainstream of human rights scholarship and advocacy.

References

Acharya, Amitav. "How Ideas Spread: Whose Norms Matter? Norm Localization and Institutional Change in Asian Regionalization," *International Organization* 58, 2 (Spring 2004): 239–75.

"Norm Subsidiarity and Regional Orders: Sovereignty, Regionalism, and Rule-Making in the Third World," *International Studies Quarterly* 55, 1 (2011): 95–123.

Aiyar, Yamini, Soumya Kapoor Mehta, and Salimah Samji. "A Guide to Conducting Social Audits: Learning from the Experience of Andhra Pradesh," Accountability Initiative working paper (not dated).

Albisa, Cathy. "Drawing Lines in the Sand: Building Economic and Social Rights Norms in the United States," in *Human Rights in the United States: Beyond Exceptionalism*, Shareen Hertel and Kathryn Libal, eds. (New York: Cambridge University Press, 2011): 68–88.

Apodaca, Clair. "Measuring the Progressive Realization of Economic, Social, and Cultural Rights," in *Economic Rights: Conceptual, Measurement, and Policy Issues*, Shareen Hertel and Lanse P. Minkler, eds. (New York: Cambridge University Press, 2007): 165–81.

Avritzer, Leonardo. *Participatory Institutions in Democratic Brazil* (Baltimore: The Johns Hopkins University Press, 2009).

Balakrishnan, Radhika and Diane Elson. *Economic Policy and Human Rights: Holding Governments to Account* (London: Zed Books, 2011)

Baviskar, Amita. "Social Movements," in *The Oxford Companion to Politics in India*, Niraja Gopal Jayal and Pratap Bhanu Mehta, eds. (Oxford/ New York: Oxford University Press, 2010): 381–90.

Birchfield, Laura and Jessica Corsi, "Between Starvation and Globalization: Realizing the Right to Food in India," *Michigan Journal of International Law* 31, 4 (Summer 2010): 691–764.

Bob, Clifford. *The Marketing of Rebellion: Insurgents, Media and International Activism* (New York: Cambridge University Press, 2005).

Brand, Danie and Sage Russell. *Exploring the Content of Socioeconomic Rights: South African and International Perspectives* (Pretoria, South Africa: Protea Boekhuis, 2002).

Center for Economic and Social Rights. *The OPERA Framework: Assessing Compliance with the Obligation to Fulfill Economic, Social, and Cultural Rights* (New York: CESR, not dated).

Chapman, Audrey. "A 'Violations Approach' for Monitoring the International Covenant on Economic, Social and Cultural Rights," *Human Rights Quarterly*, 18, 1 (1996): 23–66.

Chapman, Audrey. "The Status of Efforts to Monitor Economic, Social & Cultural Rights," in *Economic Rights: Conceptual, Measurement, and Policy Issues*, Shareen Hertel and Lanse P. Minkler, eds. (New York: Cambridge University Press, 2007): 143–64.

Chong, Daniel. *Freedom from Poverty: NGOs and Human Rights Praxis* (Philadelphia: University of Pennsylvania Press, 2010).

Cingranelli, David L. and David L. Richards. "Measuring Government Effort to Respect Economic and Social Human Rights: A Peer Benchmark," in *Economic Rights: Conceptual, Measurement, and Policy Issues*, Shareen Hertel and Lanse P. Minkler, eds. (New York: Cambridge University Press, 2007): 214–32.

Deitelhoff, Nicole and Klaus Dieter Wolf, "Business and Human Rights: How Corporate Norms Violators Become Norms Entrepreneurs," in *The Persistent Power of Human Rights: From Commitment to Compliance*, Thomas Risse, Stephen Ropp, and Kathryn Sikkink, eds. (New York: Cambridge University Press, 2013): 222–38.

Finnemore, Martha and Kathryn Sikkink. "International Norms Dynamics and Political Change," *International Organization* 52, 4 (1998): 887–917.

Fukuda-Parr, Sakiko, Terra Lawson-Remer, and Susan Randolph. "An Index of Economic and Social Rights Fulfillment: Concept and Methodology," *The Journal of Human Rights* 8, 3 (2009): 195–221.

Gargarella, Roberto, Pilar Domingo and Theunis Roux. *Courts and Social Transformation in New Democracies: An Institutional Voice for the Poor?* (Hampshire: Ashgate Publishing, Ltd., 2006).

Gauri, Varun and Daniel M. Brinks, "Introduction: The Elements of Legalization and the Triangular Shape of Social and Economic Rights," in *Courting Social*

Justice: Judicial Enforcement of Social and Economic Rights in the Developing World, Gauri & Brinks, eds. (New York/Cambridge, UK: Cambridge University Press, 2008): 1–37.

Goodale, Mark and Sally Engle Merry, eds. *The Practice of Human Rights: Tracking Law Between the Global and the Local* (Cambridge UK/New York: Cambridge University Press, 2007).

Gray, Margaret. *Labor and the Locavore: The Making of a Comprehensive Food Ethic* (Berkeley and Los Angeles: University of California Press, 2013).

Gray, Margaret and Shareen Hertel. "Immigrant Farmworker Advocacy: The Dynamics of Organizing," *Polity* 41, 4 (October 2009): 409–35.

Haglund, LaDawn and Rimjhim Aggarwal. "Test of Our Progress: The Translation of Economic and Social Rights Norms into Practice," *The Journal of Human Rights* 10, 4 (2011): 494–520.

Hertel, Shareen. "Hungry for Justice: Social Mobilization on the Right to Food in India," *Development and Change*, 46, 1 (January 2015): 72–94.

Unexpected Power: Conflict and Change Among Transnational Activists (Ithaca: Cornell University Press, 2006).

"Why Bother? Measuring Economic Rights – The Research Agenda," *International Studies Perspectives* 7, 3 (2006): 215–30.

Hertel, Shareen and Lanse P. Minkler, eds. *Economic Rights: Conceptual, Measurement, and Policy Issues* (New York: Cambridge University Press, 2007).

Human Rights Law Network (not dated). "Analysis of the Application of the International Human Rights Standards from the Perspective of Human Rights Practitioners: The Right to Food in India" (ND), www.hrln.org/hrln/right-to-food/reports/296-analysis-of-the-application-of-the-international-hu man-rights-standards-from-the-perspective-of-human-rights-practitioners-th e-right-to-food-in-india.html

Kamat, Sangeeta. *Development Hegemony: NGOs and the State in India* (New Delhi: Oxford University Press, 2002).

Keck, Margaret E. and Kathryn Sikkink. *Activists Beyond Borders: Advocacy Networks in International Politics* (Ithaca: Cornell University Press, 1998).

Klug, Heinz. "Achieving Rights to Land, Water and Health in Post-Apartheid South Africa" in *Economic, Social, and Cultural Rights: Emerging Possibilities for Social Transformation*, LaDawn Haglund and Robin Stryker, eds. (Oakland: University of California Press, 2015): 199–218.

Kimenyi, Mwangi S. "Economic Rights, Human Development Effort, and Institutions," in *Economic Rights: Conceptual, Measurement, and Policy Issues*, Shareen Hertel and Lanse P. Minkler, eds. (New York: Cambridge University Press, 2007): 182–213.

Kothari, Jayna. "Social Rights Litigation in India: Developments of the Last Decade," in *Exploring Social Rights: Between Theory and Practice*, Daphne Barak-Erez and Aeyal M. Gross, eds. (Oxford and Portland: Hart Publishing Limited, 2007): 171–92.

Law, David S. and Mila Versteeg. "The Evolution of Global Constitutionalism," Washington University in St. Louis School of Law – Legal Studies Research Paper Series No. 10–10–01 (2010).

Mander, Harsh. *Ash in the Belly: India's Unfinished Battle Against Hunger* (New Delhi/New York: Pearson, 2012).

Merry, Sally Engle. "Legal Pluralism and Transnational Culture: The Ka Ho'okolokolonui Kanaka Maoli Tribunal, Hawai'i, 1993," in *Human Rights, Culture and Context: Anthropological Perspectives*, Richard A. Wilson, ed. (London: Pluto Press, 1997): 28–48.

"Transnational Human Rights and Local Activism: Mapping the Middle," *American Anthropologist* 108, 1 (2006): 38–51.

Neier, Aryeh. *The International Human Rights Movement: A History* (Princeton: Princeton University Press, 2012).

Nelson, Paul J. and Ellen Dorsey. *New Rights Advocacy: Changing Strategies of Development and Human Rights NGOs* (Washington, DC: Georgetown University Press, 2008).

Putnam, Robert D. "Diplomacy and Domestic Politics: The Logic of Two-Level Games," *International Organization* 42, 3 (1988): 427–60.

Randolph, Susan and Shareen Hertel. "The Right to Food: A Global Perspective," in *The Right to Food in South Africa: New Directions for Economic and Social Policies,"* Viviene Taylor and Sakiko Fukuda-Parr (Cape Town, South Africa: University of Cape Town Press, 2016), 25–52. Reprinted with permission from Cambridge University Press.

Randolph, Susan, Sakiko Fukuda-Parr and Terra Lawson-Remer. "Economic and Social Rights Fulfillment Index: Country Scores and Rankings," *The Journal of Human Rights* 9, 3 (2010): 230–61.

Randolph, Susan, Michelle Prairie, and John Stewart. "Monitoring State Fulfillment of Economic and Social Rights Fulfillment in the United States," *Human Rights Review* 13, 2 (2012): 139–65.

Risse, Thomas, Stephen C. Ropp, and Kathryn Sikkink, eds. *The Persistent Power of Human Rights: From Commitment to Compliance* (New York: Cambridge University Press, 2013).

The Power of Human Rights: International Norms and Domestic Change (New York: Cambridge University Press, 1999).

Roth, Kenneth. "Defending Economic, Social and Cultural Rights: Practical Issues Faced by an International Human Rights Organization," *Human Rights Quarterly* 26, 1 (February 2004): 63–73.

Rudiger, Anja and Benjamin Mason Meier. "A Rights-based Approach to Health Care Reform," in *Rights-Based Approaches to Public Health*, Elvira Beracochea, Corey Weinstein, and Dabney Evans, eds. (New York: Springer Publishing, 2011): 69–86.

Sartori, Giovanni. "Concept Misinformation in Comparative Politics," *American Political Science Review* 64, 4 (1970): 1033–53.

Shankar, Shylashri and Pratap Bhanu Mehta, "Courts and Socioeconomic Rights in India," in *Courting Social Justice: Judicial Enforcement of Social and Economic Rights in the Developing World*, Gauri & Brinks, eds. (New York/Cambridge, UK: Cambridge University Press, 2008): 146–82.

Sikkink, Kathryn. *The Justice Cascade: How Human Rights Prosecutions Are Changing World Politics* (New York: WW Norton & Co., 2011).

Simien, Evelyn and Danielle L. McGuire, "A Tribute to the Women: Rewriting History, Retelling Herstory in Civil Rights," *Politics & Gender* 10, 3 (2014): 413–31.

Sinha, Dipa. "Social Audit of Midday Meal Scheme in AP (Andhra Pradesh)," *Economic & Political Weekly* 43, 44 (Nov. 1–7, 2008): 57–61.

Swaminathan, Madhura. *Weakening Welfare: The Public Distribution of Food in India* (New Delhi: Left World/Naya Rasta Publishers, Ltd., 2000).

Tarrow, Sidney. "Social Movements and Contentious Politics: A Review Article," *American Political Science Review* 90, 4 (1996): 874–83.

The World Bank (2011) *Social Protection for a Changing India: Volume 1.* Washington, DC: The World Bank, www-wds.worldbank.org/external/defa ult/WDSContentServer/WDSP/IB/2011/04/20/000333037_201104202355 16/Rendered/PDF/612750v10ESW0P1rt0Volume0I01PUBLIC1.pdf

Yamin, Alicia Ely and Siri Gloppen, eds. *Litigating Health Rights: Can Courts Bring More Justice to Health?* (Cambridge, MA: Harvard University Press, 2011).

Yardley, Jim. "India Asks, Should Food Be a Right for the Poor?" *The New York Times*, August 8, 2010, www.nytimes.com/2010/08/09/world/asia/09food .html

Young, Katherine G. "The Minimum Core of Economic and Social Rights: A Concept in Search of Content," *The Yale Journal of International Law* 33 (2008): 113–75.

11   Human Rights and the Crisis of Liberalism

Samuel Moyn

People often think of human rights as liberal. If they are correct, it must follow that criticisms of human rights have to be premised on a rejection of liberalism itself. Yet while human rights do incorporate historically liberal norms, they make up only one liberal project in history; indeed, it is a latecome one. In this essay, I give some reasons why it is inadequate to respond to criticisms of extant human rights agendas by claiming that those agendas simply incarnate liberalism – and that their opponents are therefore opponents of liberalism who must not accept its long-settled normative horizons.[1] In fact, the reverse is closer to the truth. One does not need to be a "radical" to be sorry about the low aspirations and minimal achievements of human rights regimes and movements today. It is enough to be a liberal.

In theory and in practice, the contemporary human rights movement exists because of an abrupt truncation of, and recent break with, the majority of liberal traditions of thought and practice in modern history. If human rights regimes and movements today preserve some central liberal norms (such as those civil and political liberties listed in the first half of the Universal Declaration of Human Rights), they are a pale imitation of liberalism as a world-historical political project. If this is true, then "liberalism" is much more a sword for criticizing contemporary human rights as a tragic failure of ambition – notably in the socioeconomic domain – than it is a shield for the movement against mounting criticism.

The main gain that contemporary human rights provide compared to past liberalism is not, as many contend, that the former are aspirationally global where the latter was generally statist. It is, rather, that liberals have recently left behind the commitments to empire that long provided their most usual foreign policy: their central program until recently for

---

[1] For full-blown presentations of human rights as the liberal view in world affairs, see John Charvet and Elisa Kaczynska-Nay, *The Liberal Project and Human Rights: The Theory and Practice of New World Order* (Cambridge: Cambridge University Press, 2008) as well as Christian Reus-Smit, *Individual Rights and the Making of the International System* (Cambridge: Cambridge University Press, 2014).

exporting liberty and equality abroad in the face of despotism and indigence. Functionally, human rights are post-imperial. But they lack cognate programs and institutions to substitute for the imperialism they have replaced. The trouble, in other words, is that proponents of human rights have no scheme of comparable ambition, opting instead for a minimalist approach to political and civil entitlements.

No liberal would have consented to this constriction and retreat before the middle of the twentieth century, when the twin specters of totalitarianism and decolonization prompted the invention of a stripped-down and minimalist "liberalism of fear" that sticks to policing the most horrendous symptoms of misrule, organizing international politics around a *summum malum* and especially around the horror of atrocity. The drastic curtailment of liberalism's ambition through the rise of its foreign policy of human rights promotion took it back to the values its belatedly canonized founders, Thomas Hobbes and John Locke, had once consecrated for domestic politics alone. They did so out of the belief that the sole plausible goal of politics in the world is the defense of order, perhaps supplemented by protection of personal liberties (and property), rather than the construction of social freedom. In setting their sights so low, today's liberals have unlearned crucial lessons they once prized about the need to augment and improve liberalism over modern history. They have broken with their own tradition as they pared it down to size. It follows that if human rights advocates were to be true to the entirety of the liberal tradition and adopt the risky attempt to envision global freedom through new and post-imperial means, they would have to abandon their exclusionary commitment to a minimal baseline of protection that they generally pursue so single-mindedly. They might even have to marginalize individual rights, as liberals historically did in domestic politics.

In recalling what liberalism has been, and how the contemporary international human rights movement breaks with it, this chapter also offers some criticisms of contemporary political science. Today, political scientists, with their empiricist fashions, engage with human rights more for the sake of disciplinary supremacy, and less for the sake of extradisciplinary relevance. An outsider might well look at human rights discussions in contemporary political science, and especially international relations, with great sadness. Human rights have mainly become fodder for prior disciplinary struggles, such as the constructivist war on "realism" or the exclusionary insistence on quantitative methods. When political scientists engage with human rights, they tend to care most about disciplinary futures, under the cover of arguing about global ones. Most ironically, they even fail to engage their own departmental colleagues, for it is political theory alone that can plausibly provide the historical and conceptual perspective to rethink the agenda of liberalism in a post-imperial age.

Mainstream political scientists who have transcended the discipline's once dismissive attitude to human rights, such as Beth Simmons or Kathryn Sikkink, appear to think that if they can quantitatively prove that human rights law and movements make the world a better place (even if only marginally), they will have struck a blow for liberalism that will matter beyond the walls of political science. Failing to engage political theory, however, they have generally skirted what liberalism actually is and has been, and why human rights do not live up to the best liberal aspirations the world has known. These include not only values that contemporary political scientists treat as competitors to human rights, such as social peace, but also an insistence on ethical diversity across the globe and the ambition to connect individual protection to economic growth and distributive equality.

It is mistaken, all things considered, to claim liberalism for human rights in their current form, as if those who worry about other values were not equally, if not more, liberal in their commitments. A corollary is that it would be far better for political scientists to start intramurally, with more engagement with theory, if the support they want to offer the human rights movement is to be more convincing than it has been so far. Most of all, political theory can remind scholars of international relations of the high aspirations liberals in modern history have entertained, before a series of catastrophic events lowered the sights of today's scholars to the defense of human rights alone.

Why Liberalism Marginalized Human Rights

Like all traditions, liberalism is an invented one. Duncan Bell has recently shown that there is no historically stable core to "liberalism," in spite of the attempts of a series of philosophers to locate it; and, if so, it is far better to write genealogically of an evolving and always contested concept that changes its own past even as it alters it present commitments.[2] With this understanding, the historian of human rights can observe that the place of her concept within the larger shifting constellation of liberal values has never been fixed. Nor is it adequate to assume that once a foundational

---

[2] Duncan Bell, "What Is Liberalism?" *Political Theory* 42, no. 6 (December 2014): 682–715. Edmund Fawcett, *Liberalism: The Life of an Idea* (Princeton: Princeton University Press, 2014), makes some of the same points in a less theoretically acute but more accessible way, though unfortunately sidelining empire. However, Fawcett plausibly writes that to grasp liberalism, "liberty is the wrong place to begin" (4; see further chapter 11 on rights as "new foundation" for liberalism).

role for rights has been laid, perhaps by John Locke, the die is cast for our own future. That approach not only mistakenly supposes that Locke stood up for liberalism in the first place, when the latter was in fact a nineteenth-century category then revised substantially in the twentieth, it also understates how much radical innovation would be required to secure the central place of rights in international affairs even later.

It is true, of course, that Locke supplemented Hobbes by making more than the right to life precede political order, and by insisting on the defeasibility of the choice of sovereign. But as Bell shows, Locke was never considered a liberal until the twentieth-century reinvention of liberalism, when it became crucial to establish a series of rights against the state as central in the face of a totalitarian enemy. Even then, however, domestic liberalism's foreign policy did not yet include international human rights, and no one claimed that it was imaginable or desirable to export Locke's theory of rights to international affairs. In this assumption, they were completely faithful to Locke's own texts. After all, Locke reserved "natural rights" for boundaried territories in which sovereign princes were to rule. He assigned to executives a wide-ranging entitlement or "prerogative" to act as prudence required in the dangerous world of international affairs – in twentieth-century parlance, Locke was a realist.[3]

If so, it follows that making the inference from rights at home to rights as central principles of the international order was a chasm to be bridged rather than a bridge to be crossed. But even framing the problem so modestly skirts how uncertain and unstable a place liberals – once they existed in the nineteenth century – assigned human rights even as a matter of domestic politics, which in turn has major implications for what sort of international policies could answer to the description "liberal" in the first place.

Of course, there is no doubt, as many historians have shown, that late-eighteenth-century natural law doctrines popular across the North Atlantic featured appeals to basic human rights. (There is persisting dispute about the sources and meanings of these appeals, though no one thinks that they had institutionally global scope for a wide range of Enlightenment thinkers.)[4] In spite of trying hard, historians of the era have not discovered widespread inferences from abstract moral principles

---

[3] For his theory of war and peace, and textual substantiation for the claims in this paragraph, see my "John Locke on Intervention, Uncertainty, and Insurgency," in Stefano Recchia and Jennifer Welsh, eds., *Just and Unjust Military Intervention: European Thinkers from Vitoria to Mill* (Cambridge: Cambridge University Press, 2013).

[4] Lynn Hunt, *Inventing Human Rights: A History* (New York: W.W. Norton, 2007); see also Kate E. Tunstall, ed., *Self-Evident Truths?: Human Rights and the Enlightenment* (New York: Continuum, 2012).

to the sort of institutional programs that political scientists now associate with human rights. Still writing in view of eighteenth-century natural law doctrine, Immanuel Kant insisted that "the rights of man" were "God's most sacred institution on earth." But by this he meant the ordering principles of domestic politics. He forbade crossborder intervention, and even tolerated East Asian state autarky, mainly because his increasingly rare hatred of colonialism overrode any leap he might otherwise have made to contemporary human rights politics.[5] Like Locke, Kant defined international ethics in terms of the relationship of states to one another in a fashion that would now be regarded as deeply traditional – if not realist. And he restricted his now much discussed category of "cosmopolitan right" to the entitlement of foreigners to present themselves at borders for the sake of commercial exchange, with no right to entry if they were unwanted. It is possible that Kant believed in a subsidiary right of entry for those who legitimately feared violence if they were rebuffed – effectively the non-refoulement provision of twentieth-century refugee law – but that is about it. Otherwise, Kant refused on principle to elevate "God's most sacred institution on earth" to the literal global order.[6]

It is not as if the domestic premises of liberals were static as their foreign policy changed, however. But if anything, their transformations stacked the deck against human rights more and more. The best candidate for a liberal who insisted on human rights as a limitation for sovereign activity in the domestic realm was the early nineteenth-century French liberal Benjamin Constant, but even he was increasingly committed to a historicist way of thinking about the evolution of political society which made it implausible to appeal to the prepolitical norms of natural rights. Of classic nineteenth-century liberals, neither John Stuart Mill, nor Alexis de Tocqueville, nor anyone else made natural or human rights foundational or central. Indeed, one reason for John Locke's absence from the self-constructed canon of liberals for a long time was that his unfashionable appeal to the unbelievable state of nature made his thought an unusable past as liberal visions were defined – even though when it

---

[5] Like several early liberals, including Edmund Burke (now routinely viewed as a liberal thinker), Kant had a healthy commitment to cultural diversity, though that commitment would increasingly disappear from the tradition, and remains peripheral in our own time. See, e.g., Sankar Muthu, *Enlightenment against Empire* (Princeton: Princeton University Press, 2003).

[6] The citation is from Immanuel Kant, *Political Writings*, ed. Hans Reiss (Cambridge: Cambridge University Press, 1991), 101. For the latest commentary, see Pauline Kleingeld, *Kant and Cosmopolitanism: The Philosophical Principles of World Citizenship* (Cambridge: Cambridge University Press, 2012) and, most incisively and historically, the relevant sections of Isaac Nakhimovsky, *The Closed Commercial State: Perpetual Peace and Commercial Society from Rousseau to Fichte* (Princeton: Princeton University Press, 2012).

came to international affairs Locke was just as much of an imperialist as the major thinkers of nineteenth-century liberalism mostly were.

The series of jostling commitments liberals made for a long time amounted to a program of what one might call "good government," with the common goal of transcending arbitrary despotic rule. Because of this core (if general) aim that united liberals for all their diversity, an agenda first adopted by aristocrats in their resistance to absolutism, liberalism would have a perpetually uneasy relationship to democracy. (Recall that the latter had always been viewed in the history of political thought, from Plato's *Republic* and Aristotle's *Politics* on, as likely to slide into a mob-rule little better than dictatorship.) Locke was a monarchist, and even when nineteenth-century liberals ruefully gave up on monarchy, they felt it most essential to seek technologies of good governance designed to achieve enlightened rule (figures such as Mill and Tocqueville differed profoundly about what these technologies were). Crucially, this emphasis on governmental limits hardly meant liberals were libertarian, whether because of commitments to natural rights or anything else. Rather, liberals always viewed the state as an indispensable tool to stave off the worse alternative of the unleashed freedoms of civil society, and so resolved to seek the proper balance between the capacitation and the constraint of government.[7] As for the deepest liberals, they regarded society as a historically evolving construction whose achievements were won at the level of social norms rather than through superficial governmental policy alone, so that history and culture were far more central fora of politics than administrative or legal fiat.

The most striking fact about any fair survey about the place of rights within liberal thought in modern times is, indeed, their etiolation within domestic argument. If human rights never made the transit above nation-states to circulate in international affairs – except for rare invocation of religious freedom in stigmatizing Ottoman misrule – they also withered within states as core liberal principles, to the extent they had ever gained a foothold to begin with. A sociological perspective never absent from the liberal tradition gained increasing ground. The greatest reason for this, perhaps, was the simple experience of citizenship politics. You assert your version and interpretation of the rights that nature dictates, and I assert mine, but if you and I disagree there is no recourse except to bargain (or fight). In real politics, rights are just a fancy name for policies, whose adoption ultimately depends on consent or force. No wonder, as Hannah

---

[7] The commitment of liberals to high capacity states is a special theme of Stephen Holmes, *Passions and Constraint: On the Theory of Liberal Democracy* (Chicago: University of Chicago Press, 1995).

Arendt observed, that rights were "treated as a sort of stepchild by nine-teenth-century political thought."[8] But liberals had a deeper reason than expediency and strategy – the lesson that assertions of human rights were at best a preliminary to bargaining or force in politics – to abjure appeal to them. As time passed, liberals came to believe, above all, in history and progress, which made any appeal to extra-social and non-temporalized account of applicable norms unbelievable, and not merely unavailing.

Following his master G.W.F. Hegel, Italian liberal Benedetto Croce, reflecting on the United Nations Universal Declaration project in the 1940s, put it best when he said "the rights of man in history" were what liberals could now make of an otherwise obsolete language: human rights were simply the set of citizenship norms to endorse for now, in a constantly evolving and progressing political society created in and through each state.[9] In their disparate national varieties, so-called new liberals across the Atlantic as the twentieth century dawned indeed went as far as to reject human rights altogether. They did not merely, as Hegel and Tocqueville had, situate them within a larger and complex picture of the achievement of individual and collective liberal freedom. They had good reason: by the late nineteenth century, the success of defenders of free enterprise in the libertarian defense of private property against state encroachment meant that progress demanded the deconstruction rather than the promotion of rights talk. In domestic politics in the North Atlantic, rights had been derided by reformers as implausible and obstructionist metaphysics as far back as Jeremy Bentham, but now under the Hegelian impress of figures such as T.H. Green, and socio-logically inspired progressives such as Léon Duguit, new liberals rallied around collective freedom as the goal for progressive societies living through historical modernization.[10] It would incorporate individual free-dom, of course, but not treat it as independently available or theoretically prior to the common good of interdependent societies.

Nor, after Kant, did rights make any headway in liberal foreign policies. It is not merely that liberalism was always statist (and typically imperial-ist) to the exclusion of anything really resembling international human rights. Its main historical project with respect to fellow whites and

---

[8] Hannah Arendt, *Origins of Totalitarianism*, new edn. (New York: Meridian, 1963), 293.

[9] Benedetto Croce, "The Rights of Man in History," in Jacques Maritain et al., *Human Rights: Comments and Interpretations* (New York: Columbia University Press, 1948), 81–5.

[10] See, e.g., the critical discussion of naturalistic rights theory, treated as a superseded mistake, in L.T. Hobhouse, *Liberalism and Other Writings*, ed. James Meadowcroft (Cambridge: Cambridge University Press, 1994), chap. 3. For the crucial intersection of liberalism and sociology in the new liberalism, see Stefan Collini, *Liberalism and Sociology: L.T. Hobhouse and Political Argument in England, 1880–1914* (Cambridge: Cambridge University Press, 1979).

Christians suffering under the wrong empire was modular nationalism. Especially in relation to the Ottoman empire, but also other faltering empires, Western European states – followed eventually by the American people – were often willing to support nineteenth-century national movements even when this meant interference with the integrity of borders. A nineteenth-century liberal nationalist such as Italian Giuseppe Mazzini was an exemplary hero. Striving in a first step for liberation of each people, the unification of humanity remained a distant goal. As a matter of fact, the combination of the proximate nation with an eventual global polity indeed ruled out anything like international human rights for a new reason – since liberals such as Kant and Mazzini long assumed that emancipated nations could not need external supervision, and if cosmopolitan unification of humanity ever took place, it would be in the form of a superstate or strong federation. It would not resemble our own "anarchical society" in international affairs, and so would not feature the same debates about sovereignty and its abrogation that our day has seen.[11]

Thus, the vanguard of progressive history for liberals was the achievement of white nations ruling the globe for reform's sake, thanks to the liberation of those nations that could govern themselves coupled with the victory of progressive empires for those not ready over merely power-hungry ones that barely improved over native misrule. To the extent so-called "liberal internationalism" existed in the nineteenth century, it was nationalist insofar as it was not imperialist: it focused on the liberation of white peoples from bad empires (and especially the Ottomans in the era of the Eastern Question). When they are not distorted by hindsight, early calls for "humanitarian intervention," starting with phil-Hellenist horror at Muslims ruling Christians, fit perfectly in this optic.[12] Of course, in most places, no liberation was imaginable, which usually meant there were no white people, either indigenous or imported. There the premium fell on the substitution of bad empires with good empires such as Great Britain, trailed by the United States as it gingerly embraced its role as "empire of liberty" in places such as Cuba and the Philippines, where Spanish domination seemed inadequate or faltered on its own.

In view of this status quo ante, the surprising rise of international human rights within liberalism could only take the form of a replacement of earlier and until then more durable nationalist and imperialist

---

[11] For more, see my "Giuseppe Mazzini in (and against) the History of Human Rights," in Miia Halme-Tuomisaari and Pamela Slotte, eds., *Revisiting the History of Human Rights* (Cambridge: Cambridge University Press, 2015), 119–39.

[12] Compare Gary J. Bass, *Freedom's Battle: The Origins of Humanitarian Intervention* (New York: A.A. Knopf, 2008).

frameworks – a substitution that occurred within living memory.[13] In the long era during which no one thought to export "human rights" to international affairs, the same broad sociological assumptions that liberals deployed to understand their own place in domestic history at home were in command when they thought about the social freedom they would bring the globe. The latter was simply far behind the former, which served as a beacon for all, except to the (sadly large) extent liberals bought into increasingly pervasive racist assumptions that made global freedom seem impossible and not merely distant. It was in part for this reason that when liberals thought globally, they bet so heavily on "civilization" as a force that, having brought Europeans out of darkness, might eventually do the same for the world's "savages" thanks to imperial rule. Indeed, liberals doubled down on sociology when in the long age of empire progress failed to materialize as quickly as Mill and others initially hoped.[14]

Reconsider from this perspective an episode often falsely made central to the "history of human rights" – the rise and fall of King Leopold's Congo (1885–1908). In a well-known bestseller, the journalist Adam Hochschild has famously portrayed the extraordinary terror Leopold brought to his own private colony, and how it was ended thanks to the mobilization of empathy that Hochschild does not hesitate to label "the first great human rights movement of the twentieth century."[15] But on second glance, it was really a story about liberalism and empire, rather than international human rights. The negotiations that first apportioned the Congo to Leopold in 1885 did so on essentially liberal grounds: the Berlin Act, as the relevant treaty was called, announced the goal of "instructing the natives and bringing home to them the blessings of civilization."[16] Figures such as E.D. Morel, lionized by Hochschild as human rights activists of their time (and understandably so, thanks to their tireless denunciation of the horrendous abuses that followed), saw no alternative to reallocating the Congo to some other empire, and preferably the British one, as a more proper steward. (Hochschild admits this decisive fact rather sheepishly.)[17] In the end, the

---

[13] For a good survey of a major recent literature, which unfortunately has not taken up the transformative era of decolonization, see Jennifer Pitts, "Political Theory of Empire and Imperialism: An Appendix," in Sankar Muthu, ed., *Empire and Modern Political Thought* (Cambridge: Cambridge University Press, 2012), 351–87.

[14] This is the lesson of Karuna Mantena, *Alibis of Empire: Henry Maine and the Ends of Imperialism* (Princeton: Princeton University Press, 2010).

[15] Adam Hochschild, *King Leopold's Ghost: A Story of Greed, Terror and Heroism in Colonial Africa* (New York: Houghton Mifflin, 1998), 2.

[16] General Act of the Berlin Conference on West Africa, February 26, 1885.

[17] "[H]umanitarians never saw themselves as being in conflict with the imperial project – as long as it was British imperialism," Hochschild writes. "This was the tradition in which

Congo was transferred to control of the Belgian state, as a more plausible trustee of civilization into an indefinite future, and it responded by replacing Leopold's atrocious governance with a forced labor regime that would not attract as much fierce international scrutiny, since it was more in step with then-current standards. As the Congolese transferred from Leopold's personal rule to Belgian sovereignty were black "savages," no one at any point, whether liberal or not, argued that they be given self-rule. Rather, the obvious remedy was to find the proper white empire that alone could bring them – as it was supposedly bringing the whole world – liberal progress.[18]

The point of this brief example is not to decry liberalism; it was a creature of its time, just like everyone and everything is. The point, rather, is to be clear that even to the extent transnational advocacy in the face of horrendous suffering took place among liberals before our age, it meant the search for good empire, and correcting mistaken allocation of benighted peoples with proper allocation. The comparison with a liberal in political science today, such as Beth Simmons, is in this regard particularly stark: when she thinks about human rights, she longs for global peoples to treat them as a powerful tool to set the terms of their own self-rule and self-emancipation through the non-imperialist mechanism of an international law they make their own. The contrast suggests that something drastic has occurred in the meantime.[19] And, in fact, it is on this

---

Morel felt at home, and ... [i]f he had believed, as we might conclude today, that Leopold's rape of the Congo was in part a logical consequence of the very idea of colonialism, of the belief that there was nothing wrong with a country being ruled other than by its own inhabitants, Morel would have been written off as being on the fringe. No one in England would have paid much attention to him" (212).

[18] Compare Jack Snyder's reading of the literature on anti-slavery in his chapter. It is crucial not to conflate the separate problem of mobilization against slavery within the British empire with that empire's subsequent fight against global slavery – the crimes of other states and empires. In the first circumstance, morality was given purchase by the loss of the American colonies and could experience relatively quick success, as visions of an "empire without slaves" compensated for political defeat. In the second, morality mattered in the geopolitical atmosphere of imperial order and rivalry, as that empire without slaves had new moral reasons for self-styled pre-eminence. Though otherwise different, neither period made the ideological language of rights central to anti-slavery. The two most crucial studies for reflecting on these problems are Christopher L. Brown, "Empire without Slaves: British Concepts of Emancipation in the Age of Revolution," *William and Mary Quarterly* 56, no. 2 (May 1999): 273–306 and Lauren Benton, "Abolition and Imperial Law, 1790–1820," *Journal of Imperial and Commonwealth History* 39, no. 3 (2011): 355–74. Snyder also fails to grapple with the reasons that current human rights movements minimalistically refuse to take up broader agendas like the imperialism I see as central to liberalism until recently and the democracy promotion that neoconservatives have captured (rhetorically, at least) over the past few decades of American policy.

[19] Human rights law, Simmons insists, is *"directly available to groups and individuals whom I view as active agents as part of a political strategy of mobilizing to formulate and demand their own liberation"* (emphasis in original). No nineteenth-century liberal would ever have

drastic transformation that emphasis needs to fall: what happened to liberalism, and surprisingly recently, to change it out of all recognition.

How Liberals Adopted Human Rights: Back to Order and Beyond Empire

That was then. Now liberalism does include rights much more prominently than ever, having undergone a "rights revolution" both in thought and in actuality, and made international human rights a policy to pursue.[20] "The history of liberalism ... is a history of constant reinvention," Bell observes. "The most sweeping of these occurred in the middle of the twentieth century, when liberalism was increasingly figured as the dominant ideology of the West – its origins retrojected back into the early modern era, it came to denote virtually all non-totalitarian forms of politics as well as a partisan political perspective within societies."[21] Disguising the novelties of its serial transformations, liberalism suddenly made several major leaps. Now, it is fully democratic, at least in its commitment to formal electoral inclusion, as well as most usually to written constitutions to organize and limit power. Above all, it is post-imperial. And, unlike in its glory years, it is chastened in its beliefs about the goals of politics and the possibilities available for progress. Liberalism went through two crucial stages to reach its elevation of international human rights to centrality. One was the antitotalitarian turn to rights, and the other their post-imperial internationalization.

The first, characteristic of "Cold War liberalism," occurred in the face of a frightening new enemy. Though the Cold War featured a commitment by liberal states to more state intervention and administrative explosion than any nineteenth-century liberal would ever have countenanced, and to more welfarist redistribution than before (or since), the spirit of Cold War liberalism changed drastically. It did so in response to the totalitarian foe that claimed for itself to be in the vanguard of moral progress and social evolution – once the greatest pride of nineteenth-century liberals. It stung liberals that Marxists took power arguing that the logic of social progress culminated in not in capitalism but in

---

worried that his tool might impose values, since such imposition is precisely what liberals believed was needed. Beth A. Simmons, *Mobilizing for Human Rights: International Law in Domestic Politics* (Cambridge: Cambridge University Press, 2011), 7.

[20] The "rights revolution" in domestic settings has to be rigorously distinguished from the liberal prioritization of human rights in international affairs, not least since the latter did not follow from the former. See, e.g., Charles R. Epps, *The Rights Revolution: Lawyers, Activists, and Supreme Courts in Comparative Perspective* (Chicago: University of Chicago Press, 1998).

[21] Bell, "What Is Liberalism?," 705.

communism, but aside from the occasional idiosyncratic "non-communist manifesto" liberals had no real reply.[22] Instead, Cold War liberals from Isaiah Berlin to Judith Shklar offered a bleak view of human affairs in which the most government can achieve is to present a space for individual freedom – most of all against the supposedly hypertrophic state itself.[23]

Yet Cold War liberals were not yet ready to criticize empire, except the Soviet one. As a matter of fact, in international affairs, even as its theoretical defenders insisted more on limits at home, the liberal state proved willing to unleash untold violence abroad. It was often the liberals who, having expanded empire in the nineteenth century, defended it to the last gasp. In America, it was the Democratic Party, rather than the Republican Party, that led the world into the Cold War and the country into the Vietnamese quagmire. No real concern for individual human rights, now more central at home thanks to Cold War liberalism and fears of state depredations toward its own citizens, obtained in international affairs, even (or especially) when liberals ruled. In the United States massive innovations such as the civil rights movement, which rewrote the social contract beyond formal racial subjugation, were carried out compatibly with massive global violence, visited upon Asians and Africans most cruelly.[24] It is ironic that contemporary liberals – including Ivy League professors, many of whose own institutional predecessors were profoundly complicit with America's Cold War violence – make broad claims about the humanity of "liberalism." After all, only shortly before our time, liberalism, including the very specific variant promoted by the American Democratic party, was entirely compatible with the pursuit of global freedom through shock and awe rather than rights and law.

But eventually the antitotalitarian constriction of liberalism converged with the loss of confidence in the tool of the imperial globalization of good government – and human rights took its place. Originally, anticolonialism had been justified on good liberal grounds, with activists around the world recalling that the first postcolonial state in world history was America's rights-based republic. In Mazzini's tracks, anticolonialists knew that there was no way to separate the protection of the individual from the emancipation of the nation, so many agitators reached the principle of "collective

[22] Cf. W.W. Rostow, *The Stages of Economic Growth: A Non-Communist Manifesto* (Cambridge: Cambridge University Press, 1960).
[23] Jan-Werner Mueller, "Fear and Freedom: On 'Cold War Liberalism,'" *European Journal of Political Theory* 7, 1 (January 2008): 45–64.
[24] Odd Arne Westad, *The Global Cold War: Third-World Interventions and the Making of Our Times* (Cambridge: Cambridge University Press, 2005).

self-determination" as a globalization rather than a qualification of liberalism. Indeed, they wondered how liberals from Mazzini, to his self-appointed heir Woodrow Wilson, to Cold War thinkers persistently restricted a liberalism of collective freedom to the white race. In response, proponents of decolonization simply resolved not to wait any longer for civilization to improve them. In their opinion, they had already waited long enough.

As the nationalist component of liberalism was allowed to trump the imperialist in the hands of global anticolonialists, international human rights were no part of the landscape. Rather, following the most ambitious version of liberalism in the North Atlantic, the new states attempted to reproduce the now welfarist nation-state around the world. It is, of course, true that anticolonialism ended up prizing sovereign equality and economic growth, treating individual protection as more of a theoretical rather than a practical priority. But then, its advocates were simply hewing to the global liberal norm in an era when state-led growth seemed to be the beacon of the future and no international human rights movement existed.[25] Autocrats and despots who trampled freedom in the third world were a sorry sight that hardly answered to liberal visions, of course, but then liberals often propped them up them to the extent they had to be supported as a lesser evil in the face of a communist threat.

Yet the liberal commitment to sociological progress counted even more, until the antitotalitarian constriction of liberalism eviscerated any attempt to retain the ambition of empire in new circumstances. It is easy to forget that it was liberals in history, not only communists, who once prioritized structural (including geopolitical) change and postponed individual protection, until they concluded that they had no working recipes for the former and ultimately risked never securing the latter. In the end, the proximate cause of the birth of international human rights politics was when liberals lost faith in their imperial and post-imperial tools to civilize the globe while also concluding that their former subjects were not up to the challenge of self-rule on their own.[26]

---

[25] Illuminatingly, as late as 1971 John Rawls was willing to relax the "lexical priority" of liberty (though not tolerate the most grievous wrongs like slavery) in view of the developmentalist imperatives of third-world states. John Rawls, *A Theory of Justice* (Cambridge, Mass.: Harvard University Press, 1971), 62–3, 247–8.

[26] See Declaration on the Inadmissibility of Intervention in the Domestic Affairs of States and the Protection of Their Independence and Sovereignty, United Nations General Assembly Res. 2131 (XX), December 21, 1965, and my "Imperialism, Self-Determination, and the Rise of Human Rights," in Akira Iriye et al., eds., *The Human Rights Revolution: An International History* (New York: Oxford University Press, 2011), 159–78.

Imperialism still haunts contemporary liberalism in many ways, at a minimum in the functional replacement of formal empire with the promotion of human rights: what rich (and generally white) people do when they feel their consciences pricked by poor (and usually black) suffering faraway.[27] But the departures from the age of liberalism and empire are in the end more compelling. The rare Niall Ferguson aside, no liberals are allowed to consider formal empire as part of the available toolbox. But other tools failed too: the Cold War versions of "civilization." To a remarkable extent, depressed by the failures of both state-led growth in the third world and what has been termed "high modernist" development brought by outsiders (including international organizations), liberals rally around human rights as the individualist salvation they feel they can plausibly defend and might work.[28] What is more impressive is not the continuity between imperial rule and human rights but the massive foreclosure of ambition involved in the substitution of the one by the other. In comparison to prior chapters in their own tradition, and not merely in the face of more ambitious rivals such as communism, liberals made international human rights their premier ideology and prestigious practice a "last utopia." Their more minimalist set of ideals and approaches – essentially the search for social order and personal freedom around the world – could seem an inspiring cause only after and instead of both the Cold War violence and the grandiose developmentalism liberals had tried first.[29] Even then, as Stephen Hopgood observes in Chapter 12, though the foundations were laid in the 1960s and 1970s, it took the end of the Cold War for human rights activism and analysis to truly surge.

To the extent all this is correct, liberalism in its antitotalitarian and post-imperialist mode is a profound break from its own prior impulses and instruments. It is so, above all, in two respects. It minimized ambition: prizing a baseline of political and civil liberties as the non-negotiable first principles and main agenda of international affairs, which had never before been the case. And it gave up the visionary character of liberalism at its welfarist (though imperialist) high tide, which defined itself as a philosophy of the *summum bonum* and the creation of the good life.

---

[27] See Jeanne Morefield, *Empires without Imperialism: Anglo-American Decline and the Politics of Deflection* (Oxford: Oxford University Press, 2014), esp. the chapter on Michael Ignatieff's thought.

[28] On high modernism, see James C. Scott, *Seeing Like a State: How Certain Schemes to Improve the Human Condition Have Failed* (New Haven: Yale University Press, 1998) and Nils Gilman, *Mandarins of the Future: Modernization Theory in Cold War American* (Baltimore: Johns Hopkins University Press, 2004).

[29] Samuel Moyn, *The Last Utopia: Human Rights in History* (Cambridge, MA: Harvard University Press, 2010).

Perhaps most deeply, liberals ditched sociology for formalism, even though generations of liberals had concluded that ambitious progress depended on the reverse move. Depressed by the betrayal of progress in false communist promises and the failure of empire (and its clientelistic successors in the newly decolonized states) to achieve freedom and equality around the world, liberals retreated to a rather different and supposedly disabused outlook. Politics seemed most likely to be a tragic recipe for evil, and suddenly the most prestigious agenda to adopt in response became to try to keep despots from killing their civilians or, when they did so anyway, to try to throw them into jail sooner or later.

All things considered, the "liberalism" that the ascendancy of international human rights epitomized, trailed as it has been by the so-called justice cascade of international criminal accountability, was a stark reversal (or even betrayal) of nineteenth-century optimism, which treated history as a forum of political opportunity rather than a charnel house of slaughter. The most cherished project of liberals – social freedom in the state with a strong welfarist dimension – was forsaken as restraining the state first at home and later abroad took pride of place. As if the high tide of liberalism had never occurred, the very rights earlier generations had found it necessary to marginalize or even abjure became in antitotalitarian and post-imperialist circumstances the highest ideals of liberals. The reasons they came to make these moves were plain. There was the totalitarian horror of Nazism and Stalinism and the travesty of progress that both represented. Even worse, there was the final indignity of concluding that empire and decolonization alike were also hollow in their common promise to bring about a better world. It must have seemed far wiser to adopt the more achievable and less risky goal of protecting individual freedoms, even though these had never been the exclusive concern of liberals in theory or in practice.

Contemporary Political Science and Human Rights

That contemporary liberals among political scientists are profoundly marked by this history is easy to show. Trailing the spike of "human rights" by a few years, "liberal internationalism" – the label to which most defenders of human rights within political science, and especially international relations, answer – is an artifact of the 1980s, as shown in Figure 11.1. The rise of liberal internationalism reflected the attempt to stake out an alternative to Cold War realism, itself mostly the creation of staunch liberals when it came to domestic politics, in the circumstances of the later Cold War once its worst excesses seemed inexcusable and international human rights were born. Like liberalism more generally, liberal internationalism has its own fabricated genealogies – Locke belatedly became the mythical founder of

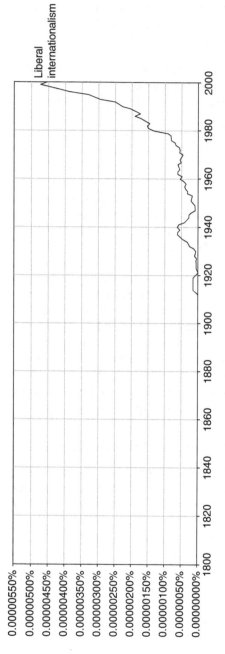

Figure 11.1: The incidence of "liberal internationalism" in the English language, as measured by the percentage of annual scanned books including the phrase. Courtesy of Google Ngram Reader.

liberalism in the early twentieth century and of liberal internationalism many decades later (perhaps most notably in Michael Doyle's well-known typology of positions in international relations).[30] As a result of their most recent reinvention of liberal tradition since the human rights revolution, the generation of theorists who really built the movement during the 1980s has not yet received the attention or credit they are due. And in spite of their creative work in building a new option in international relations theory, if the Cold War had not unexpectedly ended, liberal internationalism would not have become the prestigious success it became, either in the academy or in policy circles.

Yet instead of defending their values as rather novel and seriously controversial even within the history of liberalism, contemporary political scientists now think the premium falls on methodological battles and empirical demonstration. In large part this transformation is because of disciplinary priorities that are entirely unrelated to the topic of human rights on which they have been recently visited. The results have been extremely impressive, bringing human rights beyond the era of faith and into the era of measurement – even if cynics might observe that, surprisingly often, empirical results correlate strongly with the pre-established ideology of each empiricist. There is a deep worry, however, that the stress on empiricism functions to sideline core theoretical and prescriptive issues – in this case, what sort of hope liberals should have for the world, even before they reach the point at which they have to contend with their ideological enemies to the left or the right by converting faith into data. After all, it leads to a prestigious literature that turns out to revolve around what mechanisms (international treaties, accountability protocols, state socialization) might offer marginal improvement, as if this were the only plausible kind.[31]

That human rights have redefined liberalism profoundly predetermines the empirical investigation that Beth Simmons undertook in her extraordinary recent masterpiece, *Mobilizing for Human Rights*. If it is a liberal book, it is most of all because it is as antitotalitarian (focusing on political and civil liberties) as it is post-imperial (calling for indigenous self-liberation, and even going so far as a blanket rejection of humanitarian intervention, including under liberal auspices). In the end, Simmons argues that if polities that are neither stable autocracies nor full

---

[30] Michael Doyle, *Ways of War and Peace: Realism, Liberalism, and Socialism* (New York: W.W. Norton, 2007).

[31] See the illuminating example of Ryan Goodman and Derek Jinks, *Socializing States: Promoting Human Rights through International Law* (Oxford: Oxford University Press, 2013). See also the closely related volume: Ryan Goodman, Derek Jinks, and Andrew K. Woods, eds., *Understanding Social Action, Promoting Human Rights* (Oxford: Oxford University Press, 2012).

democracies have established a sufficient quotient of modern citizenship practices, activists can turn to international law as an additional tool to tweak citizen entitlements for the better, at least when it comes to some political and civil rights. A huge premium falls for Simmons on showing that human rights treaties make a difference at all, ruling out the "null hypothesis," even though on her own account their contribution is incremental and modest. What arguably has allowed the book to be so exciting and influential is not merely the empiricist methods it models, but the defense of world-historical minimalism in the uplifting and feel-good terms it provides.[32]

Yet if the sufficient quotient of modern citizenship is the major contribution and international human rights the minor one, even on Simmon's own account, it is justified to ask why the former rather than the latter is not the proper topic of attention and debate. It is a good question, and in fact it is a liberal one, once one drops the notion that geopolitical security and economic interests are the preserve of the "realist" from whom the liberal departs by focusing on the moral constraints of human rights. Rather, these geopolitical and sociological concerns were the central liberal goals in world history – and entirely moral ones, since the main goal was to establish the politics and material foundations of modern citizenship, and indeed in the modular boxes provided by national and often ethnic boundaries. If so, human rights are the rude interlopers into the historic agenda of liberalism, not its essential or longstanding content.

Analogous considerations apply to Kathryn Sikkink's empirical demonstration that transitional justice protocols prevent atrocities and may even – at least in Latin America, on which Sikkink predominantly focuses – have other effects in shoring up political and civil rights. In her brief for what she calls "systematic comparative empirical research," Sikkink rules out two other sets of criteria as overly optimistic, since they set up unfair standards for success that no existing movement could hope to match. The first is what she calls "comparisons to the ideal" – that is, inquiring into whether prosecutions perfectly fulfill expectations. The second is what Sikkink calls "counterfactual reasoning," which occurs when analysts measure what criminal prosecutions achieve compared to what might have happened in their absence. In other words, Sikkink rejects the first form of establishing

---

[32] For a fuller version of the criticism of Simmons as a defeatist (though not framed in terms of the liberal tradition), see my "Do Human Rights Treaties Make Enough of a Difference?" in Conor Gearty and Costas Douzinas, eds., *Cambridge Companion to Human Rights Law* (Cambridge: Cambridge University Press, 2013), 329–47. But see now Beth A. Simmons, "The Future of the Human Rights Movement," *Ethics and International Affairs* 28, no. 2 (Summer 2014): 183–96.

criteria for judgment as too utopian, and the other as too speculative, compared to an empirical comparison of real cases. And utopia and speculation can abet one another: no one knows what an alternative universe would look like – and the counterfactual scenario often simply allows projection of higher ideals, even though it is doubtful they would have been fulfilled in some alternative world. If (in Sikkink's example) the narrow set of outcomes the criminal process concerns looks better in one country that adopted prosecutions than in another that did not, then it is worth singling out. "I don't say that these prosecutions met my ideals of justice," she remarks, "but simply that countries that used them appear to be better off."[33]

But then by Sikkink's own admission, such a result is not worth praise, let alone high praise, since in the end we cannot postpone utopia or speculation forever. A difference is uninteresting or unimportant except to the extent it matters or is major. And on Sikkink's own terms, comparison of real cases forbids idealization. An empiricism that cautiously focuses on comparison of real cases, omitting or at least postponing any consideration of what justice actually is, makes it unclear how the empiricist can then celebrate a "justice cascade." Yet Sikkink allows a low bar for enthusiasm to justify high-flown rhetoric anyway. What makes good sense as a premise of research design turns out peremptorily to restrict inquiry into what sorts of ends might be worth pursuing and what sorts of outcomes worth celebrating. Thus, empiricism really functions to hide an unjustified choice of minimal ends as if it were a condition of social scientific inquiry.

And even more so than in Simmons, the human rights agenda of political science represents a narrowing of concerns. In Sikkink's work, the difference made and empirically proved in one specific domain – atrocity prevention – is now highly prized over others without justification. For understandable reasons, authors can now rely on readers to burn with outrage when crimes against humanity are in play, even though liberals have historically not placed foreign atrocity high on their list of priorities (to the extent they were not committing such atrocity themselves). These choices pass muster not only because of an empiricist vogue that ousts other priorities, including the more open-ended inquiry of political theorists down the hall, but also because modesty trumps ambition. This minimalism – seeking any tweaks in the restricted domain of political citizenship, however small so long as they are measurable – fulfills little of the liberal agenda of yesteryear. The contemporary data-driven promotion

[33] Kathryn Sikkink, *The Justice Cascade: How Human Rights Prosecutions Are Changing World Politics* (New York: W.W. Norton, 2011), 167. This paragraph follows my "Anti-Impunity as Deflection of Argument," in Dennis Davis et al., eds., *Anti-Impunity and the Human Rights Agenda* (Cambridge: Cambridge University Press, 2016), 68–94.

of human rights because they make some difference, however small, is a symptom of the silent redefinition of liberalism that scants the need to make a theoretical argument for it.

Perhaps the best imaginable defense of the empirical turn applied to unambitious ends is that, precisely because progress has failed to materialize in the guise of prior historical projects, it is now crucial to isolate the causal pathways and achieve clarity about the mechanisms of step-by-step reform. For example, perhaps democracy will prove durable only on condition of prosecuting past dictators, or economic and structural justice is only available within the terms of a democracy that provides political rights. But it is just here that the argument fails, and where it illustrates the departure from sociology that marked the liberal tradition at its best. For one thing, how plausible is it that empiricism allows the defense of human rights law and movements as they have materialized recently, among political actors who abjured long-term or structural thinking and therefore had no truck with any causal theory retroactively invoked to justify their decision to shoulder some tasks and not others? And how plausible is it that ragtag activists "mobilizing" to make use of the extra tool of international law to update their domestic citizenship in political terms will pave the way for a more generous transformation of citizenship that makes room for welfarist justice? (Did this happen thanks to the US civil rights movement, which usually provides the literature on the basis of which Simmons thinks about social movements – even though it never needed the extra tool of international law her book is designed to promote?) The very failure to make any case that initial, modest, causally secure pathways will lead to later, grander, and now more feasible futures is a glaring testament to the real constriction of the imagination that human rights scholarship in political science currently involves.

Conclusion

It is plausible to say international human rights are a liberal policy, but only with the proviso that single-minded emphasis on them breaks profoundly with historical liberalism, not only so as to correct its imperialist mistakes but also so as to foreclose its higher ambitions. Imperialism, for all its disastrous errors, represented an aspirational confidence liberals – entirely understandably – do not yet know how to replace. Creditably, Simmons insists on the need to defend human rights so as not to "overpromise," but the real worry is that, in their humility, contemporary liberals underpromise.[34]

---

[34] Simmons, *Mobilizing*, 6.

They do so thanks to the antitotalitarian constriction of liberal welfarism, which was dropped in theory under Cold War pressure and in practice once the waning of working-class movements at home and the Soviet enemy abroad prompted a massive renaissance of once-rejected economic libertarianism. And above all, they do so thanks to the post-imperial failure to reimagine global politics for the sake of the social freedom of which liberals once dreamed. Finally, they do so in search of something that works, even if its contributions are minor, on the ruins of dreams of progress that liberals, too, once entertained. The pursuit of minimal order in a vale of political tears – with securing personal freedoms and criminalizing atrocity as their highest aspirations – seems to liberals today the most they can hope for. It is true that, in Simmons's work, liberal feminism survives triage, but otherwise the shipwreck of liberalism is comprehensive.

Yet instead of facing their own situation squarely, acknowledging their surreptitious departure from their former welfarism (at home as well as abroad) and recognizing the modesty of their foreign policy, liberals today would prefer to celebrate human rights, apparently for the sake of feeling good. They do so in and through political science, which for all its scientistic pretenses often reads like little more than an attempt to raise confidence in the face of gloom and uncertainty. For this reader, at least, the extant political science literature on human rights does not work well as a psychological tonic. Rather, it inspires the thought that ambitious politics are (for the moment anyway) dead. It is a sad result for the discipline, even a disaster for the heritage of a millennium's reflection on political matters that, originating in a now marginal political theory, empirical political science generally avoids with little resistance.

On inspection, I have tried to show, the victory that self-styled liberal political scientists win in and through their promotion of human rights is one mainly aimed at their own discipline and of modest proportions. Simmons's work demonstrates that international law might help tweak domestic affairs in a positive direction if countries have already established the moral and material preconditions of modern citizenship, while Sikkink's writings show that transitional justice protocols involved in trying ex-presidents in court may improve country measurements. That empiricists think the main analytical challenge is to show that international human rights make a marginal difference is highly revealing in itself. For even if they are correct (which is by no means certain, in light of recent empirical pushback), the minimalism of these achievements is far cry from the ambitions liberals once shouldered.[35]

---

[35] For pushback, see most notably Eric Posner, *The Twilight of Human Rights Law* (Oxford: Oxford University Press, 2014).

This is especially the case insofar as the most recent liberals with whom our current ones could strive to be in communion are not Hobbes and Locke – theorists of minimal order, or at best a narrow range of personal freedoms (and property) – but the welfarist heroes whose plans at home and abroad are now broadly forsaken in the North Atlantic and as worldwide goals. If one thinks (as I do) that in real time the Universal Declaration of Human Rights announced not so much an international project of protecting life but a modular national project of renovating citizenship to incorporate welfare, the result is doubly ironic and disappointing. It is highly significant that Simmons's and Sikkink's measurement projects stick to familiar political civil and political liberties, not even aiming to vindicate the worth of human rights law and transitional justice protocols on the terrain of economic rights or broader welfarist outcomes. (One suspects they would fail to demonstrate such positive outcomes if they tried to do so.)[36]

That there are rich resources in the history of liberalism for returning to and correcting its recent truncation in and through the rise of human rights does not mean, obviously, that some earlier version of liberalism exists to surgically extract from the past for contemporary purposes. Far from it. But it does mean that earlier liberals were more aware of the range of competing ideals – social peace, national emancipation, economic growth, and collective welfare prominent among them – that in their combination marginalized anything like international human rights politics as they have risen today. It would be best, in sum, if contemporary political scientists would stop talking with such nonchalance and misinformation about "liberalism," as if the version of it they currently support were uncontested within their own tradition. The mantle of the liberal tradition is too hefty to be so easily shirked for the sake of the current fashion of human rights. This also opens the liberal canon of the past for explorations designed to help envision human rights futures. It is even possible that, just as liberals in domestic politics learned to do, advocates of international human rights will be led to put them in their place for the sake of a more sophisticated vision of social freedom.

---

[36] As Shareen Hertel's chapter shows (Chapter 10), economic rights advocacy has recently burgeoned, especially in campaigns in the global South typically marginalized both in northern non-governmental institutions and analyses, but it is far too early to tell whether such novel developments are promising. For contrasting pessimism, see my "A Powerless Companion: Human Rights in the Age of Neoliberalism," *Law and Contemporary Problems* 77, 4 (2014): 147–69.

12   Human Rights on the Road to Nowhere

Stephen Hopgood

For most of recorded human history, people have been concerned about what constitutes freedom, equality, fairness, and justice. In different eras, and different places, these ideas have had radically different answers. Any attempt to produce a grand historical account of what constitutes justice, for example, would have to deal with the many ways in which treating people justly has involved killing, torturing, enslaving, ostracizing, or exiling them. Human equality and human freedom were similarly dependent on either your identity or on any sins or crimes against gods or the social body for which you were deemed responsible. To talk of human rights as transhistorical phenomena only works, as a result, if we see them as moral (not empirical) claims, arguing that people have always had these rights in principle, whatever the reality. We have not created them; we have simply discovered them. Our forebears were either unenlightened or morally wrong. In this way, talk of empirical human rights cannot draw sustenance from the past except through reverse engineering. Some people historically may have held rights-like ideas, but "human rights" – rights that attach to all individuals on account of their simply being human – are one of our era's distinctive ideologies about right, fair and just treatment. They are reflective of a – perhaps *the* – defining feature of Western-style modernity: the emergence of the idea of rational, autonomous, self-governing individuals as the primary building blocks of political and social life and as the fundamental source of moral value. This shift has only happened in a serious way in the last two hundred or so years.

Because classic human rights are, in this sense, individual entitlements held against each other and against collective authorities, the emphasis in most arguments for rights is on the primacy of personal choice in terms of beliefs, commitments, lifestyle, and identity. This is captured in the idea of rights as trumps: winning cards in the game of life that individuals can play against any attempt to regulate, prohibit, mistreat, or disadvantage them in the name of broader social or political

283

goals, or the interests of other people.[1] Human rights make us all ends, not means, to paraphrase Kant. They carve out an inviolable and personalized private sphere. As such, they are integrally about a conception of the person who exists in some way prior to her social bonds, morally complete in and of herself. We need society to live in a practical sense, but this necessity is secondary in moral terms. That is, what has priority in a human rights world organized according to the classic conception of human rights are the lives and choices of individual human beings, not the degree to which the doctrines of nations, families, tribes, and gods are brought to life in the lives of those same individuals. Any theory of human rights that does not put this person first – that on principle (not as a lack, or oversight) allows discrimination or curtails personal choice – cannot be said to be consistent with the core inner logic of classical human rights claims, either conceptually or in their dominant historical form. How could an advocate of *human* rights accept any form of discrimination, unequal treatment, or unequal moral status *on principle*? How could any human rights agreement include such principles? Equal moral worth – and, as a logical consequence, prima facie equal individual autonomy over personal choice – are the founding principles of human rights claims. If we look at the world around us today, we see this is still a radical, even heretical, claim to make in many if not most societies.

This classic conception is not, nor has it ever been, the only option. Many places have vibrant civil societies pushing for justice, fairness, and social change – just not in the language of individual human rights (much less the idea of personal trump cards). The normative underpinnings of rights are distinct in giving social and political supremacy to the interests and choices of individuals. The classic conception does tend, it is true, to marginalize other sorts of rights claims. Demands for social and economic rights, as well as cultural and collective rights (e.g., the right to national self-determination), have always been part of the general rights discourse, with social and economic rights increasingly prominent in our era. But these claims do not map easily onto the individualist logic of the classic conception. And so they raise a critical issue of priority: for believers in the classic conception, individual rights must always come first. The collective can only legitimately claim to trump the interests of the individual person for three reasons: to prevent harm to others, to ensure the survival of the community as a whole, and for the best interests of the individual concerned. Even then, the bar is set high, the action's legitimacy will be hotly contested, and the language

---

[1] The idea of rights as trumps is indelibly associated with the work of Ronald Dworkin.

of rights will merely be temporarily suspended until the classic conception reasserts itself as the norm.

I'll suggest, in Section 1, that this classic conception has until now dominated the theory and politics of human rights, having all but monopolized rights thinking in the West. And it is Western power, for better or worse, that built the modern international system of which our current global norms and rules are integral parts. This reflects not a unified view in "the West," but a very specific sort of ideology that closely mirrors the broad needs and interests of the (middle-class) social forces that have outsize influence on life within Western societies. This raises an important question: If the momentum for globalizing human rights relies on the rights-sensitivity of growing middle classes in China and India, will these classes prove revolutionary or will they seek to support a narrower range of individual rights that mirror their interests? Section 2 considers this question, asking what implications any move to a post-Western world might have for the future of human rights in terms of state resistance. Section 3 looks at responses to human rights in terms of social ambivalence. Just as the middle classes are undergoing rapid change in Western societies, so the utility of human rights ideas as a legitimating ideology for those classes is under pressure in areas such as civil liberties and immigration.

Finally, I suggest that in this story we can see the structural limits to human rights-led progress. This has two elements. First, human rights do – as they are supposed to – strike at core aspects of sovereignty. But they have no means to make this demand for state compliance stick in the long run, beyond aiding and abetting the growth of internal and transnational forces that edge the state in that direction. The battle that must be won first is political and cultural, not legal, although these are interlinked struggles. A functioning and reasonably stable international system is a precondition for any form of generalized normative progress. Even then, there is much human rights law states can simply ignore, especially if they are powerful (the United States, China, Russia, India) or strategically important (Myanmar, Sudan, Uzbekistan, Egypt, Turkey).

Second, how effective social forces are, and their direction of travel, depends crucially on whether or not the middle class moves in a progressive direction. My hypothesis here is that, other things being equal, members of the middle classes by definition enjoy many social and economic opportunities without the need for human rights, and when they do not, they seek only those rights that will fill gaps in their own power. Chinese voters may demand more political rights over time, they may even be supportive of women's and LGBT rights, but they will not seek large-scale redistribution of their new wealth. Neither will the Indian middle class. They'll prefer to work on international issues such as human trafficking rather than see their own power and leverage dissipated. Whichever way you look at it, social and economic rights will always be more attractive for those currently without capital. A class struggle emerges between the purveyors of civil and political rights and those of social and economic rights, in other words.

1   Human Rights as a Western-led Normative Project

There is nothing inherently Western about ideas like rights, or their successor concept *human* rights. Any society or civilization could have developed similar ideas in theory. It is simply the case that it was in the West (meaning Europe, followed by its settler colonies) that this ubiquitous modern ideology came to fruition in the particular sense of becoming *an important part of the legal and cultural fabric and of having real political consequences*. Moreover, human rights are obviously not the only way to be moral. There is much in the doctrines of Islam, Judaism, Buddhism, Hinduism, and Christianity, for example, or in socialist demands for equality, or in conservative claims about the responsibilities of community, that is socially and morally valuable and/or progressive but which never mentions rights or human rights (often preferring the idea of "right" and its antithesis, "wrong"). The fact remains that it is *human rights* that have assumed the status of a modern orthodoxy at the level of international norms, succeeding Christianity in this aspiration to be universal. And the reason for this is that the dominant powers in the international system have until recently been Western liberal-democratic (and Christian) powers – Western and Northern Europe, the United States and Canada, Australia and New Zealand, and even Latin America, where legal and political systems as well as cultural and social institutions have been heavily marked by European influence, beginning with Christianity. In the Latin American case, human rights have been extremely important, even if they were also systematically abused by governments for much of the latter part of the twentieth century.

In other words, as historically situated normative innovations, there is little doubt that the West is where we must locate the drive for institutions that embed human rights globally. This does not mean that only Westerners (however we define such a problematic term) can hold those ideas – such a claim would be ridiculous, absurd, immoral, and empirically and historically false. It does not mean that a majority of Westerners actually believe in these ideas or enact them, as the callous moral failure of European states and societies to do more for destitute Syrian refugees amply demonstrates. It does not mean that Western states are not guilty of breathtaking hypocrisy and despicable historical crimes. It simply means that *the global impact of human rights in international politics in the post-1945 era is explained mostly by specifically liberal social modernization efforts (e.g., democratization) that Western states have through their greater relative power attempted to globalize, especially since the 1970s.* Not always, of course, but predominantly. Even if the expansion of human rights claims in the postwar period owes a great deal to innovations in the Global South, especially in former colonies, it is at the point that they were prioritized by Western states, and particularly the United States, that they became a significant feature of the international political system. Rights arguments were not enough. Power was essential.[2] These human rights were not necessarily adopted as aspects of Western foreign policies for human rights reasons: the spread of a particular kind of liberal individualism is just as much the ideology of hegemonic forms of capitalism emanating from the West as it is of any genuinely moral urge. It also does not mean that human rights and the institutional manifestations to which they give rise cannot, once established, be owned, changed, claimed, and otherwise used outside the West. It is simply a claim about their political origins and institutionalization *thus far.* Indeed, we may be living through the change and it is to the possible implications of that change I want to draw attention.

Major human rights innovations show this influence. Where are the major institutions of the international human rights regime? Geneva, The Hague, New York. Where are the major *global* human rights NGOs? Add London and Washington to the list. The UDHR may have had a remarkable array of states and individuals inputting into it, and it does reflect a much broader array of rights – social and economic as well as civil and political – than the classic conception. But who were its primary drafters? Rene Cassin, Eleanor Roosevelt, Charles Malik (a Lebanese Christian and Heidegger student whose commitment to the dignity of the individual was anchored in his religious faith), and John Humphrey, a Canadian international civil servant.[3] Where have regional human rights conventions and courts been most influential? Europe and the Americas.

---

[2] On the importance of the Global South in the emergence of human rights ideas after 1945, see Steven L. B. Jensen, *The Making of International Human Rights; The 1960s, Decolonization, and the Reconstruction of Global Values* (New York: Cambridge University Press, 2016).

[3] For an excellent discussion of Malik and an assessment of the claim he was a Westernized liberal, see Joe Hoover, "Remembering Charles H. Malik," (February 2011), at: http://thedisorderofthings.com/2011/02/09/remembering-charles-h-malik/.

Western Europe is routinely behind the Human Rights Council's strongest resolutions and is now the main funder of the International Criminal Court.[4] Of the P5, only the UK and France have ratified the Rome Statute. The United States, while ambivalent about the ICC, has been consistently committed (at least, in principle) to the Universal Declaration of Human Rights.[5] Which states took up the landmines treaty, or the Arms Trade Treaty, the ICC, and R2P? How many Asian or Middle Eastern states are members of the ICC? What is Africa's relationship with the ICC like? Who stands most squarely behind R2P? We can even see the West more narrowly, as Europe with Canada and the unpredictable engagement of the United States (sympathetic in principle, at least pre-Trump, conflicted in practice). Which countries in the Human Rights Council routinely lead resistance to the demands of Russia and China? European states. Who has pushed hardest for an international criminal investigation in Sri Lanka, or in North Korea? Europe and the United States. This normative architecture has been constructed under the hegemony of the West however much (or little) buy-in there has been from other states.

These rights are generally in sympathy with the political cultures of the modernizing industrial societies from which they emerged, and have been part of Western liberal discourse in broad terms dating back to the idea of natural rights (the clearest precursors to human rights). Indeed, they have come to dominate liberal discourse, relegating the utilitarian strain of liberalism culturally (if not practically) to marginal status. Human rights are not the only progressive doctrine that aims to combat injustice, nor were all the founders of human rights ideas Western. But from the UDHR onward, and especially since the 1970s, there has been a Western-led drive to globalize them for ideological and Realpolitik reasons.

It is important to note that human rights claims, while seeming to be merely political, in fact have deeper philosophical roots. There is a clear

---

[4] Stuart Ford, "How Leadership in International Criminal Law Is Shifting from the US to Europe and Asia: An Analysis of Spending on and Contributions to International Criminal Courts," *Saint Louis University Law Journal* vol. 55 (2010): 953–1000.

[5] "Remarks by President Obama in address to the United Nations General Assembly, September 24, 2014," at: www.whitehouse.gov/the-press-office/2014/09/24/remarks-president-obama-address-united-nations-general-assembly. In this speech, it is noteworthy, however, that while President Obama mentioned "human rights" twice, he did so by referring to the UDHR once and then by quoting Eleanor Roosevelt. At no point did he directly reference his commitment, nor that of US foreign policy, to protect and promote "human rights" per se. Indeed, in mentioning the UDHR he characterized its mission, along with that of the UN as a whole, as "the notion that peace is not merely the absence of war, but the presence of a better life." This is a statement of such generality no one could object. It is doubtful any statement even of this sort will be forthcoming from President Trump.

conception of the person underlying them. Thus, at the heart of Western-style modernity lies what Macpherson called "the possessive individual."[6] The moral superiority of claims to children's, women's, and LGBT rights is self-evident on this view and any social, cultural, or political norm that doesn't respect the fully autonomous individual must, again *on this view*, be regarded as wrong. That's the bottom line. The veil? Female genital mutilation (FGM)? Unspeakable wrongs, from the perspective of human rights. It is obvious to advocates that any choice to wear the veil or facilitate FGM is simply a coerced choice, shaped by structures of patriarchy that have been so deeply embedded in culture they have led to a form of false socialization that disguises the reality of human moral equality.

Eliminating discriminatory practices of this sort was once called enlightenment and civilization. In our era, it is also often about capabilities and nudging.[7] What argument to defend gender discrimination on principle could be made by any opponent of human rights and expect to be taken seriously? For human rights advocates, defending gender discrimination on principle is like defending racism on principle. In a world where human rights prescribes the limits of legitimate discourse, there is no longer any language in which to do it. These are red lines. Human rights are not a road to nowhere for their most ardent advocates, they are an often meandering and frustrating, sometimes slower, sometimes quicker journey toward a clear and predetermined *moral* destination. That destination is the legal right and social capacity, based on natural human moral equality, to make fully informed autonomous life choices *as individuals*.

This major historical shift is broadly in line with substantive moral norms within Western societies. The free societies in Freedom House's 2015 annual report are overwhelmingly in the West. The focus of global human rights is in areas such as the ICC, R2P, crimes against humanity, a world court of human rights, that place civil and political, justice and protection institutions first. The majority of research on human rights focuses on mental and bodily integrity – civil and political rights – as well. This is neither contingent nor accidental. These are the rights which work in alliance with the underlying distribution of social and economic power worldwide. The social classes who have the money or the political power – the leverage – to change things only need be

---

[6] C.B. Macpherson, *The Political Theory of Possessive Individualism: Hobbes to Locke* (Oxford: Clarendon Press, 1962).

[7] Martha C. Nussbaum, "Symposium on Amartya Sen's Philosophy: 5 Adaptive Preferences and Women's Options," *Economics and Philosophy* 17 (2001) and Richard H Thaler and Cass R Sunstein, *Nudge: Improving Decisions About Health, Wealth and Happiness* (New York: Penguin Books, 2009).

interested in the civil and political rights part of the equation. They want a voice for themselves domestically and a voice with their like-minded class compatriots internationally. They don't need to worry about social and economic rights because they can produce and consume in the private sector, which gives them access to all the goods and services they need.

As for cultural rights, I would argue these are essentially incomprehensible within the mainstream global human rights regime (hence the lack of attention they receive). They are anathema to individual rights, frequently the problem not the solution, and even if they can be made conceptually coherent, they must still be anchored in the final analysis on individual claims and entitlements, and so they are always trumped by individual rights. The same is broadly true for group rights claims as well. As Samuel Moyn has argued, the classic group right – to national self-determination – was largely killed off by the switch in the 1970s toward the classical conception of civil and political rights.[8] That this coincided with the uptake by Western middle classes and governments of human rights ideas is not incidental. This is why human rights research has discovered that human rights are best observed in the places that need them least.[9] In rights-observing societies, the public/private split and the primacy in principle of the individual, the distinctive features of modern liberalism, are marked. These are constitutively liberal spaces.[10] And they have exported and institutionalized that liberalism.

There is evidence, however, that these liberal, mainly European, states are losing influence in organizations such as the United Nations that they still do so much to fund.[11] Leaving aside the ongoing problems associated with the Euro after 2008, and fallout from Brexit and the election of Donald Trump, decreases in European defense spending represent a trend dating back to the end of the Cold War (as a share of GDP, for

[8] Samuel Moyn, *The Last Utopia: Human Rights in History* (Boston: Harvard/Belknap Press, 2010).

[9] Emilie Hafner-Burton, *Making Human Rights a Reality* (New Jersey: Princeton University Press, 2013).

[10] The metaphysical basis for this political ideology is too large a subject for analysis here; suffice it to say that the urge to rid justice of its political foundations to enhance legitimacy must co-exist with the reality that it is only as a political compromise that documents such as the Universal Declaration of Human Rights gained assent in the first place. See Joshua Cohen, "Minimalism about Human Rights: The Most we can Hope For?" *Journal of Political Philosophy* 12, no. 2 (2004), and on the problematic nature of the classic "human rights as moral rights" story, see Joseph Raz, "Human Rights without Foundations," *Oxford Legal Studies Research Paper* 14 (2007).

[11] See Richard Gowan, "Who Is Winning on Human Rights at the UN?" *European Council on Foreign Relations*, September 2012; and Richard Gowan and Franziska Brantner, "The EU and Human Rights at the UN: 2011 Review," *European Council on Foreign Relations*, at: http://www.ecfr.eu/page/-/ECFR39_UN_UPDATE_2011_MEMO_AW.pdf.

example, the UK's defense spending fell from 4.4 percent to 2.2 percent from 1989 to 2008, France's from 3.7 percent to 2.3 percent and Germany's from 2.9 percent to 1.3 percent).[12] It was still falling in all three in 2014.[13] In a recent article in *International Affairs*, Douglas Webber argues that there is a clear decline in Europe's military and economic power, which has inevitably weakened its capacity to influence world events, as revealed starkly in Crimea (and Syria and Ukraine). In Syria, in particular, the evisceration of international humanitarian law by the Assad government and by Russia has been unchecked by European protest. Even though Europe's soft power retains potency, un-backed by hard power it will further lose effectiveness, Webber claims.[14]

Freedom House recently reported an eleventh successive year of declining freedom worldwide, civil liberties and political rights being the key variables it measures annually to make this assessment.[15] Although until 2006 there had been three decades of increase in the number of democracies globally, the world has since then, argues Larry Diamond, entered a period of "democratic recession."[16] This recession has several aspects: more democratic breakdowns, declining quality of democracy in some pivotal states, deepening authoritarianism in others, and established democracies that "increasingly seem to be performing poorly and to lack the will and self-confidence to promote democracy effectively abroad."[17] The United States is front and center when it comes to lack of will, according to Diamond. Not only are its own democratic structures under-performing, but it has lost the confidence or will internationally to pursue liberal reforms. This will surely only get worse under President Trump.

---

[12] Fabio Liberti, *Defence Spending in Europe: Can We Do Better Without Spending More?* (Notre Europe, 2001), 16, at: http://www.notre-europe.eu/media/policy46_fliberti_en.pdf?pdf=ok.

[13] The Economist, "Global defence spending," (February 2015), at: www.economist.com/news/economic-and-financial-indicators/21643167-global-defence-spending?fsrc=scn/tw/te/ed/pe/globaldefencespending.

[14] Douglas Webber, "Declining Power Europe? The Evolution of the European Union's World Power in the Early 21st Century," *International Affairs* 91, no. 2 (2015). See also Christopher Hill's discussion of the decline in importance of the UK and France globally: "Powers of a Kind: The Anomalous Position of France and the United Kingdom in World Politics," *International Affairs* 92, no. 2 (2016).

[15] Freedom House, "Freedom in the World 2017," at: https://freedomhouse.org/report/freedom-world/freedom-world-2017.

[16] Larry Diamond, "Facing up to the Democratic Recession," *Journal of Democracy* 26, no. 1, January 2015.

[17] Diamond, "Facing up to the Democratic Recession," p. 144. Diamond distinguishes liberal democracies from electoral democracies, the former restricted to those scoring 1 or 2 on the Freedom House scale. In other words, to assess the state of democracy, rights and liberties, along with transparency and the rule of law, are central elements, confirming the link between rights and democracy.

Indeed, even before Trump, the United States, the engine for Western influence after 1945, was itself unsure about its strategic direction. It now faces more competition than it has since the 1980s from global rivals.[18] Attempts to shift its strategic focus to Asia have meant demanding more "burden sharing" from Europeans (and others).[19] This is a relative not absolute decline. If we take as the measure of economic power per capita GDP, not the absolute size of the economy, the United States is hugely ahead of China, as well as dwarfing all other powers in terms of its military spending.[20] According to *The Economist*, the United States in 2014 spent $581 billion on defense, compared with second-placed China at $129 billion.[21] But this was a decline in US defense spending. In Saudi Arabia spending went up by 21 percent, followed by China (up 9.7 percent) and Russia (up 8.3 percent). Russia spends more of its GDP per capita on defense than the United States, the US's share of global defense spending having fallen from 47 percent in 2010 to 38 percent in 2014.

This would seem to be consistent with the broader feelings of many Americans. After Iraq and Afghanistan, record numbers now say they want the United States to let other countries get on with their own business with less US intervention, "shared leadership" being a better model for them than hegemony.[22] And one of President Trump's key campaign promises was to put the national interests of the United States above any other consideration. This is troubling because on key human rights issues, it is often American diplomatic involvement that makes the difference – Sri Lankan war crimes investigations and action to prevent global anti-blasphemy laws just two recent examples.[23] It is difficult to

---

[18] On the decline or otherwise of American power, see Christopher Layne, "The Waning of U.S. Hegemony – Myth or Reality? A Review Essay," *International Security* 34, no. 1 (2009). See also Robert J. Lieber, *Power and Willpower in the American Future: Why the United States Is Not Destined to Decline* (New York: Cambridge University Press, 2012); Robert Kagan, "Not Fade Away: The Myth of American Decline," *National Review*, January 2012; Robert D. Kaplan, *Monsoon: The Indian Ocean and the Future of American Power* (New York: Random House, 2010); Fareed Zakaria, *The Post-American World* (New York: W. W. Norton, 2009).

[19] "Remarks by President Obama in Address to the United Nations General Assembly," September 24, 2013.

[20] Robert J Lieber, "The rise of the BRICS and American primacy," *International Politics*, pp. 1–18, 2014.

[21] The Economist, "Global defence spending," (February 2015).

[22] Pew Research Center, "Americans: Disengaged, feeling less respected, but still see US as world's military superpower," at: www.pewresearch.org/fact-tank/2014/04/01/americans-disengaged-feeling-less-respected-but-still-see-u-s-as-worlds-military-superpower/.

[23] Ronak D. Desai, "Tensions rise between the United States and Sri Lanka over human rights," *Huff Post Politics*, April 28, 2014: www.huffingtonpost.com/ronak-d-desai/a-row-emerges_b_4859375.html; Nina Shea, "An anti-blasphemy measure laid to rest," *National Review*, March 31, 2011: www.nationalreview.com/article/263450/anti-blasphemy-measure-laid-rest-nina-shea.

imagine coordinated action against ISIS without the United States as the principal military and diplomatic leader, for example.

2   Human Rights in a Post-Western World

In any post-Western world, should that emerge, Western states, particularly Europe – if it remains united – and most obviously the United States, will remain highly influential. Post-Western means more precisely post-Western *hegemony*. The West simply will not remain *as* influential. How could it, with the rise of China, India, Brazil, and Indonesia, to give just four examples? China's strategic position on the Security Council, for instance, gives it great leverage and has perhaps even emboldened Russia in pursuing a more confrontational foreign policy (e.g., over Syria). Given that there are major problems with human rights compliance even though Western states have dominated the international system for more than a century, it is not a stretch to hypothesize that this situation is only likely to get worse.

If Europe does decline in influence, this will only reveal the degree to which "the West" has been disproportionately dependent on American power. Certainly from the end of the Cold War to maybe the invasion of Iraq in 2003, it made sense to speak of world politics as unipolar, and of the United States as enjoying a "unipolar moment."[24] What we are experiencing now is a shift away from that toward either bipolarity or a qualified sort of multipolarity.[25] What might the implications of such a shift be? If the gap in power is big enough, the hegemon – or, under bipolarity, the major powers – have latitude for more expansive foreign policies. They can, in brief, afford to spend diplomatic capital on issues such as human rights which are not primary to national security. As the gap narrows, and as power comes to be in shorter supply, it must be reserved for vital interests and it is rare, aspirational rhetoric apart, that threats to human rights elsewhere represent threats to national security. Moreover, as dominant powers lose influence, that power is being dispersed to others (otherwise major powers would retain their relative advantage). Other things being equal, some medium-sized and even small powers might now drive a harder bargain for being an alliance member or refraining from joining a rival grouping. Thus, the shift to multipolarity may usher in a world where diverse norms buck the trend to isomorphism.[26] Think Central Asia and ASEAN.

---

[24] William Wohlforth, "The Stability of a Unipolar World," *International Security* 24, no. 1 (1999): 5–41.

[25] Or, in Richard Haass's view, "nonpolarity." See Haass, "The Age of Nonpolarity: What Will Follow US Dominance?" in *Foreign Affairs* (May/June 2008).

[26] Peter J Katzenstein (ed) *The Culture of National Security: Norms and Identity in World Politics* (New York: Columbia University Press, 1996), and John Boli and

For example, at a February 2015 White House conference on combatting violent extremism, President Obama's invited audience included the Egyptian foreign minister and the prosecutor general of Kazakhstan. Other attendees included officials from Bahrain, Saudi Arabia, and Uganda. The president stressed the importance of democracy and freedom in defeating terrorism, but the conference in reality highlighted the need for the US to get cooperation from governments that a Human Rights First spokesperson described as "part of the problem."[27] Human Rights Watch's chief, Kenneth Roth, called the president "Obama the disappointment."[28] In a multipolar world, these are new realities, and poor human rights compliance is not a deal breaker. It is not the 1980s, or indeed the 1990s (when US power was preponderant). The narrow self-interested focus of President Trump's foreign policy aims will likely seriously exacerbate this drift. His admiration for authoritarian leaders just compounds the problem.

Do global norms need a backer of last resort? Neorealists and many neoliberals have always thought so. Charles Kupchan says of the future that it will be *No One's World*. China, as well as India, Russia, and Brazil, will challenge rules and institutions that do not meet their interests.[29] There is no reason why mutual interests cannot be realized through norms in such a world. The question is whether a global *liberal normative* regime will be conceived of as mutually beneficial by a sufficient number of major powers. Customary international law is based on state practice, suggesting that if state practice changes – and sovereignty over the treatment of one's own citizens in opposition to R2P is re-affirmed – then customary international law will have turned away from human rights. Human rights advocates will argue this is just bad law, or no law at all.[30] But is it? The breaking of a customary norm is also potentially the beginning of a new norm.[31] In other words, it is only an assumption

George M Thomas (eds) *Constructing World Culture* (California: Stanford University Press, 1999).

[27] Peter Baker and Julie Hirschfeld Davis, "On Terror, Gentle Hand or Iron Fist," *New York Times* (February 2015), at: www.nytimes.com/2015/02/20/world/obama-extremism-summit.html?emc=edit_th_20150220&nl=todaysheadlines&nlid=18548227&_r=0.

[28] Kenneth Roth, "Obama the Disappointment," *Human Rights Watch* March 4, 2014, at: www.hrw.org/news/2014/03/03/obama-disappointment.

[29] Charles A. Kupchan, *No One's World: The West, the Rising Rest and the Coming Global Turn* (Oxford: Oxford University Press, 2012).

[30] Bringing to mind the Hart–Fuller debate of 1958 on whether law to be law must have progressive content in the broadly Kantian sense of morality. Lon L. Fuller, "Positivism and Fidelity to Law: A Reply to Professor Hart," *Harvard Law Review* 71, no. 4 (1958): 636. H.L.A. Hart, "Positivism and the Separation of Law and Morals," *Harvard Law Review* 71, no. 4 (1958): 599.

[31] Anthony D'Amato, *The Concept of Custom in International Law*. (Ithaca: Cornell University Press, 1971), p. 97.

underwritten by liberal teleology that after more than a century of humanitarian and human rights law, customary international law is perma-
nently about protecting individuals from harm, whether as civilians in war
or as regular citizens.

John Ikenberry in *Liberal Leviathan* is more optimistic than Kupchan.
Because rules and institutions are a more cost effective way of using
material power to prevail, China will eventually accept the international
order and work within it, he argues, the US-led international system's
relatively open nature making it possible to accommodate such a vast new
rising power.[32] Rule-based orders are more legitimate than non-rule-
based ones, Ikenberry says, and therefore easier and cheaper to control
because they operate on the basis of consent rather than coercion. But
here the word "liberal" has a very narrow remit. It means support for
institutions that foster cooperation on issues such as trade, security, and
arms proliferation, not support for broader norms about human rights (or
potentially even democracy). For expansive liberalism, the end of
Western hegemony means no one state or group of states can offer
sufficient incentives or punishments to ensure compliance on issues that
are not vital interests.[33] In the American case specifically, US–China
strategic competition is likely to be more central to US foreign policy
than human rights concerns about South East Asian states like Vietnam
and Thailand and even Myanmar, whose support is key to the strategy of
containing China.

One model for a world of diverse norms, where human rights are less
dominant, is legal pluralism – that is, co-existent legal regimes. This raises
the "red line" question. Negotiated compromises on the basis of the
interpretation of doctrine are one thing. Sources of agreement with
human rights-like sentiments can be found in major religious texts and
cultural traditions. But it cannot be the case that for human rights advocates the conversation with religions and cultural rights, even with social
and economic rights, has no red lines in everyday social life. If there are no
such inviolable borders, how are disputes between traditional and human
rights authorities to be reconciled? In favor of the status quo? This would
privilege all sorts of rights-violating norms: e.g., FGM, rape in marriage,
violence against LGBT people. Of course, FGM must end, like the veil
must go and domestic violence must cease. If, that is, the classic conception is to be realized. It seems to be an open-ended conversation, but it is
not. For activists this is very definitely the road to *somewhere*. At most,

---

[32] G. John Ikenberry, *Liberal Leviathan* (Princeton: Princeton University Press, 2011).
pp. 345–7.
[33] See, for a counter view, Hafner-Burton, *Making Human Rights a Reality*.

a few mildly pragmatic compromises might be made – using subtler means such as two-speed processes, nudges and gentle persuasion, and education programs, to improve human rights outcomes. But the principles at issue, the ends to be pursued, are in no sense negotiable – the priority of the individual as a self-conscious and independent moral person is the very foundation of the human rights project.

But this clear view of what human rights are is less and less consensual. Pointing to the law only takes us so far in a world of ambiguous compliance. What human rights entail is contested by governments and within societies. Even when public opinion as a whole is in favor of human rights, this tells us little about specific cases. One example is in areas where a counter-claim in the language of rights can be made, such as the rights of the unborn child – that is, the right to life – versus reproductive rights. Another is between property rights and equality rights. A third is where different kinds of freedom rights clash – between free expression and minority rights in areas like religious freedom, for example. In these cases, people on both sides try to play their trump cards. Then there is a more pernicious form of rights deployment that flourishes when the opponents of change use the language of rights to defend and promote practices that are not consistent with the basic idea of individual rights underlying the classic conception. In some cases, rights are even used to defend illiberal causes.[34]

ASEAN, for example, passed a human rights declaration which local human rights groups condemned as an "anti-human rights declaration."[35] China's response to the UN's 2014 report on North Korea, which recorded "unspeakable atrocities," was: "Of course we cannot accept this unreasonable criticism. We believe that politicizing human rights issues is not conducive towards improving a country's human rights. We believe that taking human rights issues to the International Criminal Court is not helpful to improving a country's human rights situation."[36]

In 2012, Russia promoted and passed a resolution on traditional values at the Human Rights Council, which put forward *in the name of human rights* notions about nation and family that are clearly at odds with the classic conception of human rights in that they deny individuals their veto over authority (the Russian Orthodox Church's position on human rights

---

[34] Cliff Bob, *The Global Right Wing and the Clash of World Politics* (Cambridge: Cambridge University Press, 2012).

[35] Human Rights Watch, "Civil Society Denounces Adoption of Flawed ASEAN Human Rights Declaration," at: www.hrw.org/news/2012/11/19/civil-society-denounces-adoption-flawed-asean-human-rights-declaration.

[36] Reuters, "China Rejects UN Criticism in North Korea Report, No Comment on Veto," February 18, 2014, available at: www.reuters.com/article/2014/02/18/us-china-korea-north-idUSBREA1H0E220140218.

mirrors this resolution).[37] Norway's Helsinki Committee says of the Russian resolution:

During recent years, a Russian-sponsored initiative at the UN Human Rights Council has been targeting core tenets of international human rights: their universality, their unconditional nature, and their challenge to traditions that uphold discrimination and intolerance. The proponents of the initiative have camouflaged it as laying out new ways of promoting human rights. Traditional values of humankind are a tool to strengthen and underpin human rights at the local level, they claim. In reality, the initiative threatens to destroy consensus among the states of the world on how they should honor their human rights obligations.[38]

But the elasticity of rights concepts and the interpretability of rights claims, let alone the caveats that exist even in UDHR Article 29 about "morality, public order and the general welfare in democratic societies," facilitate such a challenge to the previously hegemonic understanding of rights. Politically speaking, human rights norms are now "essentially contested concepts" where the phrases "this is a human right" and "human rights give rise to the following binding obligations" are not just disagreements about how a concept is properly used but about what the concept entails in a more foundational sense.[39] The resolution of these struggles at the international level is not to be found in discursive interaction but in the political leverage – the power – alliances can muster in global institutions. As power is increasingly dispersed, the chances of forging a global consensus recede. This is, I would argue, the coming human rights future.

The extreme version of politicization manifests itself most strongly in the cases of China and Russia. Rather than find ways to accommodate rights, they have both set themselves up broadly in opposition to the global human rights regime.[40] In the Russian case, this has led to active hostility toward human rights as a whole, and foreign-funded human rights groups in particular.[41] Even when China has used human rights language, it does so in ways that emphasize social and economic over civil and political rights, and which stress sovereignty and national

---

[37] See, for example, Cai Wilkinson, "Putting "Traditional Values" into Practice: The Rise and Contestation of Anti-homopropaganda Laws in Russia," *Journal of Human Rights* 13 (2014): 363–79.

[38] Norwegian Helsinki Committee, "Russia's Traditional Values Initiative Result [sic] in Abuse at Domestic Level," June 20, 2014, at: http://nhc.no/no/nyheter/Russia's+traditional+values+initiative+result+in+abuse+at+domestic+level.b7C_wlnKY2.ips.

[39] W B Gallie, "Essentially Contested Concepts," *Proceedings of the Aristotelian Society*, vol. 56 (1955), pp. 167–98.

[40] In "Facing up to the Democratic Recession," Diamond describes Russian-Chinese collaboration within the Shanghai Cooperation Organization as an "axis of cynical cooperation," p. 151.

[41] Tanya Lokshina, "Russia's Backward Roll," *Human Rights Watch* (July 2014), at: www.hrw.org/news/2014/07/30/russias-backward-roll.

self-determination. It is also adept at exposing Western hypocrisy by producing reports that identify human rights abuses in the West.[42] All of which does little for the legal protections that individual rights are meant to provide. In other words, human rights language might be acceptable where it is diluted of all significance, and resisted or ignored where it might still carry weight.[43]

Moving away from unipolarity, and from the hegemony of Western power, opens up space for alternative international norms. China and Russia have led the way in diffusing strategies and mechanisms by which to institutionalize authoritarian rule more effectively.[44] This creates room, especially in terms of legitimacy, for the new authoritarians to counter human rights, whether through rejection, evasion, or co-optation. To see this as merely a transient phenomenon, we would have to believe that Russia and China will at some point reverse themselves and embrace human rights norms at the international level. But the authoritarian toolkit they are exporting will blunt domestic capacity building further, thus making it even harder for rights advocates to make an impression on powerful, illiberal governments.

There are many obvious forms of pushback by states, such as the use of increasingly coercive methods to suppress dissent in Egypt, Turkey, Bahrain, Thailand, Vietnam, Pakistan, Venezuela, the Philippines, and Saudi Arabia, to name just a few cases. These methods are endemic in Central Asia and parts of the Middle East, as well as throughout many parts of Africa. Freedom House describes this as "the twilight of modern authoritarianism," arguing that the semblance of concessions (e.g., pluralistic media, political competition, rule of law) that anti-democratic regimes made for several years around the turn of the century – while the impact of unipolarity could still be felt – has now dropped away and full authoritarianism is returning.[45] Freedom House's 2015 report – which marked this shift – was titled "Return to the Iron Fist."[46] With

---

[42] Xiaoyu Pu, "Can China be a Normative Power?" *OpenGlobalRights* ((June 2013) at: www .opendemocracy.net/openglobalrights/xiaoyu-pu/can-china-be-normative-power.

[43] Tianzhao Yang and Jiangnan Zhu, "Collective Apathy: Nationalism and Human Rights in China," *OpenGlobalRights* (March 2014) at: www.opendemocracy.net/openglobal rights/tianzhao-yang-jiangnan-zhu/collective-apathy-nationalism-and-human-rights-in-china. Yang and Zhu suggest China might be more supportive of a language like "the efficient administration of justice" rather than human rights.

[44] Diamond, "Facing up to the Democratic Recession," p. 152.

[45] Tyler Roylance, "The Twilight of Modern Authoritarianism," *Freedom House* (October 2014), at: https://freedomhouse.org/blog/twilight-modern-authoritarianism# .VG7vnIfZfdk

[46] Freedom House, *Discarding Democracy: Return to the Iron Fist* (2015), at: www .freedomhouse.org/sites/default/files/01152015_FIW_2015_final.pdf.

President Trump's labeling of the American press as an "enemy of the people," authoritarianism has reached a new level of intensity.

More subtle methods can also be used, to control rather than suppress human rights activism. For example, manipulating funds is a strategy for resistors. Former United Nations human rights commissioner, Navi Pillay, warned in 2013 that human rights budgets were not keeping up with needs – the flow of money to finance wider human rights surveillance an obvious weak point in a world where the West no longer wants to pay.[47] India and Russia, to take two cases, also use laws on foreign donors to restrict flows of money to indigenous human rights NGOs. They can easily adopt similar policies internationally to control donations to organizations that propagate causes with which they disagree, and they will not be alone in doing so. In other cases, such as Egypt, denying visas to major human rights figures is another strategy.[48]

Western hypocrisy does not help. Hungary's "illiberal democracy" is an example from the Western bloc where state authoritarianism is growing, while many see Australia's immigration policy as a violation of human rights.[49] The Obama administration may have repudiated the Bush administration's interpretation of the applicability of the Convention Against Torture, but in the case of extraterritoriality and cruel, inhumane, or degrading treatment, the president was reluctant, despite the advice of State Department lawyers, to repeal Bush's interpretation in all cases.[50] President Obama was adept at lawfare himself when it came to issues such as targeted killing and Guantanamo.[51] And President Trump has openly advocated a return to torture, despite the opposition of his Defense Secretary (whose view, the new president says, he will

---

[47] OHCHR Report 2012, at: www2.ohchr.org/english/ohchrreport2012/web_en/pages/int roduction.html

[48] Reuters, "Human Rights Watch Staff Denied Entry to Egypt," *The Guardian* (August 2014), at: www.theguardian.com/world/2014/aug/11/human-rights-watch-staff-egypt.

[49] Kati Marton, "Hungary's Authoritarian Descent," *New York Times* (Nov. 2014), at: www.nytimes.com/2014/11/04/opinion/hungarys-authoritarian-descent.html?_r=2, and Helen Davidson and Ben Doherty, "Australia's 'Abusive Refugee Policies' Criticized in Damning International Report," *The Guardian* (January 2016), at: www .theguardian.com/law/2016/jan/27/australias-abusive-refugee-policies-criticised-in-da mning-international-report.

[50] Jack Goldsmith, "The debate about the extraterritorial scope of the torture Convention's provisions on cruelty is (almost certainly) not about USG interrogation policy," *Lawfare*, October 24, 2014, at: www.lawfareblog.com/2014/10/the-debate-about-the-extraterritorial-scope-of-the-torture-conventions-provisions-on-cruelty-is-almost-cer tainly-not-about-usg-interrogation-policy/.

[51] Jo Becker and Scott Shane, "Secret 'Kill List' Proves a Test of Obama's Principles and Will," *International New York Times*, May 29, 2012: www.nytimes.com/2012/05/29/world/ obamas-leadership-in-war-on-al-qaeda.html?emc=eta1.

respect).[52] In the UK case, the president of Kenya, Uhuru Kenyatta, previously indicted by the ICC for crimes against humanity, cited the British government's ambivalence about human rights as evidence that the whole human rights regime itself lacks legitimacy.[53] The ISIS fighters holding hostages in Syria dressed their captives in Guantanamo-style orange jumpsuits and water-boarded American hostage James Foley before beheading him.[54]

The use by the United States and the United Kingdom of massively intrusive surveillance is a further sign that authoritarian government is not confined to the non-West. Control of cyber-space is an issue where China and Russia have led the way, followed by a whole range of other states who fear this tool of open communication and dissent. But the response of the American and British governments – to preach open internet communications while collecting masses of data on their own and foreign citizens without oversight – seems to many an egregious example of hypocrisy.

3   Social Ambivalence

The picture I have drawn so far might suggest that pro-human rights populations are trapped inside illiberal sovereign containers, particularly outside the West. But the story at the social level is more complex than that. Human rights have always been a problem for both the left and the right.[55] Marx argued in *On the Jewish Question* in 1844 that political freedom was a poor substitute for economic freedom. Critics of major international interventions – especially Kosovo, but also Libya – have seen human rights as the vanguard of a new kind of NATO-led Western imperialism.[56] Resistance from the right comes from advocates of

---

[52] Kristina Wong, "Mattis still opposes torture despite Trump comment," *The Hill* (January 2017), at: http://thehill.com/policy/defense/316356-mattis-remains-opposed-to-torture-pentagon-says.

[53] Adam Wagner, "Kenyan President uses Tory Human Rights Plans to Defend was Crimes Charges," *UK Human Rights Blog* (October 2014), at: http://ukhumanrights blog.com/2014/10/24/kenyan-president-uses-tory-human-rights-plans-to-defend-war -crimes-charges/.

[54] Rukmini Callimachi, "The Horror before the Beheadings," *New York Times* (October 2014), at: www.nytimes.com/2014/10/26/world/middleeast/horror-before-the-beheadings-what-isis-hostages-endured-in-syria.html.

[55] See, for example, Costas Douzinas. *The End of Human Rights: Critical Legal Thought at the Turn of the Century* (Oxford: Hart Publishing, 2000), and Stephen Holmes, *The Anatomy of Antiliberalism* (Cambridge, MA: Harvard University Press, 1996).

[56] Danilo Zolo, *Invoking Humanity: War, Law, and Global Order* (London: Continuum, 2002), Jean Bricmont, *Humanitarian Imperialism: Using Human Rights to Sell War* (New York: Monthly Review Press, 2007); Robin Blackburn (ed.), *The Imperialism of Human Rights, New Left Review*, special issue 234 (1999); Ray Kiely, "Intervention: Imperialism or human rights?" *OpenDemocracy*, October 20, 2014, at: www

sovereignty and nationalism (the many right-of-center European and American politicians skeptical about immigration, for example) and also from those who see rights as a threat to traditional social values and as heralds of a more bureaucratized, rule-bound, and disenchanted world (e.g., Leo Strauss, Carl Schmitt). Rights here are seen as constraining national community, power, and mission, as undermining the traditional, embedded, and specific norms and customs that give a nation a unique identity over time. Nations become soft, engineered, bland, and weak, the rule of law overwhelms the rule of men, and manifest destiny evaporates in a cloud of bureaucracy, constraint, and mediocrity.[57] One obvious contemporary example comes from the United Kingdom, where a particular kind of anti-immigration nationalist sentiment has taken hold (fueling Brexit), pushing right-wing politicians to advocate rejection of the European Court of Human Rights (for putting rights before public order and national security) and even to demand repeal of the United Kingdom's own Human Rights Act.[58]

There are other objections to human rights – the Catholic Church and the Muslim Brotherhood together contesting women's rights at the Commission on the Status of Women, for example.[59] In terms of LGBT rights, recent setbacks in India, Jamaica, and particularly Uganda (and increasingly throughout Sub-Saharan Africa), let alone in Russia, show how little impact decades of human rights work has made to non-discrimination on the basis of sexuality.[60] Pope Francis has been savvy about counter-posing poverty and abortion and asking which should be the priority (while making more liberal gestures toward the role of women and LGBT people in religious life).[61] The language of rights can also prove

.opendemocracy.net/ray-kiely/intervention-imperialism-or-human-rights. Slavoj Zizek, "Against Human Rights," *New Left Review* 34 (2005), pp. 115–31.

[57] Holmes, *The Anatomy of Antiliberalism*.

[58] Jon Henley, "Why is the European Court of Human Rights Hated by the UK Right?" *The Guardian* (Dec 2013), at: www.theguardian.com/law/2013/dec/22/britain-european -court-human-rights. The strategy document in which any future Conservative government promises to scrap the UK's Human Rights Act is available here: www.theguardian .com/politics/interactive/2014/oct/03/conservatives-human-rights-act-full-document.

[59] Jill Filipovic, "UN Commission on the Status of Women Unmasks the Enemies of Equality," *The Guardian*, March 18, 2013:, at www.theguardian.com/commentisfree/ 2013/mar/18/un-commission-status-women-enemies-equality.

[60] Although for a more nuanced reading which problematizes the "Orientalist" divide this suggests between the civilized and uncivilized worlds, see Rahul Rao, "The Locations of Homophobia," *London Review of International Law*, vol. 2, no. 2 (2014): 169–99. In addition, the success of demands for same-sex marriage in the United States, despite conservative and religious resistance, suggests that LGBT rights might make progress where they are not seen as antithetical to core social values about the sanctity of marriage.

[61] Antonia Blumberg, "In his Speech to Congress, the Pope said 10 Times More about Poverty than Abortion," *HuffPost Religion* (September 2015), at: www.huffingtonpost .com/entry/pope-congress-poverty_us_56043b2be4b0fde8b0d1a71d.

ineffective or even counterproductive, necessitating a different approach to achieving the desired end. In the case of anti-FGM campaigns in Africa, for instance, we see how a more pragmatic approach is bringing some hope for improvement, rather than the dogmatic attachment to condemnation in the language of human rights that has been more prevalent since the 1990s.[62]

Even when there is progress in situations where religious objections to human rights remain strong, this may not take place in the way global human rights advocates expect. Kevin Ward has shown, for example, that while the law on LGBT rights is more progressive in South Africa, the treatment of gay people is significantly worse there than in Uganda, where the law is more regressive.[63]

According to one recent report on Indonesia, meanwhile, even though abortion remains technically illegal, it is tolerated both socially and religiously (Islamic authorities being more progressive here than the Catholic Church in the nearby Philippines).[64] But Indonesian politicians are loath to deal with the question formally, by changing the law, for fear that they will politicize the issue and thereby lose support (hardening positions and eroding the unspoken compromise that exists). Yet many of those who support this de facto pro-abortion status quo nevertheless do not want to advance what they call "Western values," a term connoting a loosening of public morals and validation for sexually uninhibited lifestyles. These are seen as a threat to norms of social propriety in Indonesia even though sexual and cultural freedom is a core element of human rights.[65]

Systematic data on social support for human rights is scarce, but global opinion polls certainly suggest there is widespread rhetorical enthusiasm for the idea of human rights.[66] As the global middle class grows in an era

---

[62] UNICEF, "Female Genital Mutilation/Cutting: A Statistical Overview and Exploration of the Dynamics of Change," July 2013, at: www.unicef.org/media/files/FGCM_Lo_res .pdf; Gerry Mackie and John LeJeune, "Social Dynamics of Abandonment of Harmful Practices: A New Look at the Theory," *UNICEF Innocenti Working Paper*, 2008, available at: http://pages.ucsd.edu/~gmackie/documents/UNICEF.pdf.

[63] Kevin Ward, "Religious Institutions and Actors and Religious Attitudes to Homosexual Rights: South Africa and Uganda," in Corinne Lennox and Matthew Waites (eds.) *Human Rights, Sexual Orientation and Gender Identity in the Commonwealth: Struggles for Decriminalisation and Change* (London: School of Advanced Study, 2013), pp. 409–27.

[64] Tom Hundley, "Southeast Asia: 'A Certain Medical Procedure,'" *Pulitzer Center on Crisis Reporting*, February 12, 2014, available at: http://pulitzercenter.org/reporting/asia-philippines-indonesia-abortion-underground-shame.

[65] Hundley, "Southeast Asia: 'A certain medical procedure.'"

[66] World Public Opinion.Org, "Poll Finds Strong International Consensus on Human Rights," (Dec. 2011), at: http://worldpublicopinion.net/polls-find-strong-international-consensus-on-human-rights/. For more nuanced data, see James Ron, David Crow and Shannon Golden, "The Struggle for a Truly Grassroots Human Rights Movement," *OpenGlobalRights* (June 2013), at: www.opendemocracy.net/openglobalrights/james-ron-david-crow-shannon-golden/struggle-for-truly-grassroots-human-rights-move.

of globalization, this support for liberal democracy would seem to mirror one of modernization theory's main assumptions – that liberalism (and therefore human rights) follows capitalism. In a classic of historical sociology, *The Social Origins of Dictatorship and Democracy*, Barrington Moore encapsulates this thesis in the phrase "No bourgeois, no democracy."[67] It is the bourgeoisie – the town and city dwelling, commercially active middle classes – who advance democracy as a way to protect their property and person from state power and to promote their interests. This democratic struggle seeks three things: to check arbitrary rulers, to replace arbitrary rules with just and rational ones, and to "obtain a share for the underlying population in the making of rules."[68] These demands are at the heart of the human rights project.

But how interested are the middle classes (the new bourgeoisie) beyond acquiring basic civil and political rights? These narrow first-generation rights reinforce middle-class advantage, serving as both a constraint on elite power *and* on demands for redistribution from below (e.g., property rights). Western human rights supporters (not the more highly motivated activists and advocates) may be happy working on the rights of others overseas (on issues such as child rights and sex trafficking) and less keen on turning the human rights lens on what is happening within their own societies. This position is already to some degree mirrored by the rising middle classes of Asia and Africa. It is not good news for economic, social, and cultural rights. As Moore points out, those who provide support for the revolution, those who lead it, and those who benefit from it may be three separate sets of people.[69] As he says, the price of a system that embeds bourgeois values may be "the perpetuation of a large amount of 'tolerable' abuse – which is mainly tolerable for those who profit by the system."[70]

To take an obvious example, as Martin Gilens has shown, the top 20 percent of affluent Americans tend to be more liberal than the general population on religious and moral issues (including gay rights and abortion), but more conservative than the wider populace on tax, regulation, and welfare.[71] Very wealthy Americans oppose redistribution of wealth or income by large margins.[72] The one segment of this wealthy demographic that is slightly more in favor of regulation, environmental protection,

---

[67] Barrington Moore Jnr, *The Social Origins of Dictatorship and Democracy* (London: Penguin, 1966), p. 418.

[68] Ibid., p. 414.   [69] Ibid., p. 427.   [70] Ibid., p. 426.

[71] Martin Gilens, *Affluence and Influence: Economic Inequality and Political Power in America* (Princeton, NJ: Princeton University Press, 2012); also Benjamin I Page, Larry Bartels, and Jason Seawright, "Democracy and the Policy Preferences of Wealthy Americans," *Perspectives on Politics*, v. 11, no. 1 (2013): 51–73.

[72] Page, Bartels and Seawright, "Democracy": 63.

climate change action, and economic aid abroad are professionals – specifically, doctors and lawyers (for whom income rather than wealth remains important).[73] Further work by Gilens and Benjamin Page has added to these findings by showing that the economic elite has a significantly higher influence on public policy than the average citizen.[74] And a recent analysis by Thomas Edsall of American voters in 2015 shows that even well-paid, well-educated, upper-middle-class Democrats are conservative when it comes to redistribution. As he puts it: "These voters are repelled by a social conservatism that is anti-abortion, anti-gay rights and anti-women's rights. But they are not eager to see their taxes raised."[75]

This is only a rough proxy, of course, for middle-class human rights support. It suggests, however, that whether or not this elite supports civil and political rights abroad, it does not support economic and social rights domestically – quite the opposite. The affluent represent the apex of the middle class, of course: it is far wider and more diverse in its view than this picture suggests. In the UK case, for example, opinions on the suggestion by the Conservative party that Britain might withdraw from the European Court of Human Rights split almost entirely along party lines in polls (the right favors withdrawal, the liberals and the liberal-left do not).[76]

And this is not purely a Western phenomenon. Joshua Kurlantzick has argued, building on studies by Freedom House and others, that democracy seems to be in retreat elsewhere because the middle classes in many developing countries have taken fright at the implications of democratization for their own security, wealth, and influence.[77] Other analysts have seen middle-class support for authoritarian military government in Egypt in the same light.[78] We might even see cash giveaways to public workers in Saudi Arabia as a way to stem support for any form of political

---

[73] Page, Bartels and Seawright, "Democracy": 65.

[74] Martin Gilens and Benjamin I Page, "Testing Theories of American Politics: Elites, Interest Groups, and Average Citizens," *Perspectives on Politics*, v. 12, no. 3 (2014): 564–81. See also Joseph E Stiglitz, *The Price of Inequality* (New York: WW Norton and Co, 2012).

[75] Thomas B. Edsall, "The Problem with Middle-class Populism," *New York Times* (February 2015), at: www.nytimes.com/2015/02/04/opinion/the-problem-with-middle-class-populism.html?emc=eta1&_r=0.

[76] William Jordan, "Support for Tory Human Rights Plans falls along Party Lines," *YouGov.UK* (October 2014), at: http://yougov.co.uk/news/2014/10/08/support-tory-human-rights-plans-falls-along-party-/.

[77] Joshua Kurlantzick, *Democracy in Retreat: The Revolt of the Middle Class and the Worldwide Decline of Representative Government* (New Haven: Yale University Press, 2013).

[78] Maged Mandour, "Liberalism without Democracy: The Case of Egypt," *OpenDemocracy* (February 2015), at: www.opendemocracy.net/arab-awakening/maged-mandour/liberalism-without-democracy-case-of-egypt.

liberalization at a time of regime transition.[79] More generally, Landman and Larizza have shown that income inequality correlates strongly with increased human rights abuses, particularly in terms of personal integrity rights.[80]

Tunisia might be one bright spot that provides a counter-example, having evolved more of a middle class under President Ben Ali's dictatorship and thereby laying some of the ground work for democracy.[81] Long-term middle-class pressure was important in chipping away at the foundations of the regime before the self-immolation of Mohamed Bouazizi sparked the Arab Spring.[82] Iran might be another positive case on issues such as the death penalty.[83] But in major cases like China we see a compact between the wealth-creators and the state where enrichment is the price for accepting a lack of political freedom.[84] And in India, middle-class support for Prime Minister Narendra Modi is allied to a degree of skepticism about the political process (linked to anger at corruption) and a renewed emphasis on a Hindu ethno-religious nationalism (contra human rights) which has emerged precisely as an antidote to the materialism that new wealth has brought.[85] Best-selling analyst of inequality, Thomas Piketty, has even taken the buoyant Indian middle classes to task for their lack of concern about inequality.[86]

This issue lies at the root of problems within the human rights movement more widely. There is a political economy in this movement

---

[79] Ben Hubbard, "Saudi King unleashes a torrent of money as bonuses flow to the masses," *New York Times* (February 2015), at: www.nytimes.com/2015/02/20/world/middleeast/saudi-king-unleashes-a-torrent-as-bonuses-flow-to-the-masses.html?emc=eta1.

[80] Todd Landman and Marco Larizza, "Inequality and Human Rights: Who Controls What, When and How," *International Studies Quarterly* 53 (2009).

[81] On Tunisia, see, for example, Brian Klaas and Marcel Dirsus, "The Tunisia Model: Did Tunis win the Arab Spring?" *Foreign Affairs* (October 2014), at: www.foreignaffairs.com/articles/142290/brian-klaas-and-marcel-dirsus/the-tunisia-model.

[82] Eric Goldstein, "A Middle-Class Revolution," *Foreign Policy* (January 2011), at: www.foreignpolicy.com/articles/2011/01/18/a_middle_class_revolution.

[83] Thomas Erdbrink, "Mercy and Social Media Slow the Noose in Iran," *New York Times* (March 2014), at: www.nytimes.com/2014/03/09/world/middleeast/mercy-and-social-media-slow-the-noose-in-iran.html?emc=edit_th_20140309&nl=todaysheadlines&nlid=18548227&_r=0.

[84] On China, see Kellee Tsai, *Capitalism Without Democracy: The Private Sector in Contemporary China* (Ithaca: Cornell University Press, 2007) and Yang and Zhu, "Collective Apathy."

[85] Christophe Jaffrelot, "Modi of the Middle Class," *Carnegie Endowment for International Peace* (March 2014), at: http://carnegieendowment.org/2014/03/24/modi-of-middle-class and Leela Fernandes, *India's New Middle Class: Democratic Politics in an Era of Economic Reform* (Minnesota: University of Minnesota Press, 2006).

[86] Manu Joseph, "Piketty to India's Elite: 'Learn from History,'" *New York Times*, December 2015, at: www.nytimes.com/2015/12/10/world/asia/thomas-piketty-inequality-india-mumbai.html?_r=0.

all the way down that makes it hard for the priorities of the base – the mass of people at the bottom – to really affect the priorities of global campaigns. Global human rights is in many ways conservative where grass-roots human rights work is revolutionary and much more conventionally *political*. If the people are at the bottom, the money is still at the top.

Nevertheless, having said all of this, at least two further observations might be made about the "status quo-oriented middle class" argument and the sad outlook it predicts for narrowing inequality by genuinely embracing socioeconomic rights. First, any modern democratic society cannot sustain itself indefinitely if the majority of the people are alienated from the fruits of their labor and from access to wealth. As many Western states are currently discovering, status-quo politicians are an endangered species, with increasingly angry populations on the left and the right demanding change. This suggests that the middle classes will quite possibly be forced into greater efforts at redistribution than they might otherwise choose.[87] Second, middle-class gains against the state may be hard to achieve and harder to sustain without strategic engagement and even alliance with key social interest groups and movements who bring leverage through numbers.

Indeed, these two points intersect. If the middle classes need the state to protect their wealth, having alienated other potential social allies, they will be weak bargainers when it comes to demanding the state be more accountable to them and even grant concessions. If the middle classes seek to ally with broader social forces, against the state, then they'll need to cement this alliance by embracing a more widely shared agenda that better reflects the interests of the "have-nots," including those who for reasons of identity not wealth may be marginal, as well as the "haves."

4   On the Road to Nowhere

There is no longer any hegemonic definition of what constitutes the content or foundational authority of human rights, I suggest, the conversation now being about diversity, variability, "multiple modernities,"

---

[87] This homogenizes the middle class far too much, obviously, especially where, as in the United States, the majority of people see themselves as middle class. I am using "middle class" as a proxy for those – urban, professional, well-salaried with a reasonably significant degree of equity wealth (e.g., in property and stocks) and a college or higher education – who comprise the core of the top, say, 10% of a society in terms of wealth profile.

where there are various forms of being modern, not all of which are in full alignment with the benchmark standards of universal and inalienable human rights as classically conceived and politically institutionalized.[88] In other words, there are no red lines that enjoy universal political support (even if they seem to enjoy a legal consensus). There is a further issue in that many of the most pressing human rights issues of our era will involve acts of private violence (e.g., domestic abuse, sex crimes) and these are not covered by international law, which remains principally about atrocity crimes of one sort or another committed by states and their officials. And as I have argued, human rights are not necessarily progressive – their first-generation, civil, and political variant dominates for structural (not transient) reasons over social and economic, cultural and group rights. This is a very conditional, class-specific form of liberal freedom, as Barrington Moore noted. Better, no doubt, than the alternatives glimpsed under authoritarianism, but a long way from the aspirations of many human rights advocates.

In their book *The Human Rights Paradox*, Steve Stern and Scott Straus see this conjunction between the universal and local as an irresolvable tension in all human rights work, each unable to escape the other. They must learn to co-exist. Rather than "eternal transcendent rights that emerge after a formative point of historical origin," Stern and Straus conceptualize rights as relational (between people, between local and global), and contextual, giving rise to "a shifting history and future of urgent fundamental rights attached to the human."[89] Mark Goodale echoes this, asking why "liberal (or neoliberal) legal and political theory should continue to prove so foundational when this political choice is no longer necessary."[90]

But this elides perhaps the key problem for a more pragmatic, diverse, agile, flexible, democratic global human rights movement. Many human rights advocates, in the West and elsewhere, believe in a radical moral critique of established authorities from the perspective of individual entitlements. They have a normative commitment, not

---

[88] S. N. Eisenstadt, ed., *Multiple Modernities* (New Brunswick: Transaction Publishers, 2005) but also Peter J. Katzenstein, ed., *Civilizations in World Politics: Plural and Pluralist Perspectives* (London: Routledge, 2010).

[89] Steve Stern and Scott J Straus, "Embracing Paradox: Human Rights in the Global Age," in *The Human Rights Paradox: Universality and Its Discontents*, Stern and Straus (eds.) (Madison: University of Wisconsin Press, 2014), pp. 10–11.

[90] Mark Goodale, *Surrendering to Utopia: An Anthropology of Human Rights* (Stanford: Stanford University Press, 2009), p. 10. See also Sonia Harris-Short, "International Human Rights Law: Imperialist, Inept and Ineffective? Cultural Relativism and the UN Convention on the Rights of the Child, *Human Rights Quarterly*, vol. 25 no. 1 (2003), p. 181.

a career.[91] Moreover, they hold to a version of the "Orientalist" map that separates the world into areas of concern about rights (e.g., for LGBT rights, Africa, and the Middle East), and areas where those rights are better observed (principally in the West and a few other states and societies). Where some are skeptical about the lessons to be drawn from the Pew Center's findings on anti-homosexual prejudice, most human rights advocates would see this map as an accurate reflection of where the needs are greatest in terms of LGBT activism (as one example).[92]

In other words, there is a core claim about individual autonomy and choice that in principle limits the scope of any pragmatic reorientation. Means might be adaptable, but not ends. To make the journey open-ended is to put human rights on the road to nowhere (that is, to "nowhere in particular"). But most human rights activists know the destination at which they are aiming; they just puzzle and struggle over how to get there. The power of these rights is in their clear and unequivocal codification. They are timeless principles. "Freedom" and "justice," as I argued at the outset, can accommodate diverse forms of realization. But human rights really do have some uncrossable barriers (red lines, individual trump cards, vetoes) beyond which they can no longer be called rights in a meaningful way. For advocates, human rights are on the road to *somewhere* – e.g., universal gender equality. If this isn't where Stern and Straus's negotiated tension ends up then we cannot be, for global advocates, talking about human rights any more. *But this inflexibility about ends makes human rights politically inept, even counterproductive, as humanitarians have discovered.*[93]

If global norms do get retrenched, this will reverberate through the human rights ecosystem. When China says human rights are not a global norm, or are colonial impositions, or Russia says your interpretation of human rights is not the same as ours but ours is just as valid, there is no option but to listen. Add to this the constituency of social conservatives in all societies, the West and non-West, mobilized and organized to block change even if they cannot prevail, and the angry leftists who see their lives blighted by globalization, and you have a recipe for a stalled human rights revolution at best, and for rollback

[91] Although much more could be said about this: see Stephen Hopgood, *The Endtimes of Human Rights* (Ithaca: Cornell University Press, 2013), chap. 5.

[92] Rao, "The Locations of Homophobia," pp. 169–171 and the Pew Research Center Global Attitudes Project, "The Global Divide on Homosexuality," (June 2013), at: www.pewglobal.org/2013/06/04/the-global-divide-on-homosexuality/

[93] Marie-Pierre Allié, "Introduction: Acting at Any Price?" in Claire Magone, Michaël Neuman, and Fabrice Weissman, eds., *Humanitarian Negotiations Revealed: The MSF Experience* (London: Hurst/MSF, 2011), pp. 1–11.

at worst. Populist leaders have put aspects of both the left and right critiques together to challenge liberal norms at the national level throughout the West.

One response to these anxieties has been to forge ahead, increasing the number of permanent institutions that support human rights (on the principle that even if the language is in question, the institutions, once established, are harder to disassemble and will have positive long-term effects). This is one way to see the proposed Convention on Crimes Against Humanity – as a capstone to complete the global architecture of human rights law. And it may well pass, with reservations (if the United States is to join) or without (if great powers are not to be allowed to dictate the terms of the treaty). But what difference will it make to the everyday lives of billions of people living under authoritarian rule or suffering from endemic forms of private violence, police torture, brutality, or systematic discrimination?

This rapidly transforming world can be characterized as *neo-Westphalian*.[94] Global trade and finance, essential elements of the affluence of growing powers such as China, as well as collective security concerns about transport, energy, and weapons, create shared interests in the preservation of international order. In this sense, India, China, Brazil, and perhaps even Russia have a stake in the continuation of the system (as Ikenberry argues). But there is no evidence they want to expand the hierarchical system of rules and norms centered around human rights and international justice. Great powers will break their own rules when it really matters to them. And international law will always have an element of "indeterminacy" such that competent arguments both for and against certain courses of action can be made.[95] From this it is but a short step to competing and even new norms. There may be what has been called a "structural bias" in favor of the liberal settlement, but it is precisely the survival of the preconditions for that bias that I am questioning. Or rather, it will function within *zones of relative peace, security and justice*, and not for their borderlands, which will remain *zones of conflict, poverty and injustice*. These divisions

---

[94] My understanding of NeoWestphalia is less homogeneity, less integration, more competition, and no universal norms. Jan Zielonka uses the term "neo-Westphalian" in exactly the opposite sense in the context of EU enlargement; see Jan Zielonka, "Enlargement and the Finality of European Integration," Harvard Jean Monnet Working Paper, symposium in response to Joschka Fischer, 2000, and *Europe as Empire: The Nature of the Enlarged European Union* (Oxford: Oxford University Press, 2007).

[95] Martti Koskenniemi, *From Apology to Utopia*, reissue with new epilogue (Cambridge: Cambridge University Press, 2005); David Kennedy, *A World of Struggle: How Power, Law, and Expertise Shape Global Political Economy* (Princeton: Princeton University Press, 2016).

exist within societies as well as between them. What we might have to give up, for a generation at least, is the idea that the two zones will be fused into one single glorious, universal, and liberal whole. Embracing the road to nowhere may seem like a step forward in that the newly multipolar world must be more about diversity and conversation and less about uniformity and diktat. But this may also prove to be an illusion, leaving just the lucky few still traveling the road to somewhere (most probably a gated community in an affluent suburb).

13 Conclusion: Human Rights Futures

Stephen Hopgood, Jack Snyder, and Leslie Vinjamuri

Human rights have eclipsed other forms of advocacy for progressive global change. However we date their deep origins, human rights now play a significant part in the conduct of international relations. When human rights are not on the agenda in high-level diplomatic encounters, it rarely goes unnoticed. They are a fixture of our world. Scholars who have tried to capture and explain this reality and its implications have viewed transnational civil society as the cornerstone of the mainstream model of human rights promotion. This civil society works collectively through networks to name, shame, and socialize states by drawing on rules, norms, and especially laws. Much of this early work, led by Margaret Keck, Martha Finnemore, Thomas Risse, Stephen Ropp, and Kathryn Sikkink, focused on the mechanisms by which human rights might achieve impact, giving us the influential "boomerang," "spiral," and "cascade" models of transnational advocacy.[1] The sheer scale of human rights work by international NGOs, human rights lawyers, international organizations, and the sympathetic parts of Western governments seemed evidence enough of successful impact, especially once the ICC was established. This mainstream, liberal account is at once descriptive and aspirational.

Yet, even as the apparent successes of human rights mounted up, critical voices began to be raised inside and outside the academy. Indeed, several of the authors of mainstream human rights theorizing revisited their initial model and challenged the generalizability of some of its major findings, especially in less than hospitable domestic contexts. Scholarship began to consider the real impact of law on human rights

---

[1] Thomas Risse, Stephen C. Ropp, and Kathryn Sikkink, eds., *The Power of Human Rights* (Cambridge: Cambridge University Press, 1999); Risse, Ropp, and Sikkink, eds., *The Persistent Power of Human Rights* (Cambridge: Cambridge University Press, 2013); Margaret Keck and Kathryn Sikkink, *Activists Beyond Borders: Advocacy Networks in International Politics* (Ithaca: Cornell University Press, 1998); Martha Finnemore and Kathryn Sikkink, "International Norm Dynamics and Political Change," *International Organization* 52, no. 4 (1998): 887–918. Also, Beth Simmons, *Mobilizing for Human Rights* (New York: Cambridge University Press, 2009).

outcomes. This spawned a more careful look at a series of methodological questions, from how to measure impact, to the promises and limits of quantitative as compared to qualitative analysis.[2] These issues became increasingly pressing as the tide turned against human rights advances in the years after 9/11, when civil liberties were curtailed, human rights funding was reduced, and resources for counterterrorist programs grew considerably. Rising authoritarianism, spurred on and given diplomatic cover by Russia and China, also dampened the prospects for human rights. The success of populist politicians in the West threatens to accelerate this trend. In many areas, from women's rights to LGBT rights to international criminal justice, the future looks less promising than it has for more than a decade. Our purpose in this volume has been to get a handle on these questions and to weigh their implications for the future.

We organized our discussion of human rights critiques under four headings: scope conditions, backlash, localization, and utopias and endtimes.

Mainstream human rights scholarship has been strengthened by an effort to identify *scope conditions*: what are the necessary, if not sufficient, conditions for human rights activism to succeed? Rights do not float freely. Rights need allies and supportive social institutions to flourish. Scope conditions identify what makes some cases easier and others harder for successful rights promotion. Hard cases create problems for mainstream human rights theory and practice, suggesting that new forms of pragmatism may be necessary to achieve the desired results.

Our second set of critiques we labeled *backlash*. Spoilers threatened by rights, in some liberal as well as authoritarian states, confront, evade, or instrumentalize rights to blunt their impact. Mainstream theory assumes backlash is a natural phase in the overall arc of progress toward human rights compliance, but backlash theorists underscore more pernicious, longer-term effects that may lock in regressive practices. Backlash can, for example, take us beyond resistance, leading to the creation of alternative normative or institutional structures that shrink the space for civil society activism domestically and embed permanent anti-human rights infrastructure. Rights advocates may be forced to make tactical concessions to avoid playing into the hand of rights resisters in such situations.

Our third critique, *localization*, identifies the critical role of cultural translators as brokers who are able to turn international abstract legal and moral concepts into something more resonant at the local level and, similarly, to translate local norms into the international sphere.

---

[2] Emilie Hafner-Burton and James Ron, "Seeing Double: Human Rights Impact through Qualitative and Quantitative Eyes," *World Politics* 61, no. 2 (April 2009): 360–401.

Whether translation is a mechanism that enhances the human rights project or instead impairs it is of crucial importance. One issue, focused on consequences, is whether shifting from the universalistic rhetoric of rights to local concepts such as fairness or obligation will ease the adoption of new practices or whether it will lead down a slippery slope of justification of continued abuses. A second issue is the normative justification for localization. From a liberal perspective, it is important that individuals freely adopt their normative outlook. If human rights values seek personal liberation rather than repression of social diversity, space must be reserved for negotiation, compromise, and hybrid forms of rights observance. Although this may be essential both to generate local legitimacy and to preserve the philosophical integrity of a liberal approach to rights, it raises the question of when the call for tolerating diversity is a form of backlash or backsliding masquerading as a plea for cultural protection.

Finally, we outlined what we called *utopias and endtimes*. These critiques question the feasibility of rights demands, but also whether their liberatory promise is as great as advocates claim. They worry that human rights might crowd out other forms of normative innovation, deter effective social mobilization, and replace efforts for radical transformation with superficial reform.[3] Ironically, individualism and legalism might embed inequality and injustice. These critics propose grounding rights socially and historically as a counter to teleological advocacy claims, showing where rights came from, whose interests they serve, and how they will fare in a rapidly changing world in which the hegemony of Western and liberal concepts is under challenge in new ways.

If there is an overarching theme to these critiques, echoed through much of the volume, we might label it "too-thin liberalism." By that we mean that the account widely held by mainstream human rights scholars underestimates the pivotal importance of deeper political, social, and economic structures in explaining the reception and effectiveness of rights. Human rights may require liberal-democratic societies to underwrite them. We see this possibility as analogous to Karl Polanyi's "embeddedness" claim in relation to markets – that is, that human rights are not autonomous from wider social relations but embedded in them, and only successful to the extent that they are anchored in sustainable broader social forces.[4] To evaluate this claim, we need more substantive accounts of the institutional, ideological, or class-based structures of any

[3] For a rebuttal, see Simmons and Strezhnev, this volume.
[4] Karl Polanyi, *The Great Transformation: The Political and Economic Origins of Our Time*, 2nd edn. (Boston: Beacon Press, 2001).

society marked for human rights compliance before we can understand why rights work when they work, why they fail, and what they fail to achieve even when they seem to be effective.

This will not come as news to any practitioners – they struggle constantly with the reality of these critiques. The conversation on the ground is increasingly at odds with mainstream accounts that stress the progress made by decades of human rights advocacy. The reality, whether we are talking about the ICC, R2P, women's rights, LGBT rights (outside of liberal democracies), or even those very basic civil liberties that were supposed to be the first rights to be recognized and embedded, is one of hard struggles against stiff resistance. Whether through the direct suspension of rights of association and expression (under emergency legislation) or through the use of detention for journalists and human rights defenders, heavy restrictions on funding, or onerous tax and registration requirements, the space for local human rights activism is under attack.

For both scholars and advocates, in other words, the time seems ripe for a searching assessment of the promise and possibilities of rights. The chapters in *Human Rights Futures* comprise a conversation between scholars from political science, history, and anthropology who share an interest in understanding the practical impact of human rights advocacy broadly defined, but who differ substantially in their explanations and understanding of these impacts. These can be organized into *four viewpoints:* mainstream, barriers and bargaining, the vernacular, and rights and welfare. These viewpoints recapitulate but also elaborate our initial categories (scope conditions, backlash, localization, utopias and endtimes). We then speculate on *four models of the future.* Finally, we consider implications for *future research.*

Four Viewpoints on Rights

Human Rights Mainstreaming

The mainstream view among human rights advocates, and among many scholars who study the human rights movement, is that politics under contemporary global conditions allows considerable scope for the agency of principled, transnationally connected activists to use the tools of law, moral mobilization, and shaming, sometimes backed up by coercive power, to advance the rights agenda. They think business as usual is working to spread norms and, with some important qualifications, to improve compliance. While generally adhering to the idea that core norms should be advocated universally, scholars within this tradition are alert to the difficulties of promoting rights in adverse political or cultural settings, which may require targeted tactics or, at a minimum, patience to overcome.[5] Scholars who hold this viewpoint differ in some respects when it comes to assessing the importance of scope conditions and some details of causal mechanisms, but all are united by a positive and progressive vision of the successes of contemporary human rights mobilization.[6] In our volume, the arguments of Dancy and Sikkink (2), and of Simmons and Strezhnev (3), make these points forcefully.

Barriers, Backlash, and Bargaining

Emphasizing the barriers and limitations imposed by weak institutions, powerful spoilers, and cultural differences, several of the contributors to our volume argue that contemporary social and political conditions place severe constraints on the effectiveness of mainstream tools of human rights advocacy. Their critique highlights the need to base rights advocacy on realistic calculations of social power and on pragmatic bargaining strategies. In the many and varied settings where scope conditions are unfavorable, strategies for advancing human rights need to place politics front and center. In this view, politics is based mainly on the material and ideological power and self-interest of groups that make public authority claims, which they sometimes justify using the language of rights.

Politics conducted in this register require first assessing the power and interests of social actors who may potentially support a rights agenda, of those who are likely to oppose it, leading to backlash, and of those swing constituencies who are opportunists. As Snyder's chapter (4) argues, the task for human rights advocates is then to devise a strategy based on a tailored mix of coercive force, bargaining with both allies and enemies, persuasion, institution building, and eventually law to advance their interests, taking into account interaction with other groups. Where the social power of potential constituencies for rights is weak because of underlying economic or social conditions, a human rights strategy needs to begin with a plan for changing those scope conditions.

In the era of rights, it is tempting – given that rights compliance appears better in more liberal societies – to see backlash as a feature of illiberal states where calls to arms in the language of defending the nation,

---

[5] Risse, Ropp, and Sikkink, eds., *The Persistent Power of Human Rights*.
[6] See especially Beth A. Simmons, "From Ratification to Compliance: Quantitative Evidence on the Spiral Model," in Risse, Ropp and Sikkink, eds., *The Persistent Power of Human Rights*, 43–59.

preserving ethnic purity, or resisting imperialism have often been very effective. Many commentators have issued foreboding words about democratic backsliding and authoritarian retrenchment. Freedom House claims that we have moved from the soft authoritarian era back into the world of open state violence. But the wholesale rejection of rights is rare. State elites resort to justifications that look to counterterrorism, sovereignty and non-interference, and traditional values to bolster their efforts to deflect human rights. Even where backlash is at its strongest, such as in Russia and China, outright and naked repression has been relatively rare thus far.

As Alexander Cooley has argued, for example, we still see counter-norms rather than flagrant violation.[7] Counter-norming is designed to reassure a fractious domestic audience, sway neutrals, and deflect international critics. Sometimes, it may reflect a desire to safeguard sovereignty, and protect elites, without fully undermining human rights. In Africa, Kenya led an anti-ICC backlash that sought to wrest control away from the International Criminal Court and invest it in the African Union. Rather than rejecting the basic principle of criminal accountability for atrocity crimes, this Kenyan-led initiative sought to rewrite the rules for international justice and shift the locus of authority over justice to the regional level.[8] South Africa has followed suit. The implications of counter-norming and authority contests remain unclear, however. Even if regional organizations are set up in part as a form of simple window dressing to hide repression and push back against international norms, these measures may still result in an unraveling of internationally agreed rules and standards for promoting and safeguarding human rights as universal.[9] Alternatively they might, of course, get traction despite their founders' intentions.

The prospects for spoiler backlash may be further enhanced in contexts where sectarianism and partisanship are readily available as a resource for political mobilization. In the former Yugoslavia, backlash against the ad hoc international war crimes tribunal was cast along sectarian lines. But even in consolidated democracies, backlash against accountability has leveraged prior partisan divides. The release of the US Senate torture report, for example, immediately spawned a partisan backlash that saw the production of separate counter reports with opposing findings all of which helped to inhibit further prospects for accountability.

---

[7] Alexander Cooley, "Countering Democratic Norms," *Journal of Democracy* 26, no. 3 (2015): 50–3.
[8] See Vinjamuri, Chapter 5, this volume.
[9] Cooley, "Countering Democratic Norms," 56–58.

Translating Rights into the Vernacular

The backlash critique leads directly into the questions of *localization*. Some of our authors emphasize the local and cultural basis of political action in the domain of rights, partly because differing circumstances give rise to differing concerns and feasible tactics, and partly because of differing cultural modes of expressing concerns and concepts. Cultures vary in the idiom in which they express moral concepts. Often, religious discourse is more prominent than legal framing on questions of morality and justice. Politically, some ideological climates are ultrasensitive to any appearance of cultural imperialism on the part of wealthy Northern states and societies. In this view, the effectiveness of rights promotion depends heavily on finessing those aspects of universalist discourse that play into the hands of local rights opponents and on developing two-way partnerships with local actors whose goals are compatible with a rights agenda. Theories of localization may stress normative adaptation, which consists simply of adapting norms to fit local politics and institutions, or local language and cultural practices.

Others stress a negotiation in which local brokers with an international profile play a crucial role. Sally Engle Merry and Peggy Levitt identify the role of these brokers (or "translators") as key political entrepreneurs who can forge a transnational consensus for collective action around shared goals, rather than shared principles or even shared interests. Still others see localization as a form of subsidiarity, in which local actors create norms at the regional level.[10] Localization is not always rights-respecting – on the contrary, local norm entrepreneurs may adopt strategies of localization specifically to counter human rights norms, or to displace specific strands of a broader human rights agenda but not others. This borders on backlash. In our book, chapters by Merry and Levitt (9), Hertel (10), Hurd (8), Risse (6), Vinjamuri (5), and Cooley and Schaaf (7) address various aspects of this issue.

Rights Versus Welfare

Our final set of critiques by Hopgood and Moyn, *utopias and endtimes*, question both the feasibility of rights demands but also whether their promise is as great as advocates claim. These accounts claim that human rights are philosophically weak, conceptually incoherent, lack

---

[10] Amitav Acharya, "How Ideas Spread: Whose Norms Matter? Norm Localization and Institutional Change in Asian Regionalism," *International Organization* 58, no. 2 (Spring 2004): 239–78; Acharya, *Rethinking Power, Institutions and Ideas in World Politics: Whose IR?* (London: Routledge, 2014), 217–49.

resonance with their target communities, are out of step with the times, and, most importantly from the standpoint of a positive agenda, are a distraction of progressive energies from the task of promoting a broader basis for increasing social welfare. A key question for this line of argument is whether some form of social welfarism is an alternative to human rights, a precondition for meaningful human rights, or a project that subsumes the human rights agenda under its more ambitious manifesto.

In this volume, Moyn suggests that the increasing rise of human rights since the 1970s maps onto the decline of welfare states, the pursuit of individual entitlements replacing collective political demands made on behalf of national collectives and other groups.[11] Rights, Hopgood argues, are neoliberalism's bequest to the modern middle classes, whose social and economic interests were, until the aftermath of 2008 at least, seemingly secure. From the 1970s on, demands from the "new left" for social and moral progress rooted in the choices available to individuals, including those conditioned by gender, age, sexuality, and disability, rather than collective demands for social justice on the basis of economic status, became more prominent in the developed world (in Nancy Fraser's framing, recognition replaced redistribution).[12] The decline of social welfarism, Hopgood contends, reflects a modern variant of what Polanyi called "market society," where the ideal of freedom is considered realizable only where state intervention is absent. Some form of state regulation was, for Polanyi, the only hope for genuine freedom, because without it there could be none of the justice or security upon which freedom depends.[13] Joseph Stiglitz has made similar arguments, stressing in particular how economic inequality leads to political inequality, particularly in the United States, and how this has in turn undermined democracy.[14]

On this reading, human rights have focused us on such a narrow range of social outcomes that we are left with both an impoverished view of liberalism's aspirations and little sense of its historical contingency. Thus, the mainstream account could turn out to be a success story on its own terms and still constitute an unsatisfying outcome for more substantive conceptions of human progress. The marginal achievements of human rights might have come at the cost of greater mobilization to realize real

[11] But see also Samuel Moyn, "Powerless Companion: Human Rights in the Age of Neoliberalism," *Law & Contemporary Problems* 77 (2014): 147–69.

[12] Nancy Fraser "From Redistribution to Recognition: Dilemmas of Justice in a Post-Socialist Age," *New Left Review* I, no. 212 (July-August 1995): 68–93.

[13] Polanyi, *The Great Transformation*, 262–7.

[14] Joseph E Stiglitz, *The Price of Inequality* (New York: W. W. Norton, 2012).

freedom, equality, and justice, in other words, because the middle classes may be far more interested in civil and political rights than in social and economic rights, or they may favor social welfare entitlements mainly for themselves. If human rights efforts do sometimes displace other forms of potentially more consequential activism, especially on economic inequality, then what appears to be a success story could turn out to be a hidden story of defeat.

Taken as a whole, all of the critiques of the mainstream account outlined above call for a thicker concept of political realities, taking us beyond too-thin liberalism. For the mainly empirical critiques, a thicker account of liberalism is required to re-focus on the importance of democracy, and of the to and fro of democratic politics, in explaining rights outcomes. For the more normative accounts included here, a thicker conception of liberalism helps bring wider questions of social and economic justice into the equation, questions that remain more central to the politics of the non-West where neoliberalism is less well embedded. Both empirical and normative critiques share a degree of skepticism about the mainstream model. They argue that it detaches a narrow conception of human rights from its liberal political and ethical moorings, making it hard to understand both the limits of those rights or the preconditions necessary for them to be effectively realized.

What, then, might the future hold?

Models of Human Rights Futures

From these contending viewpoints, we can now derive four possible models of the future of human rights advocacy and outcomes. Given the impossibility of predicting the future, these are obviously speculative provocations. The other contributors to this volume might have devised different scenarios, if any, and none but the editors can be held responsible for them. The usefulness of these scenarios, we hope, is in encouraging human rights practitioners to consider how strategies need to depend on what happens in the broader political world. This is the start of, not the conclusion to, a conversation.

The four models we outline are: *Staying the Course, Pragmatic Partnership, Global Welfarism,* and *Sideshow.* These are not mutually exclusive. The models might follow in a sequence where one leads to another. Periods of heightened resistance to rights might be followed by periods of more rapid gain, as more favorable conditions for rights breakthroughs emerge. Persistent struggle by human rights advocates against newly reinvigorated authoritarianism might take time to prevail, but it may succeed nonetheless.

Staying the Course

At the core of classic modernization theory was a belief in the centrality of the individual in modernity and the superiority of the Western experience (where the West went, others would follow). The nation-state was central to delivering this vision, as were elites and the technocrats who could steer the state in the right direction, meaning a democratic free market welfare state.[15] While things changed after the 1970s, and the welfare state element of this picture came under challenge, the classical model still fits with the argument that part and parcel of modernity is what Edward Shils called "civility," meaning, "a strong sense of national identity, but without excessive commitment to national symbols; a widespread interest in public affairs; a general sense of the legitimacy of the existing political order; a sense of 'rights' and the sanctity of the private; and a 'sufficient degree' of overall value consensus."[16] For the first wave of modernization theorists, development would ineluctably lead us away from "tradition toward a universal convergence on 'modernity.'"[17]

What these authors missed, however, in idealizing modernity, was the danger involved in the process of getting there. As Samuel Huntington put it: "It is not the absence of modernity but the efforts to achieve it which produce political disorder."[18] The apparent mistake of classical modernization theorists was to assume that all transitioning societies would make it through the process in a timely manner. As it turned out, some would stall, some slide back, some become trapped in destructive social conflict. Yet for those who believe in the ultimately progressive potential of the liberal model for all societies, the key virtue is perseverance. Human rights advocacy, and major liberal states, need only continue on the present trajectory. They will face lots of constraints, as outlined in the scope conditions above, and they may be forced to adapt more to what's possible rather than desirable at least in the short term. Major projects such as R2P may be a step too far and will be retained only for the easiest cases (otherwise R2P will be honored mainly in the breach). The ICC, too, will shift in a more pragmatic direction, along the lines of the qualified amnesty policies adopted by Colombia in 2015, although the ICC will maintain standard legalistic practices for the politically easy cases.

---

[15] Nils Gilman, *Mandarins of the Future: Modernization Theory in Cold War America* (Baltimore: Johns Hopkins University Press, 2003).

[16] Gilman, *Mandarins*, 141.   [17] Gilman, *Mandarins*, 100.

[18] Samuel P. Huntington, *Political Order in Changing Societies* (New Haven: Yale University Press, 1968), 41.

At the level of local implementation, the human rights community will develop a lot of pragmatic tactics, many of which will merge with humanitarian and development work. In the South, indigenous human rights movements will vernacularize where there is a real social base (e.g., Latin America). Churches will pursue a rights agenda in some places, especially in Christian communities. And in countries without much of an indigenous base, there will continue to be opportunistic, less politically mainstream rights groups with a thin base in broader society. Some countries will become more democratic due to economic development, and their human rights will improve in most cases. And while universalistic rhetoric will come to be seen as somewhat formulaic, it will retain enough attraction among donor, activist, and oppressed constituencies that on balance it will seem worth retaining, if only to document abuses that will be reckoned with later.

Pragmatic Partnership

Rather than business as usual, an alternative scenario is that a new generation of rights activists gets tired of the empty rhetoric of universalism, which fails to resonate with their hands-on experiences in the field and their "can do" ethos. They may become more flexible about working in vernacular institutional and rhetorical modes, cut deals with third-world politicians, first-world development organizations and militaries, and learn how to use law tactically rather than dogmatically. At the level of doctrine and practice, the human rights community might adopt an amalgam of mainstream, social power, and localization approaches. Activists doing so will be patient, realistic, multicultural, and dedicated. They will contribute at the margins to good outcomes, but without idealizing a utopian and universalizing vision. At the working level of the human rights movement, especially the rights-based approach to humanitarianism, such attitudes and practices are already fairly widespread.

This scenario does not exclude staying the course. The essential issue here is a pressing need to incorporate the priorities of all within the human rights movement – perhaps even to move away from the language of priorities entirely, with its connotations of hierarchy, and to allow a multitude of different claims to be brought under the mantle of human rights. Giving up the more universalistic account of rights progress and accepting strategic political alliances will potentially create more opportunities for mass mobilization. It might mean more nudging (the savvy structuring of incentives), tied perhaps to foreign aid and trade, and less international law.[19]

[19] Emilie Hafner-Burton, *Making Human Rights a Reality* (Princeton: Princeton University Press, 2013); Martha C. Nussbaum, "Symposium on Amartya Sen's Philosophy: 5

But it will also dilute the universal and indivisible nature of the global human rights regime generally. The push on all fronts for civil and political rights, economic and social rights, women's rights, LGBT rights, and environmental rights pays little or no attention to how receptive the society concerned will be to all these different manifestations of human rights. Accepting the importance of both backlash and localization is to understand that human rights will evolve at different speeds, will not be achieved in all cases any time soon, and will be defined very differently than they might be in Western capitals. Listening to local demands, compromising on human rights maximalism, and sharing resources more widely through the network of human rights supporters are identified as ways to create a more truly global movement. But by going down this pragmatic path, some of the aspirations of the mainstream model may have to be abandoned as clearly stated universal aims.

Global Welfarism

Classic modernization theory was based on the globalization of the welfare state model of economic development. On this model, social consensus was derived from the gains that the public at large received from development, even if that development disproportionately advantaged the middle classes. Since the 1970s, that compact has fallen apart, with stagnant real incomes, slow growth, rising unemployment in many countries, and growing inequality its most visible manifestations. A return to some sort of welfarist model, in response to this perceived legitimacy deficit, would emphasize collective political action and decrease the salience of individualized, rights-based, legal claim-making. Demands for economic and social justice would no longer need to be framed in the language of rights, but would be political calls made on the party of government. In this approach, neoliberalism would be, if not reversed, at least tamed though more serious social democracy. Pressure from left-leaning populists may extract commitments to expand the welfare state, increase state efforts to spur job growth, and increase wages for citizens.

Central to the emergence of this model would be American leadership, which would break with the pattern known as "the Washington consensus." How might this come about? In one answer to that question. President Trump proposed job growth through industrial protectionism

Adaptive Preferences and Women's Options," *Economics and Philosophy* 17 (2001): 67–88; Richard H. Thaler and Cass R. Sunstein, *Nudge: Improving Decisions About Health, Wealth and Happiness* (New York: Penguin Books, 2009).

and infrastructure spending. Another option might stem from demographic changes in the United States favoring immigrant and minority constituencies who tend to support governmental social welfare programs and governmental defense of human rights.

Like most powerful states, the USA seeks to project its governance formula as far as its arms can reach, including trying to bring the weighty but now stagnating BRICs into its fold through reformed and reinvigorated multilateral institutions. This might include a beefed-up global welfare bureaucracy, catering especially to social stability aspirations of the global middle class, but also promising trickle-down and safety-net benefits to the poorer classes. Global welfare (the Fourth Freedom and the second half of the UDHR) might get merged with a New Deal-style version of global human rights. Governments that are deaf to purely principled claims advanced in terms of economic and social rights might find more convincing an approach based on the coalition politics of social welfare reform.

Such a global welfarist turn might be consistent with a classical rights agenda, but it might also come to overshadow or supplant it. In the latter scenario, the Chinese Human Rights White Paper could add a short section on experimental legal aid for the poor to its 700 pages of self-praise about continued improvements in health, education, and social services, while Texas might reduce state university tuition while continuing to execute 17-year-olds with mental health problems. In other words, this model might greatly increase material welfare, but at the cost of those very rights, civil and political, that the global human rights movement has been organized to prioritize. The future of this model, given developments in Western democracies in the last few years, is perhaps less certain than any of the others. But the emphasis on meeting the demands of a working class marginalized by globalization, found in the rhetoric of populist leaders like Trump, Le Pen, Wilders and others, suggests that where rights are perceived to have failed, more traditional welfare policies might succeed.

Sideshow

Which brings us, finally, to *Sideshow*. In this model, human rights suffer an absolute decline in importance for three main reasons. First, they create backlash problems or unintentionally consolidate political identities that challenge core rights norms, as in Elizabeth Hurd's analysis of the unintended consequences of promoting religious freedom. Some have even argued that rights are being "weaponized," used to advance illiberal causes (the NRA, for example, framing its gun ownership agenda in terms of rights).[20] When we can no longer tell the good guys from the bad guys in terms of human rights claims, the language of rights will lose much of its comparative advantage. To scoff at this, suggesting that it will always be clear who the *real* supporters of human rights are, is to buy into historically unfounded assumptions about the painless automaticity of a liberal result from modernization, as well as to disregard the power of counternorms.

A second part of the Sideshow model will see human rights bypassed as the inherent tensions they obscure within liberalism are brought to the fore by growing economic and social inequality, racially based inequities, and power disparities. In this scenario, elected officials in the West may find human rights increasingly inadequate for motivating and inspiring broader public support. Those people previously inspired by human rights may also lose faith that human rights reformism will deliver tangible benefits and start to look for more radical solutions which will emphasize more fundamental change through collective grass-roots political action. Populists on the left and the right could stimulate such developments.

Third, geopolitical change challenging Western dominance could lead medium-sized and small developing states to acquiesce to the increasingly institutionalized influence of, for example, Chinese and Gulf money. A weakening of Western leverage could reduce political incentives to go along with liberal rights rhetoric. However, such consequences are by no means certain. A less assertive Western approach to rights promotion, more along the lines of current British foreign policy, might paradoxically reduce the opportunities for religious and nationalist leaders to emphasize identity, faith, and sacrifice to resist what their constituencies see as neo-imperialist cosmopolitanism. This might open a space for activism because "human rights" cannot be demonized as imperialist quite so easily when Western states are themselves ambivalent about their spread.

These four potential models draw on insights from the mainstream and its critiques. Only the first, staying the course, reflects the core of current scholarly and practitioner thinking. The other three show varying degrees of drift away from rights, which become either one strategy among others, or contested, or irrelevant. This is what makes sophisticated human rights research so vital. It is not an esoteric debate to ask whether human rights work, given the scale of the resources invested in human rights advocacy and the hope attached to them.[21] Our final substantive section asks what

---

[20] Clifford Bob, *The Global Right Wing and the Clash of World Politics* (Cambridge: Cambridge University Press, 2012).

[21] Data on human rights funding as a whole is extremely scarce. One recent estimate, from 2010, claims 703 foundations provided $1.2bn of human rights funding worldwide. If we add in government, international NGO, UN, and other sources of funding this is likely to be a significant underestimate: see Christen Dobson, Lucia Carrasco Scherer, and Emilienne

kind of future research we want human rights scholars to be doing. It identifies some key questions that should be on the human rights research agenda at the nexus where agency and structure meet, and asks what their implications are for human rights advocacy.

Implications for Further Research

Some of the disagreements we've outlined hinge on empirical questions of fact and of causality. In addition, some empirical questions arise within the context of each of the viewpoints, thinking through the analytical and prescriptive implications of its assumptions. We begin with some examples of empirical questions that arise from scholars' efforts to identify the scope conditions under which mainstream tactics work best and the harder cases where they work less well. We then look at issues that arise concerning backlash, localization and the idea of welfare versus rights.

Easy Versus Hard Cases

Research has already provided guidelines regarding the conditions under which mainstream tactics based on law, publicity, civil-society mobilization, and external sanctions are less likely to work well: e.g., when the country is at war, when the state is too strong or too weak, when the abuse is a diffusely embedded cultural or social practice, when democratic channels and legal institutions are unavailable, when poverty or illiteracy limit the skills and resources available to civil society actors, and when civil society actors are repressed or illiberal.[22] Continuing with this research agenda, scholars continue to study how strong these effects are, how best to measure these circumstantial factors, and the interaction across these dimensions.[23]

Additional factors may also be very important in distinguishing hard cases from easier cases where mainstream methods might work better. For example, research could examine whether, in contexts where alternative illiberal ideologies, cultural discourses, or sectarian histories have

de Leon, "The State of Global Human Rights Philanthropy," *openGlobalRights*, Nov. 2013, at: www.opendemocracy.net/openglobalrights/christen-dobson-luc%C3%ADa-carrasco-scherer-emilienne-de-león/state-of-global-human-righ.

[22] Risse, Ropp, and Sikkink, eds., *The Persistent Power of Human Rights*; Simmons, *Mobilizing for Human Rights;* Eric Neumayer, "Do International Human Rights Treaties Improve Respect for Human Rights?" *Journal of Conflict Resolution* 49, no. 6 (2005): 925–53.

[23] Amanda M. Murdie and David R. Davis, "Shaming and Blaming: Using Events Data to Assess the Impact of Human Rights INGOs," *International Studies Quarterly* 56, no. 1 (2012): 1–16.

strong roots and are easy to mobilize, advocacy that draws on liberal human rights discourse may face greater pushback, and therefore vernacular approaches might fare better. Likewise, where a postcolonial or anti-imperial discourse provides elites with a readily available tool to mobilize constituencies against international human rights interventions, research might ask whether the robustness of civil society has negative or positive effects on rights outcomes.

Tailoring Tactics for Hard Cases

Some might say that the line between easy and hard cases defines the scope conditions for mainstream versus social power and localization approaches to rights promotion. If so, this raises a number of researchable questions about the tactics that are best in hard cases. One important line of inquiry that will shape estimations about ideal advocacy tactics concerns the role of capacity in determining compliance gaps. In some cases, a tactical priority may be to create the conditions that make human rights possible, namely strengthening a weak state or building a literate middle class. In areas of limited statehood, localization strategies that combat culturally ingrained abuses of women's rights through vernacular techniques may have a great prospect of success. Hard cases may require sequencing of tactics, with state-building and economic development strategies unfolding gradually to strengthen scope conditions while vernacularization serves as a short-term palliative. Risse's chapter is a good start in laying a conceptual grounding for a research agenda along these lines.

What Defines the Line Between Hard and Easy Cases?

Paradoxically, research suggests that partial democracies are the states that get the most benefit from signing human rights treaties, and yet states with such mixed regimes are also among the most murderous in terms of human rights atrocities and proneness to civil war.[24] Research should be designed to help estimate whether the crucial dividing line between the successful and unsuccessful transitional states is their level of democratic participation, the strength of their legal institutions, or the strength of civil society actors. Having said this, the crucial differences between them may instead be along different dimensions, such as

---

[24] Helen Fein, "More Murder in the Middle: Life Integrity Violations and Democracy in the World, 1987," *Human Rights Quarterly* 17, no. 1 (1995): 170–91; Christian Davenport and David Armstrong, "Democracy and the Violation of Human Rights: A Statistical Analysis from 1976 to 1996," *American Journal of Political Science* 48, no. 3 (2004): 538–54.

whether the culture of civil society is liberal or illiberal, whether ethno-nationalist elites can use anti-colonial appeals to outmaneuver more liberal critics, whether the country is more economically developed, or whether its international neighbors support peaceful democratization. The answer to this question will have implications for the relevance of mainstream and more pragmatic bargaining-based approaches to cases on either side of the hard-versus-easy line.

Countering Backlash

Just as mainstream approaches give rise to a rich menu of research questions, so does the backlash critique. One obvious lacuna is the relative lack of systematic data on backlash within international and regional forums. A better understanding of the diverse array of backlash strategies, especially the roles of rhetoric, counter-norming and material coercion, will help better determine what tactics might mitigate backlash. The extent to which elite responses to human rights advocacy are conditioned by an anticipation of backlash may also affect optimal advocacy strategies. The failure of advocates and elites to anticipate backlash may lead to unexpected and unintended outcomes, many of them negative. The insights of the social power and localization approaches are essential for devising a research agenda that can capture these dynamics.

Dilemmas of Localization or Vernacularization

One topic that is ripe for research is whether, and when, localization and vernacularization of rights discourse will water down or pervert the message, leading down a slippery slope toward condoning abuses.[25] In some situations, vernacularization may unnecessarily sacrifice a powerful rhetorical tool of universalism.[26] When will it run into Merry's "resonance dilemma," wherein the effectiveness of vernacularized approaches is inversely proportional to the size of the rights goal? Legal localization may succeed by focusing on national rather than international law, as Hertel's chapter illustrates.

Localization poses the question not only of the divergence of national norms from global rights standards, but also the diversity of cultural group standards within national societies. Advocating sensitivity to community standards and local modes of normative discourse raises the

[25] Rachel Wahl, *Just Violence: Torture and Human Rights in the Eyes of the Police* (Stanford: Stanford University Press, 2017).
[26] Naz K. Modirzadeh, "Taking Islamic Law Seriously: INGOs and the Battle for Muslim Hearts and Minds," *Harvard Human Rights Journal* 19 (2006): 191–233.

328 Stephen Hopgood, Jack Snyder, and Leslie Vinjamuri

challenge of how to reconcile conflicting practices, concepts, and laws of cultural groups that live under the same state and in intertwined social relations.

We can identify three general approaches to solving this problem, two of which are rules-based, and one which rests on a logic of consequences. Each has distinct advantages but also obvious shortcomings. Human rights research can help evaluate the viability of these approaches across a range of contexts. They are not mutually exclusive, and indeed may be designed to be mutually reinforcing. The first is an individual rights approach, permitting individuals a broad scope for joining together voluntarily in culturally based group practices and legally guaranteeing non-discrimination based on religion, ethnicity, race, and analogous distinctions. This approach is rules-based and so bears a strong resemblance to mainstream approaches in form but not in substance. Its shortcoming, of course, is that this assumes voluntarism exists as a possibility and can be protected from social coercion that is facilitated by underlying power disparities that exist within social groups.

The second is a multicultural approach that decentralizes some rule-making and rule-adjudicating functions to normatively distinct communities, but where the allowable scope for those practices is subject to supervision by authorities enforcing general civic norms. Most typically, these distinct practices are recognized in areas that regulate family life or communal property where entrenched religious or communal practices pre-date the modern civic state.

Normatively, this approach tries to reconcile tensions between civic and traditional principles by giving priority to overarching civic principles, including the voluntary nature of individuals' choices to accept the authority of a communal body.[27] This approach is most likely to create significant problems for advocates of women's and especially children's rights. The prospects for success will rest on selecting diverse and representative authorities to agree on how to devise a creative, progressive reconciliation between civic norms and family life.

A third approach is political bargaining. Sometimes it might be best to avoid the bright lines of rights and law, and to work instead through political channels of redress and bargaining on a case-by-case basis, where cultural groups might find reasons based on cross-cutting interests of class or electoral expediency to respect minority practices. For example, in Myanmar's 2015 parliamentary election, ethnic minorities voted

---

[27] Will Kymlicka, *Multicultural Citizenship: A Liberal Theory of Minority Rights* (New York: Oxford University Press, 1995), 75–106.

not for their own ethnic candidates, but for Aung San Suu Kyi's Burmese National League for Democracy because they thought her party could best represent their interests against the military and because they expected her to eventually make concessions on federalism.[28]

In our volume, Hurd's chapter alerts us to the risk that advocating for the group rights of cultural minorities, such as the right to worship together freely according to their distinctive practices, can polarize and reify social identities in societies where toleration is in short supply. This issue and other dilemmas of localization point out a needed research agenda studying what tactics work best to minimize such polarization.

Crowding Out Welfare

A good deal of the bite of the Moyn and Hopgood critiques of mainstream human rights derives from the assumption that the rights movement's small-bore utopianism diverts the progressive energies that would otherwise feed into a more promising global social welfarist project. Whether there is some common ground that entails a rights strategy giving priority to economic and social rights, as discussed in Hertel's chapter, and so being less likely to crowd out welfarist concerns, is an important question. Researchers need to consider whether these hypotheses can be studied empirically.

The chapter by Simmons and Strezhnev makes a good start in a brush-clearing exercise, finding that, on average, rights progress has not come at the expense of economic welfare progress in particular states. However, Simmons' seminal book, *Mobilizing for Human Rights*, makes a powerful case that the impact of mainstream methods of rights promotion are highly conditional on a state's level of democratization, the independence of its courts, the space for civil society activism, and the issue area under consideration. This implies that a next step for the empirical research agenda on the crowding-out hypothesis should be precisely this kind of conditional and interactive relationship between mobilizing legally for rights and mobilizing politically for welfare. The analyses of Simmons and Snyder would expect broad areas of reinforcement, while Hopgood and Moyn would expect sharper trade-offs. Further research will help evaluate which of these views is right, and under what conditions.

---

[28] Daniel Maxwell, "Burma's Ethnic Minorities put their Faith in Aung San Suu Kyi," *Asian Correspondent*, Nov. 19, 2015, at https://asiancorrespondent.com/2015/11/burmas-ethnic-minorities-put-their-faith-in-aung-san-suu-kyi/.

Conclusion

The future of human rights, not unlike its past, will ultimately be heavily influenced by both politics and by social and economic development across multiple, diverse contexts. Some of the more significant factors that have shaped international human rights advocacy at the global level, perhaps most notably the Global War on Terror, have played a fairly minor role in the chapters of this volume. We have also said relatively little about the powerful political deals that are struck between major powers that often lead to the marginalization, at least temporarily, of human rights advocacy. What this volume has done, we hope, is to bring together a diverse array of theoretical and empirical perspectives. Early generations of human rights scholarship tended to err on the side of either excessive optimism or critique. Human rights scholarship frequently merged advocacy, theory, and empiricism.[29] In the last decade, international relations scholarship on human rights has become increasingly sophisticated, with more attention focused on devising clear questions and methodologies for engaging across these lines.

The contributors to this volume have suggested a variety of more specific factors that alter or even pervert the pathways through which international human rights advocacy travels. Naming, shaming, socializing, and harnessing institutions to enforce international human rights standards have had some successes, for sure, but their overall record remains mixed at best. This is hardly surprising given the magnitude of this undertaking; nonetheless, it also suggests that speaking truth to power may be insufficient or even misguided. Achieving universal human rights is unlikely to be a matter of just waiting it out, staying the course, or trying harder. As human rights advocates seek to build further on decades of discursive and institutional achievement, understanding why human rights get traction in some places and cases and not in others is a vital next step and one that may entail confronting a number of inconvenient truths. The theory and methods of social science and political analysis will be essential components in this task.

---

[29] Leslie Vinjamuri and Jack Snyder, "Advocacy and Scholarship in the Study of Transitional Justice and International War Crimes Tribunals." *Annual Review of Political Science* 7 (2004): 345–62.

Index

Abdulladjanov, Abdumalik, 182
Abortion, 302
Acharya, Amitav, 126, 163–4, 166, 170, 238–9, 244, 249
Acharya, Avidit, 72
Activists Beyond Borders (Keck and Sikkink), 239
Adcock, C.S., 206
Advocacy
  "boomerang" model of, 244, 246, 311
  review of scholarship on implications for, 14–15
  "silent victim" model of, 107
  "spiral" model of, 137–8, 311
  transnational advocacy, 38–41
Afghanistan
  amnesty laws in, 128, 129
  Bonn Agreement, 129
  freedom in, 151
  strategic importance of, 164
Afghanistan War, 292–3
Africa. *See also specific country*
  backlash in, 114
  limited statehood in, 142, 144, 146
African Court of Human and People's Rights, 130
African Court of Justice and Human Rights, 50, 130
African Union, 129–30, 134, 178
Agency for Security and Cooperation in Europe (ASCE), 177
Agenda for Peace (Boutros Ghali), 6
Alayza, M. Rosa, 217
Al-Bashir, Omar, 115, 121, 124, 125
Albright, Madeline, 232
Alfonsin, Raul, 112
Alinejad, Masih, 41
Aliyev, Ilham, 177
Al-Qaeda, 178
Alston, Philip, 68

Alvarado, Velasco, 230
American Civil Liberties Union (ACLU), 229
American Convention on Human Rights, 248
American Evangelicals, 90
Amnesty International
  generally, 6, 35–8
  Annual Report, 29
Amnesty International USA, 229
Amnesty laws, backlash and, 50, 128–9, 320
Anglicans, 110
Angola, human rights in, 144
Arab Spring, 96, 99
Arendt, Hannah, 266
Argentina
  amnesty laws in, 128
  backlash in, 132
  economic rights in, 243
  mass movements in, 112
  Mothers of the Disappeared, 112
  social movements in, 42–3
  transnational advocacy and, 38
Arms Trade Treaty, 288
Asad, Talal, 190
ASCE (Agency for Security and Cooperation in Europe), 177
Association of Southeast Asian Nations (ASEAN), 178, 293, 296
Aung San Suu Kyi, 112, 199, 329
Australia, immigration in, 299
Authoritarianism, 165–6, 299, 312
Avdeyeva, Olga, 165
Azerbaijan
  election observers in, 177
  human rights cases in, 47

"Backdoor moves," 126, 245, 247–9, 250
Backlash
  amnesty laws and, 128–9

331